# RAP MUSIC AND STREET CONSCIOUSNESS

Music in American Life

*A list of books in the series appears at the end of this book.*

# Rap Music and
# Street Consciousness

Cheryl L. Keyes

UNIVERSITY OF ILLINOIS PRESS
URBANA AND CHICAGO

Library of Congress Cataloging-in-Publication Data
Keyes, Cheryl Lynette.
Rap music and street consciousness / Cheryl L. Keyes.
p.   cm. — (Music in American life)
Includes bibliographical references (p.   ) and indexes.
Discography: p.
ISBN 0-252-02761-2 (cloth : alk. paper)
1. Rap (Music)—History and criticism.
2. Rap (Music)—Social aspects.
I. Title.
II. Series.
ML3531.K48      2002
782.421649—dc21      2002000252

*To my mother and father, Ester and Willie Keyes,*
  *for all of their love and sacrifice*
  *and for being my ideal role models.*

# Contents

# Preface

This book presents a comprehensive study of rap music and its development in the United States from the early 1970s to 2000. I address this subject from the perspectives of ethnomusicology, folklore, and cultural studies, all necessitated by the complexities of rap music in contemporary American culture.

I began studying this music in the fall of 1981 at Indiana University in Bloomington. I was enrolled in an ethnomusicology course, "Transcription and Analysis," whose main objective was unlike those of the typical Western music theory courses I had encountered in the past. "Transcription and Analysis" enabled me to modify the Western musical notation system when describing non-Western music or traditional (folk) music. Among the course's required readings was George List's article "The Boundaries of Speech and Song" (1963), which immensely impacted my thinking about black music forms. List argues that both speech and song are vocally produced, linguistically meaningful, and melodic (1963:1). In the early 1980s, scholars of African American music were engaged in detailed musical discussions that somewhat supported List's assumptions. In "The Black American Folk Preacher and the Chanted Sermon: Parallels with a West African Tradition," for example, Joyce Marie Jackson (1981) compares the varying song-speech modes of the West African *griot* performance to that of the African American folk preacher. Gerald L. Davis has also presented numerous papers on the metrical units of the performed black sermon text; his work in this area culminated with the writing of *I Got the Word in Me and I Can Sing It, You Know: A Study of the Performed African-American Sermon* (1985). While these studies further support the argument for the song-speech qualities of black music, most of them investigate black sacred expressions. I wanted to apply List's thesis to an African American popular music genre, a quest that led me to rap music.

As a teaching assistant for an African American music ensemble at Indiana University, my responsibility was to arrange music and teach it to the band's rhythm section. One day, while the students were putting away their equipment after rehearsal, accompanied by the music pouring from a boom box (a large, portable audio cassette player), I heard party rhymes recited over Chic's "Good Times." When I asked one of the students the name of this music, he replied, "Oh, this is 'Rapper's Delight,' rap music."

Although I had occasionally listened to "Rapper's Delight" on the radio, I paid little attention to its musical details until I read List's article. As I listened to the song this time, it resonated with several musical-verbal forms I had heard while growing up in southern Louisiana. Aspects of rap music resembled the cheerleaders' chants I heard during my years at an all-black high school, the whooping preaching style of the late Reverend Reuben Northern of Port Allen, Louisiana, and my Aunt Bernice's way of signifying her disapproval of someone. I decided to research rap music to determine if its style of delivery was more spoken than sung, more sung than spoken, or equally balanced between the two. In addition to matching List's points concerning the commonalities between speech and song, I discovered that rap music is also rhythmically meaningful, and in this way rap artists use speech rhythms and tonal inflections consistent with black vernacular speech patterns.

Working from the vantage point of folklore, I determined that the concept of rappin—talking in rhythm over music or to an internally realized beat—is grounded in the West African bard practice from which several African American verbal-musical forms later evolved. These genres ranged from rural southern forms, such as blues, storytelling, and game songs, to urban northern styles, such as street corner jive and radio disc jockeying. Before the style of music known as rap had emerged as a distinct form in the 1970s, the term "rap" had been used to designate a stylized way of speaking among African American urban or street speakers. In furthering my understanding of the "doing of rap," I used the performance-centered model of folklore, which was the theoretical trend of the discipline at the time. The performance-centered theory of folklore studies, which drew upon sociolinguistics and cultural anthropology, enabled me to explore the performance of rap in context (see Keyes 1984).

With this perspective in mind, I began studying the ancient storytelling tradition of the West African griot, which is believed to be the antecedent of African American oral traditions from performed sermons to rap. For a first-hand account, I visited Mali, West Africa, in the summer of 1983 through a work-travel-study program known as Operation Crossroads Africa. I hoped to observe a performance of a bard there, but my research project was confined to a survey of the Northern Mali region, a guided visit by the country's Ministry of Culture, and limited conversation with cultural specialists of the griot tradition. I also observed a folkloric dance troupe in Bamako, Mali's capitol, in which minimal storytelling took place. These observations confirmed to me the striking similarities between West African and African American musical performance practices, style, and culture, factors that later would inform aspects of this book.

During my study of rap music in the mid-1980s, I continued to observe the marginalization of rap music in the academy, where it was regarded as a fad. Other social commentators and writers, however, recognized the importance of rap as an emerging art form. Several pop culture journalists wrote what are in my opinion the most informative studies on the cultural history of rap at the time. Among these writers were David Toop (1984), Steven Hager (1984), and William H. Watkins (1984). With photographs illustrating and highlighting rap in New York City, Toop and Hager's projects positioned rap as a subgenre of the urban street culture called "hip-hop," a catch-all phrase encompassing street arts styles—breakdancing, graffiti art, disc jockeying, and emceeing—associated with African American and Latino youth in New York City.

Although I had previously conducted fieldwork on hip-hop music with local DJs at Indiana University in 1982 and during a field trip to the highly publicized Swatch Watch Rap concert tour "Fresh Fest" in Indianapolis, I did not test my hypothesis about rap music elsewhere until the summer of 1986. Using Toop and Hager's studies as models, I decided to do fieldwork in New York City, the celebrated mecca of hip-hop arts. My home base was Bedford-Stuyvesant, a Brooklyn neighborhood, though most of my research took me to other boroughs, including Manhattan, Long Island, and the Bronx, credited as the birthplace of the hip-hop arts movement. The population for this study consisted of a range of rap artists (DJs and MCs), producers, managers, promoters, club owners, music journalists, and rap music consumers. I initiated contacts with the rap community by making telephone calls to their management and record firms. Represented in my interviews are the record labels Def Jam, Flavor Unit, Nia, Reality, Select, Sugar Hill, Sutra, and Tommy Boy; and the major rap management firms Set-to-Run and Rush Productions, now known as Rush Artist Management. Most interviews were conducted at noted rap venues, including El Diablo Nes (The Devil's Nest) in the Bronx and Latin Quarters, the Underground, and recording studios such as the Shakedown Sound Studio in Manhattan.

When I was not conducting interviews or observing hip-hop venues (i.e. clubs, park concerts, subway trains/stations, and block parties), I heard rap music flowing from the boom boxes of passersby at any time of the day through my upstairs bedroom window. I remembered recording in my field journal that rap is undoubtedly a sound that underscores the rhythms of everyday inner-city life. Later, when my folklore studies led me to understand rap music as part of a continuum of black expressive forms, I realized that this music is grounded in the aesthetic and ideology of urban street culture.

There were, however, a few methodological issues I encountered during my residential stay in Brooklyn. In the area where I resided, it was common knowledge to many that I was not from their community but living there temporarily. Because of drug trafficking of crack cocaine and suspicion by some that I might be working as an undercover narcotics agent, I hesitated to openly photograph the area, for I did not want my identity to be mistaken. Instead, I periodically took pictures of artists in areas such as clubs and recording studios, while other photographs were graciously given to me by the rap management and record companies. I was advised to replace the traditional term "informant" with "consultant," because the former could be interpreted as an individual working undercover or as a "police informant."

In the fall of 1990 I visited London, England, for one week as part of a faculty exchange program. At the time of my visit, the British female rapper Monie Love was in the United States. In interviews, she talked often about growing up in Peckham, an area of Southeast London that borders the famous West Indian enclave, Brixton. I was unable to visit this area, but I did go to Brixton, a demographically similar area that is recognized for its thriving dancehall-reggae scene.

The following summer I worked as a researcher-fieldworker for the Michigan State University Museum. My task was to document rap music in Detroit and nearby areas, which afforded me the occasion to interview several rap music artists (MCs and DJs), promoters, managers, record producers, and audience members. From this research, I defined Detroit's rap style as more of a techno-and-house hybrid and began to formulate theories about the regional characteristics of rap throughout the United States. In California, the rap sound is recognized by its sampling of the funk style of Parliament-Funkadelic and its laid-back groove. In contrast, most rap music adherents define the East Coast style by its verbosity and rapid execution over musical soundtracks that vary from sparsely textured mixes to hard bop, soul, jazz, and Jamaican dancehall-sampled tracks (Keyes 1992).

While my research during the 1980s established that rap was not a fad but a thriving tradition, my research during the 1990s explored, through cultural studies, sociopolitical issues surrounding this music: the emergence, commercialization, and sensationalism of a rap subgenre dubbed "gangsta rap,"

African American and Latino working-class representation in rap music, and the cultural politics of rap. During this time, I also witnessed a proliferation of negative writings in the press that questioned rap's cultural significance, dismissed its artistic value, and claimed that it promoted violence. Despite these views, academics outside of music, namely cultural studies scholars, began seriously questioning the negative and deceptive publicity surrounding rap, thus initiating a more balanced investigation. Their studies reveal that rap music expresses poignant accounts of ghetto life along with sentiments about poverty, police repression, class and gender relations, and current social policies (e.g. Baker 1993; Rose 1994; Potter 1995; Perkins 1996; Boyd 1997; Watkins 1998). Although these works rely on lyrical analyses and minimal information from direct interviews, they have nonetheless propelled rap music research into the arena of cultural studies.

Concurrent with cultural studies scholars' growing interests in popular music in the 1990s, ethnomusicologists of popular music critically examined issues of cultural identity, mass mediation, issues of authenticity and appropriation, and local and world music markets. Such scholars include Roger Wallis and Krister Malm (1984, 1992), Peter Manuel (1988, 1993), Christopher Waterman (1990), Veit Erlmann (1991, 1996), Jocelyne Guilbault (1993), Steven Loza (1993), Charles Keil and Steven Feld (1994), Deborah Pacini Hernandez (1995), Goffredo Plastino (1996), Paul Austerlitz (1997), Gage Averill (1997), Robin Moore (1997), Harris M. Berger (1999), Kai Fikentscher (2000), and Thomas Turino (2000). In addressing these topics, ethnomusicologists veer away from being merely critics to totally immersing themselves in site-specific field research. Similar to folklorists, ethnomusicologists engage in extensive fieldwork that involves participation-observation, interviews, the videotaping of various performance events for postfield analysis, and the documentation of daily experiences in a journal.

Several ethnomusicologists have found that participation and observation prove most valuable when studying musical cultures, but this method has a few constraints. One has to balance each aspect—participation and observation—of the method to avoid giving too much weight to either role. Therefore "partial involvement or a balance between the two" (Edgerton and Langness 1974:2) is strongly encouraged. It is only at this juncture that the researcher can properly assess the tradition, values, and aesthetics of the group studied and render an accurate account of a musical culture. My role as a participant-observer enabled me to gain trust from and within the rap community, affording me opportunities to observe informal discussions or comments from concertgoers. My preperformance observations at concerts eventually led to informal interviews, in which I would pose questions to those sitting around me about the forthcoming event. While I assumed the role of participant-observer, personal interviews and feedback interviews supplemented my research. When direct interviews with hip-hop personnel were unavailable, I resorted to secondary source material such as rapzines, fanzines, talk shows, and popular books.

Upon my return to New York City in 1992, I observed that rap was no longer confined to the inner-city areas of the Bronx and Brooklyn but was heard, especially on weekends, blasting from automobiles (Jeeps in particular) along 8th Street near Washington Square Park. While I frequented major parks and a few local clubs where rap music was performed, the highlight of this research phase was attending the 18th Annual Anniversary of the Universal Zulu Nation at The Muse, a club in lower Manhattan. Although I was unable to conduct lengthy interviews there, I spent my time observing, taking photos, and briefly chatting with the veteran rap artists Afrika Islam, Mr. Biggs, Grandmaster Caz, Lovebug Starski, and members of the famed breakdance group Rock Steady Crew and saying "hello" to former interviewees Lumumba Carson (known then as Professor X of X-Clan), Afrika Bambaataa, and Grandmaster Melle Mel. On the first evening of the anniversary celebration, I heard a man explain to the audience why things seemed so relaxed or different from a rap concert during this celebration. He continued by stating, "you're going to experience 'uncut hip-hop,' the way we used to do it in the old days." Without a doubt, the hip-hop spirit was extremely apparent: aerosol art embellished the interior of the club; DJs took turns at mixing records on turntables; MCs recited rhymes over the microphone to the crowd; and breakers danced to the beats. All of the participants sported Zulu Nation memorabilia or the latest street fashions and greeted each other with the Zulu Nation's hand sign. Although the anniversary celebration took place over three days— Friday, November 13, through Sunday, November 15—videotaping was prohibited due to the onslaught of bootlegging operations.

Research in New York City culminated with my attending the annual New Music Seminar (NMS) panels on hip-hop music in 1994. The most informative of these was the "Hip-Hop Summit" panel organized by the writer Harry Allen, also known as "Hip-Hop Activist" and "Media Assassin." The panelists included KRS-One, Roxanne Shanté, Lauryn Hill, Spice-1, Large Professor, Afrika Islam, Afrika Bambaataa, Ladybug of Digable Planets, Chuck D of Public Enemy, and B-Real of Cypress Hill. Their discussions covered a broad range of issues: global marketing of rap music, the misappropriation of hip-hop, business strategies, and artist representation. The climax of the hip-hop summit were the Battles of the MCs and DJs. Because of a scheduling conflict, I was only able to attend the DJ competition. The moderator of this event was the veteran rap artist Clark Kent, with musical assistance from New York's DJ Kid Capri. The judges consisted of noted veterans such as DJ Jazzy Joyce and international figures like DJ Honda from Japan. Unlike the previous NMS that I had attended, where contestants were mainly from the East Coast, competitors for this contest came from various areas of the United States as well as Europe and Asia. The DJ who received the most applause from a majority black and Latino East Coast audience was Noize from Denmark, the winner of the 1994 NMS Battle of the DJs. It was apparent to me that rap music had indeed become a global enterprise.

In September 1994 I relocated to Los Angeles to accept a teaching position in ethnomusicology at the University of California. I anxiously looked forward to unraveling the rap scene in Los Angeles, which by that time had become a major market of this music. With fewer West Coast observations under my belt, I attempted to interview the Death Row Records artist-producer and cofounder Dr. Dre and the EastWest artist Yo-Yo, but was unsuccessful because of their busy schedules. In many instances, the classroom became a primary network through which the rap community made itself available to my research. But most of the Los Angeles artists I was able to interview were lesser known, while the remaining ones were those I have pursued over the years, including a record-producer-manager from Detroit and a noted female rap artist from New York City.

In summary, interviews generated a wealth of information about the aesthetics of style, performance practices, and the sensibilities shared by the rap community, but participant-observation proved to be the most practical investigative method for this study. Thus, it is from the juncture of all three perspectives—ethnomusicology, folklore, and cultural studies—that the nucleus of my ideas about rap music grew. Within the context of this book, I will attempt to capture the essence of the rap music tradition by examining its cultural sensibilities within its world of beats, rhymes, and street consciousness.

# Acknowledgments

This book is the result of perseverance and above all dedication. I am thus greatly indebted to many people and organizations that assisted me in this work over the many years. I would first like to extend my gratitude to the many interviewees and hip-hop community spokespersons. Their names are numerous, but they are listed in the "Interview" section at the end of the book.

I would like to express thanks to the libraries, museums, and folklore research centers whose collections supplemented my knowledge of rap music and hip-hop culture: City Lore, Experience Music Project, Michigan State University Museum, New York City Public Libraries, and the University of California at Los Angeles Libraries, including African-American Studies, the Law Library, the Music Library, College-Powell Library, Louise M. Darling Biomedical Library, and the Charles E. Young Research Library. Additionally, I express gratitude to the various archives, photographers, and collectors who generously offered the use of their photographs for this book: the Michael Ochs Archives, Alisa Childs, Brian Cross, Bill Jones, and Joe White.

The fieldwork, research, and production phases of the book were made possible by grants and fellowships. I am most grateful to the Ford Foundation Postdoctoral Fellowship for Minorities and the University of California at Los Angeles and its various research grants—Council on Research/Faculty Grants Program, Faculty Career Development Award, and Institute of American Cultures Award.

A special appreciation and recognition goes to the many scholars who organized forums and provided opportunities for me to share my research with academicians, students, and members of the hip-hop community while the book was in progress: Leonard Brown, Joyce Marie Jackson, Barbara Kirshenblatt-Gimblett, Ingrid Monson, David M. Powers, Linda Reed, Geneva Smitherman, Ronald Jemal Stephens, Earl L. Stewart, Luz Maria Umpierre, William H. Wiggins Jr., and my colleagues in the Department of Ethnomusicology at UCLA.

I wish to thank students who assisted in the final preparation of this book: Ikem Asimonye, Ray Briggs, Abimbola Cole, Vasana K. de Mel, Brana Mijatovic, Nakisha Nesmith, Rebecca Rehfeld, Charles Sharp, and Andy Connell for reproducing camera-ready musical examples. Also, my appreciation and sincere thanks go to the staff of the Center for African-American Studies and the Department of Ethnomusicology at UCLA for their assistance.

This book was further enriched by the fine eye of my editor and friend Corinne Lightweaver, whose invaluable comments contributed to the manuscript's refinement. Very special thanks go to Judith McCulloh at the University of Illinois Press and the anonymous reviewers who critically read earlier drafts of the book. With Judith's patience and, above all, persistent interest in this work, my book finally found its home. Last, but certainly not least, much thanks to Matt Mitchell, my copy editor, and Theresa L. Sears, managing editor at the University of Illinois Press.

During the long and arduous process of writing this book, I was faced with numerous challenges. However, with the moral support from friends, I found it much easier to cross fierce waters. I would like to give a shout out to Lou-Ann Crouther, Blanche Foreman, Kyra Gaunt, Paulette Gissendanner, Clarence Henry, Terrilyn Jones, Carol Kaye, C. Elizabeth Lyons, Phyllis May-Machunda, Charles E. Moore, Thomasina Neely-Chandler, Ronda R. Penrice, Kenneth Walker (my cuz), and Annie Willis. Warm appreciation is extended to the family of the late Marvin Blake, Ms. Clifford Holden, and Nesta Williams for their inspiration during the early phases of this study. Many thanks go to Harry Allen, Judy Hutson, Rachel Raimist, and Kevin Powell for their contribution and interest in my work on rap music, and Thomas "Popcorn" Doyle for sharing with me his collection of rare rap music recordings.

As I embarked on this long journey, my family provided unwavering support. Much love goes to my brother, Willie Lionel Keyes, my first musical inspiration, and to his family, Jacqueline, Jamal, and Ahmad, my extended family. Words could not capture my heartfelt sentiments for my parents, Willie and Ester Keyes. Without their consistent support and unconditional love, my educational career and musical endeavors would not have come to fruition: thanks for being the best parents that anyone could ever ask for. Finally, I would like to thank my soul mate Abdoulaye N'Gom for all of his support, especially during the times when certain energies attempted to shatter my dreams and aspirations to publish my research on rap music. Your words of wisdom made me feel so encouraged. As you said to me one day, "this book has a spirit of its own and will find its rightful home." Thanks to God for making it all possible!

Special acknowledgment is made to the following publishers and individuals who generously granted permission to reproduce music and lyrics in this book:

"America," Cory Woods, Robert Diggs Jr., Jason Hunter, W. Redd, and E. Turner. Careers-BMG (BMI) o/b/o itself, Wu-Tang Publishing, Ramecca Publishing, Cory Woods, and Robert Diggs Jr. Used by permission. All rights reserved.

"Behold a Pale Horse," words and music by Mondo McCann, Sean Pollard, and Domingo Padilla. © by 1997 EMI April Music, Inc., Rogli Music, Inc., Jugganant Plastic Music, and Deranged Music. All rights for Rogli Music, Inc., and Jugganant Plastic Music controlled and administered by EMI April Music, Inc. Used by permission. All rights reserved. International copyright secured.

"The Breaks," © 1980 by Neutral Gray Music/Funkgroove Music, J. B. Moore, Lawrence Smith, Kurtis Blow, Robert Ford, and Russell Simmons. Used by permission. All rights reserved.

"Cell Therapy" by Robert Barnett, Patrick Brown, Thomas Burton, Cameron Gipp, Willie Knighton, Raymon Ameer Murray, and Rico R. Wade. © 1996 by Songs of Windswept Pacific o/b/o Hitco Music and Organized Noize Music (BMI), and Chrysalis Songs o/b/o Goodie Mob Music. All rights o/b/o Hitco Music and Organized Noize Music administered by Windswept Pacific. Used by permission. All rights reserved. Warner Bros. Publications U.S., Inc., Miami, FL 33014.

"Don't Believe the Hype" by Public Enemy, written by Carlton Ridenhour, Hank Shocklee, and Eric Sadler. © 1988 Terrordome Music (BMI), administered by Reach Global, Inc., and Songs of Universal, Inc. Used by permission. All rights reserved.

"Don't Believe the Hype," words and music by James Henry Boxley III, Carlton Ridenhour, and Eric Sadler. © 1987 by Songs of Universal, Inc. (BMI). Claim to 43.75%. Used by permission. All rights reserved. International copyright secured.

"Everything Is Everything," © 1999 by Sony/ATV Tunes, L.L.C., and Obverse Creations Music. All rights administered by Sony/ATV Music Publishing, 8 Music Square West, Nashville, TN 37203. Used by permission. All rights reserved.

"Everything Is Everything," written by Lauryn Hill, with additional lyrical contribution by Johari Newton. © 1998 by Sony/ATV Tunes, L.L.C., Obverse Creation Music, and Jermaine Music. All rights administered by Sony/ATV Music Publishing, 8 Music Square West, Nashville, TN 37203. Used by permission. All rights reserved. International copyright secured.

"Evil That Men Do," Owens. © 1992. T-Boy Music, L.L.C, and Queen Latifah Music. Used by permission. All rights reserved.

"Fight the Power" by Public Enemy, written by Carlton Ridenhour, Keith Shocklee, and Eric Sadler. © 1990 by Terrordome Music (BMI), administered by Reach Global, Inc., and Songs of Universal, Inc. Used by permission. All rights reserved.

"Fight the Power," words and music by Eric Sadler, Keith Shocklee, and Carlton Ridenhour. © Songs of Universal, Inc. (BMI). Claim to 62.50%. Used by permission. All rights reserved. International copyright secured. "Fight the Power" transcription used by permission of Kyra Gaunt.

"Freedom" used by permission of Sugar Hill Music, Inc.

"Funkin' Lesson" used by permission of Bridgeport Music Inc. (BMI).

"Funkin' Lesson," words and music by Jason Hunter, George Clinton Jr., Garry Marshal Shider, and Walter Morrison Jr. © 1990 by Universal–Songs of Polygram International, Inc., o/b/o itself and Vanglorious Music (BMI). Claim to 50.00%. Used by permission. All rights reserved.

"Funky Beat," words and music by William Drew Carter, Lawrence Smith, Jalil Hutchins, and John Fletcher. © 1986 by Zomba Enterprises, Inc., Funk Groove Music Publishing, and Zomba Music Publishers, Ltd. All rights for Funk Groove Music Publishing administered by Zomba Enterprises for the World and all rights for Zomba Music Publishers, Ltd., administered by Zomba Enterprises, Inc., for the United States and Canada. Used by permission. All rights reserved. Warner Bros. Publications U.S., Inc., Miami, FL 33014.

# *A Note on Terminology*

The language of hip-hop culture as employed by rap music artists deviates intentionally from mainstream English. When hip-hop culture deletes the "ing" and "er" endings of words, this book remains faithful to the culture under study, retaining hip-hop spelling, pronunciation, and usage. For example, words ending in "ing" and "er" are phonetically uttered by hip-hop speakers as "in" and "ə", respectively, while the letter "f" at the beginning of a word may be replaced with "ph." Other words that have standard spellings, for example, "disrespecting" and "deft," have become "dissin" and "def." The examples below show hip-hop alterations and pronunciations, as indicated with the International Phonetic Alphabet (IPA) symbols:

| Mainstream English | Hip-Hop Alteration | IPA |
| --- | --- | --- |
| brother | brotha | ˈbr-thə |
| deft | def | ˈdef |
| disrespecting/dissing | dissin | dis-ˈsin |
| gangster | gangsta | ˈgaŋ-stə |
| rapping | rappin | ˈrap-ˌpin |
| fat | phat | ˈfat |
| sister | sista | ˈsis-tə |
| skills | skillz | ˈskilz |
| whack | wack | ˈwak |

Hip-hop spellings are intentional dialectal features, not mistakes. For a list of hip-hop words used in the text and their definitions, please refer to the Glossary.

# Introduction

Hip-hop is a youth arts mass movement that evolved in the Bronx, New York, during the early 1970s. Comprised of disc jockeys (DJs/turntablists), emcees (MCs), breakdancers (b-boys and b-girls), and graffiti writers (aerosol artists)—commonly referred to as its four elements—hip-hop further encompasses what its adherents describe as an attitude rendered in the form of stylized dress, language, and gestures associated with urban street culture. Although graffiti and breakdancing received mainstream attention during the early to mid-1980s and were showcased alongside DJs and MC in various films,[1] they do not fall within the parameters of this book. Rather, this work specifically examines rap music, a form predicated on the combined styles of delivery of the DJ and the rhymin MC, that gave birth to one of the most vital forms of popular music during the late twentieth century.[2] Rap music can be defined as a musical form that makes use of rhyme, rhythmic speech, and street vernacular, which is recited or loosely chanted over a musical soundtrack.

The rap music concept first evolved among itinerant DJs, known as mobile or street DJs, who would mix prerecorded hits alternately on two turntables while reciting into a microphone party phrases, such as "let's jam, y'all," to the crowd. When mixing records eventually developed as a competitive art in itself, street DJs supplemented their own verbal performances by hiring rhymin MCs. By the late 1970s rap had begun to attract the attention of many music entrepreneurs, including Sylvia and Joseph Robinson of Sugar Hill Records, who were enchanted with its rhyme and rhythmic aspects. The Robinsons' initial recording, "Rapper's Delight" (1979) by Sugarhill Gang, inundated the airwaves with boasting-style rhymes chanted over the disco-funk soundtrack of Chic's "Good Times." Following the Gang's commercial hit, other successful rap music acts flourished, including Grandmaster Flash and the Furious Five, Funky Four Plus One, Sequence, The Fat Boys, Whodini, Nucleus, Soul Sonic Force, and Kurtis Blow, the first rap artist to record with a major record label. Rap music not only proved to be more than a passing fad, as some first believed, but also demonstrated that it could compete and eminently thrive in a popular music industry that had so long predicated its success on vocal and instrumental acts. By the late 1980s rap music's popularity—in recordings, concert sales, television commercials, and films—led it to become a billion-dollar enterprise. As a result, it has been lauded by music critics as the most vital of new popular music forms in the music industry (Nathan 1988a).

Amid its commercial success and appeal in popular culture, rap became the site of heated controversy. In discussing these burgeoning attitudes, careful consideration was given to numerous media sources that questioned the social relevance of this youth music to a vast majority. For example, in 1981 *20/20* presented a segment on rap music, becoming perhaps the first major news magazine in the American mainstream to profile the initial years and influences of this nascent form. Noting that rap had begun to impact popular music in acts like Blondie's "Rapture" (1980), the segment also points out that rap is specific to black urban culture. The critic Lisa Robinson infers that rap's affiliation with black urban culture is seen to be threatening to the conservative middle-class ethos. "It's [rap music] not something they [middle-class America] really understand. It is very black and very urban, and people are scared of that" (Fox 1981). The music journalist and critic Nelson George counters that race is not the major issue. Rather, people make assumptions because the primary participants of rap are black urban men who "speak in a very aggressive style. They stand aggressively; they dress in an assertive manner, in a way that is not seemingly acceptable to whites in the mainstream. This turns off a lot of middle-class black folks as well. It's not racial; it's more of a class thing" ("Rap Attack" 1986). But in a 1990 *Newsweek* cover story titled "Rap Rage," Jerry Adler, Jennifer Foote, and Ray Sawhill equate "aggressive style" with "black," "male," and "violent," supplementing the stereotypes they promote in their text with photographs of African American rap performers whose gestures and facial expressions are not explained in context.

Many critics promote the common misconception that rap and violence are so intertwined as to be synonymous. Soundtracks to films like *The Lost Boys* (1987) and *Colors* (1988) reinforce the music's association with criminal and violent activities. Along similar lines, numerous articles in the news media reported violence at rap music concerts. Although most of these incidents happened outside the concert area and were unrelated to the artists or their music, some critics still postulated with a naiveté difficult to fathom that aesthetic qualities like the "beat" induce frenzied behavior. One journalist commented, "the rap today is anger and the so-called background music or scratching is so intense that it beckons you to act violent" (Thomas 1986:20).

Because of the media's proclivity toward "report[ing] even the slightest disorderly conduct incident" (Copeland 1997:100), insurance premiums for rap concerts skyrocketed, precluding the possibility of booking artists in many cases. Owing to the negative press, insurers were compelled to hire extra security and provide metal detectors, the cost of which was often exorbitant. The unspoken fear among city officials, concert venues, and insurers, noted the journalist Lee Copeland, was the massive crowds of young black men, "who, too often in America, are still viewed as a threat to law and order" (106). The rapper Boots of The Coup commented about another trend at rap concerts, the lack of a black presence in his audiences. He blames such scarceness on the manner in which promoters advertise his concerts, targeting them specifically for and to white middle-class or suburban youth venues. He calls this type of promotion and advertising to certain demographics a form of gentrification.[3] By the mid-1990s rap concerts at large venues were becoming rare. Smaller venues became more popular; the House of Blues in Los Angeles was one such outlet that invited artists to perform.[4]

Critics claim that the anxiety about black presence was exacerbated by media propaganda and conservative right-wing politics during the 1980s. The sociologist and popular culture scholar Herman Gray asserts that "the symbolic and political centerpiece of this reenergized conservative formation was Ronald Reagan, who as the embodiment of Reaganism, functioned as the cultural and historical sign, for many whites, of the 'real' America" (1995:16). The historian Robert Dallek defines Reaganism as a "return to old-fashioned Republicanism—large tax cuts for the rich, less government help for the poor, weaker enforcement of civil rights, fewer controls on industry, less protection for the environment, and emotional rhetoric on the virtues of hard work, family, religion, individualism, and patriotism" (1984:vii–viii). Thomas Edsall and Mary Edsall, in their national bestseller *Chain Reaction: The Impact of Race, Rights, and Taxes on American Politics* (1992), also found that with Reaganomics the "haves" and the "have-nots" were divided along racial lines: "to the degree that divisions between blacks and whites overlapped division between the poor and the affluent, between the dependent and the successful, and between city and suburb, race became an ally of conservatism" (1992:158).

Ronald Reagan's ideas and rhetoric were transmitted via the media, namely through television advertisements, that served as an open-book testimony to America's problems. The media targeted the young African American and Latino underclass as poor mothers or "welfare queens" and preached that teen pregnancy, drug abuse, and crime among people of color were evidence of America's eroding moral structure. In general, race—though often unnamed—operated at the center of conservative Republican political discourse. Rap music emerged as a new site from which to protest this growing negativity and—at best—apathy toward inner-city youth of color. Examples of this resistance resonate in songs like "Election '80 Rap" by The Unknown Rapper (1980), "Bad Times" by Captain Rapp (1983), and a series of sociopolitical commentary rap songs by Grandmaster Melle Mel—"The Message" and "The Message II" (1982), "White Lines" (1983), and "World War III" (1985). In "Election '80 Rap," The Unknown Rapper describes current affairs of the time, from "the hostages' release from Iran" to the CIA. "White Lines" criticizes heroin and cocaine addiction as well as the inequitable jail sentencing for black drug offenders, called the "street dealer," compared to white offenders, called the "businessman." In the refrain of "World War III," Melle Mel refer to Reagan's economic policy: "Catastrophic Reaganomics, and nobody hears what the people say."

Conservative ideology was evident on another front in the late 1980s and 1990s, through the censoring of rap music, especially among artists of the "gangsta rap" subgenre. Associated mainly with West Coast artists, gangsta rap employs graphic images of the black underworld. Although gangsta rap artists argue that the tales from the hood range from truthful accounts to exaggerated fantasies, gangsta rap's graphic lyrics caused moral panic among conservatives.

Prompting a foundation-shaking reevaluation of the First Amendment, debates surrounding the censoring of companies like Death Row Records and rap groups like 2 Live Crew, erroneously grouped as "gangsta rap," culminated in the 1994 congressional hearings. Initially inspired by right-wing organizations like the Parents' Music Resource Center (PMRC), which first gained notoriety in 1985 for its campaign against lyrics in heavy metal music as well as other pop artists' songs (e.g. Madonna's "Like a Virgin" and Prince's "Darling Nikki"), crusades against "gangsta rap" were led by Senator Bob Dole (especially during his 1996 presidential campaign), the education secretary and drug czar William Bennett, and the former civil rights activist C. Delores Tucker, the chairwoman of the National Political Congress of Black Women. Labeling gangsta rappers as misogynistic and violent, the anti-rap crusades eventually damaged Death Row Records' distribution rapport with Interscope/Time Warner, putting the company in limbo.[5]

Though the "black rage" unleased through gangsta rap was a primary concern, other critics questioned rap's artistic value. Most of these arguments point to the manner in which rap DJs create music—through digital sampling of whole musical tracks or prerecorded musical motifs—in lieu of composing newly inspired pieces. Formally trained musicians criticize rap music DJs' assumed lack of knowledge of basic Western music theory, which, for some, is the sine qua non of a composer. The musician-composer and Pulitzer Prize winner Wynton Marsalis summarizes this popular opinion: "'When you get to rap music, you can't reduce anymore. When you get past that, it's not music anymore'" (quoted in "Marsalis Rips Rap" 1989:22).

Whether or not rap is socially relevant or artistically driven, it continues to sell—and indeed flourish—in the mainstream market. The record executive Sylvia Rhone notes that rap music "'is really driving the economy of the record business these days. It's the force drawing consumers into record stores'" (quoted in Philips 1997:D4). Ben Pappas, a columnist for *Forbes* magazine, observes that "sales of the controversial but lucrative lyrics-driven music shot up 134% in the last decade, while rock sagged and country grew marginally" (1998:224). According to SoundScan, an electronic device for tracking record sales, the surge in rap music is attributable to its growth among white suburban teenagers, who account for two-thirds of its sales (Weingarten 1998b:9).

Controversial forms that threaten mainstream sensibilities will always face intense scrutiny from powerful political forces and parent watchdog groups, much in the way that rhythm and blues or its euphemism, rock 'n' roll, did during its formative years. Perhaps those who are ambivalent about or critical of rap music can move beyond essentializing it as a decadent form and, more importantly, come to realize that rap music is not an aberration of black culture but rather a part of a continuum of black expressive culture and an art form that has made an indelible entry into American history.

Fundamental to the proper interpretation of rap in this study is viewing it within the context of urban street culture. As rap artists affirm, "'rap is from the streets. If you don't know what's going on out there, you can't do rap. You can live in Beverly Hills, but your heart has to be in the streets'" (quoted in Fee 1988:R8). The video director Hype Williams asserts that the film theory and techniques he learned in the classroom only minimally inform his directing of rap videos, arguing that having firsthand experience with street culture is primary: "the 'streets' reflect in all that I do; the camera [lens] is an extension of that" (1995). Essentially, hip-hop artists state that "'you've got to be from the streets to know what rap is about, or at least be out there to know what's going on'" (quoted in Fee 1988:R21).

"The streets" is identified in this study as a subculture of the urban milieu that operates by its own rules, economics, lifestyle, language, and aesthetics. The sociologist Eugene Perkins finds that when all other institutions
within the American mainstream fail to provide the essential needs for economic survival and maintenance, individuals and communities resort to the
streets. Moreover, to survive one must become a student of the densely populated and impoverished urban landscape, a ghetto commonly known as the
"asphalt jungle" (1975:26). Primary outdoor contexts in the ghetto—ball
courts, parks, street corner hang-outs, and subway stations and trains—are
mostly inhabited by teenagers and young adults.

In hip-hop, artists bring to their performances a street culture sensibility or "attitude" and a persona that undergirds the aesthetic of style. Although
hip-hop and rap music are generally used interchangeably by the masses,
those who are followers of and participants in this arts movement think otherwise. As the MC extraordinaire KRS-One has indicated on several occa-
sions, rap is something one does or performs, whereas hip-hop is something
one lives or experiences. In the rap song "Fear Not of Man" (1999), MC Mos
Def defines hip-hop as "The People," alluding to the ebb and flow of black
life and culture in America at various times. As the cultural theorist George
Lipsitz observes, hip-hop "brings a community into being through performance, and it maps out real and imagined relations between people that
speak to the realities of displacement, disillusion, and despair created by the
austerity economy of post-industrial capitalism" (1994:36). Drawing upon
the meaning of hip-hop to its adherents, I use the term similarly; however, I
use it as an adjective as well, to define a genre of music, lifestyle, and politics. The following section explores issues of identity within the hip-hop
community and its impact on my status as both insider and outsider.

### "What's the DL on the Researcher?": Issues of Identity

Within the various rap music contexts where I was observing people or calling people to set up interviews, silent questions were insinuated by gestures
or vocal inflections from contacts: "what's the DL (down low) on her?"
"What is this woman all about?" "Who does she represent?" or simply put,
"What does she want to know about hip-hop?" It was not long before I realized that my gender, ethnicity, and occupation were primary factors by which
I was recognized and, at times, embraced by the hip-hop community while
doing research in this context. However, social scientists have wondered

whether objectivity is compromised when a researcher's identity is the same as that of the interviewee or the environment.

Most social scientists would agree that one's identity as a researcher can affect the outcome of a fieldwork experience. The researcher can assume the role of an outsider or insider: a researcher who investigates a group of people from a different cultural background than his or her own is positioned as an outsider, whereas a researcher who investigates a group of people from his or her own cultural background is positioned as an insider. The former position is most often preferred by social scientists. In the past, social scientists have argued that studying a group of people similar to one's own cultural background potentially reduces the level of objectivity. Concurring with this belief, the ethnomusicologist Bruno Nettl said, "Many would surely deny that investigation of one's own culture is ethnomusicology at all, since the idea of comparing other cultures and styles with one's own, and the principle that one can be more objective about other cultures than about one's own, are important fundamentals of our field" (1964:70).

Other evidence, however, suggests that insider or "indigenous" scholars have successfully conducted unbiased or objective studies among their own cultural traditions (Nketia 1974; Peña 1985; Loza 1993). For example, the Ghanaian ethnomusicologist J. H. Kwabena Nketia is highly extolled by scholars for his research among his people, the Asante. Although Nketia contends that his "insider" status as "a speaker of Akan [and] carrier of the tradition and its culture" contributes to the success of his research, he further credits the implementation of "proper field techniques" as paramount to one's investigation (Nketia 1962:3).

In more recent discussions, scholars such as Nettl have drastically shifted from their earlier positions. They now propose that the insider perspective commands "scholarly respect and authority" (Burnim 1985:433) and can provide importantly different interpretations than those of the outsider: "It is the insider who provides the perspective that the culture has of itself. The outsider, with an essentially comparative and universalist approach, merely adds something less significant" (Nettl 1983:262). But whether an insider or outsider, the researcher faces a variety of personal, social, and political constraints (Burnim 1985:446).

During the 1990s a growing number of ethnomusicologists shifted from thinking of fieldwork as "human culture as objectively observable" (Cooley 1997:17) to fieldwork as experience, thereby moving beyond the insider/outsider dialectic.[6] In *Shadows in the Field: New Perspectives for Fieldwork in Ethnomusicology,* Timothy J. Cooley states, "ethnographers attempt reflex-

ively to understand their positions in the cultures being studied and to represent these positions in ethnographies, including their epistemological
stances, their relations to the cultures and individuals studied, and their relationships to their own cultures" (1997:17).[7] Furthermore, contends Timothy Rice, "Rather than there being insider and outsider ways of knowing, all
who place themselves 'in front of' a tradition use the hermeneutic arc to move
from pre-understandings to explanation to new understandings" (1997:117).
As an African American woman conducting research on the music of my
respective cultural group, I initially pondered whether being an insider or
culture bearer of shared tradition would automatically guarantee my immediate acceptance and the accessibility of cooperative consultants during my
fieldwork experiences. I also became concerned about my identity as a woman researching a tradition that appeared to be male-dominated. In this regard, would gender somewhat problematize my being simply an insider, rendering me a partial insider?

Some researchers have argued against the fixity of insider status during
fieldwork because "factors such as education, gender, sexual orientation, class,
race, or sheer duration of contacts may at different times outweigh the cultural identity we associate with insider . . . status" (Narayan 1993:672). Thus,
insider status need not be static but can be seen as "shifting identifications
amid a field of interpenetrating communities and power relations; the loci
along which we are aligned with or set apart from those whom we study are
multiple and in flux" (671).

As my fieldwork progressed, I soon realized that my interpretation of
"outsider" differed from those of my consultants: for them, it signified one
who is not a music industry member. This factor, at numerous times, out-
weighed ethnicity and gender. But throughout my fieldwork it became more
apparent that my outsider status was a critical factor—both positive and
negative—in gathering information for this study.

My fieldwork investigation of the rap music tradition brought me in direct contact with the rap music industry milieu—its artists, producers, promoters, managers, music critics, club owners, and recording studios. Doing
fieldwork in this context was exciting, but at times I sensed a feeling of competition, rivalry, and suspicion among those who worked in this arena. My
first encounter with the industry occurred when I initiated contact with two
radio disc jockeys from Indianapolis and Chicago during the early stages of
fieldwork. When I asked for permission to videotape their performances, I
detected a slight hesitation in their responses. To remedy this matter, I told
them that I was a graduate student collecting data for a "class project." Ad-

ditionally, I stated that the video would be used primarily for educational and research purposes. When I presented them with a written agreement in the form of a contract and requested their signatures, they gave me permission to videotape them without hesitation.[8]

I also obtained verbal consent from the rappers' managers, as I did in October 1984 when I interviewed three rap artists at the Fresh Fest rap concert in Indianapolis. One of the managers thought that I was the usual newspaper journalist or magazine writer looking for a story. After stating to him that I was a graduate student interested in rap music from an academic perspective, he immediately granted me an interview with one of the rap groups, The Fat Boys.

While doing fieldwork in New York City during the first phase (summer 1986), I spoke daily to artists, managers, or music industry persons via telephone, hoping for interview confirmations. Since music industry personnel constantly receive telephone calls from magazine or newspaper writers demanding interviews with rap artists, they automatically assume that the potential interviewer is a music journalist. To distinguish my identity, I said I was "a student from Indiana University who is in New York City for the summer to study rap music. This study is for a class research paper. I was referred to you by. . . ." I was usually granted an interview, or at least given the name of a major contact.

Also, my student status may have made a difference to consultants and therefore facilitated the arranging of interviews. In some instances, interviews were granted in exchange for written concert reviews. For example, I was told of an up-and-coming rap group called the Nastee Boyz from New Jersey. In order to interview this group, I had to contact their manager, who told me that his group was to perform at a "Say No to Drugs" rap concert in Brooklyn's Prospect Park. He kindly suggested that I could interview the Nastee Boyz if I consented to writing a concert review for his magazine, *The Hip Hop Hit List.* He further mentioned that this concert would include other rappers from New York City who might also grant me interviews. I, of course, accepted his offer, which proved to be more than a bargain; it was the highlight of my interview experience. I was able to videotape and interview several rap artists and make further contacts in the rap community.

The pattern of identifying myself as distinct from the music industry became a primary factor in getting to interview artists, particularly during my two-week field trip for the Michigan State University Museum. Unlike the consultants I interviewed in New York City, many of those interviewed in Detroit were not as well known and thus were looking for every outlet available to expose their musical talents to the public. Upon my return to New York

City between 1992 and 1994, the rap music industry had become a major music market. Access to major rap artists was extremely difficult, compared with their accessibility during the early years of rap. When attempting to acquire an interview with an artist, especially those of reputable status, I was always asked, "What company, newspaper, or magazine do you represent?" When I answered that I was writing "a book on rap music," I was instructed to call an artist's management or to fax a letter stating why I wanted to interview a particular artist and how the interview would be used. I was never directly given a business telephone number, as was the case with writers connected with popular music trade magazines. It appeared now that being an outsider—rather than music industry personnel—did not guarantee interviews, nor did the industry mediator (i.e. managers, public relations persons, etc.) see the immediate value of my work in promoting their artists. This pattern of not obtaining interviews with major artists continued in Los Angeles as well. However, veteran and less established artists of the local scene were readily available, for they saw any interviewer as potential for exposure.

In some instances, insider and outsider status simultaneously played major roles in soliciting private information about rap artists and producers. Many of the African American consultants, for example, shared personal accounts about racist practices and commercial exploitation in the rap music industry. These consultants said that they were waiting to share their stories with someone who was "black" and preferably "outside" the music industry. Outsider status denoted to these consultants that I could be more objective about their music while simultaneously being sympathetic to their personal accounts because of our shared ethnic identity.

Another component that defined my identity was gender. I perceived that some male consultants invariably tried to impress me in a manner that went beyond the usual interaction between consultant and researcher. They would often ask, "How old are you?" and "Are you married?" I also observed how the male consultants related to other males in my presence. While speaking to other male rappers, their tone quality was heightened. However, when they spoke to me, their responses were more subdued.

There was one incident during my fieldwork investigation when my gender made a major difference in the manner in which I was perceived. One male consultant did not believe he should give me complimentary tickets to attend a particular rap concert. He candidly stated to me, "This [concert] is not a place for a 'lady' like you . . . cuz you may get hurt." I told him that "I would not be attending the concert alone . . . my escort is male." He persisted stating that this concert was "no place for a 'lady.' You have done enough work on rap music now. Uh! You are pretty good [for a woman]. But now you're getting way over your head. There are certain places of rap music which [seemingly] is no place for women researchers to be hanging around."[9] This consultant's desire to protect me left me perplexed; it confirmed that some male consultants are paternalistic, even patronizing to women who venture outside domestic space. I was also left wondering, however, if he felt that my status as a professor/educator made me naive to the street and hip-hop sensibilities that envelop most rap concerts.

Female MCs were also a part of the research population. In the early years of my study, when female artists were not the norm in rap, the few I encountered were eager to be interviewed. Some of the female artists nevertheless had to cancel at the last minute because of their maternal responsibilities. By the 1990s women artists were no longer seen as novelties in a male-dominated arena, for many had achieved gold and platinum sales status comparable to their male counterparts. Attempting to make contacts with female rappers at this point became difficult as well. But among the few I did interview, our shared ethnicity and gender created a particular openness that I did not experience with black male consultants. In this regard, there was always a willingness to share private thoughts about black femaleness that seemed to create a sense of sisterhood between me (the researcher) and the consultant, as revealed through affirmations like, "You understand where I'm coming from," or, "Yes, I see what you're sayin." What is of further significance here is how a researcher can move beyond "fixed" boundaries of identity, especially when he or she is partially or fully a part of the interview, as was the case with the female rappers. As the feminist anthropologist Lila Abu-Lughod observes:

> By working with the assumption of difference in sameness, of a self that participates in multiple identifications, and an other that is also partially the self, we might be moving beyond the impasses of the fixed self/other or subject/object divide that so disturbs the new ethnographers. To speak more plainly and concretely, imagine the woman fieldworker who does not deny that she is a woman and is attentive to gender in her own treatment, her own actions, and in the interactions of people in the community she is writing about. In coming to understand their situation, she is also coming to understand her own through a process of specifying the similarities and the differences. (1990:25–26)

This fieldwork experience further enhanced my understanding of insider and outsider status and its impact on a researcher studying a particular community. Factors of "mutually shared identity proved to be an asset in many ways, particularly in gaining full cooperation" (Burnim 1985:438) throughout my research experience. The female rap music community therefore perceived me as a cultural insider because of my ethnic and gender identities. But the status I acquired as an insider remained, nonetheless, secondary to my outsider status. My identity as a music industry outsider proved highly beneficial to my fieldwork in the earlier phases, specifically when acquiring interviews. Although being outside the circle of music industry personnel or associates (as with music critics or journalists) in this community was perceived at times with apprehension by some members of the music industry, gender and ethnicity afforded me the opportunity to obtain privileged information from African American and female interviewees. But as Michelle Kisliuk reminds us, in any role or profession, in order to act upon the world we need to continually reexpress our identities; we get to know other people by making ourselves known to them, and through them to know ourselves again, in a continuous cycle (1997:27). Fieldwork in the rap milieu enabled me to understand the constraints of outside-insider status, but it further affirmed how ethnographers reflexively understand their positions within a community by becoming a part of the experiences of others.

The interpretation of these experiences and the data gathered is elucidated in the following chapters. Part 1 presents a historical and sociocultural perspective of the rap music tradition and its aesthetics of style. Chapter 1 traces the roots of rap from its West African bardic tradition to southern black cultural forms and the transformation of these forms in the northern urban context. The latter portion of this chapter examines the concept of rappin over music through the styles of black radio DJs of the 1950s, Black Nationalist poets of the 1960s, and soul and funk music of the 1970s. Chapter 2 specifically explores the sociocultural history of rap music from circa 1972 to its early commercial years in the 1980s. It argues that rap music is a product of internal and external ruptures resulting from geopolitics, gang culture, economic cutbacks, and musical change. This chapter also examines the impact of Jamaican sound system culture in the formation of U.S. rap. Chapter 3 and chapter 4 examine the dissemination and continued growth of rap beyond the streets to the musical mainstream. Topics include rap's influence on other musical styles, its impact on the media, and its bout with U.S. copyright laws and censorship. Part 1 ends with chapter 5, which focuses on aesthetics of "street style" and its conveyance through rap music performance.

Language and rhetorical style, musical production, and paramusical-lingual qualities idiosyncratic to street style are reviewed.

Part 2 contains three chapters that incorporate cultural studies and feminist and mass mediation theories of popular culture in critically engaging with concepts of representation in rap music. Chapter 6 presents an overview of issues, conflicts, and conspiracy theories believed to be disruptive forces within the rap community. It discloses rap artists' growing concerns regarding black-on-black crime and rap turf wars, material obsessions, and intracommunity epidemics (i.e. AIDS and crack cocaine) as revealed through personal narrative accounts, conspiracy beliefs, and performance. Chapter 7 examines the gendering of rap music and the manner by which African American women's culture is articulated via the female voice. Finally, chapter 8 explores the rap music video medium as a discursive site of African American youth culture. Because of the multifaceted nature of this work, it is hoped that this book will foster a broader understanding of rap music and the hip-hop youth arts movement.

# The Sociocultural History and Aesthetics of Rap Music

*Persistence overcomes resistance.*

—Mr. Magic

# The Roots and Stylistic Foundation of the Rap Music Tradition

## 1

### *The African Nexus*

Most critics and scholars concur that rap music is a confluence of African American and Caribbean cultural expressions, such as sermons, blues, game songs, and toasts and toasting—all of which are recited in a chanted rhyme or poetic fashion. As Paul Gilroy observes, hip-hop culture grew out of the cross-fertilization of African American vernacular cultures with their Caribbean equivalents rather than springing fully formed from the entrails of the blues (1993:103). While rap artists forthrightly confirm an African American and Caribbean nexus by regarding rap as having a close resemblance to the Jamaican toast or "Jamaican rhymes," they also view their music through a historical lens by which (West) Africa is primarily perceived as the place of origin for the rap music tradition.

When I asked about the origins of rap, several veteran rap artists pointed to Africa as a reference for its performance practices. Hip-hop's proclaimed godfather Afrika Bambaataa indicated, "although it [rap] has been in the Bronx, it goes back to Africa because you had chanting style of rappin" (Bambaataa interview). Elaborating further, Lumumba "Professor X" Carson refers to an African context out of which he believes a style of rap was born: "Once upon a time ago, a long long time ago, every Friday of the month, it was the duty of the grandfather in a tribe to sit down and bring all of the immediate children around him to rap. One of the instruments that was played while grandfather rapped his father's existence was a guy playing the drum. I guess that's why we are so into rap today" (Carson interview). When I occasionally mentioned to academics how rappers would locate Africa as the foundation of the rappin style, some of them immediately marveled at this while simultaneously wondering, "Who told them that?"[1] Despite some queries by academicians about artists' knowledge of the rap music–African nexus, Bambaataa and Carson's statements suggest, nonetheless, that rappin is similar to the West African bardic tradition.

Beyond whatever traditions and history may have been passed down to African Americans through the oral traditions of their families and communities, the impact of a particular book published in the 1970s gave those who did have access to oral history a new means by which to understand their contemporary culture and practices through examining their heritage. The considerable contributions of this book may underlie the strong assertions that rhymin MCs make about the bard-rap continuum. The comparative literature scholar Thomas A. Hale notes that the West African bard's rise in popularity in the United States can be attributed to the 1976 publication of Alex Haley's *Roots: The Saga of an American Family.* The televised version of *Roots,* which was produced as a miniseries in 1977, "drew the largest audience in the history of U.S. television" (Hale 1998:2). The series retold the story of Haley's African ancestor, Kunte Kinte, who is said to have come from the Gambia. *Roots* also stimulated African Americans' interest in genealogy. *Roots* was followed by its miniseries sequel, *Roots: The Next Generations* (1979). An autobiographical sketch of Haley's life as a journalist and novelist, the sequel revealed how he embarked upon his research on Kunte Kinte. In the last episode, Haley, played by the actor James Earl Jones, travels to the Gambia where he is directed by the Ministry of Culture officials to a keeper of oral history, a *griot,* who would probably know the story of Kunte Kinte. Undoubtedly *Roots* informed viewers about the role African bards played as purveyors of the past, recorders and guardians of history, and scholars of African culture. Thomas A. Hale best summarizes the impact of *Roots:* "thanks to the continuing impact of *Roots,* West African griots have dramatically expanded their performance contexts. They have appeared on the stages of university auditoriums, in churches, and in television and recording studios in Paris, London, New York, and Tokyo" (1998:2). It would not be farfetched to presume that among the audiences of these performances were rappers, who recognized rap's strong link to an old African practice, a practice whose influence they may have unconsciously adopted from their families, churches, and cultures. To understand why rappers identify with the role of the African bard, we must examine its historical context.

In traditional African societies, the bard is a storyteller-singer and above all a historian who chronicles the nation's history and transmits cultural traditions and mores through performance. Early accounts of the bard can be found in the writings of the Syrian scholar al-'Umarī and the memoirs of the Moroccan traveler Ibn Battūta during the fourteenth century. Both al-'Umarī's work *Masālik al-absār fimamālik al amsār* (1337) and Ibn Battūta's chronicle (1355) describe a praise singer poet who serves as an intermediary and interpreter among a host of court poets. Al-'Umarī cites the following about a sultan in Mali named Sulaymān, the brother of the sultan Mansā Mūsa: "In front of him there stands a man to attend him, who is the executioner . . . and another, called shā'ir, 'poet,' who is his intermediary (safīr) between him and the people. Around all these are people with drums in their hands, which they beat" (al-'Umarī in Levtzion and Hopkins 2000:265).

Several years following al-'Umarī's visit, Ibn Battūta witnessed the following: "I arrived at the town of Mālī, the seat of the king of the Sūdān. . . . I met the interpreter Dūghā . . . one of the respected and important Sūdān. . . . I spoke with Dūghā the interpreter, who said: 'Speak with him, and I will express what you want to say in the proper fashion'" (Battūta in Levtzion and Hopkins 2000:288–89). Ibn Battūta noticed the importance of music affiliated with the interpreter and poets during council meetings and festivities associated with the sultan's court.

> Inside the council-place beneath the arches a man is standing. Anyone who wishes to address the sultan addresses Dūghā and Dūghā addresses that man standing and that man addresses the sultan. . . . The sultan comes out of a door in the corner of the palace with his bow in his hand and his quiver between his shoulders. . . . The singers come out in front of him with gold and silver stringed instruments (qunburī) in their hands. . . . As he sits the drums are beaten and the trumpets are sounded. . . . at the two festivals of the Sacrifice and the Breaking of the Fast . . . [a] seat is set up for Dūghā and he sits on it and plays the instrument which is made of reed with little gourds under it, and sings poetry in which he praises the sultan and commemorates his expeditions and exploits and the women and the slave girls sing with him and perform with bows. On the feast day, when Dūghā has finished his performance, the poets come. They are called julā, of which the singular is jālī. (291–93)[2]

In traditional West African society, the bard is a member of a caste of artisans (i.e. blacksmiths, leather workers, etc.) known among the Mande as *nyamakala*. It is believed that whenever a bard utters a word or any member of the nyamakala performs a task within their respective profession, a powerful force called *nyama* is released. Westerners have often translated *nyama* as "malevolent force," which is partially correct. But as the linguist and Mande scholar Charles Bird puts it,

> *Nyama* is essentially associated with action, acts and the individual's capacity to act. For this reason, I prefer to translate it as the energy of action. Whatever the act, the individual requires a certain amount of energy to perform it and the performance of the act itself releases a certain amount of energy. From the point of view of equilibrium, the energy of action is dangerous, since, if it is not appropriately controlled, it will lead to disequilibrium and upheaval. . . .
>
> Speech itself is considered to contain this energy as denotes the expression *Nyama be kuma la* [or] The energy of action is in speech. (1976:98)

When nyama is operative, a bard's utterance can transform chaos into peace or "transmute things and man himself" (Anyanwu 1976:576).

The words of bards abound in several quasi-song forms from epics—long narrative poems centered around a legendary hero, for example, Sunjata, a celebrated epic about the founder of the Mali Empire—to praise songs or poetry exalting a patron's namesake. While performing, a bard makes use of formulaic expressions, poetic abstractions, and rhythmic speech—all recited in a chantlike fashion that prefigures rap.

The effectiveness of a bard's performance is achieved through the use of the imagery that is created through the bard's words. As described by Leopold Senghor: "'African-Negro imagery is therefore not imagery-equation but imagery-analogy, surrealist imagery. . . . The elephant is force, the spider, prudence; horns are the moon and the moon is fecundity. Any representation is imagery, and imagery, I repeat, is not equation but symbol, ideogram.'" (quoted in Taylor 1977:25). Senghor's picturesque statement sheds light on the African aesthetic of verbal performance, that is, to paint pictures with words through the use of metaphors and symbols. Because of the masterful use of words, a bard is revered and highly respected in a community, a role claimed later in the diaspora by the most adept MCs.

A bard's performance is further advanced through the use of musical accompaniment. Most storyteller-singers are accompanied by a harp-lute (e.g. kora) or percussion instrument, whose repetitive beat interlocks with the bard's voice. A bard may also be accompanied by an apprentice, the *naamu-sayer,* who responds by singing "naamu" in affirmation of the bard's words, adding an active interchange between the bard and naamu-sayer, who represents the voice of the listener.

Alhaji Papa Susso and Mamadou Susso, griots from The Gambia. (Photo by the author)

Although the bard seemingly gives credence to the historical roots of rap's poetic performance, this aspect is not confined to the African continent alone but is rather idiosyncratic to oral traditions throughout the African World, diaspora, or what Paul Gilroy refers to as "The Black Atlantic" (1993).[3] During the trans-Atlantic slave trade, many Africans, including bards, were transplanted to the Western world. In the New World, Africans were enslaved and forced to learn a culture and language different from their own. In the face of this alien context, blacks transformed the new culture and language of the Western world through an African prism. The way in which they modified, reshaped, and transformed African systems of thought resonates in contemporary culture. For example, many rap music performance practices represent what I call cultural reversioning: the foregrounding (consciously and unconsciously) of African-centered concepts. While rap music is considered an art form indigenous to the United States, it is important to discuss its roots in this context, which I trace to early African American expressive culture. I contend, however, that the convergence of African American and Caribbean expressive culture and the influence of the latter on the former in the making of rap music occurred in a more discernible manner during the 1970s. The following section discusses African American antecedents of rap music and the basis for some of rap's verbal performance practices. The Caribbean impact on rap and hip-hop will be addressed more fully in chapter 2 and subsequent chapters.

## The Cultural Reversion of African Culture in the United States

Poetic speech remained paramount to African peoples in the New World, circumscribing their everyday experience. Essentially, "the communication system that evolved among the Africans [in America] stemmed from their creativity and their will to survive. Language quickly became not only a means of communication but also a device for personal presentation, verbal artistry, and commentary on life's circumstances. In effect the slave was . . . a poet and his language was poetic" (Baber 1987:78). Enslaved Africans devised ways by which to encode messages about their condition.

Black poetic speech is fluid and predicated on what communication scholars call *nommo*, "the power of the word," a concept derived from the Dogon of Mali.[4] Nommo permeates speech and oral performance throughout the African diaspora. In discussing the efficacy of nommo, Ceola Baber opines that it "generates the energy needed to deal with life's twists and turns; sustains our spirits in the face of insurmountable odds [and] transforms psychological suffering into external denouncements . . . and [into] verbal recognition of self-worth and personal attributes" (1987:83). These concepts will become important as we look to place rap music in a historical context.

Poetic language of African peoples eventually flourished in the New World as testimony of enslavement. Under the strictures of institutionalized slavery, blacks were forced into human bondage. Out of such conditions came black vernacular expressions that documented one's existence, hopes, and desires.

Slavery existed in varying degrees throughout the United States. The population of black enslaved persons in the North was relatively small compared to that in the South. Owing to the shorter summer months and growing antislavery sentiments, "there was no desire for slaves" (Franklin and Moss 1994:65). In the North, slavery has been described as "relatively mild, with slaves receiving fairly humane treatment and many considerations as to their personal rights" (63). A smattering of slave insurrections during the 1740s in areas like New York, however, resulted in statutes sometimes sanctioning severe punishments. Africanisms did thrive in the North, as documented with the reinterpretation of European-derived (Dutch) holiday celebrations such as Pinkster Day and the slave community's 'Lection Day.[5] But by the 1790s slavery in the North was rapidly dwindling. "The decline of slavery in the region is revealed by the fact that by 1790 there were approximately 14,000 free blacks, comprising about 28 percent of the total black population" (85). Such demographics fueled the antislavery debates in the North.

The South rose to become an economic empire on the backs of enslaved blacks. The historians John Hope Franklin and Alfred A. Moss Jr. note that when the indentured status of blacks expired between the 1640s and 1650s, southern colonists began to notice how they "fell behind in satisfying the labor need of the colony with Indians." After carefully scrutinizing the success of black slavery in the Caribbean, "it was then that the colonists began to give serious thought to the 'perpetual servitude' of blacks" (1994:56). By the 1660s slavery was institutionalized throughout the South, establishing the region as a growing reservoir of Africanisms as compared to the North. In many areas of the south, blacks outnumbered whites. As Franklin and Moss note,

> In 1790 Virginia had already taken the lead in black population, which it was to hold during the entire slave period. Virginia's 304,000 blacks were almost three times the number in South Carolina, Virginia's nearest rival. Most of the states in that region, however, presented a picture of an abundant black population. . . . By the last census before the Civil War, the slave population had grown to 3,953,760! The states of the cotton kingdom had taken the lead, with 1,998,000 slaves within their borders. Virginia was still ahead in the number of slaves in a single state, but Alabama and Mississippi were rapidly gaining ground. (1994:84, 123)

Enslaved blacks lived primarily on plantations in separate quarters from whites, with occasional interaction. Within this context evolved what the historian John W. Blassingame terms "slave culture." The plantation or slave quarter, densely populated by blacks, comprised the "primary environment" of this culture, while blacks living in contact or close confines with whites made up the "secondary environment" (see Blassingame 1979:105–6). The former environment fostered the maintenance, reinforcement, and continuation of African-derived practices in music making, oral narratives, material culture, philosophy, and belief systems. When unsupervised by whites, blacks retreated to their traditions in such contexts as the "invisible church," secluded

places in the woods aptly termed "hush harbors" or makeshift religious structures called "praise houses, and secular celebrations.[6] While it is obvious that
the art of preaching or sermonizing took precedent in black religious contexts,
expressions that emerged out of secular or recreational pastimes included storytelling and song forms such as field hollers and work songs, precursors to
the blues. Although the institution of slavery ended officially with the ratifi-
cation of the Thirteenth Amendment in 1865, African-derived locution,
phraseology, and musical forms forged in the crucible of bondage continued
to survive and evolve into newer modes of expression. The southern-based
expressions that provided a foundation for rap are storytelling, ritualized
games (i.e. "the dozens" and signifyin), blues songs, and preaching.

Stories told in rhyme have been collected throughout the rural South for
many years. One storytelling tradition that provides a structural model for
rap music is the toast. The toast is a long narrative poem composed in rhymed
couplets and recited in a humorous manner. Its text centers around the feats
and foes of a trickster, for example, the Signifying Monkey and the character Shine, or a badman hero type, such as Mr. Lion or Stackolee.[7] These stories are performed in secular contexts merely for amusement. Salient features
of the toast include the use of exaggerated language, metaphor, expletives,
boasting, repetition, formulaic expressions, and mimicry. Several verbal
forms are also structurally interwoven in the body of toast tales, such as the
dozens and signifyin. The dozens (also known in contemporary culture as
"snaps") is described as "the oldest term for the game of exchanging insults"
(Labov 1972:274). This game involves an interplay or a verbal duel between
two opponents in which one makes a direct statement about the other's family member, especially the mama, in rhymed couplets such as, "I saw yo'
mama yesterday on the welfare line / Lookin like she done drank some tur-
pentine," or "Talk about one thing, talk about another / But ef you talk about
me, I'm gwain talk about your mother" (Keyes 1982; Oliver 1968:236).

Signifyin occurs when one makes an indirect statement about a situation
or another person; the meaning is often allusive and, in some cases, indeterminate. I recall from my southern background an incident involving a married man's attempt to flirt with an unmarried woman. Aware of his marital
status, the unmarried woman reminds the man, through indirection, that he
is married. Her response places the man in an indeterminate position as to
continue or cease from flirting.

> Married Man: Hey mama, you sho' look good to me today.
> Unmarried Woman: Oh, by the way, how's yo' wife?

One popular version of the traditional "Signifying Monkey" clearly illustrates features and verbal forms—the dozens and signifyin—common to the toast tradition:

> Way down in the jungle deep,
> The baddass lion stepped on the signifying monkey's feet.
> The monkey said, "Muthafucka can't you see,
> Why you're standin' on my goddamn feet."
> The lion said, "I ain't heard a word you said. . . .
> If you say three more, I'll be steppin on yo' muthafuckin' head."
> And the monkey hid in the jungle in an old oak tree.
> Bullshittin' the lion everyday in the week.
> Everyday befo' the sun go down,
> The lion would kick his ass all through the jungle town.
> But the monkey got wise and start using his wit.
> Said "I'm gon' put a stop to this old ass kickin' shit."
> So he ran upon the lion the very next day.
> Said, "Oh Mr. Lion, there's a big bad muthafucka comin' yo' way. . . .
> He's somebody that you don't know,
> 'Cuz he just broke a loose from Ringling Brothers show.
> Said, Baby he talked about yo' people in a helluva way.
> He talked about yo' people 'til my hair turned gray.
> He said, 'Yo' daddy's a freak, and yo' moma's a whore,'
> Said he spotted you runnin through the jungle sellin' . . . from door to
> 　　door. . . ."[8]

As a rule, the effectiveness of the toast lies in its style of delivery rather than in content. Nonverbal gestures, such as facial expressions or hand movements, further enhance effective delivery of a toast. While the dozens, signifyin, metaphor, expletives, boasting, and mimicry are stylistic features of the toast, the structural unit remains the rhyming couplet. The rhyming couplet structure and the aforementioned verbal forms of the toast remain present in rap music.

Rhyme is integral to several African American expressive traditions. In the blues tradition, for example, verses are structured in an AAB rhyme scheme: "(A) I don't know where my baby done gone / (A) I don't know where my baby done gone / (B) All I can do is sing a sad sad tone." The blues singer Furry Lewis says, "If you don't rhyme it up, you don't understand nothing and you ain't gettin nowhere" (Titon 1994:47).

Rhyme is a stylistic and structural device in other African American contexts as well. For example, in the black traditional church, preachers occasionally interject rhyming verses in their sermons: "Giving honor to God, Christ Jesus, pulpit associates, members and friends. I'm glad to be here today, just to say that God is the way . . ." (Smitherman 1986:146). Rhyme also serves as a structural device in the African-derived dance-song, called "the hambone." Derived from an antebellum dance called the "juba," the hambone is executed by the patting and clapping of one's thighs, chests, and hands to rhyming verses. The hambone is commonly performed by males as a courtship game, for instance, "Hambone, hambone, ham in the shoulder / Gimme a pretty woman and I'll show you how to hold her" (Milton Lowe, personal communication, Baton Rouge, La., December 22, 1988).

Though rhyme is not germane to every African American oral expression, tonal inflections are important to the proper interpretation of an expression. Black vernacular speech utterances depend heavily on tonal contouring to convey meaning. Tonal aspects employed in the English language by African American speakers are clear evidence of African tonal language retention. The anthropologist Melville Herskovits, in his monumental study, *The Myth of the Negro Past* (1958), discusses the tonal element or "'musical' quality . . . prominent in Negro-English" (1958:291). Such vocal inflections are particularly employed in performance. For example, the preacher's most proven stylistic feature is the use of musical tone or chant in preaching (Jackson 1981:213). Blues singers talk-sing their melodies as well. Thus, it is not surprising that hip-hop MCs describe their verbal performances as "a melody in itself [or] . . . like talking" (Melle Mel interview). This concept is further discussed in chapter 5.

While tonal inflections help the performer to convey the meaning of an utterance, call and response creates a sense of cohesion between performer and auditor. Call and response is ubiquitous to the African American aesthetic in that it synchronizes speakers and listeners within a performance event, but more importantly, it is the life force of black communication. Without this interchange, black communication is lifeless. African American preachers, for example, commonly admonish their congregation that they cannot "preach to no dead church," a church in which the presence of the spirit is not made manifest by active vocal response to "the Word" as conveyed in the preached sermon (Davis 1985:27). In addition, African American artists thrive on audience response to the extent that the success of a performance is measured by the active interplay between the performer and the audience. The concept of call and response is also crucial to the status of rap artists to the extent that rappers are considered worthless by others if they do not have an entourage. For this reason, some rap artists re-create in their records a sense of liveliness by incorporating audience cheers and responses.

Rap music predominantly utilizes the artifice and art characteristic of other black oral performances. The philosopher Cornel West asserts that "'the rap artist combines the potent tradition in black culture: the preacher and singer, [who] appeals to the rhetorical practices eloquently honed in African American religious practices'" (quoted in Dyson 1993:12). While it is perhaps more apparent how rap resembles Christian preaching, its nexus in African religions is less pronounced and more subtle. Among the corpus of texts analyzed for this study there were occasional references to the West/Central African concept known as "crossroads." Crossroads represent "the juncture of the spiritual realm and the phenomenal world" (Drewal 1992:205). The art historian Robert Farris Thompson elaborates: "the points of literal intersection [are] where one might go to offer sacrifice or prayer to ancestors. . . . The crossroads, also, function as a powerful symbol in African American folklore . . . as legends of black musicians going to crossroads and trading their guitars with spirits to confirm or enhance their talents" (1990:153, 154).

The crossroads concept is not alien to black folksong traditions like the blues. For example, Robert Johnson's "Cross Road Blues" remains the most well-known of crossroads songs. Legend has it that Johnson sold his soul to the devil in exchange for his musical success. But after realizing his mistake, Johnson supposedly wrote "Cross Road Blues" as a repentant plea to God for forgiveness. The following is an excerpt from that song: "I went to the crossroad fell down on my knees / I went to the crossroad fell down on my knees / Asked the Lord above 'Have mercy, now save poor Bob, if you please'" (Thompson 1990:154). The crossroads concept is more abstract in rap than in the blues. In "To the Crossroads" (1990) Isis and Professor X of X-Clan rap about the creation of the world and humankind as evident through their deification of the ancient Kemetic (Egyptian) deities—Isis "Divine Woman/Mother" (of Horus, Son of Osiris) and Ra (Professor X), the Sun deity. Isis raps: "The I in my own song. Isis deeper and beneath those who ain't strong. / The radiant rising sun, the bright light in the world of none / . . . we'll take a walk with the black and the bold. / I'll take you there and let us meet at the crossroad." Professor X intones, "I am Ra from whom time begins. / Rising away, severing the wind, turning. / I am the hub of a wheel, a daystar hovering over in the sea. / I am not the harvest. I am the seed. Off to the crossroad we go!" The concept of crossroads is used here in a traditional African cosmic sense, meaning the place where all spiritual forces or creations are activated. In a sense,

Ra, positioned at the "hub of the wheel," parallels the deity Esu-Elegba, who in the Yoruba tradition is the guardian of the crossroads.

In another X-Clan song, "Funkin Lesson" (1990), Professor X alludes to the crossroads as a place where one goes to get in touch with spiritual forces—the ancestors—in order to empower oneself for the future. Professor X orates: "Out of the darkness, in panther's skin comes doctors, driving pink caddys, bearing the remedy of your existence. Yes, it gets blacker. With a Nat Turner-ic, Martin, Adam, Malcolm, Huey; there's a party at the crossroads." "'Driv-ing pink caddys,'" explains Professor X, is a metaphor for a "'travelling time machine.'" He adds, "'the year of that particular pink caddy is significant. It's a '59 [Cadillac]. That was another turning point of black men's existence in America. . . . The pink caddy is significant in what Detroit Red went through to become Malcolm X'" (quoted in Romain 1992:35). Professor X's teaching as a modern-day bard illuminates the continuous history of the crossroads from its place in ancient African lore to the diaspora. Today the crossroads includes not only deities and ancient ancestors but African Amer-ican leaders such as Nat Turner, Martin Luther King Jr., Adam Clayton Pow-ell, Malcolm X, and Huey Newton, who have made indelible marks on Amer-ica. In referring to what "Detroit Red went through to become Malcolm X" and later El-Hadjj Malik El-Shabazz, Professor X also clearly invokes the crossroads as the place black mortals continue to visit in contemporary times to seek guidance in preparation for change—physically, mentally, and spiri-tually—from the old self to the new self. References to the crossroads as an ancestral or spiritual gathering place are also made in "Tha Crossroads" (1998) by Bone Thugs-N-Harmony.

The African bardic tradition and its retention in southern-based oral expressions are antecedents of the rap music tradition. However, it was in the context of the urban North that rap was first introduced as a street style of speaking. It was also in this environment that rap, as a speech style, devel-oped into a distinct musical genre. The evolution of rap from a speech style to a musical form occurred during and after the migrations of southern blacks to northern urban centers.

### The Transformation of Black Vernacular Expressions

Southern traditions were transported by African Americans during their massive migration from the rural South to the urban North between the 1920s and 1950s. Southern cultural traditions were transformed and modified in the new milieu and generated expressions reflecting urban life. The rural context in which African Americans gathered in the South to hear performances of their neighborhood artists were replaced in urban centers by storefront churches, public parks, and street-corner taverns. These new gathering places comprised what urban African Americans call "the streets."

The streets are an institution as important as the church, school, and family in African American culture (Perkins 1975:26). Yet unlike the other three institutions, the survival center represented by the streets operates as a primary reference for many African Americans living in the inner city. Here one learns about the ghetto, how to survive in it, and how to combat unwarranted economic and social oppression from mainstream society. A major requisite for survival in the streets is learning how to communicate effectively.

The street context fostered a new way of speaking called "jive" talk. The word "jive" is a variation of the English word "jibe." Dan Burley, a noted scholar of jive talk, traces the appearance of the word "jive" to the streets of Chicago: "In the sense in which it came into use among Negroes in Chicago about the year 1921, it meant to taunt, to scoff, to sneer—an expression of sarcastic comment" (1981:207). Jive talk is also described as a highly effective way of talking about someone's ancestors and hereditary traits through colorful and metaphoric terms, later referred to simply as jiving someone (207). Jiving is employed in several social contexts, including intimate contexts, in which a man talks to a woman in order to win favor; however, it is more commonly used as a competitive tool, a way of establishing one's "rep" (reputation) in the streets. Speakers assess the effectiveness of jive talk in context, that is, knowing what to say and how and when to say it. What differentiates jive from its southern verbal counterparts is the use of a vocabulary derived exclusively from the urban experience. Hence, the urban term for street becomes "stroll," boy becomes "cat," girl becomes "chick," and house becomes "crib." The art of jive talk, therefore, lies in its originality. When the newness of a word wears out or the word is no longer in vogue, another word replaces it. Jive language is undoubtedly dynamic.

Jive circulated in arenas beyond the streets. In the 1920s and 1930s, prominent literary figures of the Harlem Renaissance, such as Langston Hughes and Sterling Brown, flirted with black vernacular (street) themes, speech, and music in their works. Most notable of Hughes's works are the blues poems "The Weary Blues" (1925) and "Homesick Blues" (1926) and his short stories based on a fictitious urban street character named Jesse B. Simple. The first of the Simple stories is *Simple Speaks His Mind,* in which Hughes portrays the main character as a humorous jive talker. In a similar vein, Sterling Brown wrote various poems that paid tribute to black vernacular forms like the blues. "Ma Rainey" (1930) and "Long Track Blues" (1932) rank among his premier poems. Brown's performance of "Long Track Blues," which adheres to a three-line blues structure, was spoken over live piano blues in an early Smithsonian/Folkways Recording.[9]

During the post–World War II years, jive talk had proliferated in all arenas in the urban milieu—from the church to the street corner. The English scholar Clyde Taylor notes that the tributaries of street speech are found by tracing its course in jazz (1977:30). Jive was nowhere more operative than in jazz culture. Jazz musicians employed jive in creating idiomatic expressions used exclusively to communicate to other jazz colleagues. Such words as "jam" (having a good time); "blow" (to play well); "cat" (jazz colleague); "bad" (good); and "shed" (to practice) are only a few of the many words that are commonplace in the jazz vernacular. Even prominent jazz bandleaders like Cab Calloway, Duke Ellington, Count Basie, and Louis Jordan occasionally interspersed quasi-sung narrative sections of jive into their performances to create rapport with their audiences. Louis Jordan was especially extolled for his humorous, jive-like short narratives in songs like "Caldonia" (1945) and "Saturday Nite Fish Fry" (1949). Even jazz-pop groups such as the Ink Spots utilized jive talk in their narratives when recounting aspects of romance.

The art of jiving to music over radio airwaves was introduced in the 1940s by African American radio disc jockeys. Most noted was Reverend Arthur Bernard Leaner of Mississippi, who began his career as a gospel music announcer for WGES of Chicago in 1945. When WGES refused to sell Leaner advertising in his brokered time slot because of the religious nature of the program, Leaner changed his name to Al Benson (Barlow 1999:98). In addition to his business acumen at time-brokering, Benson was known for using jive on his secular program, which helped him to connect with Chicago's black southern migrants (like himself) and its growing urban black community.[10] Undoubtedly, he "had an enormous impact upon the cultural world of the Chicago black community. He gave public visibility and legitimacy in the community to the culture of 'the street' and to the styles and perspectives of southern blacks. . . . The intermixture of Benson's southern style with the northern middle-class style resulted in a hybrid black style that evolved into a black urban language" (Spaulding 1981:123–24). In so doing, Benson was a forerunner of what critics dubbed the era of the personality jock.[11]

Credited as pioneers of jive talk in rhyme were the Chicago disc jockey Holmes Bailey, known popularly as Daddy-O Daylie of WAIT radio, and

Lavada Durst, known to his audience as "Doc Hep Cat" of KVET in Austin, Texas. As the jazz great Dizzy Gillespie recollects, "We [jazz musicians] added some colorful and creative concepts to the English language, but . . . Daddy-O-Daylie, a disc jockey in Chicago, originated much more of the hip language during our era than I did" (1979:281). Doc Hep Cat exploited rhyme, as in the following excerpt:

> "I'm hip to the tip, and bop to the top.
> I'm long time coming and I just won't stop.
> It's a real gone deal that I'm gonna reel,
> so stay tuned while I pad your skulls."
>     (quoted in Barlow 1999:106)

In addition to their artful use of jive and rhyme, early black personality jocks also employed radio sound techniques such as "talking through" and "riding gain." In the former, the disk jockey lowers the volume of the music and continues to talk as it plays, whereas riding gain occurs when the disc jockey boosts or lowers the volume on the audio board in order to accent various parts of a record (Williams 1986:81). These techniques as well as jive and rhyme were emulated by early hip-hop DJs and MCs. Numerous jockeys followed in the footsteps of Benson, Bailey, and Durst, becoming heroes in their communities. Among these are Vernon Winslow (WWEZ of New Orleans), Douglas "Jocko" Henderson (WOV of New York), Rufus Thomas (WDIA of Memphis), Tommy "Dr. Jive" Smalls (WWRL of New York), and many others.

Jive was even incorporated in the boasting poetry of certain African American sports heroes. For example, the former heavyweight champion boxer Muhammad Ali (formerly Cassius Clay) was known for his poetic prowess. Before each boxing match, Ali would taunt his opponent by boasting in rhymed couplets. Of one of his challengers, Ernie Terrell, Ali said:

> "Clay swings with a left, Clay swings with a right.
> Just look at young Cassius carry the fight.
> Terrell keeps backing but there's not enough room.
> It's a matter of time until Clay lowers the broom.
> Then Clay lands with a right—what a beautiful swing.
> And the punch raised Terrell clear out the ring. . . .
> Who on earth thought when they came to the fight
> that they would witness the launching of a human satellite?"
>     (quoted in Olsen 1967:10)

African American comedians too laced their monologues with street jive. Prior to Muhammad Ali's use of the boasting poetic style, black comedians, who used jive, flourished in 1940s Harlem, where they often hosted talent shows at theaters like the famous Apollo. Early popularizers of jive humor included Jackie "Moms" Mabley, Redd Foxx, Godfrey Cambridge, Pigmeat Markham, and Rudy Ray Moore, the man known for popularizing toasts like "Dolemite" and "The Signifying Monkey" via audio recordings as well as in film.

## The Setting of Rap as a Musical Genre

By the 1960s jive talk was redefined according to changing conditions of African American life in America (Taylor 1977:32) and reincorporated by urban speakers as "rap." Many African Americans attribute this shift from jive to rap to the Black Nationalist, Hubert or H. "Rap" Brown, whose moniker depicts his mastery of black street speech. A street-educated rapper extraordinare, Brown (also known as Jamil Abdullah Al-Amin) explains how he acquired the title "Rap": "what [I] try to do is totally destroy somebody else with words. It's that whole competition thing again, fighting each other. There'd be sometimes forty or fifty dudes standing around and the winner was determined by the way they [the crowd/audience] responded to what was said. If you fell all over each other laughing, then you knew you'd scored. It was a bad scene for the dude that was getting humiliated. I seldom was. That's why they called me Rap, 'cause I could rap" (Brown 1981:354). Brown's stylized way of speaking had gained popular acceptance among young urban speakers, who solidified the name of that style as rappin.

The 1960s also fostered a framework through which rappin was set to musical accompaniment. The Black Arts Movement (BAM) was pivotal to this occurrence. This movement began during the wake of Malcolm X's death and spanned the years 1965 to circa 1976.[12] Essential to the BAM was Leroi Jones, a poet and playwright who changed his name to Imamu Amiri Baraka, meaning "Blessed Priest and Warrior."[13] After the death of Malcolm X, Jones sent a letter to black artists summoning them to work for the black community and themselves, to use their art to "pick up and continue where Malcolm ended" (*I'll Make Me a World* [video] 1999). Baraka describes the mission of the BAM: "'when we went Uptown to Harlem in the Black Arts Repertory School, we said we wanted to do three things. We wanted to create an art or a poetry that was African American, let's say, as African American as Bessie Smith or Duke Ellington. We wanted to create an art that was mass-oriented, that would come out of the universities, that would get into the street, that would reach our people. . . . And the third thing we wanted to do was create an art that was revolutionary'" (quoted in Alim 2000:16).

Following Baraka's lead, young African American artists began rejecting European literary canons and replacing them with African-derived ones or something uniquely black in expression. They espoused that art should be functional, community-based, and it should resonate with real-life black experience, establishing a mandate for what would soon be termed "the new black aesthetic." Afrocentric and Black Nationalist themes and Islamic ideology were all fundamental to the expression of the new black aesthetic formulated by the BAM. In keeping with Afrocentric themes, adherents of the BAM donned Afros or natural hairdos and African dress. They used certain gestures that signified Black Nationalism (e.g. the clenched fist for black power), replaced their anglicized birth names with African and Islamic ones, established the Afrocentric national holiday Kwanzaa (founded by Maulana Karenga in 1966), sought to define the meaning of black, and continued to popularize rappin through the recitations of BAM's poets. Poetic skills were not judged on rhyme per se but rather on one's ability to articulate themes relevant to African American life. Poetic lines were executed in a rhythmic

Amiri Baraka. (Courtesy of Joe White)

fashion using breath cadences, alliteration, repetition, and expletives for emphasis. Performances included shifts from casual talk to heightened speech and sometimes to musical chant. It is for these reasons that I define BAM poetry as song poems. Among those who championed the artistic explosion that Baraka initiated are the literary artists Larry Neal, Nikki Giovanni, Don Lee (known as Haki Mabhubuti), Sonia Sanchez, Toni Cade Bambara, Ishmael Reed, June Jordan, and Audre Lorde; the composer Oscar Brown Jr.; the visual artists Benny Andrews and Faith Ringgold; the filmmakers Melvin Van Peebles and Gordon Parks Sr. and Jr.; and ensembles such as the Dance Theater of Harlem and the Art Ensemble of Chicago.[14]

Various cultural organizations also sprang up during the heyday of the BAM, including the Umbra Writers Workshop in Greenwich Village, the Organization of Black American Culture (OBAC) in Chicago, and the Art Ensemble of Chicago's Association for the Advancement of Creative Musicians (AACM). Black filmmakers explored black urban America from an insider's viewpoint. Following the BAM mandate that African Americans should create art without apology, black independent publishing companies such as Broadside Press in Detroit and Third World Press of the OBAC rose to this charge.

A number of writer's workshops espousing the new black aesthetic produced a legion of poets who recited their poetry to musical accompaniment, thus advancing the popularity and influence of song poems. The Watts Prophets of the Watts Writers Workshop stand out in this regard. Although The Watts Prophets were regionally known, The Last Poets of Harlem succeeded in becoming nationally recognized via their recordings and spoken word tours. For this reason, they are recognized by rap artists as "the first or original style rappers" (Bambaataa interview).

The Poets' first album, *The Last Poets* (1970), which sold more than eight hundred thousand copies, featured poems of political commentary like "New York, New York," "Niggers Are Scared of Revolution," and "When the Revolution Comes" rendered over African-derived percussion (i.e. congas).

In 1973, Jalal "Lightnin' Rod" Uridin, a member of The Last Poets, recorded a solo album called *Hustler's Convention*. Unlike the political poetry on the first album, *Hustler's Convention* featured a series of toasts about two fictitious urban badman characters, Sport "The Gambler" and his buddy Spoon. The album chronicled the street adventures of Sport and Spoon, from their wins at craps, pool, and poker to Sport's bout with the cops that almost leads to his demise (Toop 2000:119). Because of its close association with street language and lore, *Hustler's Convention* was recognized by early rap artists as a prototype of rap music. As the rap music veteran Grandmaster Caz re-

The Last Poets. (Courtesy of Michael Ochs Archives)

called: "'I knew the entire *Hustler's Convention* by heart. That was rap, but we didn't know it at the time'" (quoted in Hager 1984:49). Another New York poet-musician known for his political songs and lauded as a major influence on rap music was Gil Scott-Heron. He considered himself "neither poet, composer or musician" (liner notes, Scott-Heron 1970). But to many, his lyrics captured the essence of rappin through their language, rhythm, and technique of indirection. One popularly known song poem by Scott-Heron is "The Revolution Will Not Be Televised," from his 1970 album *A New Black Poet: Small Talk at 125th and Lenox.* In this poem, Scott-Heron informs his listening audience that there will be no commercials, soap operas, reruns with white actors, nor processed hair worn by those African Americans ascribing to white beauty standards; rather, the revolution will be a group action by which black people take to the streets in search of a brighter day. In the album's liner notes, the critic Nat Hentoff includes excerpts from Scott-Heron's song poem "Plastic Pattern People," which employs the BAM's poetry writing—a negation of European grammar rules. Note the use of an uncapitalized "i" for the first-person pronoun, the use of capitalization for certain letters in a word, and the use of varied indentations—all capturing the asymmetric motion of black art sensibilities espoused by the Black Arts Movement.

Gil Scott-Heron. (Courtesy
of TVT Records)

> STP and LSD. SpEed kiLs and some-/-times
> music's call to the Black is confused. . . .
> i beg you to escape
>     and live[15]

Often overlooked as a forerunner of rappin style over music is Nikki
Giovanni. On her widely acclaimed spoken word album *Truth Is On Its Way*
(1971), Giovanni experiments with music and poetry by reciting her poems
in various black musical styles. For example, "Ego-Tripping" is recited to
African percussion, while the remaining songs, "Woman Poem," "All I Got-
ta Do" (or "sitting and waiting 'cuz I'm a woman"), "Poem for Aretha," and
"Great Pax Whitey" are performed to the gospel sounds of the New York
Community Choir. More importantly, unlike the song poems of The Watts
Prophets, The Last Poets, and Gil Scott-Heron, Giovanni's poetry gave voice
to an African American woman's perspective and to black feminist thinking.

In growing numbers, balladeers and funk performers incorporated rap
into their songs, a style initially popularized by Larry Darnell and Arthur

Nikki Giovanni speaking at the California African-American Museum in Los Angeles, 2000. (Photo by Bill Jones)

Prysock in the 1940s and 1950s and by certain soul music artists—Ray Charles, James Brown, Aretha Franklin, and Lou Rawls—who integrated short rappin sections in their music to establish a rapport with their listeners. By the late 1960s, rappin emerged as a distinct song style all its own. It took the form of a monologue that celebrated the feats and woes of love and party-oriented themes. The songwriter-singer-musician Isaac Hayes led the way in this style. Hayes's unique way of setting the tone of songs by speaking loosely in a stylized manner over a repetitive accompaniment, as with his rendition of "By the Time I Get to Phoenix" (1969), was emulated by his contemporaries Millie Jackson and Barry White. In contrast, the monologue raps of funk performers during the 1970s centered on topics such as "partying," or having a good time. The funk artist George Clinton and his groups Parliament and Funkadelic were considered popularizers of this rappin style, which was grounded in the concept of "being cool": behaving in an emotionally re-strained manner, being laid-back, and moving at a moderate tempo. Clinton emphasized this concept in "P-Funk" (1975) when he declared: "the law around here is to wear your sunglasses so you can feel cool." Unlike the rappin style of the early entertainers, the love ballad and funk-styled raps were not in rhyme but were loosely chanted over a repetitive instrumental accompaniment. By the early 1990s Clinton's music would become the centerpiece for a West Coast subgenre of rap music known as gangsta rap.

Though the roots of rap music reside in the African bardic traditions, they continued to penetrate African American oral traditions from the rural South to the urban North. During the 1930s through the 1950s, southern expressions were transplanted in the urban context, fostering a new way of speaking: jive talk. Jive was incorporated in the verbal performances of sacred and secular African American performers. By the late 1960s African American political nationalists renamed jive talk as rap. The Black Arts Movement, I assert, set the tone for hip-hop, a youth arts movement. Drastic social, political, eco-nomic, and musical changes external to and internal to black urban commu-nities, particularly in New York City, gave rise to rappin as a musical genre during the early 1970s. Rap music emerged, then, as an expressive tool through which its creators responded creatively to changes in their environ-ment. The following chapter addresses these issues in more depth.

# The Development of the
# Rap Music Tradition

2

The previous chapter revealed that the concept of rappin can be traced from African bardic traditions to black oral expressive forms of the South and their transformation in the urban North. Although the pretext for rap is embedded in past oral traditions, its development as a discernible musical genre began in the 1970s during the wake of the Civil Rights and Black Nationalist movements of the 1960s. New social policies fostered by the Civil Rights Act of 1964 and Affirmative Action, implemented by the Department of Health, Education, and Welfare in 1967, helped to propel African Americans into full participation in various areas of mainstream American society that were formerly closed to them. But in spite of these political measures, some sectors of the African American community grew pessimistic when these policies made little impact on black Americans in the ghetto, where living conditions steadily worsened, youth gangs multiplied at alarming proportions, and drugs ravaged the communities. The new political incentives brought about by legislation and policy did, however, affect blacks in the music industry positively, fostering a new atmosphere of artistic freedom and a more powerful platform from which to reach a much wider audience. And those who reached the hallowed halls of the industry took the opportunity to give voice to those still struggling in the ghetto and to those who made it out. As Nelson George eloquently states, "The struggle to overcome overt apartheid of America had given blacks an energy, a motivating dream, that inspired the music's makers" (1988b:147).

Black popular music of the 1970s tended to reflect African Americans' split reactions to integration. Some artists made conscious aesthetic choices to launch black musical styles further into mainstream acceptance, while others struggled to keep the music "real" in allegiance to a disenchanted black public. Rap music developed in the United States in complex relation to diverse factors that include geopolitics, shifts in the music industry and the music of the streets, and changes in federal government policies. In response to these factors, inner-city youths—DJs, MCs, graffiti writers, and b-boys and b-girls—forged an arts movement that evolved in the streets called hip-hop. A closer look at the interdependent relationship between musical change and sociocultural factors sheds much light on the maturation of rap.

### Musical and Social Change

The 1970s ushered in a new era of black popular music in the United States. Drawing from and expanding on musical concepts associated with past styles of jazz, blues, gospel, rhythm and blues, black rock 'n' roll, and soul, black artists created new and diverse forms of contemporary black popular music (Maultsby 1979:BM10). The three most distinct black popular styles of the 1970s were funk, disco, and rap. Funk and disco were catalysts in the developmental stages of rap as a musical genre.

Funk was a term brought to musical prominence in the title of a jazz tune called "Funky Butt" by a New Orleans jazz cornetist, Buddy Bolden, around the 1900s. In 1953 the term was employed by the hard bop pianist Horace Silver to define "the return to the evocative feeling and expressiveness of traditional blues" as captured in his "Opus de Funk" (Shaw 1986:257). Funk in the jazz culture of the 1950s was a style countering "the coldness, complexity, and intellectualism introduced into the music by Bop, Cool, West Coast, and Third Stream jazz" (257). By the late 1960s, the term was reformulated by the soul singer James Brown to denote an earthy and gritty sonority characterized specifically by Brown's preachy vocal style and his horn and rhythm section's interlocking rhythmic "grooves."[1]

Brown's funk style was recycled later in the music of Sly and the Family Stone and Kool and the Gang, who produced "Thank You (Falettinme Be Mice Elf Agin)" (1970) and "Funky Stuff" (1973), respectively. The style was further advanced by Larry Graham (the former bass player of Sly and the Family Stone) with Graham Central Station and George Clinton of Parlia-

James Brown at the Universal Amphitheatre in Los Angeles, 1995. (Photo by Bill Jones)

ment-Funkadelic. Both Graham's and Clinton's songs were party-oriented, but they differed in many ways.

Clinton, who coined the term "P-Funk," or pure/uncut funk, viewed his music as a way to induce a relaxed mood in his listeners. In establishing this mood, Clinton manipulated varied sound effects produced on the synthesizer and dictated to his audience via an accompanying rappin monologue loosely chanted over music how to be and feel "cool." James Brown's stylistic influence on P-Funk is most prevalent via Parliament-Funkadelic's horn section, which was comprised chiefly of Brown's former instrumentalists. However, in discussing what he contends was the underlying essence of funk, Clinton states, "'We [Parliament] realized that blues was the key to that music. We just speeded blues up and called it "funk" 'cause we knew it was a bad word to a lot of people'" (quoted in Reid 1993:45).[2] Underscoring the P-Funk vision, Clinton expanded on Sly Stone's soul-punk attire and added special effects. He augmented Parliament-Funkadelic's extravagant galactic-centered live shows with the landing of a spaceship called the Mothership. Another trademark of Clinton's image is the popularization of the funk sign—a clenched fist with a raised forefinger and pinky (a salute appropriated by hip-hop's godfather Afrika Bambaataa and his Zulu Nation).

In contrast, Larry Graham's "churchy" music used a Hammond B-3 organ (commonly used in black gospel music) and gospel-based vocals. More importantly, Graham's music was dominated by his playing style: his pulling, thumping, and slapping the bass guitar strings, "which became the trademark for defining the funk style" (Maultsby 1979:BM22).

In contrast, the historical precedent for 1970s disco music was the work of the African American artist Barry White and the musical production of Philadelphia International Records, a black-owned company started by Kenny Gamble and Leon Huff.[3] Tunes by White and his forty-piece Love Unlimited Orchestra, such as "Love's Theme" (1974) and MFSB's "TSOP" (The Sound of Philadelphia, 1974), the original theme for the syndicated television dance program "Soul Train," are typical of this music. The musical basis of

George Clinton speaking to an audience at the Baldwin Hills Crenshaw Mall, Los Angeles, 1993. (Photo by Alisa Childs)

disco was an orchestral arrangement over a rhythm section, soul vocals, and an underlying bass-drum rhythm that accented all four beats subdivided by the hi-hat cymbal beats. The role of the disc jockey in disco foreshadowed the same in rap: "disco gave prominence to the record producer and the disc jockey—the former for his skill in manipulating the new sophisticated recording technology, and the latter for his ability to use changes in tempo, volume, and mood to manipulate dancers on the floor" (Shaw 1986:251).

By the mid-1970s, European producers, including Pete Bellotte and Giorgio Moroder, entered the disco scene and modified it with female soloists, an eighth-note bass line figure that outlined the notes of a chord, and a shift in tempo from a moderate to a faster beat. Nelson George contends,

> Disco movers and shakers were not record executives but club deejays. Most were gay men with a singular attitude toward American culture, black as well as white. They elevated female vocalists like [Donna] Summer, Gloria Gaynor, Diana Ross, Loleatta Holloway, Melba Moore, and Grace Jones to diva status, while black male singers were essentially shunned. Funk, which in the late-70s was enjoying great popularity in the South and Midwest, was rarely on their playlists. It was too raw and unsophisticated, and one thing dear to the hearts of disco fans, gay and straight, was feeling a pseudosophistication. (George 1988b:154)

"In the quest for commercial success, creativity had given way to formula, and the very excitement and challenge for which the music makers had long striven began to fade" (Joe 1980:31). As a result of being farther removed from its cultural base, 1970s disco became distorted, altered, and less dynamic. It was recognized as "a white, middle-class, youth-to-middle age phenomenon" (Shaw 1986:250).

Black musicians like George Clinton responded to the disco commercial fever by signifyin on its tempo à la funk style, which was the aim of Funkadelic's signature song, "One Nation Under a Groove" (1978). Carl "Butch" Small explains, "'One Nation' was a snub at disco. You know how we were used to hearing the 'lily white' disco with heavy percussion. I did so many sessions in the disco era. During the disco era I worked from sunup to sundown. 'One Nation' was conceived with a tempo like 120 beats per minute. Yeah, a disco dance tempo, but it was black rhythm" (Small interview). A similar radical reaction toward disco occurred among black youth, particularly those in New York City. Bill Adler, an independent rap music publicist and critic, observed:

In New York City in the mid-70s, the dominant black popular music was
disco as it was every place else. The difference about New York was that kids
were funk fiends who weren't getting their vitamins from disco music. It was
"too nervous," in their terminology, which meant too fast. It was too gay. It
was something, but it just didn't move them, and so they were thrown back
into their own resources, and what happened was that they started to . . . play
a lot of James Brown. . . . His old records were . . . staples, and Kool and the
Gang, and heavy funk like that developed. I mean, part of it just had to do
with there being a lot of neighborhood parks in New York City . . . and what
kind of music was played in those parks by the disc jockeys there. (Adler
interview)

While the commercialization of disco did indeed make an impact on the
redirection of black popular music in the United States, some have argued
that rap music was a consequence of geopolitical factors idiosyncratic to New
York, particularly the Bronx. Drawing from the works of Mollenkopf (1983),
Walkowitz (1990), and Mollenkopf and Castells (1991), the rap music scholar Tricia Rose points out how postindustrial conditions, such as the replace-
ment of industrial factories with information service corporations and the
changes in the federal governmental policies, reshaped the economic structures of cities like New York during the 1970s (1994:27–34). For instance, the
dwindling federal funding for the arts had a profound effect on extracurric-
ular school programs for inner-city youth and the public school system's arts
programs as well. At the National Endowment for the Arts (NEA) conference
in Chicago on April 14, 1994, the author Thulani Davis delivered the keynote
address, "The Artist in Society." Davis stated that the days of classroom in-
struction in music have been replaced by "street arts like rap . . . those little
instruments we once learned to play in the classroom, those [days] are gone."
This statement fueled a discussion among audience members about the "demise of black music"; the majority of the audience concurred that the lack
of funding for the arts in public schools was a major contributor to rap's
evolution. In the face of decreased financial support for New York City's
public school music programs, particularly the instrumental music curric-
ulum, inner-city youth reacted creatively by relying on their own voices,
launching the resurgence of street-corner a cappella singing and popularizing the human beat box (vocal rhythmic simulation of a drum). They also
became more interested in musical technology ushered in by disco from turntables to synthesizers.

In addition to the changes in federal education policy, radical changes in
housing had a profound effect by institutionalizing poverty and distilling the

concentration of the mostly black and Latino underclass into condensed pockets of the urban environment. In New York City, as throughout the country, "deep social service cuts were part of a larger trend in unequal wealth distribution and were accompanied by a housing crisis" (Rose 1994:28). The housing crisis negatively impacted people of color, who comprised more than half of the inner city's working class and underclass. In *Organizing the South Bronx* (1995), the urban crusader Jim Rooney notes that prior to the 1960s, public housing was basically for those who were temporarily "down on their luck" and not for "long term welfare families and unwed mothers." But by the 1960s, "this concept had been discarded, and admission policies were changed to allow welfare recipients into the structures. Thereafter, public housing came to be seen as the shelter of last resort, as a permanent home for the underclass rather than a temporary refuge for 'respectable families'" (1995:46).

By the 1970s, most of the federal monies allocated for inner-city housing were transferred to upscale suburbia and funneled into housing construction there. In the phenomenon known as "white flight," these areas had now become a refuge for whites fleeing the poorly neglected inner cities that had an increasing black and Latino underclass. The disproportionate distribution of monies to build suburbs rather than rebuild the inner city divided the races, causing people of color throughout the nation's urban centers to be segregated and ghettoized. Thus, "modest blocks were bulldozed flat in the name of social progress, and the promise of these high-rise projects [in the inner city] rapidly soured" (Rooney 1995:46).

### New York City Gang Culture

Numerous U.S. cities were impacted by similar policy initiatives similar to those affecting New York City. Among those areas profoundly disturbed by the unstable economy in New York was the Bronx, whose decline begin rapidly after World War II. Jim Rooney identifies two primary culprits in the disintegration of the Bronx: postwar federal housing and highway initiatives (1995:43). These factors are also catalytic to the evolution of hip-hop culture and music.

In discussing the geopolitics of the region in the 1950s, the rap music journalist Steven Hager writes, "the Bronx was known as the borough of apartment buildings where rent controls . . . were usually kept in the family, handed down" (1984:1). After New York's park commissioner, Robert Moses, ordered that the Cross Bronx Expressway be built through the Bronx in 1959, "the middle-class Italian, German, Irish, and Jewish neighborhoods disappeared overnight. Impoverished black and Hispanic families, who dominated the southern end of the borough, drifted north. Along with the poor came their perennial problems: crime, drug addiction, [and] unemployment" (2–3). Rooney notes that while the Cross Bronx Expressway enabled some people to move to the suburbs and still retain their jobs in the city, "this gargantuan expressway disrupted neighborhoods and destroy[ed] viable parts of the South Bronx. The expressway became the de facto northern border of the South Bronx" (Rooney 1995:59). As a result, property owners sold apartments at lower rates to avaricious landlords, who neglected apartment upkeep yet charged exorbitant rent. Black and Latino residents were forced to live in dilapidated, rodent-infested housing. Exacerbating matters, some landlords devised lucrative schemes to evade taxes by hiring stooges to force residents out by burning down the apartments so they could receive insurance payoffs (Henry Chalfant, personal communication, Manhattan, June 23, 1993). Between 1970 and 1975, there were 68,456 fires in the Bronx—more than thirty-three each night (Rooney 1995:56).[4]

As conditions worsened, crime escalated. Some youths formed neighborhood groups or gangs to police their apartments, projects, streets, and neighborhoods from outside invaders. As soon as one gang formed, others formed in response, eventually leading to fierce territorial rivalry (see the video documentary *Flyin' Cut Sleeves,* 1993). By the 1960s the South Bronx was regarded as a leading headquarters of street gang violence. Numerous brutal gang encounters, particularly around intraterritorial rivalries and sexual assault of female victims by male gang members, were common headlines in local newspapers, as were rapes, murders, and, as one writer recalls, "unspeakable rites of passage" (Hager 1984:5–11). By 1973 statistics revealed that New York City gangs totalled 315 with over nineteen thousand members (George 1992:11), though toward the end of that year gang activity slowly dissipated in part because of a peace meeting between rival gangs in the Bronx. According to *Flyin' Cut Sleeves,* this gang truce was initiated by the Ghetto Brothers, a nonviolent gang, after the death of one of their members, Cornell "Black Benji" Benjamin, who was fatally wounded while trying to stop a fight among rivals of the Seven Mortals, Black Spades, and Mongols gangs.

Other factors that ultimately led to the collapse of street gangs included homicide among gang members, maternal responsibilities of female gang members, and the introduction of heroin. The following best summarizes the disintegration of New York City street gangs as recalled by one member:

"'Some gangs got into drugs. Other gangs got wiped out by other gangs. Others got so big that members didn't want to be involved no more. Girls got tired [and] wanted to have children. Plus times were changin'" (Bambaataa quoted in Hager 1984:10).[5]

In the wake of street gang violence, Afrika Bambaataa, deemed the "Godfather of Hip-Hop," asserted his concept of youth solidarity by rechanneling violent competition into artistic contests. Prior to his vision, like many youth in the Bronx, Bambaataa had been a member of the notorious street gang Black Spades. When the Spades established a division in his neighborhood in 1969, Bambaataa had joined them because "'it was all part of growing up in the southeast Bronx'" (quoted in Hager 1984:73).

By the early 1970s Bambaataa had slowly retreated from the Spades by following his passion for DJing at local venues. In an effort to curtail violence, he drifted toward religious and political organizations, including the Nation

Afrika Bambaataa, Founder of the Zulu Nation, mid-1980s. (Photo by Lisa Haun/ Michael Ochs Archives)

of Islam (NOI), that deterred street youth from gang activity. He explains his attraction to Islam and its influence in his life: "'What got me excited first was when James Brown came out with "Say it Loud, I'm Black and I'm Proud." . . . I decided to get into the Nation of Islam. It put a change on me. It got me to respect people even though they might not like us because we [were] Muslims. The Nation of Islam was doing things that America had been trying to [do] for a while—taking people from the streets like junkies and prostitutes and cleaning them up. Rehabilitating them like the jail system wasn't doing'" (quoted in Toop 2000:59). Through the teachings and philosophy of the NOI, Bambaataa envisioned a way to terminate street violence in the Bronx River housing project. In 1973 he formed a nonviolent organization called the Youth Organization, which he eventually renamed Zulu Nation. The Zulu Nation is "a huge young adult and youth organization which incorporates people that are into breakdancing, DJing, and graffiti. I had them to battle against each other in a nonviolent way, like rapper against rapper rather than knife against knife" (Bambaataa interview). The creative forces of this youth community, who shared a common historical and political space, were realized via the unification of spiritual, psychological, and linguistic factors.

The Zulu Nation's idea was inspired by the 1964 British film *Zulu*, starring Michael Caine and directed by Cy Endfield. In an interview conducted by the hip-hop critic David Toop (2000), Bambaataa recalls:

> "The Zulu Nation. I got the idea [from] . . . this movie called *Zulu* which featured Michael Caine. They [the Zulus] were proud warriors and . . . fighting very well against bullets, canons and stuff. They fought like warriors for a land which was theirs. . . . And then, as the years went by, through all the civil rights movement, human rights, Vietnam war, and all the folk and rock that was happening—all the change of '60s that was happening to the whole world—it just stayed with me to have some type of group like that."
> (quoted in Toop 2000:57)

Years after seeing the film, Bambaataa visited Africa, where his idea of nation was solidified. Bambaataa's metamorphosis continued as he rejected Western influences and Judeo-Christianity. He believed that Christianity contributed to the acceptance of black cultural stereotypes: "'black was evil, and turn the other cheek . . .'" (quoted in Toop 2000:57). His religious passion for Islam shaped his perception of the Civil Rights movement and the Nation of Islam. The former seemed passive to him: "'So Martin Luther King was the thing that was happening because he was fighting for civil rights, but

Malcolm X was more on the aggressive side. Myself, I was more on the Malcolm X way of thinking'" (quoted in Toop 2000:57).

Following in the tradition of the Nation of Islam, he rejected his anglicized name—"I never speak of my real name, 'cuz I don't consider it my real name anyway" (Bambaataa interview)—and adopted the name Afrika Bambaataa in honor of the legendary African Zulu warrior, whose name means "affectionate leader." Despite his rejection of the nonviolent tactics of Martin Luther King, he cites as influences a wide range of the viewpoints represented by black leaders: "'I always had an understanding of teachers such as the Honorable Elijah Muhammad and Minister Louis Farrakhan and in the '60s watching the Black Panthers, Martin Luther King and the rest of our great leaders that were doing a strong knowledge thing. . . . So by pulling all factions together, we made this whole cultural movement called Hip-Hop'" (quoted in Webb 1992:56).

According to Bambaataa, the word "hip-hop" can be traced to Lovebug Starski, a South Bronx disc jockey. He indicated that at Starski's parties, the DJ would always say, "hip hop you don't stop that makes your body rock." "So I just coined a word myself and started using the word 'hip-hop' to name this type of culture, and then it caught on" (Bambaataa interview). Bambaataa's concept of hip-hop encompassed urban street expressions and embodied a street attitude through gestures, language, and stylized dress associated with street culture.

Hip-hop, as well as the Zulu Nation, was not conceived as an ethnically homogeneous expression or unit comprised solely of and for African Americans. During its early development, many hip-hop innovators were of African Caribbean and Latino (mainly Puerto Rican) descent. DJs like Kool "DJ" Herc, Bambaataa, and Grandmaster Flash were African Caribbean, and Charlie Chase, who deejayed for the Cold Crush Brothers, was Puerto Rican (see Toop 2000; Hebdige 1987; Flores 2000). Graffiti artists were ethnically diverse overall, but Puerto Rican hip-hoppers dominated in breakdancing, while African Americans and African Caribbeans mainly performed as DJs and MCs. It is this cultural intersection of African diasporic blending that ultimately provided the basis for a hip-hop aesthetic (see chapter 5).

Full discussion of all the artistic expression encompassed by the youth arts mass movement known as hip-hop and led by Afrika Bambaataa is beyond the scope of this book. The following section will focus primarily on the development of two aspects of this artistic movement—DJing and MCing—which, as a consequence of geopolitics, gang violence, and the commercialization of disco music, became hip-hop's driving force.

## From Kingston to the Bronx: The Rise of the Street DJ

Gang activity affected not only the outdoor environs but also the club scene in which hip-hop music was performed. One of the major problems party-goers consistently encountered at the clubs was gang violence. The violence ultimately led to the temporary suspension of DJ performances at local clubs, particularly in areas like the South Bronx, where club gang violence predom-inated. As one jockey recalls, "'it got too dangerous for people to go to discos'" (quoted in Hager 1984:32). As a result, a few of the South Bronx jockeys like Kool "DJ" Herc and Afrika Bambaataa took their talent to settings remote from neighborhood clubs, such as local parks. These itinerant disc jockeys' mastery on the turntables made them instant heroes in their respective communities. Such itinerant disc jockeys became known in the hip-hop community as street or mobile DJs, as opposed to those who performed in clubs or on the radio. These DJs played an important role in the growing influence of rap music.

Mobile disc jockeys drew their inheritance from radio disc jockeys. A number of DJs and MCs interviewed stated that they took their initial in-spiration from and patterned themselves after New York radio personalities such as Frankie Crocker, Gary Byrd, Hank Spann, and others. In exploring the link between radio DJs and mobile DJs, it is apparent that the street DJs, similar to radio jockeys, speak to their audiences in a stylized manner and make an art of dovetailing one record into another. In the early days, street DJs also incorporated sound techniques popularized by radio jockeys, such as "talking through" and "riding gain" in performances. But when I asked them about the roots of the street DJ, they would continually assert that rap music evolved also from toasting. When I asked whether they were referring to toast narratives like "The Signifying Monkey" and "Dolemite," though they knew of these toasts, they cited a different toast tradition known as Ja-maican rhymes. One rap artists stated, "we had a lot of toasters coming out of Kingston" (Carson interview).

The link between the Bronx and Kingston is substantial, though in gen-eral it has been unmentioned or simply glossed over in previous works on rap music and hip-hop culture. Toasting and DJing were initially employed simultaneously in the Jamaican tradition. The model for this combination can be traced to Kingston and the development of sound system or dance-hall culture.

During the 1930s, swing bands dominated the music scene in Kingston, Jamaica. Most of the bands' repertory consisted of American-style music performed primarily in local clubs and rented-out lodges called dancehalls.

By the end of World War II, the swing band scene waned. At this time, in desperate need of labor in order to rebuild, Britain passed the British Nationality Act of 1948, conferring citizenship to subjects of the Commonwealth in the West Indies.[6] In discussing the demise of the swing band scene in Kingston, the dancehall scholar Norman C. Stolzoff notes, "Because Britain was in need of massive rebuilding after World War II, the British government turned to the colonies as a source of cheap labor. Given this open-door policy, Jamaicans and other West Indians left home 'seeking greener pastures.' . . . Among them were a significant fraction of Jamaica's trained [swing] musicians" (2000:41). DJs in search of musical alternatives were hired merely to spin records at dancehall parties. With the booming DJ culture came powerful amplifiers or sound systems. According to Stolzoff, the prototype of the dancehall sound system was the PA (public address) system first rented-out and used at political rallies in Jamaica. He credits Hedley Jones, however, as a builder of the first sound system. From an interview with Bunny "the Mighty Burner" Goodison, Stolzoff determines that "from its genesis as a PA system for political rallies, the sound system went on to become the basis of an enterprising dancehall scene" (42).

The new dancehall scene became a phenomenon among Kingston's black working class. Because Jamaica's radio airwaves were dominated by black popular music or rhythm and blues during the 1950s, DJs often spun U.S. imports on their record players. The dancehall scene expanded to outdoor contexts. As one patron described, "'you just pay a sound system man about three or five pounds, as [was] the case in them day. Bring his equipment stick it up on the sidewalk, or inna the yard, and bring in the boxes of beer and thing, and you have a dance and make some money'" (quoted in Stolzoff 2000:42 [bracketed note in original]). The Jamaican producer Junior Lincoln observed, "'A sound system is just like what you call a disco. But the only thing is, it is not as sophisticated as a disco set. The amplifiers are huge, well now amplifiers are as big as 2,000 watts. They emphasise a lot on the bass. And they play sometimes twenty or twenty-four inch speakers. So it really thump, y'know. The bass line is really heavy. You've never heard anything so heavy in all your life'" (quoted in Hebdige 1987:63).

Setting the criterion for who ranks the best in the world of the DJ, Jamaican DJs led the way in using massive sound systems to "try and 'blow' the other off the stage with rawer and rougher sounds" (Hebdige 1987:63). Signifying on their unique skills, sound system DJs created catchy names for themselves and their two-to-three-man crews, such as Duke Reid's Trojan, Sir Coxsone's Downbeat, and Tom Wong, also known as Tom the Great Se-

U-Roy. (Photo by David
Corio/Michael Ochs Ar-
chives)

bastian, who was Chinese Jamaican. Count Matchukie, a major innovator in
the dancehall sound system scene, is considered an originator and master
performer of toasting. Matchukie, who once deejayed with Sir Coxsone, recited his rhymes in Jamaican Patois, formal English, and even Spanish to show
off his versatility at the microphone. The famous U-Roy was one of a number of other DJs who advanced toasting in their performances.

By the late 1950s, Jamaican DJs shifted their musical taste from American popular music to something uniquely Jamaican. Prince Buster, a sound
system DJ, provided this transition. At the time, the Jamaican popular music scene turned toward its own musical resources in the invention of "ska,"
a forerunner of rocksteady, reggae, and dancehall. Unlike rhythm and blues,
in which the rhythmic accents occurred on beats 2 and 4, the rhythmic accents in ska fall on the "and" of beats 1, 2, 3, and 4. Ska makes use of the sax-
ophone and trombone as well. Jamaican-owned and -operated recording
studios, including Ken Khouri's Federal Records (founded in 1954) and Ed-

ward Seaga's West Indies Records (founded in 1958) produced a number of ska recordings.[7] Ska artists include the Skatalites, the Vikings, Prince Buster, and Justin Hines and the Dominoes. Ska was soon replaced by a slower and more bassy sound called "rocksteady." Unlike ska, rocksteady made little or no use of horns. Alton Ellis, Delroy Wilson, and the Vendors rank among the top rocksteady performers in Jamaica.

Alongside ska, several changes took place in Jamaica during the 1960s: the proliferation of the Rastafari movement; the change in political power; and the maturation and globalization of Jamaica's popular musical culture (through the reggae music of Bob Marley and the Wailers). These musical and sociopolitical tides were most evident with Jamaica's youth culture. Dancehall or sound system culture remained closely linked to Jamaica's working class. Soon it would be emblematic of a thriving youth culture, known as "rude boys" or "rudies."

Rudies hung out on Kingston's ghetto street corners. Disenchanted with Jamaica's economy, rudies sported handguns and knives and donned certain clothes: "very short green serge trousers, leather or gangster-style suit jackets, and . . . shades" (Hebdige 1987:72). Caught between the political rivalry of Michael Manley's People's National Party (PNP) and Edward Seaga's Jamaica Labour Party (JLP), rudies fell into youth gangs divided along political lines and recruited by constituents of each party to instigate political resistance. By 1966 political gang warfare escalated. "Gang warfare, political violence between supporters of the PNP and JLP, and clashes between gangs and security forces began in February and March 1966 and continued, except for certain pauses, until after 22 February, the polling day of the 1967 General Election" (Lacey 1977:87). Toward the end of the 1960s, the economic situation worsened in Jamaica, creating growing disenchantment among the poor toward outsiders, particularly British and U.S. businesses in Jamaica. Among the most notorious riots in Jamaica's political history were the Rodney Riots of October 1968, named after Walter Rodney, the alleged conspirator behind the formation of political youth gangs or posses. "The city of Kingston was divided like a checkerboard into political garrisons controlled by the gangs under the patronage of party leadership" (Stolzoff 2000:84).[8]

Gang attacks ensued, spilling into the dancehall scene. When the gang's rudies invaded the dancehalls, DJs retreated from the dancehall scenes to the recording studio. By the late 1960s, a studio-produced form of Jamaican pop called "dubs" emerged. While mixing tracks for Sir Coxsone, the sound engineer Osbourne "King Tubby" Ruddock accidentally stumbled across a way to fade out the vocal and instrumental parts on the two-track recording machine.

"He began fading out the instrumental track, to make sure that the vocals sounded right. . . . So instead of mixing the specials in the usual way, he cut back and forth between the vocal and instrumental tracks and played with the bass and treble knobs until he changed the original tapes into something else entirely" (Hebdige 1987:83). The technique of fading certain parts in and out or altering them in creating several varied cuts from the original resulted in dub versions. Alongside King Tubby's invention of the dub concept came "riddims." Riddims are rhythmic reggae grooves consisting of a distinct reggae-style bass line. Leroy Sibbles, the bassist for the Heptones, is acknowledged as a creator of several bass riddims. The riddims grooves Sibbles helped create include "Full Up," "Satta Massagana," "Declaration of Rights," "No Man Is an Island," "Ten to One," "Things a Come to Bump," "Sweet Talking," "Freedom Blues" or "MPLA," "School Riddims," "Book of Rules," "Midnight," "Love I Can Feel," "In Cold Blood," and "Baby Why" (Chang and Chen 1998:77). Riddims become a trademark of reggae and reggae dancehall.

In the past, DJs toasted over live music. The 1970s ushered in toasting over recorded or dub versions called "talk overs." U-Roy, mentioned previously for his influence in toasting, is the person most often credited as the "grandfather" of the contemporary DJ phenomenon. Among his contenders include Big Youth, I-Roy, Linton Kwesi Johnson, and Mutabaruka.

Undoubtedly the talk overs and the sound system concept had a direct impact on musical production throughout the West Indies and eventually the United States through West Indian immigrants. Thus it is not surprising that the three recognized innovators of rap music—Kool "DJ" Herc, Afrika Bambaataa, and Grandmaster Flash—are of West Indian heritage. Their parents were among the many who emigrated from the West Indies to the United States during the 1960s. Although West Indians had migrated to the United States before 1960, a large influx of West Indians occurred after the termination of Britain's Commonwealth Immigrants Act in 1962 and the independence of Jamaica and Trinidad and Tobago from England in 1962, followed by Guyana and Barbados in 1966. Accordingly, West Indians comprised one-third of Caribbean immigrants living in the United States in the 1960s. According to the economist Ransford W. Palmer, the majority came from Jamaica. "The U.S. Census [also] reported 171,525 immigrants from the West Indies in New York City [which] represented 73 percent of all West Indian immigrants in the United States, 48 percent of whom arrived between 1965 and 1970" (1995:20).

With a large concentration of West Indians in New York City, the musical scene would soon be altered. In an effort to create contexts similar to Jamaican dancehall culture, U.S. street DJs followed suit, creating outdoor discotheques in local parks. The rap music artist The Real Roxanne said, "People used to do jams [parties] outside in the schoolyard or handball court. Someone used to bring their two turntables out and plug it into the lamp post outside and that's how they got their power. People would listen and dance to the music out in the streets" (The Real Roxanne interview).

Street DJs were well known in their own boroughs and were supported by local followers. Popular jockeys included Pete "DJ" Jones of the Bronx and Grandmaster Flowers and Maboya of Brooklyn. They occasionally spoke to their audiences in a legato-mellow style reminiscent of early African American radio disc jockeys of the 1950s and 1960s. According to DJ Hollywood of Harlem, New York street DJs, like Jamaican DJs, were evaluated on the size and sound of their sound systems and their loudness rather than their technical abilities to spin or rap to a crowd in the early 1970s: "Pete 'DJ' Jones, Flowers and Maboya, they weren't microphone DJs, they were DJs that just had big big sound systems and big equipment; and this is what people were into at that particular time. Who had the biggest one, who had the biggest sound. So when I looked back at the concept of what was happening, I said to myself, 'I wanted to be the best'" (DJ Hollywood interview). Although many street DJs were males, there was a noted female from Brooklyn by the name of Lady J. The music promoter Dennis Shaw recognized Lady J as a pioneer and credits her as "very unique for her time. She was a forerunner of lady DJs, who was very adept at mixing" (Shaw interview).

The most innovative of the mobile disc jockeys was the Jamaican-born Clive Campbell, known as Kool "DJ" Herc, whose mixing technique immensely influenced the future direction and production of rap music. Herc emigrated to the Bronx from Kingston, Jamaica, in 1967, when he was only twelve years old.

By 1972, Herc began DJing throughout the Bronx, though his approach to this form contrasted with that of the U.S. jockeys. Instead of simply dovetailing one record after another and talking intermittently to the crowd, Herc recited rhymes over the microphone while mixing. In mixing, the DJ places a disc on each of two turntables and attempts to match their speed with a pitch control device on the turntable system. With the use of an audio-mixer, which sits between the turntables, and its cross-fader lever, a DJ can smoothly shift from one turntable to the next. Simultaneously, Herc also added electronic sound effects—"echoing and reverbing back and forth between the vocal and instrument track; [while manipulating] the treble and bass knobs" (Hebdige 1987:83).

Kool "DJ" Herc and Grand-
master Flash receive the
Hip-Hop Pioneer Awards at
the Source Hip-Hop Music
Awards, Los Angeles, 1999.
(Photo by Alisa Childs)

Herc tailored his DJing style after the dub music jockeys of Jamaica by
mixing musical fragments referred to by street jockeys as "breaks" or "break-
beats"[9] from various recordings to create an entirely new soundtrack. Afrika Bambaataa recalls in an interview that Herc "'knew that a lot of American
blacks were not getting into reggae. He took the same thing that the deejays
[were] doing—toasting—and did it with American records. . . . He would
call out the names of people who were at the party, just like the microphone
personalities who deejayed back in Jamaica'" (quoted in Chang and Chen
1998:72). Bambaataa recalls how Herc "'took the music of . . . Mandrill, like
"Fencewalk," certain disco records that had funky percussion breaks like
The Incredible Bongo Band [a Jamaican disco group] when they came out
with "Apache" and he just kept that beat going. It might be that certain part
of the record that everybody waits for—they just let their inner self go and
get wild. The next thing you know the singer comes back in and you'd be

mad'" (quoted in Toop 2000:60). The "certain part of the record that every-body waited for" consisted of an African Latin percussion soundtrack—con-gas and timbales—called the "break" section. In addition, as Herc went back and forth between breaks and the microphone, his MC, Coke La Rock, con-tinued giving props to various members of Herc's crew. Indeed, Herc's DJ parties fostered an atmosphere of hip-hop arts with his accompanying breakdancers or b-boys, known as the Nigger Twins.

Because of his enormous sound system, Kool Herc could be heard per-forming at a distance throughout the Bronx. His mixing concept inspired many itinerant jockeys in the Bronx, including Afrika Bambaataa, who even-tually perfected this technique. The rap music producer Larry Smith contends that Afrika Bambaataa possessed the most incredible ear for finding beats from all over and using all genres of music in his mixes, a talent that earned him the title "Master of Records" (Smith interview). The "breaks" that con-tained these beats represented a variety of musical styles, ranging from soul, funk, and disco to commercial jingles and television themes. Most of Bam-baataa's favorite break-beat records—including "Funky Drummer" by James Brown, "Take Me to the Mardi Gras" by Bob James, "Think" by Lynn Col-lins, and "Dance to the Drummer's Beat" by the Herman Kelly Band—have gone on to become the foundation for numerous hip-hop tracks (Fernando 1994:54). L Ju, an admirer of Bambaataa, also notes, "'he blended tracks from Germany, Jamaica, the Philippines, Cali[fornia] and the South Bronx into a beautiful collage called hip-hop jams in the park and created a movement that turned into a world-wide musical and cultural revolution, as well as a billion dollar industry. His parties lifted the dancer into a spiritual state of euphoria based on his overstanding of vibrations, rhythms, cadence, tone, melody and mood'" (quoted in Emery 1998:26)

Another Bronx disc jockey influenced by Kool "DJ" Herc was Joseph Sadler, better known as Grandmaster Flash. Flash began his career as a DJ for neighborhood block parties, but he realized his skills were limited because of his mixing board. Flash felt intimidated by Kool Herc's huge sound sys-tem and enormous volume, even though he later discerned that Herc had less than perfect mixing skills.

"With the monstrous power he had he couldn't mix too well. He was play-ing little breaks but it would sound so sloppy. I noticed that the mixer he was using was a GLI 3800. It was a very popular mixer at that time. It's a scarcity today but it's still one of the best mixers GLI ever made. At the time he wasn't using no cueing. In other words, the hole was there for a headphone to go in but I remember he never had headphones over his ears. All of a sudden, Herc had headphones but I guess he was so used to dropping the needle down by eyesight and trying to mix it that from the audio part of it he couldn't get into it too well." (quoted in Toop 2000:62)

Flash began going to discotheques to observe other jockeys in performance. At a Manhattan disco club, he met Pete "DJ" Jones. Though Jones performed for a conservative audience, Flash noticed that Jones was more accurate in mixing records than Kool Herc. Also, Jones was known for his extended play concept. Commenting on "the way Pete would connect the records," Flash says, "some of the DJs I used to watch [back then] used to let the record play all the way to the end then play the next one with the gap in between. I found it quite amazing that Pete kept the record going, going, going, all night long. That's how he acquired the name Pete 'With the Funky Beat DJ' Jones" (Grandmaster Flash interview). In addition, Jones had a switch on the system that allowed him to hear what was playing on one turntable before playing it aloud. Grandmaster Flash, a student of electronics, later invented an apparatus allowing him to cue up a record while the other is played through the speak-

Grandmaster Flash and the Furious Five. Top row, left to right: Scorpio, Kid Creole, Raheim, Melle Mel, Cowboy (center, kneeling), Grandmaster Flash (front), 1980s. (Courtesy of Micheal Ochs Archives)

ers. He accomplished this with an external amplifier, headphones (later a one-ear headphone), and a single-pole, double-throw switch, which he glued to his audio-mixer. Through experimenting with this apparatus, Flash pioneered two turntable techniques popularly known as "backspinning" and "phasing."

Backspinning, which requires having a copy of the same record on two turntables, is executed by rotating one record counterclockwise to the desired beat then rotating the second record counterclockwise to the same musical phrase, creating a loop-like effect. In phasing (also known as "punch-phrasing"), the DJ accents a short phrase of a recording during the playing of a second record by manipulating the turntable's cross-fader. This technique is somewhat similar to the previously discussed "riding gain" technique employed by black radio jockey personalities of the 1950s, but phasing is done with two turntables. While Flash perfected his inventions, other disc jockeys experimented with new mixing concepts.

Grand Wizard Theodore from the Bronx, a protégé of Grandmaster Flash, is credited with inventing another mixing technique called "scratching," moving a record back and forth in a rhythmic manner while the tone arm's needle remains in the groove of the record, producing a scratching sound. Although in 1978 Theodore was only thirteen years old, the youngest of the hip-hop DJs at the time, he was considered one of the few who could mix records with skill comparable to that of Flash.

New York DJs like Davy DMX and Grandmixer D.ST perfected Theodore's scratching invention. Grandmixer D.ST is responsible for popularizing scratching as a primary musical feature in the hit single "Rockit" (1983) by Herbie Hancock.[10] Other noted New York street DJs of the time who used various mixing innovations were Junebug, Charlie Chase, Sweet G, Jazzy Jay, Disco Wiz, Disco King Mario, DJ Tex, Afrika Islam, Smokey, Kurtis Blow, DJ Hollywood, the Whiz Kid, and the female DJ RD Smiley.[11] As the mostly male DJ circuit expanded, some jockeys underwent apprenticeship with other better-known DJs. This usually took the form of an exchange wherein the apprentice disassembled the mentor's sound equipment after performances and in turn received personalized professional advice about the art of DJing. The master-student relationships that developed are often indicated by "surrogate father-and-son" titles. For instance, DJ Afrika Islam is considered the Son of Bambaataa; Joseph "Run" Simmons of Run-D.M.C. is considered the Son of Kurtis Blow; and DJ Funkmaster Flex is recognized as the Son of DJ Chuck Chillout. Since mixing records had become an art in itself, some DJs felt the need for MCs. The next section explores the context in which this merge took place, eventually setting the stage for the rhymin MC.

Hip-Hop veteran MC Grandmaster Caz of the Cold Crush Brothers (front, center), along with colleagues, including Afrika Islam and Lovebug Starski (3d and 4th from the left), at the 18th Annual Universal Zulu Nation Anniversary held at The Muse, New York, 1992. (Photo by the author)

### The Rhymin MC and the Emergence of a Rap Music Genre

By the mid-1970s gang-related violence had declined in many areas of New York City, including the Bronx. In response to this change, a few neighborhood clubs reopened their doors, while others remained ambivalent about hiring street DJs because of potential gang violence. As one club owner observed, "club owners didn't like little young kids from the streets" (Abbatiello interview). Nevertheless, a few clubs, including the Dixie Club, Club 371 of the Bronx, and Harlem World of Manhattan, remained common venues for hip-hop music. Some clubs promoted this music in a series of one-night acts called "one-nighters." One club owner explained this trend pioneered by promoters:

> rap music must have been in the streets for about three or four years. The year that I went over there [it] was just startin' to get the attention of promoters' eyes—street promoters. What they were doing with these popular

people . . . they were puttin' them up in one-nighters. . . . What they would do was they would hire ten of them [DJs], rent out a ballroom that held three or four thousand people, throw in a sound system, and give everybody ten dollars apiece and charge like seven, eight, or ten dollars at the door, and they would make a fortune. . . . The promoters were making so much money they had to start giving them something. (Abbatiello interview)

The most important street music club was Disco Fever in the South Bronx, which began as an anonymous neighborhood bar. By 1976, Sal Abbatiello had acquired it as a gift from his father. He converted the bar, often referred to as "The Fever," into a dance club, and promoted street music on an every-night-of-the-week basis, rather than the usual one night of the week. Abbatiello's club featured a different DJ each night: "Eddie Cheeba was on Sundays, Love-bug Starski on Monday nights, Flash on Tuesdays, DJ Hollywood on Wednesdays, and Sweet G and Junebug, the house DJs, on Thursdays, Fridays and Saturdays" (Abbatiello interview). Because the club catered strictly to DJs and their music, Disco Fever became the hottest hip-hop dance club in New York

Sal Abbatiello, owner of Disco Fever, Bronx, New York, 1996. (Photo by the author)

City as well as a main attraction for music business entrepreneurs, leading the South Bronx to surface as a major creative center of rap music.[12]

Since playing records on turntables had become an art as well as a business, some jockeys felt the need for MCs. For example, with the hiring of Clark Kent, Jay Cee, and Pebblee-Poo,[13] Herc became the leader of the Herculords. At many of his DJ performances, Bambaataa was also accompanied by three MCs, Cowboy (not Cowboy of the Furious Five), Mr. Biggs, and Queen Kenya. The MC talked intermittently, using phrases like "get up" and "jam to the beat" to motivate the audience to dance while the DJ mixed records. The MC rapped to excite the crowd and engage them in call and response. The DJ spun the records and "played that certain part of the record and made the crowd . . . wild" (Bambaataa interview). The MC could compensate for any musical beat lapse or gaps that sometimes occurred during the DJ's mix. Flowers's MC, Sidley B, was adept at doing so, recalls Carson: "Flowers used to play with Sidley B. He [Sidley] built them [the crowd]. He helped make it go up, the excitement. It was a great timing job . . . between the DJ and whoever was vocalizing on it like Sidley B" (Shaw and Carson interview).

With the popularity of the group Grandmaster Flash and the Three MCs, the rhymin MC emerged as a distinct and primary feature. As one observer explains, "Flash was a great DJ, but his MCs were so different from the other MCs" (Abbatiello interview). Instead of simply talking intermittently to the dancing crowd while the DJ spun records, each of Flash's MCs executed their phrases in a rhyming and rhythmic fashion. Flash notes, "Melvin Glover had . . . a scholastic-type style. . . . Danny could say rhymes from now to doomsday. . . . There's some that can't really catch on when the music's being phased in and out to the beat. Cowboy, he was superb at it. As far as that 'Ho,' 'Clap your hands to the beat' and 'Say oh yeah,' I'd have to give him credit for being one of the creators of that" (quoted in Toop 2000:72).

The Three MCs popularized the concept of "trading phrases," the exchange of phrases between MCs as illustrated in example 1 by The Furious Five. They also introduced a percussive style of talk, giving rise to what rap artists call a "party-style" rap. This style features phrases in rhyme, rhythmic chanting, and synchronous timing with the disc jockey, all of which provided the underpinnings of rap as a distinct music genre.

The most acclaimed MC of the party style was DJ Hollywood of Harlem. Although little footage of DJ Hollywood's live performances at The Fever exists, he was nonetheless regarded by almost all the "rappin deejays" and their followers as a trailblazer ("Rap Records" 1980:57). As one critic

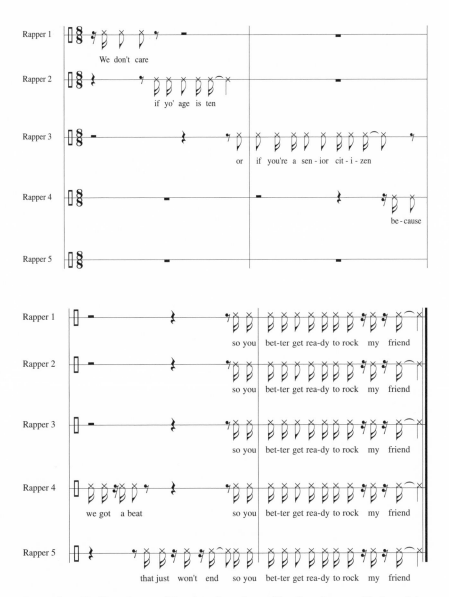

*Example 1:* Trading phrases; "Freedom," performed by Grandmaster Flash and the Furious Five (1979).

remembered, "Hollywood can shut people up. After Hollywood, a lot of people won't grab a microphone. They can't say rhymes because he's so witty . . . he's so . . . he's rhythmic. He's everything. He's rap music" (Smith interview). Abbatiello remembered, "I searched all over for the most popular guy. His name was Hollywood. He was the best rapper. He was the greatest . . . the fastest. He was the only rapper I ever saw get applause" (Abbatiello interview).

As the reputations of Grandmaster Flash and The Three MCs and Hollywood spread throughout the Bronx, other DJs began using MCs in a similar manner. Street DJs, for example, featured two or more MCs who called themselves "crews," among them Cheeba Crew, Fantastic 5 MCs, The Mercedes Ladies, and The Malachi Crew. Meanwhile, other jockeys, including Eddie Cheeba, Sweet G, Lovebug Starski, Busy Bee of the Bronx, and Kurtis Blow of Harlem, tried their hands at rappin in the party style popularized by The Three MCs.

By 1979 the rhymin MC and DJ concept had become the norm throughout New York City. The symbiotic relationship they established became the model for rap music and would soon be introduced to audiences outside of the South Bronx by two routes: the promotion of rap music in Manhattan, particularly its DJs at Manhattan's mainstream disco clubs, and the commercial recording of Sugarhill Gang's "Rapper's Delight" by the successful independent record company, Sugar Hill Records. By the early 1980s, clubs in lower Manhattan, like The Roxy (a former skating rink) and Negril, began catering solely to a hip-hop clientele. Additionally, street DJs had evolved as popular acts in the disco club circuits among Manhattan's mostly white clientele. One person who was responsible for exposing hip-hop music in the Manhattan area was Kool Lady Blue of London, England. She was initially sent to New York City to operate Malcolm McLaren's World's End punk clothing store for one year. After witnessing the burgeoning hip-hop scene in the Bronx, Kool Lady Blue began promoting hip-hop arts at The Roxy and Negril. Several celebrities visited these clubs, and some of them, like Herbie Hancock, eventually collaborated with artists such as Grandmixer D.ST.

Other music observers from the Manhattan area in turn began to frequent the Bronx. Prominent entrepreneurs like the British punk promotor Malcolm McLaren, the soon-to-be Tommy Boy Records rap mogul Tom Silverman, and Arthur Baker, the owner of Shakedown Sound Studio, frequented Afrika Bambaataa's DJ battles and performances in the Bronx and noticed the musical diversity of his record repertory. Bambaataa recalled, "'First Malcolm McLaren came, 'cause he said, "There's this Black kid playin' all this rock and other types of music to a Black and Spanish audience." ' . . . He invited me to

The legendary DJ Hollywood with the author, Harlem, 1986. (Photo by the author)

come play at the Ritz with [his group] Bow Wow Wow. So when I came and did this show, I brought everybody together like Rock Steady [breakdancers] and all the groups. . . . We went to the Danceteria and got too big for that until finally the Roxy became our home'" (quoted in George 1993:50).

In *Billboard,* a music trade magazine deemed as the bible of the music industry, Radcliffe Joe and Nelson George used the term "rapping deejay" to describe the result of the merge of the rhymin MC and the street DJ. They noticed that the change in disco "fostered the growth in the popularity of the rapping deejay; and [as a consequence], a number of recordings by rapping deejays are beginning to have an impact on the soul and disco charts of various music publications" (Joe and George 1979:4). "Rapper's Delight" bombarded the airwaves in October 1979. Considered by critics as the first successful commercial rap music recording by any record company, this song initiated an avalanche of similar recordings by makeshift independent record companies and eventually by major labels.

The musical fusion of Jamaican dancehall and African American–based funk music and the verbal art performance of both cultures contributes to the distinctiveness of rap music. Other factors, such as geopolitics, street gang culture, and lack of monies allocated to New York public schools, further fueled a response among inner-city youth like Afrika Bambaataa, whose creative insight laid the foundation for the arts movement known as hip-hop. The next chapter covers the commercialization of hip-hop music, its explosion in the musical mainstream, and the various street music promotion tactics employed in making rap a vital genre of popular music in the late twentieth century.

# The Explosion of
# Rap Music in the
# Musical Mainstream

*3*

## *The Early Commercial Years of Rap Music, 1979–85*

In the previous chapter I discussed the emergence of rap music as a distinct musical genre. The Bronx was the primary context in which street DJs with massive sound systems experimented with sound production using two turntables. By the mid-1970s, DJs sought out MCs who could recite phrases on the microphone while the DJs created the musical mix. The confluence of the street DJ and the rhymin MC became the trademark for what soon would be recognized as rap music in the musical mainstream. This chapter discusses the early commercial success of rap music with small independent record companies and its diversified musical directions and examines alternative marketing and promotional strategies within the music industry in general.

Prior to its first commercial recording, rap music was usually recorded on homemade cassettes or eight-track tapes and sold at a high price to fans or friends. DJ Hollywood explained that during his early career, after learning that one could use two turntables to make a tape, he would sell eight-track tapes for twelve dollars apiece (DJ Hollywood interview). From New York street corners to subway stations, rap music poured from large, portable cassette players called "ghetto blasters." The rap sound eventually spread to neighboring northeastern cities via homemade tapes and DJ mix tapes. The first commercial producers of rap music were rhythm and blues veterans:

Bobby Robinson (Enjoy Records), Paul Winley (Winley Records), and Joe and Sylvia Robinson (Sugar Hill Records).

Bobby Robinson, who founded Enjoy Records in 1951 and produced such rhythm and blues sensations as Gladys Knight and the Pips and King Curtis, heard about the rap scene in the Bronx from his nephew, Spoonie Gee. He sent Enjoy's A&R (artist repertoire) personnel to the Bronx to look for potential rap acts, where they discovered two rap groups: Grandmaster Flash and the Furious Five and another group with one female member, Funky Four Plus One.[1] In 1979, the latter group released its first and only successful recording on Enjoy, "Rapping and Rocking the House." Grandmaster Flash and the Furious Five recorded "Superrappin Part I and Part II," their only cut with Enjoy.[2] Robinson also produced The Treacherous Three (L.A. Sunshine, Kool Moe Dee, and Positive K) and Spoonie Gee.

Paul Winley, a veteran rhythm and blues producer and songwriter, founded Winley Records in 1956. By the 1970s he had acquired an interest in rap music. His first rap recording collection, *Super Disco Brakes, Vols. 1–4,* contained rap artists' most common disco break beats.[3] Winley also recorded "Vicious Rap" by his daughter Sweet Tee, one of the earliest female solo rap artists. Because Winley had primarily worked with rhythm and blues in the past, he used a rhythm and blues–style accompaniment for Sweet Tee's rap. As a result, "Vicious Rap" lacked the authentic, street-edge sound that was characteristic of the MC and DJ format. Winley continued to record Sweet Tee along with her sister Paulette Tee on "Rhymin and Rappin," a song produced by his wife, Ann Winley. In addition, Winley produced and released two singles by Afrika Bambaataa and his groups: Soul Sonic Force, including G.L.O.B.E., Mr. Biggs, Pow Wow, and DJ Jazzy Jay, and Cosmic Force, whose members included Master Bee, Queen Lisa Lee, Prince Ikey C, Ice Ice, Mr. Freeze, and Kool DJ Red Alert, to name a few. Bambaataa's groups recorded two singles, "Zulu Nation Throwdown Part One," by Cosmic Force, and "Zulu Throwdown Part Two," by Soul Sonic Force. Once more, Winley lacked the musical understanding and marketing strategy for Bambaataa's material. Bambaataa eventually left Winley Records and was later signed by Tom Silverman of Tommy Boy Records in 1982.

Among the first music producers to achieve national exposure for rap music were the former rhythm and blues singer Sylvia Vanderpool and her husband, Joe Robinson. Like Winley and Bobby Robinson, Sylvia and Joe Robinson discovered rap music by coincidence. Sylvia remembers the first time she was introduced to rap music: "'You know, I almost didn't go to that club [Harlem World] that night, but I promised my niece that I'd get there.

Well, I walked in and heard these fellahs rappin and saw how much the people were enjoying it. What they were doing had a different feel than just singing and I said to myself, "What a hell of a concept. I think that it would be great on record!"'" (quoted in Gillespie 1983:32). In 1979 the Robinsons recorded their first rap act, a trio from Englewood, New Jersey, the area where the Robinsons lived. The Sugarhill Gang, named after an area in Harlem, consisted of Mike "Wonder Mike" Wright, a friend of the Robinsons' eldest son, Hank "Big Bank Hank" Jackson, a club bouncer, and Guy "Master G" O'Brien, a New Jersey street artist.

The Gang's first rap single was "Rapper's Delight," performed to the bass break from the disco group Chic's "Good Times." "Rapper's Delight" was notable as the longest rap recording at the time.[4] Prior to "Rapper's Delight," rap recordings were first played and promoted in local clubs, but the Robinsons sought to promote "Rapper's Delight" via the airwaves, perhaps the first rap music entrepreneurs to do so. WKTU was among the initial New York radio stations to play the Gang's recording. Sal Abbatiello recalls that WKTU's disc jockey, Carlos De Jesus, played "Rapper's Delight" as a joke: "Carlos [De] Jesus was telling me the story. He'd played it as a joke, and when he put it on the air, thousands and thousands of calls was comin' in to play it again. . . . So the next day he played it as a joke, and the joke became real. It was unbe-

The Sugarhill Gang, 1979. (Courtesy of Michael Ochs Archives)

lievable. The sales were going crazy" (Abbatiello interview). The song's popularity grew exponentially. Within a few months, "Rapper's Delight" had sold two million copies.

Although the Sugarhill Gang is credited as the first rap group to receive national exposure, the New Jersey–based group may owe that success in part to the talents of New York's leading MCs. Members of the New York rap tradition claimed that the Gang used rhymes originally created by New York MCs: "They just took all the sayings from DJ Hollywood and Starski [for example, 'hip hop you don't stop'] . . . the record was goin' crazy" (Blake interview). Additionally, the hip-hop photojournalist Steven Hager found that some of Big Bank Hank's rhymes in "Rapper's Delight" were originally composed by a New York MC, Grandmaster Caz (Casanova), the main lyricist for the punk-style rap group Cold Crush Brothers (Hager 1984:57). New York MCs credited the song "King Tim III" (1979) to the New York–based funk group the Fatback Band. Jerry Thomas, the coproducer of the Fatback Band, told of the event leading to the recording of "King Tim III": "'I recalled hearing a rappin deejay in action at the Apollo Theater. The spinner I heard was Hollywood, one of New York's most celebrated exponents of rappin. Later I heard a cassette of Roy Ayres' "Running Away," with a "rap" recorded over it. I made some inquiries and found that the voice was that of King Tim III, a local deejay. Me and other members of the Fatback Band decided to record a disk with Tim, and the result was "King Tim III"'" (quoted in Joe and George 1979:64).

In 1979, Sugar Hill Records bought Enjoy's rap acts and signed others, thereby expanding their record label. During a national tour of Sugar Hill's artists, the Robinsons discovered a female singing/rapping trio in Columbia, South Carolina. Sequence, whose members were Angie B, Cheryl the Pearl, and Blondie, recorded their most popular rap hit, "Funk You Up," in 1981, establishing a model for other female trios such as Salt-N-Pepa. Other Sugar Hill rap acts included Superwolf, The Treacherous Three (formerly with Enjoy), Crash Crew, and the Philadelphia female rap artist Lady B.

Sugar Hill's most successful and innovative act was Grandmaster Flash and the Furious Five. In the premier recording to showcase a disc jockey as a solo artist, Sugar Hill featured Flash's mixing dexterity on the turntables in "The Adventures of Grandmaster Flash on the Wheels of Steel" (1981). A year later, Sugar Hill Records released the first rap music video, "The Message" (1982), by Grandmaster Flash and the Furious Five, featuring Melle Mel.

Most early rap recordings mixed in party sounds, such as audience cheers and kazoos, along with percussive breaks accompanied by a back-up band.

Sequence—Blondie, Cheryl the Pearl, and Angie B, 1981. (Courtesy of Michael Ochs Archives)

Rap artists often brought neighborhood friends to studio sessions to provide "live" audience cheers reminiscent of the street discotheques. "Freedom," a party-style rap recorded by Flash and his famous crew and accompanied by kazoos and audience cheers, was immediately accepted by a rapidly growing youth audience. Within six months it achieved gold-record status.

The early Sugar Hill recordings also used a back-up band instead of a DJ accompaniment. The initial house band included drummer Keith LeBlanc, bassist Doug Wimbish, guitarist Bernard Alexander, and a horn section called Chops. Later additions included guitarist Skip MacDonald, percussionist Ed Fletcher (Duke Bootee of "The Message" and "Survival" fame), and keyboardists Gary Henry, Duane Mitchell, Reggie Griffen, and [arranger-organist] Clifton "Jiggs" Chase (Toop 2000:105).

After the commercial success of Sugar Hill Records, other artists received recording contracts with independent record companies (e.g. Sweet G with West End and Dr. Jeckyll and Mr. Hyde with Profile). The first major company to become involved with rap was Mercury Records, with the signing of Kurtis Blow in the late 1970s (Nathan 1988b:R18).[5] In 1980, Blow's first two twelve-inch singles—"Christmas Rapping" and "The Breaks"—were the first two records by a solo rap artist to certify gold.

Between 1980 and 1982, a few white rock performers and comedians began to record rap music. In so doing, some white performers began collaborating with rap artists. "Rapture" (1980) by Blondie, which featured Deborah Harry rappin, and "Buffalo Gals" (1982), by the British punk-stylist Malcolm McLaren, were among these productions. In addition, the white comedians Mel Brooks, Rich Little, and Rodney Dangerfield adapted the rap style (i.e. rhymed couplets) for their monologue materials. Little's "President's Rap" (1982) is perhaps the most popular and comical rap during this period.

In 1979 the first rap radio show aired on WHBI in Newark, New Jersey. Its

Kurtis Blow (front, center) with The Fat Boys, left to right: Kool Rock Ski, the Human Beat Box, and Prince Markie Dee, mid-1980s. (Courtesy of Michael Ochs Archives)

host, Mr. Magic, named the show "Mr. Magic's Rap Attack." Magic traces the early days of his career to 1973, when he worked as an itinerant DJ in Bedford-Stuyvesant, Brooklyn. "'For four years, I was the top mobile jock. I was out there doing my thing and making money but I still had a dream that had always been with me and that was to be a radio disc jockey'" (quoted in Rogers 1983:8). That same year, Magic's dream became a reality. He discovered a station, WHBI, purchased air time, and sold commercials. Magic claims that "many of the first rap records were heard first on his show" (Rogers 1983:8). By 1982, Frankie Crocker, a long-time radio personality on WBLS in New York, invited Magic to continue his show at WBLS. Crocker assigned the sportscaster Tyrone Williams as Magic's manager and a young DJ, Marley Marl, as Magic's sound engineer. Magic, Marl, and Williams began to refer to themselves collectively as the "Juice Crew."[6] Magic's show aired on Friday and Saturday evenings from 9 P.M. to midnight. Magic's radio concept established the trend for other rap-oriented stations, such as Greg Mack's all-rap radio station KDAY in Los Angeles and the declared "pioneers of underground rap radio," Stretch Armstrong and Bobbito "The Barber" Garcia, whose rap show was launched on WKCR-FM, Columbia University's radio station.

Mr. Magic and Marley Marl working at WBLS, mid-1980s. (Courtesy of Michael Ochs Archives)

The Juice Crew later added MCs, notably MC Shan and Roxanne Shan-té, who advanced answer-back raps, such as the renowned verbal battle on the airwaves between the rappers MC Shan and KRS-One of Boogie Down Productions (BDP). WBLS played MC Shan's verbal taunts of BDP, and DJ Red Alert of KISS-FM played BDP's response. In his single "The Bridge" (1986), produced by Marley Marl, Shan boasted about the Queensbridge sound of Long Island City, New York, and dissed the Bronx. KRS-One's "South Bronx" (1986) and "The Bridge is Over" (1987), both produced by Scott La Rock, responded to Shan's rap.[7] The hip-hop biographer Steven Stancell notes how "these back-and-forth radio battles were also good for both stations [KISS-FM and WBLS], raking in listeners by the numbers on the weekends" (1996:194). The Juice Crew eventually expanded to include other MCs. Most notable are Kool G Rap and DJ Polo, Big Daddy Kane, Masta Ace, Biz Markie, and Intelligent Hoodlum (also known as Tragedy).

While rap's popularity grew on the airwaves, in the studio there remained shortcomings in producing and promoting this new sound. Early producers lacked an understanding of street music concepts; they used, instead, the conventional horns, rhythm sections, and vocal formulas associated with the rhythm and blues tradition and often made musical decisions without the input of rap artists. The newly formed, independent, street-oriented record companies established by 1982 used the production concepts rendered by street DJs—the circulation of mix tapes—and refrained from controlling or stifling artists' unique styles. Bill Stephney, the former vice president of Def Jam Records and cofounder of SOUL Records, recalls that Def Jam's production of rap music remained very much "at street level" (Nathan 1988b:R10). This philosophy was key to the success of Russell Simmons, Def Jam's cofounder and the founder of Rush Artist Management. He opines that producers only help while artists are people who have their own concept, who create and develop things themselves, express themselves, and appreciate what they do. Simmons notes further, "They [rap artists] are not people that some guy comes along and stands up and says 'Talk this way, walk this way.' They come to you with their own ideas. My feel about production is that you [as the producer] know you didn't write it, you only shape it" (Simmons interview). With producers who appreciated street-level production concepts, rap artists were able to create, shape, and control their own products while experimenting with sound possibilities ad infinitum. This freedom afforded by the independent companies gave rise to a plethora of diverse styles and content in rap music.

Afrika Bambaataa, a seminal figure in reshaping the direction of rap, led the transition from the "Old School Style" of the early performers and pio-

Russell Simmons receives the Lifetime Achievement Award at the Source Hip-Hop Music Awards, Los Angeles, 1999. (Photo by Alisa Childs)

neers of rap music (including himself) to the "New School Style." Building on the turntable techniques of scratching, Bambaataa added synthesizers, drum machines, and computerized arcade sounds, producing a techno sound.

Immensely influenced by the computerized sound called "techno-pop" created by European and Asian pop artists, Bambaataa wanted to experiment with it in rap music. He says,

> At the time, a lot of rap records was about boasting . . . how many young ladies they could get. I wanted a sound that nobody had before. I looked at all the black music in the industry and I said, "There's no electronic or singing group or funk group or whatever style". Techno-pop at the time was only for Europeans from the [German] group Kraftwerk or . . . a Japanese group called Yellow Magic Orchestra. I was influenced a lot from Kraftwerk. . . . The synthesizer, I say, this is the music of the future. (Bambaataa interview)

Bambaataa modified the techno sound in his works by fusing it with the funk music styles of James Brown and Sly and the Family Stone. This hybrid sound created by Bambaataa is referred to as "electro funk."

In 1982 Bambaataa and his group Soul Sonic Force recorded "Planet Rock" on the new independent rap label Tommy Boy Records. The recording made extensive use of electronic instruments—synthesizers and drum machines—rather than the band sound popularized in "Rapper's Delight." With the collaboration of Arthur Baker, the owner and producer of Shakedown Sound Studio (where "Planet Rock" was recorded), Tom Silverman, and Afrika Bambaataa and the Soul Sonic Force, "Planet Rock" revolutionized rap music.[8]

By 1982 rap music had sparked the interest of European recording companies like British-based Jive Records. After Jive's executive director Barry Weiss witnessed the initial impact of American rap music in the United Kingdom, he went to the label's owner, Clive Caulder, to discuss the possibility of producing a rap record with Mr. Magic of WBLS. Though Mr. Magic could not accept Jive's invitation because of a contract agreement with WBLS, he referred Weiss to Jalil Hutchins, another prominent MC from Brooklyn. Hutchins con-

Whodini (Ecstacy, Grand-
master Dee, and Jalil), 1985.
(Courtesy of Michael Ochs
Archives)

tacted his fellow rap friend John "Ecstacy" Fletcher. Magic added Drew "Grandmaster Dee" Carter, creating Jive's first prized rap group, Whodini.

In the fall of 1982, Jive Records released "Magic's Wand," Whodini's debut twelve-inch single, coproduced by Mr. Magic and Thomas Dolby, England's techno-pop whiz. Though critics described this trio's sound as heavy funk, Whodini asserted, "'We've got a more European techno-sound'" (quoted in Stuart 1986:21). In fall 1984, Whodini released its debut album, *Escape*, which achieved gold-record status. The success of this album is attributed to Larry Smith, a funk musician, songwriter, and producer. Smith became Whodini's main music consultant and produced Whodini's sophomore album, *Back in Black* (1986), which became a platinum success.

Following the breakthrough success of Whodini, rap became more diverse. In May 1983, Disco 3 earned their way to the rap stage by winning the Tin Pan Apple Rap Contest (cosponsored by Coca-Cola and WBLS). The group consisted of Mark "Prince Markie" Dee, Damon "Kool Rock-Ski" Wimbley, and Darren "The Human Beat Box" Robinson. Robinson, who earned his moniker for his vocal talent in imitating an electronic drum machine, provided the accompaniment. Their victory culminated in a recording contract with the contest's organizer, Charles Stettler, the founder of Sutra Records. Released in October 1983, Disco 3's record "Reality," featuring "The Human Beat Box," was the first to showcase the commercial potential of this vocal technique.

Capitalizing on their weight, Disco 3 changed their name to The Fat Boys. They continued to profile Robinson as the original human beat box on their popular twelve-inch single, "Jail House Rap," recorded in 1984. Although some critics say the human beat box sound was in existence prior to its commercialization by The Fat Boys, Robinson was nevertheless known for popularizing the use of the voice as a rhythmic accompaniment in rap music. Doug E. Fresh, who considers himself the originator of the human beat box, exhibited his skills in "All the Way to Heaven" (1986), succeeded by Run of Run-D.M.C. in "Hit It Run" (1986).

In 1984, the Select Records group UTFO initiated another trend in rap music—the answer raps—with their recording of "Roxanne, Roxanne." "Roxanne" was a term used in New York among black males to depict a snobbish girl. UTFO and their producer/band, Full Force, conceived of the "Roxanne" idea as a possible rap theme during a flirtation with a waitress. According to the group, a waitress made a snotty remark to Paul Anthony, one of the members of Full Force. This waitress was soon to become The Real Roxanne immortalized by UTFO. The Real Roxanne recalls her day of discovery:

Well it came when UTFO and Full Force got together and wanted to make
this song about a girl called Roxanne, and Bryan from Full Force came up
with the name Roxanne. They came up with the rhyme and everything; but
what happened was that they needed the girl to fit this role. You know the
Roxanne role. . . . It all happened when I met Paul Anthony from Full Force
at the restaurant I used to work in downtown [Brooklyn], Fulton Street. It
was this snotty remark that I gave him and he gave me that role, Roxanne.
(The Real Roxanne interview)

The Roxanne sequels were initiated by "Roxanne, Roxanne," by The Real
Roxanne with UTFO in 1984, followed by a series of Roxanne-inspired raps
during 1985, in this order: "Roxanne's Revenge" by Roxanne Shanté, "The

The Real Roxanne, 1980s.
(Courtesy of Michael Ochs
Archives)

Real Roxanne" with The Real Roxanne featuring UTFO, "Sparky's Turn" by Sparky Dee (in response to "Roxanne's Revenge"), "Queen of Rox" by Roxanne Shanté, and finally a verbal battle between Sparky D and Roxanne Shanté on "Round 1." The Roxanne raps resulted in other male/female answer sequels, including "A Fly Girl" by the Boogie Boys, "A Fly Guy" by Pebblee-Poo, "Girls Ain't Nothing but Trouble" by DJ Jazzy Jeff and the Fresh Prince, and "Guys Ain't Nothing but Trouble" by Ice Cream Tee. The popularity of the male-female sequel raps provided additional opportunities for and interest in female rap artists.

### East Coast in the House, 1986–89

Rap music gradually moved from the streets into the music mainstream. This progression was facilitated by rap's fusion with rock, a sound largely attributed to the innovation of rap artists from Hollis, Queens. Accordingly, the Queens cultural landscape in contrast to the other boroughs—Brooklyn, Bronx, and Manhattan—played a major role in the shaping of its rap style. The rapper LL Cool J explains: "'Atmosphere always bears on what you write. . . . I'm from a middle-class, not upper, upper middle-class, but from a nice, middle-class home. I got grass and trees. . . . Rappers from other parts of the city will reveal their environment in the music and poetry they create. The Bronx kids are always rappin about the street, being bums and stuff like that because that's their life. Brooklyn boys rap about sticking up places, robbing things. And us [Queens rappers], we just *rock* this shit'" (quoted in Fuentes 1985:20). LL Cool J and Run-D.M.C. were instrumental in inaugurating a distinct Queens sound. From a middle-class neighborhood in Hollis, Queens, Joseph "Run" Simmons began his rap career in 1977 under the tutelage of the Old School rapper Kurtis Blow. Because of his apprenticeship with Blow, with whom he honed his rhymin skills, Run acquired the title "Son of Kurtis Blow." In 1982 the DJ and former bass guitarist Jam Master Jay teamed up with Simmons and Darryl "D.M.C." McDaniels, to form the group Run-D.M.C., one of Rush's earliest major rap acts. They were managed by Run's brother, Russell Simmons, who also managed Kurtis Blow's career.

Their first two singles, "It's Like That" and "Sucker M.C.s," coproduced by Russell Simmons and Larry Smith, became hits in 1983. In 1984 Run-D.M.C released their first album, *Run-D.M.C.,* which certified gold on Profile Records. One of the selections, "Rock Box," which featured the heavy metal guitar work of Eddie Martinez, broke new ground in rap music because it

D.M.C., Run, and Jam Master Jay of Run-D.M.C. backstage at The Source Hip-Hop
Music Awards, Los Angeles, 1999. (Photo by Alisa Childs)

fused heavy metal with rap. This song became the first rap song aired on the
syndicated rock video station MTV. Run-D.M.C.'s second album, *King of
Rock* (1985), also achieved gold status. In addition to their penchant for rock,
Run-D.M.C. collaborated with the Jamaican dancehall artist Yellowman in
recording a rap-dancehall mix, "Roots, Rap, Reggae," on the *King of Rock* LP.

By the summer of 1986, their third album, *Raising Hell,* coproduced by
Russell Simmons and Rick Rubin (the cofounders of Def Jam Records), was
the first rap album to go triple-platinum. The album's success was attributed to the extensive fusion of hard rock with rap, as best illustrated with the
trio's remake of Aerosmith's "Walk This Way." According to Joseph "Run"
Simmons, the idea of crossing rock with rap had been on the streets for a long
time: "'I think Aerosmith [a hard rock band] was more popular as a street
thing '79, '80. It was our favorite thing. We didn't even know the name of the
group . . . all we knew was we liked the beat. There's a breaking part in the
record where the drums just play a little, the guitar comes in. You just cut the
start of it, scratch it from record to record, keep cutting the break part'"
(quoted in Cummings 1986:58).

The rap-rock fusion sound introduced by Run-D.M.C. is characterized
by a piercing guitar, extensive sampling (of former rhythm and blues tracks),

and funk-style drum rhythms with a heavy bass drum. Because of the minimal instrumentation, heavy metal accompaniment, sparse arrangements, piercing sound quality, boisterous-aggressive tone, and use of expletives, this style has been dubbed by rap critics as having a "hardcore" sound (see chapter 5). Run-D.M.C.'s fourth album, *Tougher Than Leather* (1988), achieved platinum status and was the soundtrack for the group's movie by the same name, which was directed by Rick Rubin.

James Todd "LL Cool J" Smith, another artist from Hollis, Queens, launched his recording career as one of Def Jam Records' premier recording artists with the single "I Need a Beat" (1984). Using a Korg rhythm machine, the song was recorded in Rick Rubin's dorm room at New York University for seven hundred dollars. His album *Radio* (1985) became Def Jam's first album release. On his triple-platinum album *Bigger and Deffer*, LL Cool J also led the way with the rhymin love rap in his single, "I Need Love" (1988).[9] Although LL Cool J's third album, *Walking with a Panther* (1989), also went platinum, his hardcore credibility among hip-hop fans began to wane. With the recording of "Jingling Baby" on *Mama Said Knock You Out* (1990), produced by Marley Marl, LL Cool J regained his reputation for a street-edge style among his fans.

After the tremendous commercial success and impact of *Raising Hell* and *Radio,* non-black groups like the punk-style Beastie Boys (Adam "King Ad-Rock" Horovitz, Adam "MCA" Yauch, and Michael "Mike D" Diamond) began to emulate the hardcore sound of rap-rock fusion à la punk. The Beastie Boys' debut album for Def Jam, *Licensed to Ill* (1986), sold five million copies, which at the time was the largest record sale for any rap LP. Because of royalty disputes, they eventually sued Russell Simmons and Rick Rubin. They later left Def Jam and switched to the Capitol label, recording *Paul's Boutique* (1989), which certified gold. The group subsequently created their own label, Grand Royal, distributed by Capitol. Under this label the group released *Check Your Head* (1992), *Some Old Bullshit* (1994), and *Ill Communication* (1994), which went platinum.

During the 1980s, several artists brought a new sound to rap by incorporating a semi-humorous or a softer (less street-edged) style to their performances. Forerunners in this category include Dana Dane, known as "The Comedian of Rap," and Doug E. Fresh, dubbed "The World's Greatest Entertainer." Those who further shaped this style (with the aid of music video) include Biz Markie, DJ Jazzy Jeff and the Fresh Prince, De La Soul, and Kid 'N' Play. Marcel "Biz Markie" Hall entered the rap arena with his twelve-inch single "Vapors," penned by Antonio Hardy, who was soon to be known

The Beastie Boys—MCA, King Ad-Rock, and Mike D—in concert, 1985. (Courtesy of Michael Ochs Archives)

as Big Daddy Kane. "Vapors" appears on Markie's debut album *Goin' Off* (1988). While *Goin' Off* did not sell astronomically, his second album, *The Biz Never Sleeps* (1989), which includes the single "Just a Friend," certified platinum. Biz Markie's comedic flare is vividly illustrated in his videos, in which he delivers his rap while wearing a colonial-style wig and attire or simply posturing in a humorous manner. The critics Havelock Nelson and Michael A. Gonzales comment that Biz Markie is "more than a rapper, [he] can be placed in the context of black comedians from Redd Foxx to Richard Pryor" (1991:26).

The rap duo DJ Jazzy Jeff and the Fresh Prince, lauded as the "Cosby Kids" of rap, also followed the comedic tradition. Originally from suburban Philadelphia, in 1989 DJ Jeff Townes and rapper-soon-turned-actor Will Smith became the first to receive the Grammy award in a new rap category for "Parents Just Don't Understand" from their album *He's the DJ, I'm the Rapper*. Their success was attributed to a nonhardcore style that seemed acceptable to middle-class American taste, contributing to rap's growing acceptance in the mainstream.

Wearing 1960s hippie-style clothing, Tommy Boy Records' group De La Soul (Kelvin "Posdnuos" Mercer, Dave "Trugoy the Dove" Jolicoeur, and

Vincent "Maseo" Mason) promoted a concept they called "Da Inner Sound Y'all" (D.A.I.S.Y). Their major single, "Me, Myself, and I," from their LP *3 Feet High and Rising* (1989), produced by Prince Paul of the group Stetsasonic, showcased De La Soul's limerick-laden rhymes. Prince Paul's aptitude for selecting unique breaks for the accompanying soundtracks (e.g. the use of Funkadelic's funk classic "(Not Just) Knee Deep" for their hit single, "Me, Myself, and I") enhanced De La Soul's music. Recognized for his funky beats, Paul credits P-Funk master George Clinton for influencing his vision for De La Soul: "'I evolved the whole De La Soul thing around George Clinton at first, the characters, the visuals, the illness'" (quoted in Ro 1991:22).[10] However, De La Soul's image and music was not well-taken by some hip-hop heads, who felt that the group's sound was too soft. De La Soul refuted this claim by changing their New Age/hippy-style dress and releasing *De La Soul Is Dead* (1991), considered by critics and fans as a masterpiece in street-edged rhymin. Despite their enigmatic persona, De La Soul is a part of a fictive kinship unit known as the Native Tongues, comprised of the black-conscious group the Jungle Brothers and the jazz-inspired group A Tribe Called Quest. These groups are mentioned in subsequent sections of this chapter.

Along with humor, some rap artists brought "light" dance moves to rap. The dance moves and high fade hairstyles of Kid 'N' Play, composed of Christopher "Kid" Reid and Christopher "Play" Martin, captured the attention of many hip-hop fashion heads. Their humorous, party-dance rap style is evident in "Rollin' with Kid 'N' Play" from their platinum debut LP, *2 Hype*. Under the production and management of Hurby "Luv Bug" Azor, Kid 'N' Play's music fuses house and go-go styles with rap. Though some critics have accused the duo of "selling out" to a wider audience because of their appeal to non-hip-hop dance-oriented audiences (Nelson and Gonzales 1991), their fusion of dance styles with hip-hop was in line with artists such as Rob Base and DJ E-Z Rock. Base's 1988 hit "It Takes Two"—"built with samples from Strafe's 'Set It Off' and Lynn Collins's single 'Think (About It),' produced by James Brown—is recognized [as ushering] in the hip-house genre" (Stancell 1996:244). Kid 'N' Play's dance performances dovetail with other hip-hop dance acts, such as MC Hammer and his female dancers Oaktown 3-5-7. The duo also ventured into cartoons with *Street Frogs,* rap music's first morning cartoon, and *Kid 'N' Play* in 1990. Their hip-hop cartoon concept paved the way for Aaron McGruder's comic strip *The Boondocks,* which began to appear in several major U.S. newspapers during the late 1990s.

Verbal dexterity is one of the distinguishing features of New York or East Coast MCs. The exhibition of this skill inundated the rhymes of many MCs.

Lawrence Krisna Parker of Boogie Down Productions is no stranger to verbal artistry. Parker, better known in hip-hop circles as KRS-One, a partial acronym for Knowledge Reigns Supreme Over Nearly Everyone. Parker, who at one point in his life was homeless, met Scott La Rock, then a social worker, at a shelter. The two formed BDP, and Scott La Rock served as the primary DJ and producer. Their first album, *Criminal Minded* (1987), which featured "9mm Goes Bang" and "The Bridge Is Over," became a hip-hop classic. While the latter song was an answer-back to the Juice Crew, "9mm Goes Bang" shares similarities with Jamaican dancehall rhymin style. After this album, BDP received a recording contract from Jive Records for their follow-up work *By All Means Necessary*. But during its conception, La Rock was fatally wounded while trying to break up a fight. Although BDP had grown in membership with D-Nice and Parker's brother Kenny, *By All Means Necessary* was released after Scott La Rock's death. Its title and album cover is a spin-off from Malcolm X's words "by any means necessary." The album shows KRS-One posed similarly as X's famous photograph, only with the AK-47 rifle replaced by an Uzi. In 1989, KRS-One and BDP released the album *Ghetto Music: The Blueprint of Hip Hop.* What contributes to his long-standing popularity among

KRS-One performing at 92.3 The Beat Summer Jam, Irvine Meadows Amphitheatre, 1998. (Photo by Alisa Childs)

MCs is his ability to address various subjects in his rhymes from drug dealing in "9mm Goes Bang" and black-on-black crime in "Stop the Violence," from *By All Means Necessary,* to lessons about black history in "You Must Learn" from *Ghetto Music.* For this reason, KRS-One labels his rhymes as "edutainment" and refers to himself as a communicator and a teacher.

Another one of Jive's recording artists during this time was Mohandas "Kool Moe Dee" Dewese, a former member of The Treacherous Three. Kool Moe Dee launched a solo career with his single about safe sex, "Go See the Doctor," from his debut album *Kool Moe Dee* (1986). Kool Moe Dee's second album, *How Ya Like Me Now,* contains hits like the title track, in which the horn lines from James Brown's 1960s hit "Papa Got a Brand New Bag" is heard, and the controversial "Wild Wild West." While the album went platinum, some critics misinterpreted the lyrics in "Wild Wild West" as promoting violence. Careful attention to the wordplay, however, reveals the artist urging his audience to fight opponents figuratively with their hands instead of with guns and knives, as he indicated in several interviews. Kool Moe Dee's famed "Let's Go" (1988) is an answer-back rap to LL Cool J's "Jack the Ripper" (1998), following the verbal battle tradition, which will be discussed further in chapter 5.

Among other MCs from the East Coast who reigned supreme during this time were Big Daddy Kane, Chubb Rock, Just Ice, Kool G Rap of Kool G Rap and DJ Polo, Freddie Foxxx, EPMD, Rakim, Schoolly D (an innovator of gangsta-style), Slick Rick, T La Rock, the group Stetsasonic, and the Ultramagnetic MCs, to name a few.

Perhaps the most controversial of politically styled rap groups is Def Jam's Public Enemy (PE), also known as "The Prophets of Rage." PE's organizer, Carlton "Chuck D" Ridenhour, began his career in the early 1980s as a member of Spectrum City, a group of DJs and MCs who appeared on Adelphi University's radio station WBAU of Long Island. WBAU was the venue where Chuck D conceptualized and formed the group Public Enemy, whose members included Chuck D, "Messenger of Prophecy"; Flavor Flav "The Cold Lamper"; Terminator X, "Assault Technician"; and Professor Griff, "Minister of Information." Professor Griff, who was the group's sole security guard, later organized a component of PE called the Security of the First World (S1W). Griff's assigned title, "Minister of Information," notes Chuck D, "is a spinoff of Eldrige Cleaver of the Black Panther Party" (Chuck D 1997:216). S1W's dress code of army fatigues also recalls the Black Panthers.

The Prophets of Rage's first album, *Yo! Bum Rush the Show* (1987), sold 270,000 copies in the first run. With their subsequent release, *It Takes a Na-*

Chuck D and Flavor Flav
(with large clock) of Public
Enemy on the video set of
"Fight the Power," 1988.
(Courtesy of Michael Ochs
Archives)

*tion of Millions to Hold Us Back,* PE's lyrics became more political and controversial. Chuck D's poignant lyrics and no-nonsense demeanor are complemented by Flavor Flav's performance. Flavor Flav responds to Chuck D's lyrics with a "Yeeeah boyeee," resembling the cartoonish voice of Popeye. He dons a large clock as a necklace to symbolize that it is time for black people to mentally wake up.[11] Flav responds to PE's music with jerky or exaggerated body gestures. Because his performance is designed to offset the seriousness of Chuck D's nationalist message, Flavor Flav parallels the trickster figure common in black oral narratives, and in this respect he becomes Chuck D's alter ego. Chuck D comments:

> "The simple reason why we work together is just the contrast in our voices. People try to come up with intellectual reasons for 'the noise' and it ain't nothing intellectual. We was just making BAU [WBAU] tapes and needed voices to cut through that shit. Flavor got a powerful trebly voice, with cut. I got some bass with treble and pitch, which also cuts. So you put me and Flavor together and it's basically like Bobby Bird and James Brown—*Everybody over here? Get on Up!* The Bird/Brown combination set off everything." (quoted in Marriott 1994:76)

The controversy surrounding PE stems from their potent Black Nationalist messages. As Chuck D explains, "'We're out for one thing only, and that's to bring back the resurgence of Black power. But we're not racist. We're nationalist, people who have pride and who want to build a sense of unity amongst our people. . . . You hear Public Enemy, you hear a tone that say, "Look Out! This is some serious shit comin'!"'" (quoted in Elliot 1988:15). Interwoven with their music is a collage of material from famous speeches by Black Nationalist spokespersons from Gil Scott-Heron to the Nation of Islam leader Louis Farrakhan. For example, Chuck D discusses how he sought to evoke Farrakhan on *It Takes a Nation of Millions to Hold Us Back* (1988) in the lyrics of "Bring the Noise," with the line, "Farrakhan's a prophet I think you ought to listen to," and in "Don't Believe the Hype" with the line, "A follower of Farrakhan, don't tell me that you understand, until you hear the man" (Chuck D 1997:229). PE's third album, *Fear of a Black Planet* (1990), was released during a tumultuous period in which the group was accused of being anti-Semitic as a result of an interview with Professor Griff.[12] This album contains the classics "Welcome to the Terrordome," "911 Is a Joke," featuring Flavor Flav, and "Fight the Power," which appears on the soundtrack of Spike Lee's film *Do the Right Thing* (1989). More importantly, "Fight the Power" brought major attention to PE's production team, the Bomb Squad (Hank Shocklee, Keith Shocklee, Eric Sadler, and Chuck D), because of the extensive musical samples over James Brown's grooves (see chapter 5). The unprecedented digital sampling from more than twenty popular songs pushed the boundaries of sound polarities in mixing rap music soundtracks.

PE blazed the trail for other nationalist rap artists, dubbed "nation-conscious" rappers, whose lyrics endorsed Afrocentricity and the religio-nationalist beliefs of the Nation of Islam (Eure and Spady 1991). They include Black Star, Brand Nubian, the Jungle Brothers, King Sun, Lakim Shabazz, Nefertiti, Poor Righteous Teachers, Sister Souljah, and X-Clan, as well as the San Francisco Bay Area rappers Paris and Boots of The Coup. (See chapter 6.)

By the late-1980s, the so-called New School of rap had expanded its roster to include a growing number of female artists. Salt-N-Pepa are recognized as the first female rappers to successfully make it to the charts with the single "Push It." Produced and managed by their mentor, Hurby "Luv Bug" Azor, the trio is composed of Cheryl "Salt" James, Sandra "Pepa" Denton, and Deidre "Spinderella" Roper, who replaced Latoya Hanson. The platinum success of their debut album, *Hot, Cool & Vicious* (1987), paved the way for other female rap artists. For example, *Lyte as a Rock* (1988), the debut album of female Lana "MC Lyte" Moorer, sold seventy-five thousand copies in a month with virtually no airplay (Coleman 1988:29).

Prior to 1988, no distinct "female" style existed per se. Female rap artists used the hardcore vocal style and stylized behavior typical of male rappers. They wore stylish attire, patterned after male rappers' attire—leather outfits, name-brand sweatsuits, sneakers, jeans, brass name buckles, and fingerless leather gloves. Yet, unlike their male counterparts, female MCs offered a woman's perspective on female and male relationships in their raps.

In the late 1980s, Dana "Queen Latifah" Owens introduced a feminist-Afrocentric message. Unlike women artists who preferred to sport unisex clothing (e.g. MC Lyte) or those who donned revealing clothing (e.g. Sequence or Salt-N-Pepa), Latifah opted to wear Afrocentric attire that underscored her message. Her "Ladies First" (1989) the first political commentary rap by a female artist, commented on men's stereotypes about female rappers. Subsequent to Queen Latifah's success, a few female rappers, including Harmony and Isis, also adopted traditional African women's attire and dealt with black political issues in their raps. Chapter 7 discusses female rap artists in more detail.

### West Coast G-Funk in the House, 1985–89

The late 1980s marked a drastic change in rap music history when artists from California introduced to rap a more bassy sound with a laid-back feel heavily rooted in 1970s funk music. The funk sound that became the basic soundtrack for the music of the West Coast, aptly called G-Funk, initially had been affiliated with a unique dance culture that grew out of the club parties or jams in the early 1970s.

Thomas Guzman-Sanchez produced and directed *Underground Dance Masters: History of a Forgotten Era,* a controversial documentary about the evolution of vernacular dance in Los Angeles in the 1970s and its infusion in contemporary popular dance across the globe. He notes that the dancer Don Campbell, the founder of Campbellock Dancers who initially appeared on the nationally syndicated dance show "Soul Train," is credited with creating the robotic "locking" dance technique that accompanies the funk sound. The hip-hop critic R. J. Smith writes, "Campbell's jerky but controlled gestures sparked a new way of dancing that turned into a movement. First came the Los Angeles–based Campbellock Dancers (later known as the Lockers), who performed [on] numerous TV programs, including *The Carol Burnett Show* and *Saturday Night Live*. Then came [the] Guzman-Sanchez Chain Reaction ensemble and 'Boogalo Sam' Solomon's Electronic Boogaloo Lockers [of Fresno], who perfected a more robotic locking style called popping, back in the early '80s" (Smith 1998:268).[13] The Lockers and the celebrated Electronic Boogaloo Lockers contributed to the popularity of locking and popping styles. Members of the original Lockers also included Shabba Doo, who appeared in the movie *Breakin'* (1984) and its sequel *Breakin' 2: Electric Boogaloo* (1984), and Fred Berry, most remembered as Rerun in the 1970s television series "What's Happening!!"

While funk music accompanied L.A.'s dance scene, it was also incorporated in MC and DJ performances as well. Early hip-hop artists from Los Angeles say, however, that their rhymin and turntable techniques were influenced by New York's MCs and DJs. Michael Mixxin Moor recalls how he "'saw the two turntables, then in New York . . . [and] was always gettin' cues from N.Y.'" Ice-T reminisces about the SpinMasters, Evil E and Henry G from Brooklyn, whom he credits with bringing the New York beats to Los Angeles (quoted in Cross 1993:121, 184). Early L.A. hip-hop clubs included Radio (renamed Radiotron in the film *Breakin'*) and Rhythm Lounge. Other venues for funk music were skating rinks such as Skateland USA and World on Wheels, which were equally as popular with L.A. hip-hoppers. Among L.A.'s pioneering rap acts were Egyptian Lover, Captain Rapp, Arabian Prince, Skatemaster Tate, DJ Flash and Lovin C, Toddy Tee, Mixmaster Spade, World Class Wreckin' Cru, The Dream Team, King Tee, and Roger Clayton's Uncle Jam's Army, an itinerant group of DJs and MCs whose name derives from an album by George Clinton's Funkadelic. Ice-T distinguishes New York and Los Angeles hip-hop scenes thus: "'Hip-hop started in N.Y. They had graffiti artists, breakdancers, we [L.A.] didn't have any of that, we had gangs'" (quoted in Cross 1993:183). Toddy Tee, along with his DJ, Mixmaster Spade, is most celebrated among Los Angeles rappers for ushering in a prototype of gangsta rap with his street (underground) mix tape "Batterram" (1985), which exposes the devastation of crack cocaine and was eventually re-released as a commercial single in 1986.[14]

Aspects of contemporary Chicano gang culture, or *cholo,* permeates much of the West Coast rap scene. Cholo is characterized by "a distinctive street style of dress, speech [*caló*/Spanglish], gestures, tattoos, and graffiti that is a direct outgrowth of a 1930s-1940s second-generation Mexican subculture called *pachuco*" (Vigil 1994:3). West Coast artists are credited with popularizing baggy khaki pants and jeans, oversized shirts, baseball caps, bandanas, and lowriders—all idiosyncratic to cholo identity.

By the late 1980s, the West Coast's indelible mark infused rap music from coast to coast. The heavy bass sound, sampled Parliament-Funkadelic break beats, and laid-back tempo became the backdrop for powerful depictions of gang life on the streets of Los Angeles. The lyrics West Coasters introduced conveyed the gritty and dangerous aspects of hustling (drug dealing), gang-banging and drive-by shootings, and police repression. For this reason, the West Coast is credited with ushering in a subgenre called "gangsta rap." Because gangsta rap proponents claim that they are "telling the real story of what it's like living in places like Compton," this subgenre is also known as reality rap (Hunt 1989:80).

Prior to the commercialization of gangsta rap, Boogie Down Productions addressed East Coast street gang themes in "9mm Goes Bang." Despite the West Coast's advancement of the gangsta rap subgenre, one cannot disregard its origins in the Jamaican dancehall tradition. As chapter 2 explained, an era of political rivalry began in Jamaica during the 1960s. In the wake of Jamaica's independence, two political parties emerged, the People's National Party headed by Michael Manley and the Jamaica Labour Party led by Edward Seaga. In response to political dissension between the parties and a fallen economy, rude boy youth culture represented the voices of disillusioned youth. Rudies adopted an aggressive pose, as indicated by the wearing of certain clothes, and they carried knives and handguns. Rudies also formed gangs, which were divided along political lines. As a result of Jamaica's first election since its independence, Michael Manley rose to power. With the shift in political power from Manley to Seaga in the late 1970s, followed by the untimely death of Bob Marley—a symbol of working-class sentiments—in 1981, rudies responded with more riotous behavior. They use DJ sound system culture or dancehall to subvert the new government. Their resistance was conveyed through an attitude called "slackness." The cultural critic Carolyn Cooper observes that "slackness is a metaphorical revolt against law and order; an undermining of consensual standards of decency" (1995:143). Slackness ushered in a hypermasculine posture indicative of sexually explicit language and misogynistic references. In some instances, slackness extends to the use of violent lyrics or "gun lyrics." Jamaican dancehall artists also started wearing lock hairstyles reminiscent of the Rastafari movement and Marley and incorporated more reggae-inspired rhythms. The Jamaican rude boy or slackness is depicted in the musical performances of Yellowman, Shabba Ranks, Mad Cobra, Bounty Killer, Buju Banton, Ninja Man, Beenie Man, and the "rude girl" Lady Saw.[15] Note the use of certain stage names, such as Mad Cobra and Bounty Killer, which make very powerful statements about law and order or the new ruling order by subverting mainstream ideology of civility. Gangsta rap artists also use their stage names in strikingly similar ways and with the same purpose as Jamaican dancehall artists.

Concomitant with the Jamaican dancehall gun lyrics style is Philadelphia's Schoolly D, whom some credit with making the first gangsta rap recording. Schoolly D debuted the single "Gangster Boogie" (1984), followed by "PSK What Does It Mean?" (1985), a rap about the Philadelphia gang Parkside Killers.[16] Schoolly D's recordings, known for their risqué content, garnered an underground audience at the time. But on the West Coast, the rapper Ice-T, apparently unaware of Schoolly D's activities at that time, identified himself as the "original gangsta" (O.G.). His single "Six in the Morning" (1985) is considered to be the first commercial West Coast gangsta rap recording.

Tracy "Ice-T" Marrow grew up in Newark, New Jersey. After the untimely deaths of his parents, he moved to Los Angeles to live with his aunt, Rosa Lee.

Schoolly D, 1989. (Courtesy of Michael Ochs Archives)

During his years at Crenshaw High School in South Central Los Angeles, he became intrigued with rapping through the writings of the former pimp Robert Beck, known in literary circles as Iceberg Slim. "'I used to read books by Iceberg Slim, a pimp who wrote street poetry. He would talk in rhyme—hustler-like stuff—and I would memorize lines. People in school would always ask me to recite them'" (quoted in Nelson and Gonzales 1991:110). Because of his love and admiration of Iceberg Slim, Marrow took the name Ice-T. He soon paired with the Chicano MC Kid Frost, performing on the local circuit.

During the early 1980s, after spending four years in the army, Ice-T decided to use Iceberg Slim's hustler-style poetry in rap. In honing his craft, he traveled to New York and hung out with noted rap artists there. Before landing a record deal with Sire/Warner Bros., he appeared in the film *Breakin'*. Because at the time most films about hip-hop centered on New York–style breakdancing, Ice-T wore the East Coast uniform, a sweatsuit with sneakers. He recalls, in Brian Cross's book *It's Not about a Salary*, "'[W]hen I was in gangs and when I was in the army and shit, I was out here stealin' and gangbangin', and pimpin' women, and hanging out with drug dealers. Then I'd go into a club dressed like a breakdancer and tryin' to rap. My boys was like, "Hey man, you gotta rap about what we do, do some of that gangsta shit"'" (1993:183). In 1985, Ice-T released "Doggin' tha Wax" on a twelve-inch single (with "Six in the Morning" on its B-side) that was coincidentally released during the same year as Schoolly D's "PSK What Does It Mean."

In 1987, Afrika Islam, a member of Afrika Bambaataa's Zulu Nation who worked on the production of Ice-T's music, formed the Rhyme Syndicate, a management company, and they recorded and released Ice-T's first album, *Rhyme Pays* (1987), on the Sire/Warner Bros. label. When Ice-T's "Colors" became the title track for Dennis Hopper's *Colors* (1988), a Hollywood film about L.A. gangs and the crack cocaine economy, Ice-T's music reached a national audience, setting the stage for his subsequent recordings, *Power* (1988) and *Freedom of Speech . . . Just Watch What You Say* (1989). With the national success of Ice-T's music in *Colors,* the group N.W.A. (Niggaz with Attitude), organized by Eazy-E, found a ready-made audience for "gangsta rap."

Eazy-E, who described himself as a former drug dealer, founded Ruthless Records in March 1987. He appointed his longtime manager Jerry Heller to be the executive of Ruthless. Eazy-E formed N.W.A. in the fall of 1987 with Andre "Dr. Dre" Young and Antoine "DJ Yella" Carraby (members of Compton's World Class Wreckin' Cru), Lorenzo "MC Ren" Patterson of Compton, and O'Shea "Ice Cube" Jackson of a South Central L.A. group, CIA.[17]

Kid Frost, 1980s. (Courtesy
of Michael Ochs Archives)

Ice-T on a video set in Sylmar, California, 1998. (Photo by Alisa Childs)

Eazy-E with original members and associates of N.W.A., 1989. (Photo by Raymond Boyd/Michael Ochs Archives)

The following year, Eazy-E produced N.W.A's first album, *Straight Outta Compton,* which certified double platinum, and his own solo debut, *Eazy-Duz-It,* which certified platinum. Because of the antipolice sentiment in N.W.A.'s "Fuck tha Police"—which ridiculed the Los Angeles Police Department (LAPD)—the group received a warning letter from the FBI that chided them about their verbal assault on police officers. In defense of N.W.A., "California Congressman Don Edwards, a former FBI officer himself, contacted the FBI, objecting to its letter to N.W.A. calling it a form of censorship" (Brodeur 1995:55). "Fuck tha Police" is also interpreted as a verbal prelude to the 1992 Los Angeles uprising, resulting from the acquittal of three white LAPD officers for the brutal beating of a black man, Rodney King. Ensuing actions by government bodies and the powers that be provide the backdrop to a series of censorship cases regarding gangsta rap during the 1990s. These cases are discussed in more detail in chapter 4.

In addition to N.W.A., Ruthless recorded the female trio JJ Fad, the singer Michel'le, the rapper the D.O.C., the Jewish rap group Blood of Abraham, Above the Law, and Bone Thugs-N-Harmony. JJ Fad's self-titled single and their album *Supersonic* (1988) went platinum. *Supersonic* was the company's first platinum LP. Much of the trio's commercial success was based on their techno-pop soundtrack and their spandex costumes.

Another burgeoning style in California was the party-oriented sound promoted by the Los Angeles–based MC Anthony "Tone-Lōc" Smith, whose single "Wild Thing" (1988) on Delicious Vinyl Records was credited as the second-best-selling single since "We Are the World" (1985) at the time. Lōc's deep, gravelly vocal delivery punctuated by a catchy guitar riff advanced the song's distinctiveness and uniqueness. His album, *Lōc-ed after Dark,* sold over two million copies. Tone-Lōc followed up the single "Wild Thing"[18] with the equally successful "Funky Cold Medina."

Marvin Young, who at the time was studying economics at the University of Southern California, penned the lyrics to Tone-Lōc's most memorable songs. Young, better known to audiences as "Young MC," also recorded on Lōc's label. He was introduced as an MC with his multiplatinum rap song "Bust a Move" (1989), followed by the album *Stone Cold Rhymin',* which certified platinum. In the following year, Young MC earned several music awards, including the coveted Grammy for Best Rap Performance.

Two noted artists, Stanley "MC Hammer" Burrell and Todd "Too $hort" Shaw, put Oakland (or "Oaktown") on the map of rap, displacing the L.A./N.Y.C. duality and establishing their city as a thriving hip-hop mecca. The rapper MC Hammer revolutionized a quick-stepping dance with multiple splits that resembled the celebrated movements of James Brown. In the mid-1980s, Hammer recorded his first single, "Ring 'Em," which was released on his independent label Bustin Records. With Hammer "selling 12-inch copies of the single from the trunk of his car, it became number one in the San Francisco Bay area" (Stancell 1996:125). Following the success of his single and local production of an album, *Let's Get It Started* (which sold fifty thousand), he signed with Capitol Records in 1988.

Hammer's rappin and dance style created a trend that was followed by many hip-hop artists, including Heavy D and the Boyz. Hammer said, " 'I'm taking it [rap] in that [dance] direction. I'm tired of rap artists pacing the stages . . . and not putting on a show. . . . The acts I am going to produce will be dance. Rap is changing, and each artist will have [a] distinctive style' " (quoted in Fee 1988:R-8). In defining his rap style of delivery, he says, " 'I'm an entertainer. My music has as much singing and dancing as any other pop record. I want to be a pop star'" (quoted in James T. Jones 1990:13). The popular raps "Turn This Mutha Out" and "U Can't Touch This" propelled Hammer's debut album into the top ten. "It became the third rap album to hit number one on the pop charts (behind the Beastie Boys' *Licensed to Ill* and Tone-Lōc's *Lōc-ed after Dark*)" (Stancell 1996:125). Hammer's musical success was not only derived from his consummate dance moves but his subtle use of recycled funk "jams" and past rhythm and blues hits as background music in his rap songs. For example, "U Can't Touch This" uses the music from Rick James's "Super Freak." "Help the Children" makes use of Marvin Gaye's "Mercy, Mercy Me."

Hammer's second album, *Please Hammer Don't Hurt 'Em* (1990), sold nearly five million copies within fourteen weeks, making it the top-selling rap record at the time. It soared simultaneously on *Billboard's* pop chart and rhythm and blues listings to number one.

Todd "Too $hort" Shaw evolved his style in the underground rap scene of East Oakland in the early 1980s. Between 1983 and 1985 he recorded three albums—*Don't Stop Rappin, 75 Girls Present Too Short,* and *Players*—on the local 75 Girls record label. These albums were distributed locally. The actor and Oakland native Mark Curry of ABC's television series "Hangin' with Mr. Cooper" recollects Too $hort's early popularity: "'His was the underground tape to have. The way Short was spittin' game about the 57 bus line and cruisin' Foothill Boulevard? He's a legend in the O [Oakland]'" (quoted in Jenkins 1996:63). In these recordings Too $hort cultivated a subdued rappin style that belied his street hustler's rhymes about pimping (or macking) and ghetto lore.[19] Because of his enormous success on the local circuit, he attracted the attention of Jive/RCA Records. In 1988 he released *Born to Mack,* which went gold. Although the "mack" image was not all that new to rap—Big Daddy Kane's debut album *Long Live the Kane* was also recorded in 1988—Too $hort elevated this image with a succession of platinum albums, including *Life is . . . Too $hort* (1989), *$hort Dog's in the House* (1990), *$horty the Pimp* (1993), and *Get In Where Ya Fit In* (1993). After moving to Atlanta, Too $hort continues to stay true to the pimp music game. In his work, Too $hort laid the groundwork for the other Bay Area artists to come, such as Rappin 4-Tay, Spice 1, E-40, Digital Underground, The Luniz, and underground sensations including Hieroglyphics, Blackalicious, Planet Asia, and Mystic Journeymen, among a host of others.

Too $hort, late 1980s.
(Courtesy of Michael Ochs
Archives)

## All Coasts in the House, 1987–89

Between 1987 and 1989, rap artists from around the country staked out vital
territories in rap. Sir Mix-A-Lot (Nastymix) of Seattle, Washington, produced
several platinum recordings—"Square Dance Rap" (1985), *Swass* (1987), and
*Seminar* (1989)—as well as hits such as the techno-funk mix "Baby Got Back"
from *Mack Daddy* (1992), released on his own label, Rhyme Cartel. 2 Live
Crew of Miami, Florida's Luke Records, founded by Luther "Luke Skyywalk-
er" Campbell, emerged with sexually explicit lyrics and song titles, such as
"Throw the D [Dick]" (1986). Their controversial 1989 album, *As Nasty as
They Wanna Be*, initiated numerous attempts to ban it for obscenity. Another
group to emerge in the mid-1980s was the Geto Boys (formerly the Ghetto
Boys) from the Fifth Ward section of Houston, Texas. Conceived by James

Smith (also known as James Prince), the founder of Rap-A-Lot records, they flirted with gangsta themes, as is apparent in their single "Assassins" (1988) and their first album, *Makin' Trouble* (1988), which was a local success. Although the group's membership fluctuated, the primary members consisted of Big Mike, Bushwick Bill, Scarface, and Willie D. It was not until their controversial album *Grip It! On That Other Level* (1989), rereleased as *Geto Boys* (1990) on Rick Rubin's newly formed Def American label, did the group receive national exposure (see chapter 4). Def Jam Records recorded other artists during the late 1980s: 3rd Bass, an integrated rap trio comprised of two white MCs, Michael "MC Serch" Berrin and Peter "Prime Minister Pete Nice" Nash, and black DJ Richard "Richie Rich" Lawson, recorded *The Cactus Album* (1989), which went gold; and Slick Rick (formerly MC Ricky D with Doug E. Fresh) recorded *The Great Adventures of Slick Rick* (1988), which certified platinum.

While Latino artists had been a part of the rap scene since its formative years, Spanish-speaking rappers did not become fully integrated into rap's mainstream until 1990. Instrumental in catapulting Spanish-speaking MCs to the rap scene was the Cuban-born rapper Mellow Man Ace. Ace landed a recording contract with Capitol Records and released the single "Mentirosa" from his debut album *Escape from Havana*, certifying gold within a month. What contributed to its success was the use of *caló*, a mixture of Spanish and English words. According to Craig Rosen of *Billboard*, *Escape from Havana* was released in August 1989, but "the album did not start breaking [into the musical mainstream] until nearly a year later" (1990:70). Kid Frost, who once performed alongside Ice-T, gained mainstream acceptance with his debut album *Hispanic Causing Panic* (1990) on Virgin Records, featuring the celebrated "La Raza." Set to the music of "Viva Tirado" by the famed bandleader-composer Gerald Wilson, "La Raza" (the race) promoted Chicano pride and unity among Chicano gangs. Frost organized the Latin Alliance, described as "a collective of rappers that included Mellow Man Ace and ALT" (Ro 1996:15). Following the success of Frost and Mellow Man Ace, Latino rappers such as Lighter Shade of Brown, Gerardo, and Cypress Hill gained mainstream prominence, while the Aztec-inspired nationalist collectives Ozomatli and Aztlan Underground championed hip-hop underground circuits. A group closely allied with Chicano gang-style MCs was the Samoan group the Boo-Yaa T.R.I.B.E., with their only LP to date, *New Funky Nation* (1990).

### Rap Music and the Media

Ultimately rap found its way onto the silver screen. Its artists have appeared in *Wild Style* (1983), *Beat Street* (1984), *Breakin'* and *Breakin' 2* (1984), *Krush Groove* (1985), and in other feature-length films. Run-D.M.C. starred in *Tougher Than Leather* (1987), and The Fat Boys took the leads in *Disorderlies* (1987).

During the 1980s, rap music was shunned by many radio programmers. They said their listeners complained that its language and music were too coarse or "streetified" for the airwaves. A few stations, such as WBLS and WRKS (KISS-FM) of New York and KDAY of Los Angeles catered to rap music listeners. KDAY, as shaped and guided by its program director, Greg "Mack Daddy" Mack, was developing a large consumer market while maintaining its street sensibilities.

KDAY was also the first radio station to have an all-rap format. "Credited for broadcasting and spreading West Coast rap music outside the confines of local neighborhoods as well as breaking a lot of East Coast artists locally," it soon received national attention from the music industry and was frequented by many rap music businesspersons and artists ("Hey DJ" 2000:115). When the station was bought from Heritage, the original owners, the new owner, Fred Sands Realty, closed the station with two hours' notice. KDAY went off the air officially at 1 P.M. on March 11, 1991.[20] Despite this blow to rap, the rise of music video television supplemented radio airplay and was instrumental in further cultivating this youth market.

MTV, a rock-oriented cable music video network, was championed by Ted Demme, the nephew of MTV's then-director, Jonathan Demme. MTV's first rap show, "Rap Sunday," premiered on August 6, 1988. Because of rave reviews from young viewers, the program paved the way for a weekly show, "Yo! MTV Raps," which premiered on September 24, 1988. Lee Masters, MTV's executive vice president and general manager, noticed that "'the show *Yo! MTV Raps* does fifty percent to sixty percent better than the videos that used to run during its time slot. If I could get from all our shows the kind of results I'm getting from *Yo!*, the results would be unbelievable'" (quoted in Malanowski 1989:77).

The graffiti veteran Fred Brathwaite, better known as Fab Five Freddy, was chosen as the program's video jockey (VJ). Wearing ultra-cool sunglasses, Fab Five Freddy introduced each video clip with hip-hop language and gestures that underscored the authenticity of his knowledge. Some programs were taped at video shoots, concerts, or college campuses, where Fab Five Freddy would interview the artists. In addition to entertainment, "Yo!" served as a tutoring program for hip-hop fans. "'Hip-hop fans were able to get the styles, the dance steps and the right parts in their heads, and go out and represent shit correctly,'" says Fab Five Freddy (quoted in Hampton 1992:54). "Yo!" soon added the comedic duo Ed Lover and Dr. Dre (a former member of Original Concept, not the L.A. rap music producer with the same name), as hosts for a primetime weekday program that supplemented the weekend rap music program. As MTV continued to broaden its viewership, its rap music programs were eventually seen abroad, thus contributing to the globalization of hip-hop arts.

MTV was only one avenue by which rap music was introduced to the rock and pop-oriented viewing public. With rap's growing commercial success, other cable television networks opened their doors to rap music videos.

Launched in fall 1995, Video Jukebox, also known as "The Box," used the tag-line, "The Jukebox Network—Music Television You Control."[21] The Box afforded viewers an alternative to the sequenced or preprogrammed airing

Fab Five Freddy delivering the keynote address at the Power Moves hip-hop conference at UCLA, 1999. (Photo by Alisa Childs)

of music videos based on *Billboard* chart ratings. Instead, viewers would be charged a fee to call and request a particular video. The cultural critic Andrew Ross notes The Box's "reputation as an alternative for those fans who are fed up with urban radio's disdain for and MTV's marginalizing of rap" (1995:17). But while Video Jukebox may have been perceived as a way out of the predetermined MTV format, rap fans still had to compete with other viewers to get their requests aired.

The Black Entertainment Television network (BET) showcased a variety of rap music acts. Conceived in 1980 by the black media mogul Robert Johnson, BET began broadcasting music video programs, "Video Soul" and "Video Vibrations," in its program lineup. BET specifically targeted black viewers by programming rhythm and blues and other diverse black music acts not shown on MTV or any other network at the time. By fall 1989, BET added "Rap City" (pronounced "rhapsody") to its program lineup. Initially hosted by the black comedian Chris Thomas, "Rap City" aired ninety minutes on weekdays and sixty minutes on weekends.[22]

All three music video cable networks—MTV, BET, and The Box—were based on the East Coast. Meanwhile, in fall 1989, the FOX TV network of Los Angeles developed its rap video show, "Pump It Up," hosted by Dee Dee Barnes, formerly of the rap duo Body and Soul. I call "Pump It Up" hip-hop's "American Bandstand" because of its dancing audience, interviews with guest hip-hop artists, and music videos. Although the program ended rather abruptly in the early 1990s, "Pump It Up" was the first rap music show to be picked up by a major network.

"Video Music Box" is lauded as the first music video program to have an all-rap format. It deserves special attention because of its significant role in the development of rap music video production. Launched in 1984, "Video Music Box" was veejayed by a former itinerant DJ, Ralph McDaniels, described by fans as "having an ear" for street music. His early training in the street DJ tradition occurred in Queens and neighboring New York boroughs. McDaniels attended LaGuardia Community College, where he studied communications, and continued his study at the New York Institute of the Arts (Stancell 1996:238). McDaniels, along with the show's producer Lionel Martin, pioneered rap music video production with Classic Concepts, the first black-owned music video production company. Others proceeded to establish video production outlets for rap music videos, for example, Paris Barclay's Black and White Television, founded in 1988.

Toward the end of the 1980s, rap music had become the most vital popular musical form since the days of rhythm and blues. Monica Lynch, the president of Tommy Boy Records, observed that the versatility of rap was boundless because of the music's ability at "'reinventing itself. Every six months, there's a new wrinkle in the fabric'" (quoted in Henderson 1988a:R6). In 1988, the National Academy of Recording Arts and Sciences established a category for Best Rap Performance, and by March 1989, *Billboard* initiated its "Hot Rap Singles" chart. In the international market, while rap music had gained acceptance in Denmark, France, and Germany, its popularity was short-lived because of poor marketing strategies. However, the presence of many U.S. rap artists in London, where they recorded on English subsidiary labels (e.g. Whodini with Jive Records), has created productive interactions between hip-hop artists from the two countries. Most noteworthy are North London's reggae-house sound, spearheaded by Funki Dreds (out of which Jazzie B emerged with the act Soul II Soul), and the U.S. artist Teddy Riley, known for his mixture of hip-hop and rhythm and blues called "new jack swing." The British sociologist Paul Gilroy writes, "[Soul II Soul's] song, 'Keep On Movin',' was notable for having been produced in England by the children of Caribbean settlers and then re-mixed in a (Jamaican) dub format in the United States by Teddy Riley, an African American. It included segments or samples of music taken from American and Jamaican records by the JBs and Mikey Dread, respectively" (Gilroy 1993:16).[23] With the growing influence of rap in England, Rush Artist Management (soon to be renamed Rush Communications), the world's largest rap entertainment firm, established a branch in London.

Between 1984 and 1989, rap music concerts and recordings had grossed over three hundred million dollars (see Collins 1988). Much of this can be attributed to rap's diverse and growing audience. Moreover, advertisers added to the mix by making rap music a consumer commodity. For example, after the release of Run-D.M.C.'s "My Adidas" in 1986, the group signed a twenty-million-dollar contract with Adidas. In 1988 Reebok began a thirty-five-million-dollar advertising campaign that featured Run-D.M.C. Designer sweatsuits worn by rap artists in their videos have generated burgeoning sales for fashion labels such as British Knights, Troop, Kangol, Gucci, and Louis Vuitton. Rap artists began appearing in commercials to advertise Pepsi (Young MC) and Sprite (Heavy-D).

By the end of the 1980s, several trends occurred in rap that undoubtedly expanded the parameters of music production. DJs revolutionized sound production concepts from manual mixing (break beats and scratching) to electronic mixing and digital sampling. Additionally, rhythm and blues performers teamed up with rap singers, creating a new hybrid genre. Examples include Chaka Khan's "I Feel for You" (1984), featuring Melle Mel; Midnight Star's "Don't Rock the Boat" (1987), featuring Ecstacy of Whodini; and Jody Watley's "Friends" (1989), featuring Eric B. and Rakim. Al B. Sure's "Off on Your Own Girl" (1988) and Bobby Brown's "Don't Be Cruel" (1988) include rap segments. By the late 1980s, the producer-songwriter-musician Teddy Riley established the group Guy with lead singer Aaron Hall and advanced the "new jack swing" concept. Finally, gospel artists began incorporating raps in numbers such as The Clark Sisters' "Computers Rule the World" (1988), featuring Melle Mel. Even Christian evangelists such as Michael Peace and DC Talk have found rap to be an appropriate medium of expression.

While rap music continued to bum rush the mainstream on its own terms during the 1990s, its popularity did not come without a price. Its artists encountered a deluge of legal battles from copyright infringement to obscenity charges and censorship. In the midst of controversy, some critics predicted the demise of rap. The next chapter explores rap's resiliency as it rises to become a thriving empire against all odds.

# Expanding Frontiers:
# Rap Music, 1990–2000

### *Guilty until Proven Innocent: Rap's Bout with the Law*

Reproducing portions of a song via digital sampling had become a common practice in creating a rap music soundtrack. The practice seen by hip-hop musicians as signifying on and giving props to respected artists and favorite songs was never challenged until rap began to gain commercial notoriety in the musical mainstream with De La Soul's sampling of the Turtles' music during the late 1980s. Sampling continued to be of major concern during the 1990s as well. For example, in Biz Markie's "On N On" from his album *I Need a Haircut* (1991), he sampled eight bars of the singer-songwriter Gilbert O'Sullivan's 1972 hit "Alone Again (Naturally)." O'Sullivan sued Markie's affiliated label, Cold Chillin', and its distributor, Warner Bros., which prompted a New York federal judge to have Markie's album removed from retail stores until the case was settled. As a result, record companies imposed stringent sampling clearance policies, involving compensations to the artists and publishers of sampled music.

The advent of gangsta and explicit rap resulted in a wave of censorship hearings in the 1990s. Among the first was the case of 2 Live Crew and their album *As Nasty as They Wanna Be,* deemed to be so sexually explicit that the district attorney's offices of Florida and Alabama charged 2 Live Crew with violating their states' obscenity laws. Citing the First Amendment, the Court of New York found the group not guilty.

Despite censorship, the statistics gathered by using SoundScan showed that gangsta rap's popularity was surging. N.W.A.'s second LP, *Efil4zaggin* (a backward spelling of Niggaz 4 Life), released in 1991, became the first gangsta rap album to reach number two on the *Billboard* pop chart. It soon became number one, "the highest album debut since Michael Jackson's *Bad*. It sold 1 million copies in two weeks" (Allen 1994:74). Ice Cube's solo debut LP *AmeriKKKa's Most Wanted* (1990), produced by Da Lench Mob and Public Enemy's Bomb Squad, followed *Efil4zaggin* on the *Billboard* pop chart, selling nearly two hundred thousand copies in its first week. Another controversial release, "the album, which ultimately [went] platinum, [set] off protests against what [were] perceived as anti-Korean, anti-Jewish, and anti-gay lyrics in songs like 'Black Korea' and 'No Vaseline'" (Allen 1994:74). Numerous gangsta and explicit rap recordings were considered not only sexually explicit but misogynist: AMG's "Bitch Betta Have My Money" (1991), Ice Cube's "Nappy Dugout" (1991), and Apache's "Gangsta Bitch" (1993). The Geto Boys' "Mind of a Lunatic" (1990) and 2Pac's "Soulja's Story"[1] (1991) generated heated controversy because of necrophilic and cop-killing themes. Additionally, the Geto Boys' self-titled LP, which contained "Mind of a Lunatic," was deemed too violent by Geffen Records, the distributor for their label at the time, Def American. As a result, Geto Boys released subsequent recordings on Rap-A-Lot.

Ice-T and the black Marxist rapper Paris were pressured to leave their record companies, Sire/Warner Bros. and Tommy Boy, respectively, because of the criticism of their explicit lyrics. Police officers had led a boycott of Sire Records, the label that released *Body Count* (1992), by Ice-T's heavy metal band of the same name, because of their song "Cop Killer." Paris's "Bush Killa," from the album *Sleeping with the Enemy* (1992), had appeared to describe a mock assassination of President Bush, alarming U.S. national security forces. As a result, both artists left their labels. Paris released *Sleeping with the Enemy* on his own label, Scarface, only to follow with his third album, *Guerilla Funk* (1994), on Priority. Sister Souljah also received much criticism in 1992 from presidential candidate Bill Clinton, who took seriously her sarcastic, offhanded comment to black youth about black-on-black crime, advocating black-on-white violence at Jesse Jackson's Rainbow Coalition Leadership Summit.

Gangsta rap or so-called porno rap was the subject of congressional subcommittee hearings on Capitol Hill between February 11 and May 5, 1994. Although the PMRC initiated similar hearings in 1985 against heavy metal music, resulting in mandatory warning labels on records with explicit lyrics, the 1994 hearings did not have such a concrete outcome as a goal. Instead, it seemed that the instigators sought to create a blanket condemnation of music by black males and of black male sexuality. Numerous spokespersons—high-powered activists and politicians, music executives, scholars, and a female rap artist—addressed gangsta rap. Rap artists and fans of gangsta rap were noticeably excluded from testifying. Some observers described these proceedings as a showcase for the elite rather than a forum to elucidate the inner-city issues to which gangsta rap draws attention. These hearings, notes Paul D. Fischer, reflected "the 1985 pattern where the spouses of numerous PMRC members were on the Subcommittee [Tipper Gore, for example] and in the high level government positions. Second, with no legislation or other action contemplated by the Subcommittees, none of this information has gone forward to inform discussion of the larger issues it raised about the chronic and critical problems of the communities that produce the most potent rap" (1996:53).

While the 1994 congressional hearings did not harm rap music record sales, the debates prompted the Federal Communications Commission (FCC) to demand that artists using expletives in their songs provide the radio industry with "clean" versions for broadcast. Speaking about 2 Live Crew's single "Where Them Ho's At" and the clean version "Where Them Girls At," Luther Campbell concedes, "'You gotta deal with the FCC regulations. That's their law. But you still got that ghetto law. They want to deal with the real thing. The streets want to hear the uncensored version. On the other hand, it's good to have that clean version, because you run into situations where you want to get played at malls and skating rinks'" (quoted in Benesch 1994:42). Radio airplay of hardcore rap music declined slightly, but word of mouth via DJ mix tapes supplemented promotion. Rap music sales continued to soar, in part because of the sensationalism of the hearings and also through underground promotion.

The hearings also affected the programming of explicit music videos. Video producers intentionally obscured weapons and risqué views of women.[2] Time Warner replaced The Box with the History Channel. "Yo! MTV Raps" was soon reformatted and faded from the music video network's lineup. Ralph McDaniel's "Video Music Box" suffered a loss when it was dropped for a six-month period from one of New York's PBS stations during its purchase by ITT/Dow Jones in 1997. Another New York PBS station, channel 25, significantly reduced broadcasts of "Video Music Box." Despite these changes, BET's "Rap City" (subtitled "Tha Bassment") thrived, eventually augmenting its video lineups with "Hits from the Streets," as MTV did with its "Jams Countdown."

### Blending and Shaping Styles: Rap and Other Musical Voices

Undaunted by ongoing censorship and vilification of rap, artists active in the 1980s continued to flourish within the musical mainstream during the 1990s: A Tribe Called Quest (with Q-Tip going solo), the Beastie Boys, Brand Nubian, DJ Jazzy Jeff and the Fresh Prince, Dr. Dre and Ice Cube (former members of N.W.A.), Kool Keith (also known as Dr. Octagon), Hammer, Heavy D, Ice-T, KRS-One, LL Cool J, MC Lyte, N.W.A., Public Enemy, Queen Latifah, Rakim, Salt-N-Pepa, and Too $hort, to name a few. Rap music also welcomed a new breed of MCs, the white artists, who contributed to the dynamism and hybridity of the genre.

Blondie is an example of a white act that experimented with rap during the early 1980s with their song "Rapture." Although Deborah Harry's rhymes were somewhat abstract (e.g. "the man from Mars stopped eatin' cars") the mere notion that Blondie was a well-established punk group led some critics to falsely assume that they were the originators of rap. But the group that perfected what Blondie was attempting to do by mixing punk with rap was the Beastie Boys. Considered rap's first successful white act, their success stemmed from a strong affiliation with rap moguls Rick Rubin and Russell Simmons, the cofounders of Def Jam Records. However, it was Run-D.M.C. that laid the foundation for the mixing of rock-oriented music with rap. Other thriving white rap/hip-hop acts soon followed suit during the 1990s: House of Pain, Icy Blu, Marky Mark and the Funky Bunch (featuring the actor Mark Wahlberg), 3rd Bass, Biggie Smallz,[3] and Vanilla Ice. While acts like House of Pain and 3rd Bass pursued a more hardcore image, others, like Marky Mark and Vanilla Ice, were more dance-oriented, a trend made popular by Hammer. But it was Vanilla Ice, declared by critics as "rap's first white superstar," who became the subject of controversy during the early 1990s.

Vanilla Ice, born Robert Van Winkle, rose to the forefront of rap despite questions about whether he actually was tutored by hardcore rappers, as he had claimed. Although his debut album *To the Extreme* (1990), which contained the single "Ice Ice Baby," went from gold to quadruple platinum status within a month, critics questioned the originality of his music, particularly when the hit "Ice Ice Baby" was recognized as the signature chant of the national black fraternity Alpha Phi Alpha (Morthland 1991).[4] In addition, it was discovered that Ice was not from the hood, as he had claimed, but had been reared in the suburbs.

In the wake of Vanilla Ice's demise, a newer breed of white MCs emerged. These acts continued where Ice-T and his heavy metal band Body Count and

Run-D.M.C. left off. Advancing the marriage of heavy metal and rap is Detroit's underground artist, Esham, who is credited for "acid rap." Esham defines acid rap as analogous to "'modern day blues [or] heavy metal'" (quoted in Alert 2000:107). Rap acts that exploit the acid rap style include Kid Rock and his band Twisted Brown Trucker (who coined the term "hickhop"), Korn, Limp Bizkit, Everlast (formerly of House of Pain), Insane Clown Posse, and Kottonmouth Kings' metal sound with a hip-hop feel.

Alternative rock artists topped the charts with quasi-rap styles, such as Beck's "Loser" (1994), or the multi-ethnic rap-rock alternative band Rage against the Machine. Beck and Rage against the Machine both garnered Grammys for their creative efforts. As one critic states, these artists "are gaining strength in the alternative rock scene and finding a young, suburban male audience that in the past has embraced heavy metal and hard-core rap" (Boucher 1999:F10).

Perhaps the most enigmatic yet controversial white act is the Grammy award winner Eminem (born Marshall Mathers) of Detroit. Dubbing himself "Slim Shady," Eminem's *The Slim Shady LP* (1999) was his first on Dr. Dre's label, Aftermath. Eminem's follow-up LP, *The Marshall Mathers LP*, sold 1.7 million units in its first week, the largest sale in the history of hip-hop music to date. However, he received much flack from the gay community concerning the homophobic content of this album as well as from the American mainstream for the LP's graphic depictions of rape, murder, and incest. Moreover, the LP's single, "Stan," a rap composed as a series of letters written by an emotionally disturbed fan named Stan, concludes with the protagonist's suicide. Considered a rapper with tight lyrical skillz, Eminem's music is further enhanced by the trademark funk sounds of Dr. Dre. Some rap culture bearers undoubtedly find that Emimen's ability to flow "like the brothas" put him in a higher league than other white rap acts. Some rappers assert that his lyrics embrace the hardcore realities of growing up white, poor, and feeling like a loser in contemporary society.[5]

Rap's dynamism continued to lie in its ability to fuse comfortably with other styles. In the 1980s the industry witnessed this confluence with Run-D.M.C. and the rock group Aerosmith. In the 1990s, KRS-One provided a guest rap on the single "Radio Song" (1991) by the alternative rock group R.E.M., Public Enemy revisited their 1988 hit "Bring the Noise" with the heavy metal band Anthrax in 1991, and DMX, Redman, and Xzibit performed on Limp Bizkit's album *Chocolate Starfish and the Hotdog Flavored Water* (2000). Wyclef Jean of the Fugees used classical music on his solo album, *Wyclef Jean Presents the Carnival, featuring the Refugees All Stars* (1997), and Cheryl "Salt"

Eminem performing on The Lyricist Lounge Tour at House of Blues, Los Angeles, 1999. (Photo by Alisa Childs)

James of Salt-N-Pepa rapped with the contemporary gospel music of Kirk Franklin and his choir God's Property's in "Stomp" (1997). Hip-hop also introduced the "rap singer," as best exemplified by the "Queen of Hip-Hop Soul" Mary J. Blige and her cohorts Erykah Badu, Lauryn Hill, LV, and Nate Dogg, most of whom perform guest solo vocals on rap music recordings. With the emergence of reggae dancehall, rap artists such as KRS-One, Heavy D, and Queen Latifah collaborated with dancehall artists or stylistic tributes to this form. Totally unanticipated, however, was rap's fusion with jazz, a genre so harmonically distinct from hip-hop music.

Some legendary jazz artists like Quincy Jones (1990) and Max Roach (in Owen 1988) have speculated that hip-hop and jazz were destined to meet because of their "renegade" nature. Jones explains: "Hip hop is in many ways the same as Bebop, because it was renegade-type music. I came from a disenfranchised sub-culture that got thrown out of the way. They said, 'We'll make up our own life. We'll have our own language'" (1990:167). On his album *Back on the Block* (1989), Jones paid homage to the synergy of hip-hop and jazz with his use of musicians from each musical camp. The jazz pianist Herbie Hancock was the first of the jazz disciples to venture into the experimental sounds of hip-hop with the 1983 hit "Rockit," highlighting the art of scratching with

DJ Grandmixer D.ST. Hancock's *Dis Is Da Drum* (1994) also drew upon hip-hop music and jazz. The final album produced by the legendary jazz trumpeter Miles Davis was the experimental work *Doo-Bop* (1992) with the DJ/hip-hop producer Easy Mo Bee. This work was released posthumously.

Noted contemporary jazz artists continued in the same fashion. The saxophonist Greg Osby, a disciple of the Brooklyn-based jazz collective movement M-BASE, produced *3-D Lifestyles* (1993), which used the talents of the rap DJs Eric Sadler of Public Enemy and Ali Shaheed Muhammad of A Tribe Called Quest. The following year, the saxophonist Branford Marsalis made *Buckshot LeFonque* (1994), with tracks produced by DJ Premier of Gang Starr.

Hip-hop artists' involvement with jazz can be traced to the 1970s, when Grandmaster Flash would mix jazz breaks over funk tracks. But in 1988 the group Stetsasonic released "Talkin' All That Jazz" from *In Full Gear* (1988), a tune that incorporated sampled jazz breaks from Lonnie Liston Smith's "Expansions" and Donald Byrd's "(Fallin Like) Dominoes." Following "Talkin' All That Jazz," the duo Gang Starr (Guru and DJ Premier) recorded a song called "Manifest" on the LP *No More Mr. Nice Guy* (1989) and sampled the well-known bass line intro from Dizzy Gillespie's "A Night in Tunisia." Gang Starr's album also contained the song "Jazz Music," which was later revived as "Jazz Thing" in collaboration with Branford Marsalis for the soundtrack of Spike Lee's film *Mo' Better Blues* (1990). Other groups continued producing tunes with jazz-like breaks, including the following: A Tribe Called Quest's hip-hop classic album, *The Low End Theory* (1991), with the respected jazz bassist Ron Carter; US$_3$'s *Hand on the Torch*, with samples from Herbie Hancock's "Cantaloupe Island," Thelonious Monk's "Straight, No Chaser," and Horace Silver's "Filthy McNasty"; and Digable Planets' "Rebirth of Slick (It's Cool Like Dat)" from *Reachin' (A New Refutation of Time and Space)* (1993), which contained a sample from Art Blakey and the Messengers' performance of "Stretchin'."

Freestyle Fellowship and The Pharcyde underscore their sing-song style with tinges of jazz. Both groups honed their rappin skills at experimental hip-hop "hang-outs" like the Good Life Cafe and Project Blowed in the Leimert Park area of South Central Los Angeles, which hosted open-mic poetic jams. Similar clubs flourished on the East Coast as well. The most popular of these include the Fez, S.O.B.s, the Nyuorican Poets Cafe, and Giant Steps. At the latter, artists from coast to coast, including Michael Franti from the San Francisco Bay Area, The Roots from Philadelphia, or Sha-Key from New York, performed hip-hop-inspired poems a cappella.[6] However, groups like Free-

Gang Starr members DJ
Premier and Guru backstage
at House of Blues Smokin'
Grooves concert, Universal
Amphitheatre, Los Angeles,
1998. (Photo by Alisa
Childs)

style Fellowship and The Pharcyde, with their respective albums, *Innercity Griots* (1993) and *Bizarre Ride II the Pharcyde* (1992), extend open-mic poetry to that of a song-like rap style over jazz-tinged breaks and drum beats.

Hip-hop artists such as Guru of Gang Starr and The Roots experimented with live instrumental performances in making soundtracks for their albums. While making his revolutionary *Jazzmatazz: Volume 1* (1993), Guru invited the jazz musicians Donald Byrd, Roy Ayres, Courtney Pine, and Lonnie Liston Smith among others to perform on his album. The album also featured a duet with Guru and the French/Senegalese rap sensation MC Solaar on the song "Le Bien, Le Mal." The Roots experimented with the live band concept, as heard on their recordings *Do You Want More?!!!??!* (1994) and *Things Fall Apart* (1999). The latter featured the hip-hop/soul vocals of Erykah Badu on the song "You Got Me," written by the poet-songwriter-singer Jill Scott.[7] In 2000, Scott released her debut LP, *Who Is Jill Scott?* coproduced by Jeff "DJ Jazzy Jeff" Townes. The joining of Scott with Townes captured the growing jazz-hip-hop hybrid mixture. By the end of the millennium, hip-hop had extended its live music repertoire to the symphonic medium, pioneered by Dakah, a hip-hop orchestra that features various MCs.

### From the Streets to the Boardroom: Rap's Growing Empire

With the ingenuity, vision, and street promotion tactics inspired by independent black music entrepreneurs like Russell Simmons and Eric "Eazy-E" Wright, rap became a multimillion dollar enterprise that major record companies could no longer afford to ignore. As a result, some of the majors established distribution and marketing deals with independent rap music labels (i.e. Def Jam/Universal), while others bought out or created labels divisions that solely catered to rap music (i.e. Elektra/EastWest). Select, Priority, NastyMix, and Rap-A-Lot were among the few independent rap music labels that remained unaffiliated for some time. As the 1990s progressed, rap music witnessed the trend of "rap-artist-turned-mogul," as artists established their own labels with which they were able to take control of their careers and influence the tide of up-and-coming artists.

Andre Harrell, a former member of the early 1980s rap duo Dr. Jeckyll and Mr. Hyde, established a position with Russell Simmons's management company. In 1986 he moved on to start his own record label, Uptown Entertainment. His intern Sean "P. Diddy" Combs (also known as Puffy or Puff Daddy) discovered and nurtured Mary J. Blige, Jodeci, Heavy D, and The Notorious B.I.G. After a conflict with Harrell, Combs left Uptown Entertainment to head up his own company, Bad Boy Entertainment.[8] Adding The Notorious B.I.G. to his newly formed company, Puffy also ventured into rapping, producing, and finding other rap talents, such as Mase, Lil' Kim, and Lil' Cease of Junior M.A.F.I.A.[9]

After discovering the platinum-selling rap trio Naughty by Nature for her home-label Tommy Boy, Queen Latifah's management company became Flavor Unit Records in 1993. She severed her ties with Tommy Boy and produced the rhythm and blues duo Zhané, the solo artist Apache, and herself. By September 1999 Queen Latifah was host of her own daytime television talk show on the FOX network, receiving top ratings.

The West Coast dominated the gangsta rap scene. Eazy-E's Los Angeles label, Ruthless Records, led the way. With growing discontent among members of N.W.A., Ice Cube left in 1989 to record as a solo artist. Soon to follow was the group's top producer, Dr. Dre, who joined forces with an ex–college football player and former bodyguard, Marion "Suge" Knight, to form Death Row Records in 1992. So named because of its affiliated artists' bouts with the law and Knight's brutal business tactics,[10] Death Row garnered over one hundred million dollars within few years from the multiplatinum sales of Dr. Dre's *The Chronic* (1992), Snoop Doggy Dogg's *Doggystyle* (1993), and Tha Dogg Pound's *Dogg Food* (1995), becoming the most successful gangsta rap label of the 1990s. After Suge Knight posted $1.4 million bail for the release of the rapper-actor Tupac "2Pac" Shakur, who was serving a sentence for sexual assault, Shakur was released from Riker's Island prison in New York in fall 1995 and joined Death Row's roster. On February 13, 1996, he released *All Eyez on Me,* the first double CD in rap's history. By April it had gone quintuple platinum.

With political watchdogs working against Death Row Records and gangsta rap, Dr. Dre and Interscope (Death Row's distributor) severed their ties with the label. Another blow to Death Row was the untimely death of Tupac Shakur, the label's most prolific artist.[11] Although problems combined with criminal allegations levied against Knight forced the company to slowly close its doors, Death Row's meteoric rise to success as a major independent player in the history of rap music remained uncontested at the end of the century. By summer 2001, Knight had restructured Death Row records and changed its name to Tha Row Records.[12] Dr. Dre, who formed Aftermath Entertainment in 1996, rose to success with Xzibit and the award-winning MC Eminem, as well as earning a Grammy himself.

Cedric Singleton founded Black Market Records out of Sacamento in the early 1980s. A former DJ turned producer, Singleton has aided in developing a rap scene in Sacramento with local talents such as Da Lynch Hung and X-Raided. Jermaine Dupri's Atlanta-based company So So Def, distributed by Columbia, produced tracks for the platinum-selling artists Kriss Kross and Da Brat. By the beginning of the new millennium, Dupri had further extended his record empire into sports management.

Among the rap music executives who have achieved phenomenal success in the medium is Percy "Master P" Miller. Master P grew up in New Orleans' Calliope projects and relocated to Richmond, California, north of Oakland, where he opened a record store called No Limit. While in the San Francisco Bay Area, Master P (the P stands for Profit) performed as a rapper on the local underground scene. After an unsuccessful record deal with Solar Music Group and the untimely death of his brother Kevin, P shifted direction and launched No Limit Records.

Prior to 1996, Master P had made several solo albums and produced others, though most of his clout remained underground. By his third solo album, *Ice Cream Man,* Master P eased into the musical mainstream as a major player. Establishing a home office in Baton Rouge, Louisiana, he relied upon the talents of TRU, consisting of his brothers Vyshonn (Silkk the Shocker) and Corey (C-Murder). Other No Limit artists include Mia-X and Mystikal (formerly with Jive Records) of New Orleans, Sons of Funk and Steady Mobb'n of the Bay Area, Snoop Dogg (formerly Snoop Doggy Dogg of Death Row Records), No Limit's five-man music production team The Medicine Men (formerly known as Beats by the Pound), and many others.

Master P augmented his rhymin and entrepreneurial crafts with the semi-autobiographical film *I'm Bout It* (1997), which he wrote, directed, and produced. Bypassing the film-to-video format, P's direct-to-video movie sold 250,000 copies within months of its release. His 1998 film project *I Got the Hook-Up,* directed by Michael Martin, caught the attention of a major film distributor, Miramax/Dimension. This film tallied $4.4 million the first weekend, clearing $10.3 million in total (Brown 1999). Because of Master P's "Midas touch" reputation, his distributor, Priority Records, settled for a mere 20 percent of No Limit's profits. Master P diversified to include a telecommunications service and a sports entertainment branch. This diversification was unprecedented for any independent label in the history of the music business. *Forbes* magazine listed Percy "Master P" Miller entered as 1998's tenth highest paid entertainer in America, grossing $56.5 million.[13]

Cash Money Records, another company in the deep South, has been instrumental in making New Orleans (the "Crescent City") a thriving hip-hop arena. Most of the hits produced by Cash Money Records, founded in 1991 by brothers Brian "Baby" and Ron "Suga Slim" Williams, were produced by underground acts known throughout Louisiana and Texas. By 1998, New Orleans' Juvenile, a member of The Hot Boys (Lil' Wayne, B.G., and Turk), helped placed Cash Money in the mainstream of hip-hop music with the songs "Ha" and "Back That Azz Up" from his multiplatinum album *400 Degreez* (1998). The latter hit was a remake of a bounce tune by New Orleans' DJ Jubilee, hailed as the "King of Bounce" (Wade 2001:52). Without a doubt, "Ha," a common verbal exclamation used in black New Orleans speech, was immensely popular among hip-hop adherents. Cash Money's musical production is masterminded by Mannie "Fresh" Byron, who complements sampled "bounce" tracks (an underlying techno-funk-driven accompaniment) with originally composed music grooves.

Other rap music artists established their own businesses in the late 1990s. The MC extraordinaire Shawn "Jay-Z" or "Jigga" Carter, along with Damon

Dash and Kareem Burke, co-CEO's of Roc-A-Fella Records (distributed by Def Jam), founded a clothing line, Rocawear.[14] Lil' Kim founded Queen Bee Records, and Snoop Dogg founded Dogghouse Records.

## Coastal Rap and Other Growing Trends

The 1990s witnessed a burgeoning of regional rap scenes with sounds idiosyncratic to certain areas. While gangsta-funk and mack-daddy styles thrived in California and parts of Texas, such as Houston with Geto Boys, techno sounds à la "porno" became a fixture with Miami's 2 Live Crew, Trick Daddy, and Trina. The ever-present bass sounds of DJ Magic Mike and his cohorts (i.e. 95 South and the 69 Boyz) were characteristic of Orlando, but became the model for the Miami bass sound.

The millennium ended with two unexpected trends. Preceded by Atlanta-based acts such as Kriss Kross, the rap–rhythm and blues hybrid act TLC, Arrested Development, and Da Brat (of Chicago), a "dirtier" sound emerged from Atlanta and New Orleans, commonly referred to as "The Dirty South." Although some critics often include Texas and Florida rap music scenes as part of the Dirty South, I contend that there is a distinction. The artists of Atlanta and New Orleans introduced to rap a distinct style of rhymin characterized by a more singsongy, freeflowing style. The Dirty South style makes use of vernacular expressions peculiar to black southern life (e.g. "Clampett," "Miss Ann," "Hoody Hoo," "ha," "you heard me," and "bling, bling") and incorporates the names of southern icons in their performances (e.g. the Mardi Gras Indians and the names of neighborhood streets and projects). The accompanying soundtracks are composed of funk-driven beats and, as with the New Orleans sound, a techno-funk sound called "bounce." The term "The Dirty South" is derived from the title of a song from the Goodie MOb's debut LP, *Soul Food* (1995). On the Atlanta-based LaFace label (founded by Kenny "Babyface" Edmonds and L. A. Reid), Goodie MOb, whose name is a loose acronym for "the good die mostly over bullshit," consists of Big Gipp, Cee-Lo, Khujo, and T-Mo. LaFace Records also represents OutKast, the duo composed of Big Boi and André, which has produced a string of innovative recordings, from their debut LP *Southernplayalisticadillacmuzik* (1994), *AT-Liens* (1995; the title comes from a term embraced to identify Atlanta-based artists), *Aquemini* (1998), and *Stankonia* (2000). Making use of varied sounds, from sampled tracks to live instruments, OutKast and Goodie MOb popularized a freeflowing rap style with chanted refrains. Underpinning the unique sounds of these two acts is the production crew known as Organized Noize, which started in the basement of its mastermind, Rico Wade. Wade is accompanied by Raymond Murray and Pat "Sleepy" Brown. Along with Goodie MOb, OutKast, and other affiliates, such as Witchdoctor and Cool Breeze, they form the ATLien collective called "The Dungeon." Acts such as Young Bleed of Baton Rouge and Ludacris of Atlanta continue to expand the southern sound and garner wide audiences.

A city often considered southern in style, St. Louis made audiences take notice when Cornell Haynes, better known as Nelly, entered the top *Billboard* spot with "Country Grammar" followed by "EI" from the LP *Country Grammar*. Nelly, a Grammy nominee and a member of the crew St. Lunatics (Kyjuan, Murph, Slo Down, and Ali) continued the familiar singsongy style used by the Dirty South acts.

At the close of the 1990s black and Latino MCs continued to dominate the U.S. pop and rap music charts. While it is impossible to mention every prominent artist, the following list includes the most recognized artists on the contemporary rap music scene who have not been mentioned previously: Bahamadia, Beanie Sigel, Beatnuts, Black Eyed Peas, Black Moon, Black

Goodie MOb promoting their debut album, *Soul Food* (left to right: Big Gipp, T-Mo, Khujo, and Cee-lo), 1996. (Photo by Alisa Childs)

Rob, Boogiemonsters, Busta Rhymes, Cam'ron, Canibus, Capone, Chanel Live, Cocoa Brovaz, Common, Coolio from W.C. and the MADD Circle, Crucial Conflict, Cypress Hill, Da Brat, Daz, dead prez, Dilated Peoples, DJ Quik, DMX, Drama, Eve, Fat Joe and his Terror Squad (including Armaggedon, Big Punisher, Cuban Link, Prospect, and Triple Seis), Foxy Brown, the Haitian-reggae-hip-hop trio the Fugees (who now perform as the solo acts Wyclef Jean, Pras, and Lauryn Hill), Chinese philosophical groups such as the kung-fu-styled groups Fu Schnickens and the Shaolin-inspired collective Wu-Tang Clan (i.e. The Rza, Method Man, Ghostface Killah, Raekwon, Inspectah Deck, U-God, The Gza, Masta Killa, Ol' Dirty Bastard, and Cappadonna), Ja Rule, Jeru the Damaja, J. T. Money, Jurassic 5, K-Solo, Keith Murray, Kurupt, Lil' Bow Wow, Lil' Kim, Lil' Romeo, Lord Tariq and Peter Gunz, LOX, Mack 10, Memphis Bleek, Missy "Misdemeanor" Elliott, Mobb Deep, M.O.P., Mos Def, Nas, Naughty by Nature, Noreaga, Pharoahe Monch, Outsidaz, Rah Digga, Ras Kass, Redman, Scarface of Geto Boys, Screwball, Shaquille O'Neal, Shyne, Soul Assassins, Souls of Mischief, Tha Eastsidaz, The Coup, The Luniz, and Warren G.

Alongside the success of rap's MCs are the hip-hop DJs, who provide the soundtrack. While some DJs work independently, most are a part of a rap music ensemble. When rap music recordings are made, DJs take on the role of producer, gaining a reputation through successful affiliation with particular MCs. Well-known production partnerships include Ant Banks for Too $hort; Blaze for Amil, Busta Rhymes, DMX, Jay-Z, and Prodigy; the Bomb Squad for Public Enemy; Buckwild for Black Rob's "Whoa," Big Punisher, and Beanie Sigel; DJ Mark the 45 King for Queen Latifah and Jay-Z; DJ Premier of Gang Starr, Common, Rakim, and Nas; DJ Scratch for Busta Rhymes/Flipmode Squad; Dr. Dre for Snoop Doggy Dogg, Eminem, Xzibit, and for himself; Easy Mo Bee for Busta Rhymes and Biggie; Hi-Tek for Mos Def, Talib Kweli, dead prez, Big L, and the Cocoa Brovaz; Hitman Howie Tee for The Real Roxanne and Chubb Rock; Irv Gotti for Ja Rule and The Murderers; Jermaine Dupri for LL Cool J, Da Brat, and Kriss Kross; Large Professor for Main Source, Kool G Rap and DJ Polo; Mannie Fresh for Juvenile and The Hot Boys; Marley Marl of the Juice Crew for a number of artists; The Medicine Men for Master P; Neptunes for Mystikal's "Shake Ya Ass"; Organized Noize for OutKast and Goodie MOb; Pete Rock for CL Smooth; Prince Paul of Stetsasonic for De La Soul; Rockwilder for Jay-Z, Method Man and Redman, and Rah Digga; The RZA for Wu-Tang Clan's collective; Swizz Beatz for Ruff Ryders (including DMX); Timbaland for Missy Elliott, among others; and Trackmasters, for Nas as well as other artists or groups.

Another important hip-hop music scene is that of the DJ soloist. With the innovations of mobile DJs from the early years of rap—Bambaataa, Herc, Flash, and Theodore—and Grandmixer D.ST's performance on Herbie Hancock's "Rockit," DJing as an art form rose to the forefront. Artists who have mastered various turntable techniques and showcase themselves as DJs began referring to themselves as "turntable technicians" or "turntablists." Some of these DJs and collectives are the Beat Junkies, Cut Chemist and Nu-Mark of Jurassic 5, DJ Apollo, DJ Shadow, DJ Honda, DJ Symphony, Invisibl Skratch Piklz (DJ Disk, D-Styles, Mix Master Mike, DJ Q-Bert, Shortkut, and Yoga Frog), and X-ecutioners (Mista Sinista, Roc Raida, Rob Swift, and Total Eclipse), to name a few.[15]

With the fast-growing sale of rap music to a large youth constituent, the film industry cashed in on hip-hop's expressiveness, using numerous rap artists to add realism to its narratives. The 1990s also ushered in a wave of young black male filmmakers called "new jacks" (Jones 1991). Barry Cooper, a co-screenwriter for Mario Van Peebles's appropriately titled film *New Jack City* (1991), coined the term to describe the young black newcomer in the filmmaking profession. New jack films expose their audiences to urban street culture and aesthetics and the perils of ghetto life from the perspective of a young black protagonist much in the same manner as gangsta rap. Rap music is central to these films' soundtracks because it establishes a sense of time and place, reinforces the raw texture of the "new jack" aesthetic, and educates viewers about the realities of street life for contemporary youth. To bring a sense of realism to certain roles, rap artists were often cast as leads or co-stars: Ice Cube in *Boyz 'N the Hood* (1991), Tupac Shakur in *Juice* (1991), and Ice-T in *New Jack City* (1991).[16] Some new jack/hip-hop cult classics, however, like *House Party* (1990) and its sequels, starring Kid 'N' Play, are contemporary satires of urban black youth culture, where party, dance, and frivolity bring comic relief to ghetto life. Many rap music video directors went on to produce and direct new jack or urban films. F. Gary Gray's *Set It Off* (1996), starring Queen Latifah, captures the urban lifestyles of four black women. Hype Williams's *Belly* (1998) follows the new jack aesthetic, casting rappers DMX, Nas, and Method Man as leads.

Rap artists were in demand in the 1990s as leads in other mediums, such as sitcoms and mainstream films, where they appeared alongside well-known Hollywood actors: LL Cool J in *The Hard Way* (1991) with Michael J. Fox; Queen Latifah in *Living Out Loud* (1998) with Holly Hunter and Danny Devito; Will Smith in the long-running sitcom "The Fresh Prince of Bel Air" and in the blockbuster flicks *Men in Black* (1997) with Tommy Lee Jones and

*Enemy of the State* (1998) with Gene Hackman; and Busta Rhymes in *Shaft* (2000) with Samuel L. Jackson and *Finding Forrester* (2000) with Sean Connery. By the late 1990s, hip-hop filmmaking was undertaken by the renowned actor-director Warren Beatty, who became the first Hollywood luminary to produce, write, and star in a hip-hop spoof in his film *Bulworth* (1998). To prepare for *Bulworth*, Beatty consulted with the mogul Suge Knight in an attempt to understand hip-hop politics. Warren Beatty explains why he wanted to make a hip-hop-oriented film: "'Rap gave me a great comic contrast. Here's this white, middle-aged politician going nuts with a young rapper's voice coming out of his mouth'" (quoted in Goldstein 1998:92). While not a major hit with Beatty's Hollywood cohorts, the *Bulworth* screenplay, co-written by Beatty and Jeremy Pikser and based on Beatty's original story, received an Oscar nomination for best original screenplay in 1999. Its soundtrack gained popularity among hip-hop heads.

The film industry continues to pursue other avenues with rap music. By 2000, Artists Management Group (AMG) created by Hollywood entertainment magnates Michael Ovitz, Julie Silverman-Yorn, and Rick Yorn, lured the talents of hip-hop executives Chris Lighty and his business partner, Mona Scott. Lighty, founder of Violator Records and Management, and Scott, who oversees Violator Management, have been successful in landing television commercial spots for clients Busta Rhymes with Mountain Dew (soft drink) and for Missy "Misdemeanor" Elliott with the Gap clothing line as well as developing the film careers of LL Cool J and Q-Tip, among others. With the move to AMG, Scott and Lighty head up the new urban entertainment division, whose sole responsibility is to develop music-related programming for film, television, animation, and new media ("Busta Rhymes, Missy Elliott" 2000:48). In commenting on the inclusion of Lighty and Scott with AMG, Ovitz states that "hip-hop has become a cultural reference point for the world, and Chris Lighty and his partner Mona Scott have stayed on the cutting edge of this revolution. They are forward-thinkers who anticipate these trends in music and have a keen awareness of what the audience wants" ("Violator" 2001).

Film directors also produced hip-hop documentaries containing live concert footage enhanced by interviews. These documentaries captured the effervescence of hip-hop performance as seen in *The Show* (1994), *Rhyme and Reason* (1997), *Nobody Knows My Name* (1999), *Freestyle: The Art of Rhyme* (2000), and *Scratch* (2001).

By the end of the century, the promotion of rap music via the touring circuit soared again. Concert promoters in the early days of rap expressed anxiety because of past violent incidents, but in the late 1990s rap music artists and entrepreneurs took matters into their own hands by organizing and promoting their own tours (e.g. the Ruff Ryders/Cash Money Tour, Jay-Z's "Hard Knock Life" tour, and Dr. Dre's "Up in Smoke" tour).

Remaining somewhat peripheral to mainstream rap is the "underground" scene, where many of the up-and-coming hip-hop artists, such as Mos Def, Talib Kweli, Rah Digga, and Eminem, first tested their verbal dexterity. One such itinerant circuit is The Lyricist Lounge. The Lounge was established by Anthony Marshall and Danny Castro in Manhattan's Lower East Side in 1991. When the "bumpin beats and lyrical traffic" generated from the Lounge began aggravating nearby tenants, the Lounge eventually became mobile. Promoted among hip-hoppers by word of mouth and flyers, the Lounge moved from venue to venue. At a typical Lounge event, MCs would elicit their rhymes in "freestyle," the execution of extemporaneous rhymes, and passing rhymes around from one person to the next in a circular formation known as a cipher (see chapter 5). Rawkus Records has released recordings of The Lyricist Lounge performances. In February 2000, MTV aired the hip-hop program "The Lyricist Lounge Show," based on the Lounge's concept.

Finally, with the enormous growth of rap music in the 1990s, a number of music trade magazines specializing in hip-hop culture appeared in paper and on the Internet. Among the most popular trade magazines are *Hip-Hop Connection, The Source, Vibe, Urb,* and *XXL,* while the hip-hop Internet magazines, including Contrabandit.com, Daveyd.com, and Rapstation.com, are steadily becoming primary outlets for the circulation of hip-hop's latest news.

Internal and external forces stimulated the maturation of rap music as a distinct genre. Rap artists responded to these forces by forging new directions for rap music. Using their creative ingenuity, rap artists and entrepreneurs explored and widened the parameters in sound technology and musical production. Because this tradition has attracted a culturally diverse audience, rap music has become the most vital of popular music forms—becoming a billion-dollar enterprise. *Rolling Stone* magazine reported that "rap album sales shot up thirty-two percent in just twelve months, breaking the 80 million-album-a-year mark for the first time. Superstar releases by Lauryn Hill, Jay-Z, and DMX (each of which outsold records from Pearl Jam, the Smashing Pumpkins, and Dave Matthews Band) proved that rap acts can not only score big first week gains but [maintain a presence in] the Top Ten for months at a time" (Boehlert 1999:15). Clearly, youth tastes in rap range from the moderate to the hardcore street-edge artists. In accommodating the varied musical tastes, rap music artists have experimented with other musical styles, from alternative rock to jazz. The music industry has also witnessed the unprecedented acceptance of non-black and Latino artists and the influence of rap music from regions between the East and West coasts. Record companies abroad that specialize in rap and mass-mediation (i.e. Jive Records) also account for much of rap's global evolution.[17]

Before the 1990s, black artists exploited by ruthless music executives ended up broke, destitute, and bitter. But out of the years of struggle and the experiences of jilted black artists of the past, a new breed of black executives emerged during the latter years of the twentieth century. Rap music spearheaded "a return to those concepts of self-sufficiency, self-ownership, and self-validation, and [rap artists are] more aware of the parasitic nature of the industry than ever before" (Taha 1999:128).

Rap's commercial potential rests with its inventiveness and unique aesthetic. To fully understand the complexity of its production techniques and performance practices, the following chapter explores hip-hop's musical aesthetic in depth.

# Street Production:
# The Aesthetics of Style
# and Performance in the
# Rap Music Tradition

5

Most scholars have placed rap music in the urban context, describing it alternately as "the black urban beat" (Baker 1993:33), "a product of African-American urban cultures" (Potter 1995:53), or "a form that prioritizes black cultural voices from the margins of urban America" (Rose 1994:2). While rap music is undoubtedly urban and a medium by which segments of a disenfranchised urban youth speak, its artists prefer to reclaim the word "ghetto" as a marker of power and identity, thus referring to rap music as "ghetto music" or music from the "underground." In the rap song "Ghetto Music" (1989), KRS-One says that "underground" defines a sound that is "raw," a sonic depiction of the grit and grime of the urban ghetto landscape. While rap continues to cross over into wider acceptance, many rap artists strive to remain "underground," refusing to identify with a pop market and insisting that staying "real" necessitates rawness, authenticity, and a continued connection with the streets. The streets nurture, shape, and embody the hip-hop music aesthetic, creating a genre distinct from other forms of black popular music that evolved after World War II.[1] Through a critical assessment of this tradition from within the culture of its birth, we can begin to adequately analyze rap's performance and aesthetic qualities, interpret its lyrics, and define its height of style. The following sections provide a model by which to interpret the performance practices and aesthetics of style of rap music.

## Rap Music 101

During my study of rap music, I discovered that people who react negative-ly to this music are often unable to decode its lyrics, style, and message. Rap's verbal style derives from a nonstandard dialect that thrives within African American street culture, properly called black street speech (Baugh 1983:5). The term "nonstandard" defines the constant reinvention and variation in new terminologies associated with street speech. For example, since the 1960s, black street speakers have used the word "bad" to mean good or exception-al. To determine whether "bad" means atrocious or "good," the listener re-lies on the speaker's vocal inflections, verbal stress, and facial expression as well as the context. In the 1980s, rap artists replaced "bad" with "def," "dope," and "phat" to describe something good or exceptional.[2]

Street speech in hip-hop has its own distinct style. Style translates among black innovators of hip-hop "as that unique, individualistic ambience with which a person invests his or her presence and being; the appropriate com-bination of timing, tempo, rhythm, words, and sounds for an established context; and the aesthetic finesse with which any kind of statement, attitude, or value is delivered. It is carriage and persona! It is poetry in motion—life, living, exuberance, and energy" (Gay 1987:8–9). Moreover, style for hip-hop artists is predicated on being original. Some artists affirm their distinctive-ness of style in lines such as: "I've got a style that's all my own / You've got Lady B on the microphone" ("To the Beat Y'all," by Lady B [1980]), or "You've gotta have style. / You've gotta be original" ("My Philosophy," by Boogie Down Productions [1988]).

Establishing one's rep is highly valued, even revered in the hip-hop com-munity. The individual's ability to develop a distinctive style, also known as "freshness," forms the criterion for such achievement. If someone bites or uses another MC's rhymes or lacks originality, rap artists call the offender a "sucker," a "perpetrator," or "wack." Rap artists often establish their style through a "trademark" text. Run-D.M.C. is credited as the first to popularly define a "sucker" in the recording "Sucker M.C.s" (1984): "you're a sucker MC and you're my fan . . . / you try to bite lines, your rhymes are mine. / You's the sucker MC."

"Hip-hop attitude" is another manifestation of a street style specific to rap music. Although "hip-hop" embraces urban street expressions in gen-eral, it also defines specific gestures and stylized dress (e.g. sneakers, leather, monogrammed jewelry, gold or silver chain necklaces, large gold earrings, and designer clothing). The hip-hop attitude conveys how rap artists wish to be perceived by others. The MC's use of street speech, dress, and body gestures authenticates his or her association with a street aesthetic. Some rap artists present themselves as hardcore and aggressive. The veteran DJ Jam Master Jay for the duo Run-D.M.C. attributes the group's success to this type of street attitude. He explains: "'That's part of what makes us so good. We're aggressive. We walk with a strut. We wear our hats a certain way. We've got the feeling. Street feeling'" (quoted in Hinckley 1986:21).

The social structure of the inner-city street gangs in the rap music tradition is a "crew," also referred to as a "posse." A crew consists of support members of a rap group (e.g. Doug E. Fresh and the Get Fresh Crew). Sal Abbatiello, a club owner and the founder of Fever Records, defines a crew as "a group of people that are down with a particular rapper. The crew sounds like a gang, which is a gang, but it's an organization of rappers and their followers" (Abbatiello interview). The crew in many ways parallels the amen corner, the responsorial comments from the congregation that characterize black worship services. It also delivers essential parts of the rapper's text and helps focus attention on important lines to which rappers wish their audiences to respond: "Every rapper tried to recruit, and the crews wanted to be with them 'cause they were popular. If a rapper would say, 'What's that word when you're bustin' loose?' The crew knew to yell out, 'Juice, Juice!' The rapper would say a line and they [the crew] would just say the answer after that. So everybody [rappers] had to have their own crew or then they didn't look like they had any clout" (Abbatiello interview).

The number of members in a crew signifies the leader's power, status, and merit as an MC. On more contemporary fronts, being down with an artist is like being hooked up, suggests the rap critic Russell A. Potter. "Record companies for their own motives are receptive to these chains. This structure gives them a free connection to other potential successes" (1995:115). For instance, C-Murder, Mia X, Mystikal, Silkk the Shocker, and Snoop Dogg are "down with" the producer-rapper-mogul Master P and record on P's No Limit record label. To further distinguish their type of posse or crew, the artists on No Limit are dubbed as No Limit Soldiers.

Another network system for MCs is the "cipha" or cipher. A term popularized by the Five Percenters (or the Five Percent Nation) and adopted by hip-hop speakers, rhymin MCs refer to a cipher as a circle of three or more people.[3] MCs "feed off of one another" in keeping a rhyme going in a cyclical fashion. As one participant summarizes, "'The cipher basically is the circle and you know it's like the energy . . . you come full circle, everything is just goin' around and everybody is gettin hyped off of each other's rhymes'"

(ICD quoted in Balde 1999:81). The prerequisite for participating in a cipher session is the ability to create rhymes instantaneously. Hence, ciphers are likened to freestyling sessions.[4]

Apart from crews, ciphers, and freestyling sessions, rappers underscore their self-styled rep through self-appointed titles or earned praise names that indicate merit or distinction. Kool Moe Dee is cool; Doug E. Fresh offers something new or fresh; Heavy D defines himself as an overweight lover; Queen Latifah means queen of royal "badness"; Grandmaster Flash exhibits extraordinary speed (flash) at mixing; and H. "Rap" Brown demonstrates verbal dexterity. While many of the names adopted by rap artists define the individual's prowess, other names adopted by rap artists, such as Intelligent Hoodlum, Public Enemy, The Lady of Rage, Special Ed, Kurupt, Bytches with Problems, OutKast, and Niggaz with Attitude, "quite consciously recode mainstream values by employing so-called 'negative images' to communicate very powerful messages . . . about issues of self-respect" (Lott 1992:84).

Hip-hop artists often adopt various street personae through which they portray or salute those who impacted their lives while growing up in the hood. The late Tupac Shakur (or "2Pac") once stated in an interview: "I spent a lot of my times in the street. Because the words I say [don't] come from a mother's mouth or a father's mouth, they're words that come from a pimp's mouth, a ho's mouth, or a prostitute's, or a hustler's, or a drug dealer's. . . . These were my role models" ("Conversation" 1994).

The sociologist Eugene Perkins identifies five personalities typical to street culture: street man, hustler, pimp (or mack), working-class man, and militant (1975:76). Although Perkins limits his examination to males, rap artists recognize other street archetypes, like the gangsta or thug. For example, Snoop Dogg[5] and Too $hort depict the mack image, while Ice-T takes on dual roles as an O.G. (original gangsta) and pimp; MC Eiht, Geto Boys, and the female artists Gangsta Boo and Boss represent gangsta lifestyles; 2Pac identified himself as a "thug";[6] Public Enemy, Sister Souljah, Paris, and X-Clan bring to their performances a Black Nationalist stance through their clothing (army fatigues or African apparel). Rap artists' portrayals of street characters make statements about being down or keepin it real with the streets.

The conceptual base of rap music is rooted in a street style. An artist's use of speech, characters, attitude, and crews asserts that the rapper is down with the street. Rap artists measure the success of their performances by signals, cues, and expressions from the audience, such as verbal exclamations, handclapping, and dancing. An excellent performance is defined by lyrical fluidity, rhythm and timing, articulation, voice quality, musical mix, stage presence, and above all, originality. These qualities can be examined under the broad categories of black language and rhetorical style, music-making practices, and paramusical-lingual features.

### Language and Rhetorical Style: The Artifice of Rhyme

MCs are evaluated on their ability to "rock the microphone." A rapper "must have the rhythm, coordination, and timing" (DJ Hollywood interview). Rocking the microphone occurs through lyrical style or the fluidity or flow of their rhymes.[7] Rap artists demonstrate their flowing skillz in catchy rhymes that capture the essence or manner of their flow as "smooth like liquid": "some think that we can't flow, / stereotypes they got to go" (Queen Latifah, "Ladies First" [1989]). In this regard, flow involves synchronizing text with the beat of the music or, as MCs assert, "rappin to the beat" or "riding a beat." One performer asserts that "the rhythm of the beat and music . . . got to be there for the lyrics [to] like join into one" (Dynasty interview). In this sense, the rhythm track functions as a time organizer around which the rhymed couplet unit weaves. The interlocking of text and accompaniment creates the Western music concept hocket, whereby all of the parts fit together to form a whole rhythmic idea. In the introduction of "Peter Piper," for example, the MCs Run and D.M.C. rhythmically interlock the text to form a cohesive unit (see example 2). MCs can also exhibit their ability to flow by interweaving rhymes to an internalized beat, as rendered in an a cappella rap song or freestyling.

The ideal rendering of lyrics must be grounded in poetic flow, but there remain several factors that determine lyrical competency among MCs. They include semantics and its various aspects. According to the Black English scholar Geneva Smitherman, "Black Semantics is broadly conceived to encompass the totality of idioms, terms, and expressions that are commonly used by Black Americans; it is highly metaphorical and imagistic" (1986:42–43). Rappers also use linguistic devices that entail syllabic stress, melodic-rhythmic contouring, vocal timbre, and signification. To understand how these devices work in rap, it is important to examine the construction of rap music lyrics.

Rap lyrics are grouped as rhymed couplets. Following traditional African American poetic forms (i.e. the blues and toasts), the couplet rhyme, according to Doug E. Fresh, "is just a more condensed way of saying something" (Doug E. Fresh interview). Effective rhyming in rap, as with most poetic forms, requires selecting words for both sound and sense. Standard poetry commonly uses assonance, a juxtaposition of similar vowel sounds,

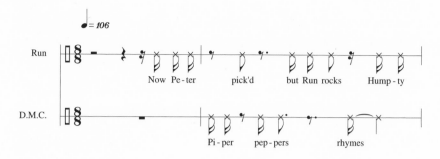

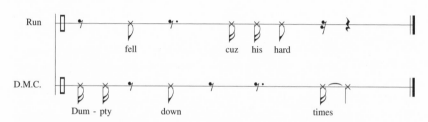

*Example 2:* Interlocking of text or hocket concept, illustrated in "Peter Piper," performed by Run-D.M.C. (1986).

noted for its sonorous quality. This type of rhyme formation commonly comprises rap lyrics, occurring either through monosyllabic words, final endings of bi- or multisyllabic words, or a combination of the two. For example, monosyllabic words in rhyme can occur in the following manner: "I am woman, hear me *roar* / When I grab the mike it's never a *bore*" (MC Lyte, "I Am Woman" [1988]), or, "But hardcore my science for *pain,* / I spent time in the *game,* / kept my mind on *fame*" (Nas, "Nas Is Like" [1998]). Bi- or multisyllabic rhymes on final endings may result, as follows: "Drones and mu*tations* and devi*ations,* / and there is no one that can escape the nuclear reve*lation*" (Melle Mel, "World War III" [1985]), or, "So God will turn me to my *essence,* / 'cuz even as an adole*scent,* / I refused to be a conva*lescent*" (2Pac, "I Ain't Mad at Cha," [1995]). Assonance specific to black speech may also occur with word alteration when an MC purposefully changes a letter in a word for rhyming purposes. For example, in MC Lyte's "I Am Woman," she states, "That's right, I'm well *respected.* / Don't get stupid, I'm well *pretected.*" The invented word "*pretected*" replaces "*protected*" in order to achieve rhyme with "*respected.*" Example 3 illustrates the manner in which a monosyllabic rhyme occurs within four beats, on or nearly on the beat. Notice how the

*Example 3:* Monosyllabic rhyme and the interlocking of text with the beat in "Nas Is Like," performed by Nas (1998).

accenting of beats 2 and 4 and the basic outline of the rhythm section track interlocks with the lyrics in "Nas Is Like."

Some MCs use an overlapping style of rhyme that is typical in a cappella freestyle. MCs may alternate rhyming words in between the beats, on the ending of measure lines, or after the beat of 4 as best illustrated in example 4 by T-Mo of Goodie MOb in "Cell Therapy" (1995): "on the average 'bout four or *five* I'm lucky to be *alive* / at sun*rise* now I rea*lize* the *cost.* After I *lost* / my best friend *Bean* I recognize as a *King.*"

The "use of voice rhythm and vocal inflections" is what performers define as melodic qualities in rap (Smitherman 1986:134). Hence, it is not surprising that MCs interpret their art as "talking but . . . [creating] a melody in itself" (Bambaataa interview), "a rhythm in itself" (Blake interview), and "rhythmic chanting" (Melle Mel interview). MCs manipulate meaning in the text by accenting certain words or syllables in a melodic-rhythmic manner, thereby creating fluidity of a line. Note the use of accent marks (>) over certain words to indicate emphasis and a downward accent mark (∨) to denote stress with lower vocal inflection—a common stylistic device similar to a

*Example 4:* The alternation of rhyme in between the beats in "Cell Therapy," by T-Mo of the Goodie MOb (1995).

musical cadence—as seen in example 5, "Don't Believe the Hype" (Public Enemy, 1988).

*Example 5:* Melodic-rhythmic treatment of rhyme in "Don't Believe the Hype," by Chuck D of Public Enemy (1988).

Some MCs use rhythmic execution of mnemonic syllables or syllabic sound carriers to fill the gaps between words. Syllabic repetitions, commonly known as mnemonic syllables, "convey a great deal of meaning regarding how a rhythm is to be realized in terms of timbre and timing" (Kubik 1972:169). Grandmaster Melle Mel describes his frequent use of "ha-ha-ha-ha-ha-ha-ha!" as "just something to fill in the space on the record" (Melle Mel interview). Although rappers commonly describe these syllables as mere space fillers, these rhythmic structural devices become essential to the musical idea and rhyme as well, as with the "iggedy-diggedy" used by Das EFX, "Ha!" used by Juvenile, or "ha-ha-ha-ha-ha-ha-ha!" used by Melle Mel.

Consistent with the application of syllabic stress is accenting certain syllables within a word, similar to an accent mark over certain musical notes. Meaning is conveyed by a raised vocal inflection as indicated in capital letters in "The Message" (1982), performed by Melle Mel (see example 6).

By the 1990s, rap artists begin to include a more tonal lyrical style known as "raggamuffin," a trademark of the Jamaican rude boy style associated with reggae dancehall music in the 1980s.[8] Although a few U.S.-based artists, like KRS-One, Queen Latifah, and the Jamaican-born Shinehead employed a quasi-ragga style in their songs, this style of delivery is rooted in the Jamaican dub poet and toasting styles in which English is spoken with more tonal

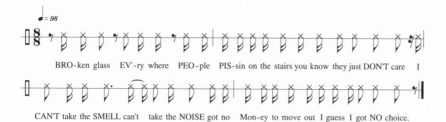

♩ = 98

BRO-ken glass   EV'-ry where   PEO-ple   PIS-sin on the stairs you know they just DON'T care   I

CAN'T take the SMELL can't   take the NOISE got no   Mon-ey to move out I guess I got NO choice.

*Example 6:* An illustration of vocal inflection in "The Message," by Melle Mel (1982).

nuances than it is among African Americans.[9] A feature of this style is a kind of melodic-rhythmic device described by increasing the speed of a rhyming couplet or lines within a measure. Monie Love refers to this as "flipping" (Green 1991:52), whereas the rapper Ant Knox of Detroit calls it "stutter steppin" (Courtland interview). This fast flipping or stutter steppin style is also utilized by U.S.-based artists like Big Daddy Kane, Tung Twista, and the group Bone Thugs-N-Harmony.

Vocal timbre is another stylistic component. In rap, timbre entails the synchronicity of tonal quality and articulation. A mellow quality associated with rappers who pose as macks or pimp-like characters, for example, corresponds with a smooth/legato articulation, while those who project a hardcore image employ heightened speech with percussive articulation. But with digital sampling, MCs have increased the use of vocalizations as "breaks," as with, for instance, James Brown's yells and screams as popularized in "It Takes Two" (1988) by Rob Base and DJ E-Z Rock.

### The Art of Signifyin

Signification—the application of metaphor, allusions, and imagery—is further exploited by MCs to manipulate meaning. In his groundbreaking study *The Signifying Monkey: A Theory of African-American Literary Criticism,* Henry Louis Gates Jr. explores the relationship between African and African American vernacular tradition through the art of signification or "signifyin," as pronounced among African Americans. Drawing upon the seminal work on signifyin by the linguist-anthropologist Claudia Mitchell-Kernan, he agrees that "the Black concept of signifying incorporates essentially a folk notion that dictionary entries for words are not always sufficient for interpreting meanings or messages, or that meaning goes beyond such interpretations" (Mitchell-Kernan 1981:314). As Mitchell-Kernan observes, "complimentary remarks may be delivered in a left-handed fashion. A particular utterance may be an insult in one context and not another. What pretends to be informative may intend to be persuasive. The hearer is thus constrained to attend to all potential meaning carrying symbolic systems in speech events—the total universe" (1981:314). Thus, signifyin is to rap lyrics as icing is to cake.

Signifyin, as outlined in Mitchell-Kernan's thesis—indirection, apparent meaning, and metaphorical reference—is advanced in rap lyrics mainly through the use of words or statements. Words such as *cut, bite, dope, dog,* and *chill-out* have alternative meanings beyond their conventional interpretation. *Cut,* for example, refers to a turntable technique; *bite* refers to the act of stealing or plagiarizing someone's rhymes; *dope* means great or incredible; *dog* is a male friend, as in "what's up dog?"; and *chill-out* or *chillin* means to relax. Some words that go beyond their usual meaning may also adhere to the rule of word or syllabic deletion/contraction, for example, "whack" and "deaf," which become "w*a*ck" and "d*e*f," respectively. According to the rap music publicist Bill Adler, "'def' unless I'm mistaken is a deviation of d*e*af, you know, in the same fashion that black culture turns around the meaning of 'bad' to mean 'good.' I think they [rappers] use 'def' to mean vital—all. It's spelled d-e-f. So something 'def' is just great . . . just as opposed to 'whack' [meaning to strike] is rendered w-a-c-k, which is something awful or terrible" (Adler interview). Other street speakers contend that "def" is a shorter version of "definite," meaning distinct or positive, while others say that "def" is derivative of "deft," meaning skillful or dexterous.

While many words and expressions that originated in rap music (e.g. "chillin") have now been adopted by the American mainstream, including those specific to artists—like "edutainment" with KRS-One, "flamboasting" with E-40, and "raptivist" with Chuck D—others are exclusive to African American street speech, where the commonplace rap lexicon used in everyday speech may not readily be understood outside by cultural outsiders or outside of its cultural context. *Project gold* and *skeezer* are just few of the many culture-bound terms used exclusively in the streets and adopted by rap artists. (For further references, see the glossary.)

Indirect commentary is delivered in rap lyrics through ambiguity, allusion, imagery, metaphor, braggadocio, or insults. In many instances, an MC subtly uses a word or phrase in varied forms that go beyond what the title of a song suggests. For example, in the 1980s hit "The Breaks" by Kurtis Blow, homonyms unify the sound while playing on multiple meanings:

Brakes in a bus, brakes on a car.
Breaks that make you a superstar.
Breaks to win and breaks to lose,
and these here breaks will rock your shoes.
And these are the breaks.
Break it up! Break it up! Break it up! [instrumental interlude (vamp)]

After each rhymed narrative section, Blow chants "break it up" to give a cue to the musicians and audience that the "break" section (the instrumental interlude) is to follow. Blow manipulates "breaks/brakes" to refer to either bad circumstances in life, a vehicular mechanism, or breaks, such as the instrumental vamp. Other examples of alternate meaning in rap lyrics are "Let's Go Go" (1986) by The Real Roxanne, "Come into My House" (1989) by Queen Latifah, "Doggy Dogg World" (1993) by Snoop Doggy Dogg, "Rosa Parks" by OutKast (1998), and "Fight the Power" by Public Enemy (1989). In "Let's Go Go," The Real Roxanne interchangeably uses "go go" as the directive "let's dance" or to refer to a type of regional dance music called "go-go" that is associated with the Washington, D.C., club.[10] The latter is suggested, though nonverbally, by the timbales' rhythm, distinctive to go-go percussive tracks. In "Come into My House," Queen Latifah uses "house" to refer to her abode and to a dance culture associated with Chicago. Snoop Doggy Dogg in "Doggy Dogg World" signifies on his moniker to suggest in the lyrics and video a place where he rules as the big dog or where the small players could get "dogged" by the big players.

Public Enemy's "Fight the Power" (1989) incorporates musical samples that some scholars say allude to several of hip-hop's most saluted artists, including James Brown, whose "Funky Drummer" underscores PE's song. The song's title and refrain, "fight the power . . . you got to fight the powers that be," chanted by Flavor Flav and Chuck D, recall the Isley Brothers's 1975 sociopolitical hit "Fight the Power." As with the Isleys' message, PE's lyrics call for defying the hegemony, "the powers that be."

In the rap duo OutKast's "Rosa Parks" (1998), the civil rights matriarch, who was asked to give up her seat for a white person, is never directly mentioned by name, rather recalled by the song's title and OutKast's refrain ordering all wack MCs to move to the back of the bus. Andre of OutKast explains that "move to the back of the bus" is "'lettin' people [other MCs] know that we are back in the game, so go ahead and prepare to move to the back of the bus'" (quoted in Gill 1998:46).

The hip-hop scholar Russell A. Potter points to other examples of signifyin, ambiguity through recoding, or the turning around of a stereotype for alternative, positive meaning, particularly with the "gorilla trope." The play on "gorilla" emerged during the wake of the Rodney King beating, when "transcripts from car-to-car radios used by the L.A.P.D (Los Angeles Police Department) recorded one [white] cop's use of the memorable phrase 'It was straight out of the Gorillas in the Mist'" (1995:77). Following this incident came a battery of allusions to the "gorilla" themes via recoding and hom-onymic treatment of gorilla to mean "guerilla." The nation-conscious rap-per Paris, for example, refers to himself as a "Black Guerilla," and Ice Cube's group, Da Lench Mob, signifies on "gorilla" via visual and rhetorical strate-gies. As Potter observes, "The cover photos on their debut album *Guerillas in tha Mist* show the members of Da Lench Mob wearing black ski masks and carrying automatic rifles (=guerillas), and yet places them in the midst of a dense forest with a heavy undergrowth of ferns (=gorillas)" (78).

Rap artists create rhymes in which their listeners can actually visualize scenes through "lyrical movies" (Singleton interview). Ice Cube applauded this quality in rapper Mack 10: "'When I met Mack 10, I saw that he had a deep knowledge of how the street game worked and he knew how to put it in rhyme. But he was more visual than most people'" (quoted in Williams 1997:78). The artist most celebrated for his talent in metaphorical imagery is Grandmaster Melle Mel. The rap music producer Larry Smith describes him as "the Langston Hughes of rap. I'm saying when he paints [raps], he paints a picture. He describes with words, and you see everything Mel tells you. Everything! Everything!" (Smith interview). In "The Message" (1982),[11] Melle Mel alludes to the ghetto as "a jungle," thereby creating for his listeners an illusion through metaphor of the ghetto in the refrain: "Don't push me 'cause I'm close to the edge. / I'm trying not to lose my head. / Ha, ha, ha, ha, ha! / It's like a jungle sometimes, it makes me wonder how I keep from going under." The song unfolds through vivid imagery about the grim realities of ghetto life. Here, the average inner-city youth grows up "livin' second rate, / [where one's] eyes . . . sing a song of deep hate." The lyrics describe cogent-ly the lifestyles—"thugs, pimps, [drug] pushers"—for which many ghetto youth are destined, mourning "how [one] lived so fast and died so young."

Since the release of "The Message," similar rap songs have recounted ghetto life, for example, Ice-T's "Escape from the Killing Fields," whose title is "based on a movie about the conflict in Cambodia as a metaphor for the warlike conditions in today's ghetto" (Kelley 1996:124). Additional songs about ghetto lore include "Growing Up in the Hood" (1991) by Compton's Most Wanted, "Ghetto Bastard" (1991) by Naughty By Nature, "The Ghetto" (1990) by Too $hort, "A Gangsta's Fairytale" (1990) and "The Drive-By" (1990) by Ice Cube, and "Hard Knock Life (Ghetto Anthem)" (1998) by Jay-Z. The ongoing afflictions of black inner-city youth who experience political, economic, and social isolation from and marginalization in mainstream America continue as a prevalent theme in rap music.

Certain terms used by MCs may be perceived as negative or vulgar by mainstream English speakers, however, their actual meaning depends on the context. Some words may be interpreted either as insults, gender-specific terms, or terms of endearment. Words such as "bitch" and "ho" can be insults. When referring to females, rappers, like male street speakers, commonly use "bitch" and "ho" to refer to non-kindred females. The street-educated journalist Nathan McCall explains: "According to street wisdom, there were two types of females: There were women, such as your mother, sister, and teacher, and there were bitches and 'hoes [whores]. Bitches and hoes were good for one thing—boning [sexual intercourse]" (1994:40; 42). Some contemporary black male speakers trace the popularity of "bitch" and "ho" to the celebrated black action film classic *The Mack* (1973), in which Goldie the pimp refers to his female sex employees as "bitches" or "hoes." The majority of male rappers I interviewed concur with street conventional meanings of these words, that these words are meant in a pejorative way.

There are, nonetheless, alternative readings of "bitch" and "ho" in the rap community. The rap music entrepreneur Leyla Turkkan has observed that males sometimes refer to each other as "bitches" as a form of play: "They'll [men] call each other a bitch. It's really a linguistic thing. It's just [used in] a bunch of boast raps and exaggerated tales. It's just kind of like flexing their muscles, and kind of how they talk when they're hanging out together, but it's not to be taken literally" (Turkkan interview). The use of "bitch" in this case parallels that of "ho," as when some male MCs use the word to refer to a sexually promiscuous man (rather than woman), as in Whodini's "I'm a Ho" (1986):

Cuz I'm a ho, you know I'm a ho.
I rock three different freaks after every show
Cuz I'm a ho, you know I'm a ho.
How do you know? Because I told you so.

KRS-One views capitalism as a metaphor for the pimp and ho, particularly when the latter is subjected to audits by the pimp (the Internal Revenue Service). KRS-One explains that the song "Who Are the Pimps?" from his album

*Sex and Violence* (1992), is about "'the I.R.S. Capitalism is a pimp and ho system . . . the I.R.S. don't care if you're white or black'" (quoted in Foxxx 1992:36).

While McCall, Turkkan, and Whodini are among those who express how
males commonly refer to both women and men as bitches or hoes, other
women, like Queen Latifah, adamantly feel that some rappers are "gettin' a
little carried away with that" (Queen Latifah interview). As a result, Latifah
wrote the rap song "U.N.I.T.Y." (1993) as a rejection of the words "bitch" and
"ho." Although Latifah never states directly that she is referring specifically
to those men who call black women bitches and hoes, she uses "U.N.I.T.Y."
as a statement to remind them of black women's limitless and unconquerable spirits "from infinity to infinity." Similar to Latifah, the rapper Yo-Yo
founded the Intelligent Black Women's Coalition in response to the vilification of black women in rap. The female rap artists Bytches with Problems
and Hoes with Attitude, however, have reclaimed the words in the names of
their groups. The male rapper Too $hort reports that it pays for him to use
the word "bitch" in his recordings: "Long time ago I couldn't use the term
bitch without being look down upon by the community; but now I can use
the term and get paid" (*Rap City Rhapsody* 1990)

But despite twofold meanings of "bitch" and "ho," these gendered terms
can be powerful, especially when "bitch" is used to refer to a physically, emotionally, or sexually frail male as a "bitch-nigga" or "acting *fruitio*," as heard
in Busta Rhymes's "Put Your Hands Where My Eyes Could See" (1997). "Fruitio" here could mean a male homosexual or an easily intimidated man.
Furthermore, some vernacular speakers argue that while "bitch" and "ho"
function as humor within a specific social context, they frequently reinforce
patterns of social power while giving men "privileges to perpetuate misogynistic humor against Black women" (Crenshaw 1991:32).

Other controversial words used by MCs are "muthafucka" and "nigga."
Commonly used by both African Americans and persons of other races to
refer to a low-life person or as a racial epithet, these words are reclaimed from
their negative associations by hip-hop speakers. For example, "muthafucka"
can describe a person of distinction. LL Cool J uses "muthafucka" to say that
he has not met anyone who can rhyme as well as he does: "If you think you
can out rhyme me, ya' boy I'll bet / 'cuz I ain't met a muthafucka that can
do that yet" ("I'm Bad" [1987]). In both street speech and hip-hop argot,
"fuck" or "fuckin" is used as a superlative or a grammatical intensifier. One
MC explains the manner in which it is used as a superlative to get "across a
point even stronger sometimes, such as 'Hey don't do that' or 'Hey don't fuck
with that.' The effect is much stronger" (Doug E. Fresh interview). The su-

perlative and nominal versions of "fuck" are sometimes used simultaneously, as I observed while attending the Battle of MCs and DJs competition held at the New Music Seminar in New York City in 1986. In the midst of a finalist's performance, a few rappers from the audience loudly blurted that they wanted to challenge Grandmaster Melle Mel, one of the honored judges of the competition. Infuriated by this interruption, the finalist Grandmaster Caz stated that "if someone like me don't want to challenge him [Melle Mel], and all these muthafuckas that got the caliber to challenge him don't, y'all bums just stay where the fuck you're at. . . . This is my show, he's judgin' my shit, and you back the fuck off until this is over with." Caz's words were effective, for the competition resumed without further delay.

When used as a term of endearment among black speakers, "nigga" is reclaimed, referring to one's buddy, neighborhood friend, and, if spoken by a female MC, a male lover. However, the meaning of this term is solely determined by the adjective or possessive that precedes it: *my* nigga, *main* nigga, *real* nigga, or its acronymic rendering as in 2Pac's song "Strictly 4 My N.I.G.G.A.Z." (1993).[12] Variations on the theme are its negative usage: "two-minute motherfucka" (a sexually inept man),[13] "house nigga" (an Uncle Tom),[14] "fake nigga" (phony person), or "sucka nigga"[15] and "bitch nigga" (flimsy person).

MCs advance signifyin with lyrical wit via braggadocio. As boasting and exaggerated language escalates, it evolves into a form of signifyin known to the rap community as *dissin,* the act of *dis*respecting or downplaying someone else's attributes while praising one's own. During the formative years of rap music, it was not unusual for an MC to verbally challenge an opponent through freestylin, the extemporaneous recitation of rhyming couplets. Many of these verbal battles (e.g. Busy Bee versus Kool Moe Dee) were live, unrehearsed performances, but as rap music grew into a commercial music industry, verbal battles ensued on record. Among these recordings was the battle between LL Cool J, the young challenger, with his single "Jack the Ripper" (1988), and the veteran Kool Moe Dee, with his response "Let's Go" (1988). In the following excerpt, LL Cool J makes use of dissin:

> How ya like me now, punk?
> . . . Here's what my game is.
> Here's what my aim is . . .
> My name is Jack the Ripper.
> How ya like me now? I'm gettin busier.
> I'm double-platinum; I'm watchin you get dizzier.

LL Cool J and Kool Moe
Dee, 1980s. (Courtesy of
Michael Ochs Archives)

Though Kool Moe Dee's name is never directly mentioned, "How Ya Like Me Now" is the title of a rap song by Kool Moe Dee. LL Cool J demeans his manhood by calling him a "punk," meaning a homosexual.

Kool Moe Dee answers LL Cool J by ridiculing him in "Let's Go." First, he dismisses LL Cool J by addressing him by his birth name, James Todd Smith; and second, he directly insults LL Cool J by emasculating him:

> Now you go on *Todd,* try to talk that talk.
> Try to act like you're a big man,
> but you're a big *fag.*
> . . . You ain't got a chance in the world.
> Your records were smokin but you sound like a girl.
> "Right now, I'm gettin busier,
> I'm double-platinum" [an imitation of LL Cool J's voice].
> Hold up, is he a man or a girl?
> What in the world? You sound like Cheryl the Pearl.
> and you want to battle me on the microphone?
> Leave that crack alone.[16]

In constructing a rhyme, MCs must remain cognizant of their communities' concerns about everyday issues and life in the hood. Some rappers are associated with specific topics. West Coast artists popularized "reality raps" or gangsta rap. Ice Cube once stated that his former group, N.W.A., "'deals with reality. Violence is reality; You're supposed to picture life as a bowl of cherries, but it's not. So we don't do nothin' fake'" (quoted in Hochman 1989:24). MCs compose rhymes on topics ranging from lyrical dexterity, comical satire, and sexually risqué stories to sociopolitical concerns such as police brutality (most common in the West Coast style), drug addiction, feminist issues, and nationalist themes.[17] Essentially, some rappers believe that rap text is a form of catharsis by which to "release all the anger, all the aggravation; / convert it into words, it's sort of like conversation" (from MC Lyte, "Lyte the MC" [1988]). Lauryn Hill prompts her audience to listen to the "mixture where hip hop meets scripture. / Develop a negative into a positive picture" in the song "Everything Is Everything" (1998).

These language and rhetorical practices do not, however, stand alone but are synchronized into a complex musical accompaniment provided by the DJ. The following section discusses aesthetic choices involved in creating a music soundtrack.

## The Musical Mix and All That Jazz: "Breaking Beats"

As rap artists will forthrightly admit,

> . . . rap groups don't need no band.
> All we need in order to achieve
> is some help from the master [DJ] you better believe . . .
> The DJ will give you one hundred percent. (Whodini, "Funky Beat" [1986])

Each MC has a DJ whose sole responsibility is to provide the musical soundtrack to which MCs construct rhyming couplets and to which the dancers rock. The DJ who supplies "one hundred percent" possesses an excellent sense of timing and a mastery of turntable techniques. "You need something [a track] with a heavy beat," says Cut Master DC ("Say No to Drugs" interview).

In a DJ's performance, time is technically complex. Scholars concur that the Western concept of linear time is not sufficient in the analysis of African-derived music: time in this context may be viewed as an overlay of structures (see Nketia 1974; Chernoff 1979; Stone 1985; Jackson 1988). Outer time is measured by "homogeneous and measurable devices, clocks and metronomes" (Stone 1982:9), whereas inner time is unmeasurable but consciously experienced. The African concepts of outer and inner time have also been applied to the study of African-derived musical forms in the United States (Burnim 1985; Jackson 1988). Joyce Marie Jackson, a scholar of the black sacred music tradition, describes an interdependent relationship between outer and inner time. She notes that the reckoning of time "does not totally operate in a Western mode or meter, but rather in an additional internal mode or inner time. Inner timing . . . [is] implied or suggested by outer timing and actions" (1988:171).

Rap music participants broadly conceive of time in a musical and social sense, where it is delineated as outer and inner time. First, there is a special concept of timing; it is first realized in an inner sense as "the beat" or pulse. To audience members who want to dance, a rap song must have a certain beat within the tempo. One audience member indicates that the right "beat" is felt through a certain tempo: "The beat is important. . . . More people like a beat to dance to, and rap music has that downbeat to dance to it. It's easier for us to dance to [that beat]; when we go to a garage and hear that fast upbeat music and can't dance to that" (Vicki and Valerie interview). The "downbeat" refers to a moderate-paced tempo that may vary from slow $\mathbf{J}$ = 80–88 beats per minute (bpm) to moderate $\mathbf{J}$ = 92–116 bpm.

The beat is set by the rap disc jockey, the timekeeper, who must rely on an inner sense to determine the tempo. As one interviewee remarked, "The DJ is like the drummer. His job is to make sure everything goes steady, and if the beat messes up, everybody is going to know because everybody wasn't on the beat" (Dynasty interview). The DJ uses the pitch control, a built-in mechanism on the turntable, to accelerate or decelerate the tempo. Thus, the beat is first reckoned through inner timing and later coordinated through outer time by a pitch control.

The manner in which DJs alter time is attributable to an in-depth knowledge of turntable techniques. Several turntable techniques—backspinning, phasing (also known as punch-phrasing), and scratching—were discussed in Chapter 2. DJs also use mixing techniques called "cutting" and "blending." In cutting, the DJ repeats a word or musical phrase through editing. In blending, the DJ combines music or text from two different discs to create a new piece of music (White 1996). The ethnomusicologist Miles White, who conducted an organological study of the turntable, divided mixing techniques into those using a single turntable or dual turntables. He found that while backspinning, scratching, and cutting can all be executed on a single turntable, mixing, blending, and punch-phrasing require two turntables. Furthermore, with the use of two turntables, DJs can fuse break-beats or collages of sound from prerecorded discs into one cohesive unit. Sound is further filtered through an audio-mixer that is positioned between turntables. The most important feature on the mixer is the cross-fader, a device that allows a DJ to switch back and forth between turntables while executing various turntable techniques. DJs also use the cross-fader to produce various forms of scratching, most notably "crabs," a signature of DJ Q-Bert, and "transforming," introduced by DJ Spinbad and perfected by DJs Jazzy Jeff and Cash Money.[18]

Equipment is essential to carrying out turntable techniques. Effective execution of these techniques requires the best, most flexible and steady turntable unit. "First of all," says Grandmaster Flash, "the tone arm's needle [stylus] has to be conical [for me]; it's like a nail, so that [it] will sit in the [disc's] groove better" (Grandmaster Flash interview). The preferred turntables are the Technics SL-1200 models because of their pitch-control capability and action-stability control. During the 1990s, Gemini Sound Products, a longtime manufacturer of DJ mixers, introduced the now-popular PT-2000, modeled similarly to the Technics SL-1200. The quartz lock defeat button on the PT-2000 returns the speed to exactly 33⅓ or 45 RPM when the pitch

A DJ operating dual turntables at the Attic in South Central Los Angeles, 1992. (Photo by Brian Cross)

Kiilu, JMD, and Mattematicks working on tracks at a rehearsal studio, North Hollywood, 1992. (Photo by Brian Cross)

control is positioned off-center, a feature now included on Technics SL-1200 MKII (Glazer 1999:58–59).[19] The most popular mixers are the Gemini, Numark, and Vestax models.

In addition to turntable techniques and the finest of equipment, hip-hop musicians are forever in search of the perfect beat. Developing an acuity for break-beats requires a knowledge of black dance favorites from percussion-oriented songs such as early classics like "Apache" by Incredible Bongo Band and "It's Just Begun" by Jimmy Castor to heavy funk tunes like "Funky Drummer" by James Brown, "Flash Light" by Parliament, or the mellow sounds of "Between the Sheets" by the Isley Brothers. Although the success of a DJ is based on his or her repertory of break-beats, uncovering them and then protecting one's "trade secret" can be quite tedious. During the 1970s, DJs like Afrika Bambaataa and Kool "DJ" Herc, for example, were known to soak record labels off so other jockeys would not know the names of their break-beats. According to Jazzy Jay, a protégé of Afrika Bambaataa, "'We'd find these beats, these heavy percussive beats . . . a lot of times it would be a two-second spot, a drum beat, a drum break, and we'd mix that back and forth, extend it, make it 20 minutes long'" (quoted in Leland and Stein 1988:26). In the 1980s, shopping for break-beats presented a few problems because of existing compilations. The record collector Lenny Roberts compiled more than twenty volumes of break-beats in *Ultimate Breaks and Beats*. Roberts's series was distributed by the late Stanley Platzer, a well-known hip-hop record dealer, at the famous Music Factory in New York City (Leland and Stein 1988:26–28).

With the growing value placed on originality, DJs shifted from compilations to searching out their own beat material. As the ethnomusicologist Joseph Schloss notes, "the process of acquiring rare, usually out-of-print, vinyl records for sampling purposes has become a highly developed skill, and is referred to with the term 'digging in the crates' [or 'digging']" (2000:95). For example, DJ Diamond of the Bronx, who owns thousands of old recordings, believes that "'there's an art to finding a break that somebody else doesn't know about. . . . It makes people go, "Oh shit, where'd he get that from?" That's part of the mystique'" (quoted in Fernando 1994:54).

By the mid-1980s, DJs were supplementing the manual process of mixing music with electronic instruments—digital samplers, drum machines, sequencers, and synthesizers. Using the built-in sequencer on most samplers, artists extend the duration of a sound—from long to short fragments—through looping. DJs use sampling to mix and mingle bits and pieces of "breaks" from records, "mix and mingle [them] into musical collages of sounds" (Kemp 1989:68). While some of the most popular samplers, like the Akai S900, are hard to find, the Emu SP-1200 and the Roland TR-808 sampling drum machines are the most coveted among rap music DJs because of their "raw" sound quality (Fernando 1994:55) and heavy "kick" or bass drum sound, respectively. Mixes with the heavy "kick" characteristic of the Roland TR-808 are known as "boom-bap." By 1999, the TR-808 was updated to the SP-808, which still maintains a heavy kick sound.

Sampling has undoubtedly revolutionized the art of creating music, but turntablism is complicated further with other aspects. In his study on DJs as producers, Joseph Schloss delineates four sampling ethics observed by DJs in the production aspect of hip-hop music: "biting," a pejorative term meaning stealing someone's beats; "flipping" (not to be confused with the melodic-rhythmic device) the alteration of a prerecorded beat; "chopping," a type of flipping in which the DJ alters a sampled phrase by dividing it into smaller segments and reconfiguring them in a different order; and "looping," or taking a beat and repeating it (2000:125). More importantly, when DJs create a track, they are forbidden to steal another DJ's beats. However, flipping, chopping, and looping are sampling techniques most coveted by hip-hop musicians in creating versions from prerecorded beats.

Some DJs foray into production and promotion. According to DJ Oliver Wang, there is a thin line between DJing and producing:

> "It's definitely not a coincidence that most producers start off as DJs. Because not only were they exposed to music in a very significant sense, they were basically exposed to music a lot, in volume. And also they have access to music, which is always important in sampling. A lot of DJs are also record collectors, which transitions well to becoming a producer, since you have a source of sampling to work from. And because deejaying works as a profession, that can earn you the capital that you would need to become a producer as well. So I think all those different things kind of work together." (quoted in Schloss 2000:68)

In bridging the two, hip-hop musicians have formed teams to accomplish the dual job of DJing and producing, for example, Hank Shocklee and the Bomb Squad for Public Enemy and Rico Wade and his production team, Organized Noize, for Goodie MOb and OutKast.

In promotion, some hip-hop DJs like DJ Clue and Funkmaster Flex provide a powerful service by introducing an artist to fans prior to the release of an authorized recording. Record companies often encourage DJs to record live or studio performances or give them a sample tape to remix it, distribute it, or play the recording to a local dance crowd as a way to test the artist's street credibility. Joseph Schloss further notes that when DJs record a performance to create a mix tape, they then become "sole authors" of the tape. DJs release the mix tape for sale to a distributor, who in turn passes it on to a potential "vendor" (Schloss 1997). Although this type of promotion bypasses protection and risks royalty payments to an artist, it is a sure way to gauge an artist's success and commercial viability.

## Hip-Hop Sound Culture

The legendary jazz drummer Max Roach once stated, "'Hip hop lives in the world of sound—not the world of music—and that's why it's so revolutionary. . . . There are many areas that fall outside the narrow Western definition of music and hip-hop is one of them'" (quoted in Owen 1988:61). The juxtaposition of timbre and texture are important to the aesthetics. Hip-hop DJs bend the Western norms of timbre and texture homogeneity to produce an aesthetic that is consistent with the "heterogeneous sound ideal tendency" (see Wilson 1983). The ethnomusicologist Portia K. Maultsby notes that "the unique sound associated with black music results from the manipulation of timbre, texture and shaping in ways uncommon to Western practice. Musicians bring intensity to their performance by alternating lyrical, percussive, and raspy timbres; juxtaposing vocal and instrumental textures; changing pitch and dynamic levels; alternating straight with vibrato tones; and weaving moans, shouts, grunts, hollers, and screams into the melody" (1990:191–92).

Through digital sampling, DJs fuse various timbres and textures: voluminous bass sounds (bass guitar and drum), strident piercing sounds (e.g. high glissandi sounds), static "noise," harmonic dissonance, and a battery of vocal ornamentations from James Brown's yells, grunts, moans, and shouts to speech excerpts. According to Cedric Singleton of Black Market Records, the music of Public Enemy represents the aesthetic quintessence of the fusing concept because of the group's use of "a whole lot of sampling. They get a groove going and build on top of that groove, and build on top of that groove; they just build on top of grooves" (Singleton interview). PE's "wall of noise" concept,[20] which is the distinguishing feature of the Bomb Squad's production, employs dissonant sonorities—booming bass guitar and kick, interlocking speech and music rhythms, and a boisterous-aggressive rap style as best exemplified in Kyra Gaunt's transcription (1993) of "Fight the Power" (see example 7).

Example 7: The fusing of timbres and textures via digital sampling in "Fight the Power," by Public Enemy (1989).

Texture and timbre qualities are distinct to geographical regions. In areas like Miami and Los Angeles, where a vibrant car culture reigns, the booming bass and closed-kick (short delay in sound) created on the Roland TR-808 tends to dominate in mixes, as DJs create soundtracks for car rather than home stereo systems. Thus, rap musicians coined the term "jeep beats" when referring to booming bass soundtracks. The DJ-producer Marley Marl contends that rap is music "made for" steering or cruising, as in volumes 1 and 2 of his album *Steering Pleasure*. Marl states that he made his album "'for people who wanna have som'n cool playin in their rides. You won't get the same effect if you play the tracks through a regular system; you need a hype car system. The beats are programmed to make the speakers howl, you know what I'm sayin'" (quoted in Nelson 1991:39).

Marley Marl takes credit for specifically introducing what has come to be known as the Miami bass sound. He recalls,

> "I went down to Miami with Roxanne Shanté. She would go freestyle in the middle of the show [at Luke Campbell's] club. I pressed 'start' on the [Roland-TR] 808. Everybody was like . . . 'What is dat?!' Luke ran, started staring at the machine like it was an alien. Then, he started asking a whole bunch of questions. Next thing you know . . . they didn't have the Miami bass until me and Shanté brought it down, like all those Arthur Baker jams, 'Planet Rock,' 'Play at Your Own Risk.'" (quoted in Nelson 1991:39)

DJs use the Roland TR-808 for different effects in different regions. For example, in Oakland and the Bay Area, Cedric Singleton observes that "they use the sound kick [bass] drum, but they use it in a different manner. See, it's a Miami sound. In Oakland it's more . . . of the same thing, but it's not opened-up. The delay on it is not as long as in Miami. It's more like 'boom,' like in a hall coming out of Miami, than more of a solid kick coming from Oakland. The sound in Los Angeles is more of a sample-driven type of sound" (Singleton interview). The Los Angeles sound is dominated by the rapper-producer Dr. Dre, who creates "a variation on the theme of a bass sound" adapted from the music of the group Parliament (Singleton interview). The East Coast punctuates the heavy bass with horn riffs (James Brown and bebop/fusion jazz influences) as well as Jamaican reggae dancehall music.

Most DJs prefer a certain "noise" level in their finished mix. The propensity for certain "noises" or "buzzy-like" musical timbres peculiar to African-derived music depends on "an artist's preference . . . for environmental factors as part of the musical event" (Wilson 1974:70). Environmental sonorities in rap are what I call cityscape sounds: sirens, blaring automobile horns, etcetera. One of the earliest rap songs to incorporate cityscape sounds is "The Message." In the last segment of the song, Grandmaster Flash incorporates sounds of the urban landscape from automobile horns to sirens, underscoring a conversation among members of his group, The Furious Five. These sounds, along with the members speaking in street language, intensify the ambience of city life depicted in the song's lyrics.

Another factor consistent with environmental sounds yet idiosyncratic to hip-hop music is "popping," the scratching sound that is heard on old records. When interviewing rap DJs, I discovered, to my amazement, their knack for acquiring "old records for that popping sound" in producing a "dirty" mix (Singleton interview). Hence, it is not assumed that if a person has been formally trained as a sound engineer or has mixed other styles of pop music that this would automatically qualify them to mix a hip-hop track. As one rap music producer recalls,

> I had a guy mix it [a rap tune] that does rock. A guy that mixes rock, he's not a rap mixer. I could have mixed the record better than he could 'cause I did the record and I know what the record's supposed to sound like. They got reverb on stuff that didn't need to have reverb. They got it sounding nice and clean. And every record that I've done since then, I've done on eight-tracks. I haven't done it on twenty-four-track studio, even though we can afford to do it on twenty-four. We've done it real grimy and dirty, and it works better. The popping on the record is the essence of the music. After a while, you listen to some old record, hear that popping; it takes you back. That's really the aesthetic value to it. (Singleton interview)

Other hip-hop DJs, like Cool DJ OC of HardKnox Productions of Detroit, opine that the "dirty" mix is consistent with what is known as the "basement" sound. Due to economics and practical reasons, most hip-hop DJs practiced their craft in their home basements. As they garnered reputations among their peers, many DJs began recording local artists in their converted basement studios, a choice made for both aesthetic and financial reasons. Along with microphones, turntables, samplers, drum machines, and a keyboard synthesizer, a typical basement studio may have anywhere from an eight- to a twenty-four-track mixing board and a computer with MIDI capability. In the finished mix, the lyrics should be "clean" or free from distortion, but the accompaniment should incorporate a heavy kick or "boom-bap" quality. The mix should be grimy.

"Passin Me By" (1993) by The Pharcyde stands out among the many raps that use popping. At the beginning of the song, auditors hear a sampled excerpt of Quincy Jones's arrangement of the Lovin' Spoonful's "Summer in the City" (1973), accompanied by a constant popping sound, seemingly the result of a poorly preserved record. To rappers however, popping undoubtedly expresses the essence of "funk": a return to fundamentals, to the earthiness represented by old, scratched-up records.

Because dissonant sonorities are ubiquitous in rap music, some outsiders conclude that hip-hop musicians have limited or no knowledge of musical harmony. The jazz pianist-composer Herbie Hancock surmises, "'There's no regard for harmonic rules. Like in the case of sampling one harmonic texture and juxtaposing that with another that has the same beat, but is in a totally different key. They're just kind of thrown together. Sometimes when you're ignorant you can do something that no one has done, because you're not aware of what the rules and the habits are'" (quoted in Norris 1993:85). According to Hank Shocklee, dissonance in rap is a preference, an aesthetic; it does not occur because of lack of knowledge about conventional (Western) music harmony. In a provocative article by the music critic Tom Moon, Shocklee justifies his use of harmonic dissonance: "'Eric [Sadler] sings on key, while I'm like, fuck the key. I'm looking for a mood, a feeling. So some things are purposely out of key. Like Son of Bazerk. I work with him by having what's behind him in key, otherwise you lose Bazerk. If I put things in key behind Chuck D, you lose Chuck, because his vocal is smooth. So you have to put it against abrasion'" (1991:72). The abrasive aesthetic of dissonance underscores the disharmony expressed in rap's urban-centered lyrics. Ambience ("mood") and the juxtaposition of timbres ("smooth/abrasive") interlock purposely to create sound polarities.

By the 1990s, hip-hop DJs began experimenting with extended jazz breaks in sound mixes, narrowing the gap between dissonant and harmonic sounds. Mixing jazz with hip-hop music is not a new idea, according to Grandmaster Flash,, who used to mix jazz breaks in his music during the early days of rap (Grandmaster Flash interview). But in the late 1980s his concept was advanced by A Tribe Called Quest, followed by DJ Premier of Gang Starr and Digable Planets and US$_3$ in the 1990s.[21] Some rap critics note that because of the overly used funk breaks, some rap artists were pushed to seek other musical styles to sample, including jazz (Norris 1993:82–87). The most common styles of jazz sampled are hard-bop and soul jazz, identified by a driving drum beat, blues form and tonality, and a laid-back, mellow feel. In mixing jazz with hip-hop music, rap musicians assure the predominance of the street sound through the use of "jeep beats." For example, on *Jazzmatazz* (1993), Guru strove to ensure the street style by recording cityscape sounds and funky grooves first, then having the jazz performers Courtney Pine, Donald Byrd, and Branford Marsalis "play behind the rhymes and over the [jeep] beats" rather than in the foreground (Norris 1993:83). The rap/jazz fusion has inspired some rappers to deliver in a quasi-scatting manner, as Mikah Nine of Freestyle Fellowship does in "Innercity Boundaries" (1993). Mikah Nine, whose rap style alludes to Jon Hendricks's scat singing, cautions that one should not assume that scat-like rap will ultimately mitigate rap's "hardcoreness," because rawness can be lyrically maintained via gangsta-lore rhymes (Norris 1993:83). The rap/jazz fusion demonstrates another successful juxtaposition of textural polarities—hardcore/rawness (i.e. jeep beats) and smoothness/mellowness (e.g. hard bop)—while simultaneously expanding the frontiers of jazz by placing it in a hip-hop context.

In the world of hip-hop DJs, creating a soundtrack is predicated on having a unique ear for the most obscure beats that complement the MC's style or beats that could move a dance crowd. Because of their ability at cutting and mixing break-beats, one critic concludes that "[h]ip-hop humanizes technology and makes it tactile. In hip-hop, [DJs] make the technology do the stuff that it isn't supposed to do, get music out of something that's not supposed to give you music quite that way. [They] squeeze it, rip at it, and do other things with the equipment that mess viciously with [the] warranty" (Allen 1988:10). Thus, when deemed necessary, DJs rely totally on ingenuity to manipulate state-of-the-art technology by conforming to African-derived cultural practices in search of the perfect beat.

### Paramusical-Lingual Qualities

Rap music is an amalgam of street language coding, style, and raw beats. The rap music performance event is one in which dance, drama, music, and visual arts are inseparable. On a paramusical-lingual level, particular posturing, street dress, jewelry, and hairstyles underscore the message of the music.

Performers establish an image, communicate a philosophy, and create an atmosphere of "aliveness" through the colorful and flamboyant costumes they wear during a performance (Maultsby 1990:189). Aliveness means bringing a hip-hop attitude to the stage through styling and profiling or strutting and bopping: "You've got to give them [audience] a good performance. It has a lot of acting to do with it. You have to act it out. You've got to make the audience feel what you're saying and understand it as well, sort of like a hip-hop thing in the street. The young kids relate to the hand movements when they talk, you know, and when they see you doing that on stage, they could really relate to that" (The Real Roxanne interview). Using the latest street dance steps to foster "aliveness," rap artists dazzle their audiences with energetic, pulsating dance movements or bopping struts. The audience, in turn, responds physically to rap artists with handclapping and verbal replies.

Call and response is often an essential component of aliveness in which time is manipulated by the performers who engage the audience. Hence, expanding or stretching the duration of performance is "contingent upon the relationship between participants—performer and audience" (Jackson 1988:174). This effect is achieved in rap performance in several ways. Performers begin by verbally introducing themselves or saluting the audience as means of setting the atmosphere, through such phrases as "Do You Wanna Have a Party?" or "Is Compton in the House? Let Me Hear You Scream!" In this way, time is effectively manipulated to build intensity (Burnim 1985a:163).

As a performance continues, rap artists may interject formulaic expressions, "something everybody might say" (Dynasty interview). Since adherents of rap are very familiar with certain common expressions, MCs use them as climax builders and as means of promoting interaction. Common formulaic expressions include "Hip Hop You Don't Stop," "Everybody Say Part*ay*," and "Wave yo' hands in the air, wave 'em like you just don't care."

A performance is also expanded by inserting "break" sections between each poetic narrative group. During the breaks, MCs may strut from one side of the stage to the other, beckoning their audience to respond by dancing or asking them to "wave yo' hands from side-to-side," encouraging verbal and physical interplay between themselves and the audience.

Certain gestures mirror a street attitude peculiar to rap music performance. For example, some artists perceive smiling during performance as suggestive of being soft rather than "hardcore" or no-nonsense; for "'you have to come hard. If you come soft, you get booed off the stage; and you can't smile'" (Sparky Dee quoted in Pearlman 1988:27). The libation gesture seen in videos finds its roots in a ceremony derived from West African rituals. Following that tradition, rap artists occasionally pour the contents of a bottle onto the ground in recognition of dead homies who have been stricken by gang-related violence.

Rap artists regard clothing as "a way to make the most powerful statement about themselves" (Kochman 1981:132). Attire visually conveys the message, image, and style of a rap artist. For example, Flavor Flav of Public Enemy wears a huge clock strung around his neck to signify that it is time for black advancement; the group members also dress in army fatigues to represent their "militant" stance. West Coast gangsta-style rappers appropriate the Chicano cholo style with the wearing of bandanas, "baggies" (oversized pants), and shirt tails outside. The duo Kriss Kross popularized baggy pants worn backwards; mack style rappers wear designer suits by Versace, for example, and "fly girls" sport brief, tight-fitting "batty riders" shorts characteristic of reggae dancehall culture. With the resurgence of Black Nationalism in rap, some artists choose to wear traditional African clothes. In the late 1980s, dance-oriented rap acts such as Hammer inaugurated extra-blousy pants. Other rap artists have worn Kente cloth hats, fezzes, or kufis (crowns) with the Kemetic ankh emblem. By the 1990s, fashion designers created clothing lines that were advertised in rapzines and stage performance or modeled by hip-hop artists in their videos. Designers who market hip-hop clothing include Avirex, Davoucci, Echō Unlimited, Enyce, FUBU (For Us, By Us), Hood Wear, Johnny Blaze, Karl Kani, Nike, No Limit, Phat Farm, Tommy Hilfiger, and footwear brands like Lugz and Timberland. Some noted hip-hop artists have created their own signature clothing lines, for example, Sean "Puffy" Combs's Sean John and Jay-Z's Rocawear.

Gold chains, bracelets, earrings, and gold teeth are considered trademarks of many rappers. Male artists are known for wearing large, seemingly heavy gold necklaces, whereas females place more emphasis on large, seemingly heavy gold earrings. While wearing gold suggests style, prestige, and wealth in the world of hip-hop, the veteran MC Schoolly D connects this practice to an Africanism. Wearing gold, he says, "is not something that was born in America. This goes back to Africa. The gold chains are basically for warriors. The artists in the rap field are battling. We're the head warrior. We got to stand up and say we're winning battles, and this is how we're doing it" (Schoolly D 1988:52).

By the late 1980s, some rap artists began replacing gold jewelry with the soul-on-a-rope leather medallion, in which the continent of Africa or the African Nationalist Congress's colors—red, black, and yellow—are represented. However, gold jewelry was practically replaced by platinum and diamond-studded jewelry in the mid- to late 1990s. The critic David Wall Rice finds that, similar to gold jewelry, platinum was "prized by the ancient Egyptians and [even] proclaimed by France's King Louis XVI as the only metal fit for royalty" (2000:74). Rice credits the hip-hop MC-entrepreneur Jay-Z as ushering in this trend, and I would add Juvenile and The Hot Boys of Cash Money Records.[22]

From elaborate braids, locks, Afros, and fades[23] to shaved heads, hairstyles and wear accentuate an artist's personal style. Head pieces also accentuate style, as in the leather fezz worn by Kool Moe Dee or brand-name hats by Kangol popularized by LL Cool J to bun wraps occasionally worn by Jay-Z and the hip-hop soul artist Musiq Soulchild.

Additional paraphernalia include sunglasses, which convey "coolness." Though a posture adopted by African American males, "coolness is observed to enhance one's social competence, pride, dignity, self-esteem, and respect" (Majors and Billson 1992:105). Cool posing may derive from or be influenced by the Yoruba of Nigeria, for whom "'coolness' is a part of character, and character objectifies proper custom. To the degree that we live generously and discreetly, exhibiting grace under pressure, our appearance and our acts gradually assume virtual royal power" (Thompson 1983:16). Some may approach such a comparison with a bit of skepticism, but it is nonetheless striking how rap artists execute their rhymes in a reposeful manner while strutting or dancing on stage to the beat, appearing in total control without sweating profusely. While watching Kool Moe Dee perform "I Go to Work" on "The Arsenio Hall Show," I noticed that although he was dressed in a leather long-sleeve outfit with fez and sunglasses, he appeared not to perspire when strutting from side to side and mingling with the audience during the musical interludes. As one of my students commented, rap artists often carry to the stage a street persona. Thus, it is important in the hood that no matter how tough a situation is, one should not break or lose his cool; if he does, then he loses his clout among peers and is considered a wimp or a punk. Perhaps Kool Moe Dee's name is appropriate because of his ability to remain cool, calm, and controlled under the spotlight.

The effectiveness of a performance involves careful execution of flow, timing, rhetorical devices, soundtrack mix, sound quality, and paramusical-lingual features. Through these combined components, rap unfolds as a complex form that is rooted in a street aesthetic in which rawness, realness, ingenuity, and, above all, style are essential. It has permeated the cultural mainstream on its own aesthetic terms while simultaneously giving voice to a disenfranchised segment of urban America.

# The Critical Perspectives of Rap Music and the Hip-Hop Nation

WE MUST *unite and stand for what is right in the music society and world society itself.*

—Afrika Bambaataa

# Issues, Conflicts, and Conspiracies: The Hip-Hop Nation at a Crossroad

# 6

The Hip-Hop Nation comprises a community of artists and adherents who espouse street performance aesthetics as expressed through the four elements of hip-hop. At the hem of the nation's ideology is Afrika Bambaataa, the organizer and founder of the Zulu Nation. Hence, the ideology of the Hip-Hop Nation is encapsulated under the rubric of Bambaataa's Zulu Nation, a youth organization spawned in the Bronx River district in 1973. Following its gender-cooperative beliefs, it consists of both men and women. Senior members are referred to as Zulu Kings or Zulu Queens. Because of its growing popularity abroad, the Zulu Nation has renamed itself the Universal Zulu Nation. Owing to its international recognition, hip-hop has become a youth arts *mass* movement. Although the Hip-Hop Nation embraces anyone who performs any of its artistic forms, a follower or member of the Zulu Nation, the philosophy that undergirds its beliefs is guided by black nationalism and street consciousness.

During the formative years in the Bronx, hip-hop arts were merely seen as a passing fad by many spectators. Despite this assumption, Bambaataa and the burgeoning hip-hop arts captured the fascination of journalists, independent filmmakers, and music entrepreneurs. In January 1988, the avant-garde newspaper the *Village Voice* presented a special section called "The Hip Hop Nation," in which popular music critics drew attention to the movement, particularly its historical significance to American popular culture.

During the late 1980s, several U.S. hip-hop artists dubbed "nation-con-

Afrika Bambaataa (center) surrounded by members of the Zulu Nation, 1990s. (Photo by Al Pereira/Michael Ochs Archives)

scious rappers" (Eure and Spady 1991) popularized the Black Nationalist message as a theme of hip-hop music. These artists impart a form of "nationalism like black nationalism that provides inspirational territory for African Americans" (Decker 1993:55). Using the rhetoric of the Nation of Islam, Rastafarianism, the styles and expressions of Black Panthers and Black Nationalist poets of the 1960s, and the wearing of African garb, nation-conscious rappers address the political and economic disenfranchisement of black people in mainstream America. Their songs are designed to promote empowerment, awareness, and ethnic pride among black youths. Included among these rappers are Arrested Development, Black Star (Mos Def and Talib Kweli), Brand Nubian, dead prez, Jungle Brothers, KRS-One, Lakim Shabazz, Nefertiti, Paris, Poor Righteous Teachers, Public Enemy, Sister Souljah, The Coup, Wise Intelligent, and X-Clan, to name a few.

As hip-hop continued to garner popular acceptance in the U.S. mainstream during the 1990s, some artists veered away from a nationalist tone. Segments of the hip-hop community were troubled with this metamorphosis, especially when certain artists began using rap as a vehicle to glorify a gangsta image, utilize gendered expletives (e.g. "bitches and hoes"), and exploit drug lore, violence, and sexual promiscuity on and off the stage.[1] The new trend presented a sharp contrast to the message of black pride and self-respect that nation-conscious rappers promoted.

Commercial exploitation of and within the hip-hop community also contributes to a growing polarization. As a result, some artists believe that hip-hop is headed for its demise. Afrika Bambaataa cautioned adherents of hip-hop about the devious tactics that are devised to divide them and informed them of these crises with a tract he published in the black trade publication *Jack the Rapper:*

> YES BROTHERS AND SISTERS, there is a plot to destroy the Hip-Hop Culture. If you don't think so, just look at the news around you. . . . The news media and radio on some parts helped to destroy it [by] not writing on any positive things like how many of the rap groups did benefits for anti-crack and drugs, homeless people . . . and many radio stations who still don't like to play Hip Hop records. . . . *WE MUST* stop disrespecting each other on records, magazines or the streets. *WE MUST* stop selling our souls just to make money. . . .
>
> *WE MUST* unite and stand for what is right in the music society and world society itself. *WE MUST* stop the destruction of Hip Hop and make Hip Hop respected all over the world again. (Bambaataa 1986:1–2)

This chapter outlines the basic concerns that the Hip-Hop Nation believes are oppositional to its ideology, which I refer to as the political dialectics of hip-hop nationalism. Before discussing these concerns, it is necessary to define what the concept "nation" means in the context of hip-hop and to examine the ideology that shaped and developed the Hip-Hop Nation.

### The Political Precedence for a Unified Hip-Hop Nation

Defining "nation" is polemical because of its intangible essence. The political scientist Walker Connor views this essence as a psychological bond that joins a people and differentiates the subconscious convictions of its members from all other peoples' in a most vital way (1978:379). Perhaps the most widely quoted scholar on this topic is Benedict Anderson, who expands on Connor's definition of nation to mean an "imagined political community" that is "both inherently limited and sovereign" (1983:6). Drawing from the writings on "nation" by Anderson in particular, scholars of hip-hop concur that the nation idea is an "imagined community" and a created one, "both intangibly dreamt up and tangibly shaped, produced and constructed, [albeit] based less on its realization of state formation" (Decker 1993:54). According to the cultural studies critic Josh Kun, the hip-hop "nation" concept is "an effort by communities of black youth to establish political, philosophical, and racial identity through an accessible framework of recognizable linguistic, historical, and cultural markers" (1994:25). Moreover, "nationalism of the Hip-Hop Nation picks and chooses from the various black nationalist movements of the sixties, combining ideologies that were once held separate from each other, and shaping them together into a brand of what is perhaps best described as a 'cultural nationalism' that remains fluid, changing, and unfixed" (25). Such a philosophy lends itself "to dynamic reformulation and reinterpretation as the time arises" within the Hip-Hop Nation (Zook 1992:260). While hip-hop nationalism is founded upon the guiding elements of the Black Nationalist movement, the hip-hop arts movement is nonetheless a continuum of the Black Arts Movement as discussed in chapter 1.

Instrumental to the shaping of the Hip-Hop Nation and hip-hop nationalism is Afrika Bambaataa. Chapter 2 explained how he envisioned a way to mitigate youth gang violence in his neighborhood by galvanizing black and Latino youths' creative efforts. He had rival gang members compete artistically against one another as MCs versus MCs and breakdancers against breakdancers rather than fighting each other with knives. Influenced by Cy Endfield's film *Zulu*, a visit to West Africa, the Nation of Islam, Malcolm X's philosophy, and James Brown's music, Bambaataa promoted unity and the hip-hop arts movement through the formation of the Zulu Nation, whose members included blacks as well as Latinos. Bambaataa fervently believes Latinos are a part of and connected to the African diaspora and share similar political struggles with African Americans.[2] In an interview in *The Source*, Bambaataa says, "'Now one thing people must know, that when we say black we mean all our Puerto Rican or Dominican brothers. Wherever hip-hop was and the blacks was, the Latinos and the Puerto Ricans was too'" (quoted in George 1993:48). As the popular music reporter Mandalit del Barco comments, "the godfather of hip hop, Afrika Bambaataa, gives much respect to the Latino members . . . then and now" (1996:67). Some of the early Latino members of the Zulu Nation include the b-boy Richie "Crazy Legs" Colon and members of the renowned breakdancers group the Rock Steady Crew.

The Universal Zulu Nation (UZN) is guided by fifteen principles.[3] It is a nonsectarian organization that advocates a universal recognition of One God—whether that be Allah, Jehovah, Yahweh, Eloahim, Jah, or the Judeo-Christian God—and promotes the quest for knowledge, wisdom, mathematics, science, life, equality, love, truth, and facts ("Beliefs" 1993:49). Although the UZN is not a religious organization per se, certain principles are informed by Islam. The second principle states the belief "in the Holy Bible and the Glorious Qur'ān." The Zulu Nation's thirteenth principle, for example, indicates that while Amazulu (members of the Zulu Nation) are people of peace and respect, to those who give respect and peace, so is it given. "But if we are attacked by an aggressor then [we] should fight back in the name of Allah, Jah, Yahweh, Eloahim." A similar statement appears as a verse in the Qur'ān: "And fight in the way of Allah against those who fight against you but be not aggressive. Surely Allah loves not the aggressors" (Sura 2:190).

The fifteenth principle makes reference to "mathematics," a concept that stems from the Five Percenters, a splinter group of the Nation of Islam: "everything is based on mathematics." Founded in Harlem in 1964 by Clarence 13X, this group believes that only five percent of the earth's population, dubbed as poor righteous teachers, possess self-knowledge. They also consider the original human to be the Asiatic black man.[4] Most reinterpretations of the Nation of Islam are rendered by the Five Percenters in the form of lessons based on a Supreme Alphabet and Supreme Mathematics system (Nuruddin 1994). For example, the significance and meaning of a number are derived from a mathematical computation of each letter of the alphabet. Certain members of the Hip-Hop Nation have publicly identified themselves with this Five Percenters sect, including Big Daddy Kane, Brand Nubian, Busta Rhymes, Lakim Shabazz, Poor Righteous Teachers, Rakim, and Wu-Tang Clan.[5]

There remain other influences borrowed from Islam. The Shaka Zulu, the security force of the Zulu Nation, recalls the Fruit of Islam, the Nation of Islam's security force.

While conservative Muslims find that the Five Percenters' beliefs are extreme because they depart from conventional Qur'ānic interpretations, semi-liberal Muslims assert that being a follower of any sect of Islam serves as a gateway to Islam. Because the former Nation of Islam cleric Conrad Muhammad, the founder of Conscious Hip-Hop Activism Necessary for Global Empowerment (CHHANGE), recognizes rap as a musical catalyst for the conversion of many young blacks to Islam, he declares Islam to be the unofficial religion of the Hip-Hop Nation (Allen 1996). It is this identity and reverence for Islam that contributes to the religio-political foundation of the hip-hop community.

Rastafari and African spiritualism also influence the Hip-Hop Nation. Among those who come to mind here are Lauryn Hill of the Fugees, who makes references to the Rastafarian concepts of Zion and Jah, and Arrested Development and the hip-hop singer Erykah Badu, who demonstrate in performances and personal interviews their connection with African spiritualism or naturalist practices through the use of incense, candles, libations, and more.

The Zulu Nation further inspires and promotes musical enclaves within its organization, such as Bambaataa's groups, Soul Sonic Force and Cosmic Force. Several of the earlier hip-hop enclaves, including the Rock Steady Crew, were initiated by Zulu members. The Zulu Nation organization concept serves as an inspiration for other music enclaves that promote a form of hip-hop nationalism and group cohesion. Among these are Boogie Down Productions' Stop the Violence Movement, Fat Joe/Big Pun's Terror Squad (of Latino MCs), Ice-T and Afrika Islam's Rhyme Syndicate, Medusa's Feline Science, Public Enemy's the Bomb Squad (a production team), A Tribe Called Quest, De La Soul, and the Jungle Brothers' Native Tongues, Queen Latifah, Chill Rob G, Lakim Shabazz, Apache, and Lord Alibaski's Flavor Unit collective, Yo-Yo's Intelligent Black Women's Coalition, and X-Clan's Blackwatch Movement. Additionally, many followers of hip-hop nationalism choose to de-anglicize their names by adopting African and Afro-Asiatic-derived names. Among these artists are Kwame, Queen Latifah, Rakim, Lakim Shabazz, Ahmad, and Nefertiti, to name a few.

## Change in the Message

Despite the global success of hip-hop arts, its musical component became the center of controversy in the mid-1980s. News reporters focused on concert fights and deaths at rap music concerts and remained silent about the various benefit rap concerts, such as "Say No to Drugs," that concluded peacefully. Meanwhile, as "more positive acts were trying to steer the audience into nationalism, unity and political awareness" (Ro 1996:6), West Coast groups like N.W.A. and South Central Cartel veered away from this stance toward the controversial rap subgenre labeled "gangsta rap." In the sensationalism generated by this subgenre, non–gangsta rap artists fell by the wayside "while the one-dimensional gangsta [rappers] signed six-figure album deals and dragged hip-hop away from its roots" (7). Rappers' portrayals of gangstas, thugs, pushers, pimps, and sex kittens—complicated by the artists' real-life brushes with the law (life imitating art or vice versa)—led the public to question the moral value of all rap music. As a result, rap music encountered much hostility from urban radio supporters who coerced certain stations to curtail their airplay of rap records or forced them to stop playing rap music altogether.[6]

By the 1990s, this music also encountered countless foes, including the Parents' Music Resource Center, the Anti-Defamation League, former civil rights advocates and politicians, and Christian ministers, all of whom rejected the street bravado and explicit lyrics that began to reach mainstream America. The cultural critic Michael Eric Dyson notes that tactics against gangsta rap appear in two forms: censorship and civil responsibility. The former "seeks to prevent the sale of vulgar music that offends mainstream moral sensibilities by suppressing the First Amendment. The latter, however, is a more difficult but rewarding task [in that] it seeks to oppose the expression of misogynistic and sexist sentiments in hip-hop culture through protest and pamphleteering, through boycotts and consciousness raising" (1996:103).

The most notable case of censorship involved the Miami-based rap trio 2 Live Crew and their album *As Nasty as They Wanna Be* (1989). This album, whose song titles included "Me So Horny" and "Bad Ass Bitch," was condemned by the PMRC for polluting the minds of American youth and aestheticizing and glorifying sexual violence against women. As a result of the controversy, 2 Live Crew's album, according to one critic, "'was the first in the United States to be banned by a federal judge; members of the group were arrested at a live performance in Florida, and the controversy surrounding the Crew became all the rage in the 1990s'" (quoted in Baker 1993:63).[7]

Censorship in the form of "civil responsibility" emerged in meetings with record executives and the 1994 congressional hearings. William Bennett, the former U.S. education secretary and drug czar, and C. Delores Tucker, the chairwoman of the National Political Congress of Black Women, began meeting with record executives at Time-Warner, which, at the time, was a distributing arm of the gangsta rap label Death Row Records.[8] The Reverend Calvin Butts III, the minister of the Abyssinian Baptist Church in Harlem, destroyed gangsta rap CDs and cassettes with a steamroller. The anti–gangsta rap faction convinced record companies to use warning labels on CDs containing explicit lyrics. These groups also demanded that major record companies halt their manufacturing of gangsta rap and that they terminate relationships with rap artists whose music they deemed too risqué, sexist, militant, or crude in tone.

At the 1994 congressional hearings, those testifying against gangsta rap included Tucker and the singer Dionne Warwick. While Yo-Yo, a non–gangsta rapper, was invited to testify on behalf of rap music, no gangsta rap artist was invited to testify. Among those less offensive toward of gangsta rap was California State Congresswoman Maxine Waters, who saw the anti–gangsta rap crusade as an attempt to marginalize black youth. She and the Reverend Jesse Jackson used the hearings to try to convince the public that the problem was not with the lyrics but with the devastating realities and consequences of ghetto life.

In the wake of the protests, it appeared to the Hip-Hop Nation that segments of the black community conspired with the powers that be to destroy rap music, placing rap music at a crossroad. Meanwhile, members of the Hip-Hop Nation faced other major challenges in their inner-city neighborhoods, such as drug abuse and AIDS, which steadily worsened. Turf wars within the Hip-Hop Nation (e.g. East versus West Coast rappers) sparked both verbal and violent confrontations antithetical to the Nation's purpose of unifying and supporting rappers and their communities. Furthermore, some artists overindulged in material possessions, prompting disapproval by Nation members as well. Bambaataa cautioned the Hip-Hop Nation in 1986, "*WE MUST* unite and stand for what is right in the music society and world society itself." Now it seemed that issues of black-on-black crime, turf wars, materialism, and the intracommunity epidemics of AIDS and substance abuse might lead the Hip-Hop Nation to self-destruction. These are the issues that I examine in the following sections.

### Black-on-Black Crime and Turf Wars: Message to the Peeps

During the early years of hip-hop's development, its musical component supplied a beat by which its audience could party. But as rap music moved into mainstream popular culture during the mid-1980s, it began to address themes of violence, and negative coverage of this genre began to appear in the media. For example, media coverage often reported violence at rap music concerts and called this music the catalyst for violent behavior. Even though most of these incidents were instigated by "posses of black and Hispanic gangsters, with the intention of robbing and harassing innocent concertgoers" (George 1990:11), rap music and its artists became the scapegoats for the troublemakers who attended the concerts.

The fatal stabbing of a nineteen-year-old concertgoer, Julio Fuentes, at the "Dope Jam" rap concert at Long Island's Nassau Coliseum on September 10, 1987, prompted rap artists to crusade against violence at their concerts and within their communities. In the wake of Fuentes's death, Boogie Down Productions, spearheaded by KRS-One, along with other rap music artists wanted to set the record straight about rappers and concert violence. Their collaborative efforts led to the creation of the Stop the Violence Movement and its theme song, which appeared on BDP's second album, *My Phi-losophy* (1988). Besides addressing crime at rap concerts, the movement sought to raise public awareness of black-on-black crime, to point out its real causes and social costs, to raise funds for a charitable organization already dealing with the problems of illiteracy and crime in the inner city, and to show that rap music is a viable tool for stimulating reading and writing skills among inner-city kids (George 1990:12).

Their efforts culminated with the song and video "Self-Destruction" (1989), which featured rhymes by KRS-One, Kool Moe Dee, Just Ice, Chuck D and Flavor Flav of Public Enemy, MC Lyte, Daddy-O, Delite, Fruitkwan, Wise of Stetsasonic, Heavy D, D-Nice, Ms. Melodie, and Doug E. Fresh. The black music journalist Nelson George and the rap music entrepreneur Ann Carli, the executive producers of the "Self-Destruction" video, convinced the National Urban League to sponsor the project. According to the league's executive vice president, Frank Lomax III, the main objective of "Self-Destruction" coincided with the Urban League's mission to communicate that "crime is not acceptable in the African American communities and crime is not part of our black heritage" (Lomax 1990:21–22). The National Urban League provided statistics and footage for the book *Stop the Violence* (1990) and the "Self-Destruction" video. The statistics cited homicide as the leading cause of death among black males between the ages of fifteen and twenty-four. In addition, the statistics showed that black youths are twice as likely as white youths to be unemployed and that a black child's father is twice as likely as a white child's father to be unemployed (George 1990:43, 51).

The initial release of "Self-Destruction" was scheduled for late 1988; however, it was rescheduled and released on January 15, 1989, in honor of the Martin Luther King Jr.'s national birthday celebration. While the crux of "Self-Destruction" was to foster King's nonviolence stance, Malcolm X epitomizes to the Hip-Hop Nation a northern urban black experience against racial injustice and the zeal for redefinition, redirection, and self-respect that is reinforced in the mandate of the Universal Zulu Nation. The introduction of this rap song commences with an excerpt from Malcolm X's "Message to the Grass Roots" (1963) speech: "We all agree tonight, all of the speakers have agreed that America has a very serious problem. Not only does America have a very serious problem, but our people have a very serious problem. America's problem is. . . ." Following the speech excerpt, rappers chant the chorus "self-destruction, you headed for self-destruction," and exchange rhymes in which they address black-on-black and concert violence. In the "Self-

Destruction" video, the rappers Heavy D and Fruitkwan rap in front of a mural of Malcolm X in Harlem.

Although the primary performers on "Self-Destruction" are from the East Coast, artists from the West Coast—Young MC and Tone-Lōc—flew to New York from Los Angeles to join in the video production. The Stop the Violence Movement donated two hundred thousand dollars in profits to the National Urban League in support of its mission to foster literacy programs and eradicate black-on-black crime.[9] After the success of "Self-Destruction," similar collective efforts against black-on-black crime evolved, such as a recording by the West Coast Rap All-Stars, "We're All in the Same Gang" (1990), as well as "Bangin' on Wax" (1993) by the Bloods and the Crips gang members, which they produced as part of a truce after the Los Angeles uprising of 1992. Despite the Stop the Violence Movement's efforts, rap's association with violence continued to escalate with gangsta rap's popularity.

The American public's insatiable appetite for violence plays out in over-the-top ticket sales for gangster films, such as Francis Ford Coppola's *Godfather* trilogy (1972, 1974, 1990), Brian DePalma's *Scarface* (1983), Martin Scorsese's *Goodfellas* (1990), and Quentin Tarantino's *Pulp Fiction* (1994). Gangsta rap also details gangster life, though its setting is different. Described by one rap music producer as a "lyrical movie" (Singleton interview), gangsta rap graphically depicts life in ghetto America, including economic deprivation, drive-by shootings, drug dealing, police brutality, and broken dreams. It is clear to me that the standard of evaluation for artistic depictions of white gangsters and black gangsters is blatantly biased. While the gangster lifestyle portrayed by white male characters in films by well-known directors is romanticized and exulted by the mainstream entertainment industry, black male characters who appear on wax (music recordings) and in videos are ridiculed as degenerate gangsters by the same cadre.

Because gangsta rap vividly conveys the brutality of street life, West Coast rappers prefer to call this style "reality rap" (see Marriott, Bernard, and Gordon 1994). Gangsta or reality rap gives voice to a young or adult black protagonist who lives where the rule is survival of the fittest. Life becomes hopeless and meaningless: "the frightening result is a numbing detachment from others and a self-destructive disposition toward the world" (West 1994:23). Tragically, the protagonist meets his or her demise at the hands of the law or by violent means, often as a result of a drug deal gone sour, a robbery, or simply being in the wrong place at the wrong time, as described in the reality rap "Gangsta's Paradise" (1995) by Coolio:

As I walk through the valley of the shadow of death,
I take a look at my life and realize there's nothing
    left. . . .
Death ain't nothing but a heartbeat away. . . .
I'm twenty-three, never will I live to see twenty-four.
The way things are going I don't know.

In "It Was a Good Day" (1992), Ice Cube raps, "So hooked it up for later as I hit the door [left home] / thinking, will I live another twenty-four?"

While these texts may appear to be simply fatalistic in tone to outsiders, they reflect candid feelings of many inside the hood. Before I interviewed some rap artists from Brooklyn in March 1993, the mother of one artist interjected her feelings about increased violence in the hood and her fear that her sons might die at the hands of another young black youth over something trivial or material. At the time her sons ranged from fifteen to twenty-one years old. One of the artists said that he would be thankful if he reached thirty years of age. The philosopher Cornel West believes that the growing sense of nihilism in impoverished areas is the result of many complexities beyond the economic and political control of those living in the hood (1994:22–25).

### Clash of the Turfs

While rappers rhymed about ongoing afflictions in their neighborhoods, violent turf wars ignited between East and West Coast artists. Claiming one's turf via rhyme was a skill cultivated by hip-hop's godfather Afrika Bambaataa as an alternative to violence. Verbal dueling was the norm. In New York City, through borough taunts—"Manhattan keeps on makin' it, Brooklyn keeps on takin it, Bronx keeps on creating it, and Queens keeps on fakin' it"—MCs let tongues rather than bullets fly. Rhyme was also a considerable weapon for demanding respect from another rapper who might have "dissed" you publicly: examples include the answer-back raps of "Jack the Ripper" (1988) by LL Cool J and "Let's Go" (1988) Kool Moe Dee, or "The Bridge" (1986) by MC Shan and "The Bridge is Over" (1987) by KRS-One/BDP. Whenever there was a disagreement between two rappers, it was resolved peacefully with meetings between opposing parties, sometimes facilitated by the Zulu Nation. By the 1990s, however, verbal intraborough battles gradually escalated into bicoastal beefs or feuds between East and West Coast hip-hoppers: Tim Dog's "Fuck Compton" (1991), followed by Rodney O and Joe Cooley's "Fuck New York" (1992), and the West Coast group Tha Dogg Pound's "New York, New York" (1995), followed by Capone-N-Noreaga's "L.A., L.A." (1996).

The reported tension between the rap music record executives Sean "Puffy" Combs of Bad Boy Entertainment of Manhattan and Marion "Suge" Knight of Death Row Records of Los Angeles furthered the burgeoning bicoastal war. When Knight's cousin, Jake Robles, was murdered at a birthday party for the hip-hop producer Jermaine Dupri (a friend of Combs's) at Atlanta's Platinum House on September 24, 1995, Knight accused Combs and his bodyguard of the murder (Blackspot 1996:103). Following this incident, the taunts and threats continued. Gunshots were fired at Knight's group, Tha Dogg Pound, during a video shoot in Brooklyn, New York.

None of these feuds attracted the level of media coverage given to the East Coast/West Coast beef between the late Christopher "The Notorious B.I.G." Wallace (a.k.a. Biggie Smalls), who recorded for Bad Boy Entertainment, and the late Tupac "2Pac" Shakur, who recorded for Death Row Records. Some feel the feud sparked the murders of each artist in fatal gangland/drive-by shootings that occurred no more than six months apart. The violence began on November 30, 1994, when Shakur was shot several times while in the lobby of the Quad Recording Studios in New York's Times Square. In a *Vibe* magazine interview (Powell 1995), Tupac Shakur implicated members of Bad Boy Entertainment.

Several weeks after the shooting, Shakur was sentenced to serve four and a half years in New York's Rikers Island for sexual assault. Within eight months, Suge Knight posted a $1.4 million bond for Shakur's early release. After his release, Shakur recorded the single "Hit 'em Up" (1995), with lyrics expressing veiled threats toward The Notorious B.I.G. and Puffy Combs and announcing Shakur's alleged affair with Faith Evans, Smalls's wife. Shakur stated that he recorded the song "Hit 'em Up" in retaliation for Biggie Smalls's 1995 song "Who Shot Ya," which Shakur took as a personal comment on his attack at the Quad Recording studios. Smalls denied the connection, stating that "Who Shot Ya" preceded Shakur's shooting (Blackspot 1996:103; Fab Five Freddy 1995:25–29).

Shakur was attacked again on September 7, 1996, after the Mike Tyson–Bruce Seldon boxing match in Las Vegas. He died on September 13 from multiple gunshot wounds. Six months after 2Pac's death, Smalls was fatally wounded and died on March 9, 1997, the day after the Soul Train Awards and a party in Los Angeles. The Hip-Hop Nation stated that stories about the ongoing beef between Wallace and Shakur, which appeared in *Vibe* maga-

2Pac (center) with Biggie Smalls (left) and Redman (right), at the Palladium in New York, 1993. (Photo by Al Pereira/Michael Ochs Archives)

zine (April and August 1995, February and September 1996) further agitated hostile sentiments between East Coast and West Coast hip-hop communities.[10] Fans of The Notorious B.I.G. and 2Pac as well as the general public perceived these deaths to be another gang-related statistic.

After Tupac Shakur's death, black entertainment figures and black community spokespersons attempted to dismiss and repudiate any assumption of an ongoing East Coast/West Coast war. Before Wallace's death, the comedian Steve Harvey brought together Puffy Combs and the Death Row artist Snoop Doggy Dogg on national television on February 23, 1997, to openly state that the tension between East and West Coast rappers was a myth. Their attempt to dismantle this notion concluded with a handshake. But a few weeks later, The Notorious B.I.G. was slain in a drive-by shooting similar to 2Pac's, igniting the feud once again. The Hip-Hop Nation reexamined its agenda with urgency, promoting unity on television and radio talk shows. 2Pac and The Notorious B.I.G.'s murders prompted the BET show "Rap City" to temporarily insert the slogan "Unifying a Hip Hop Nation" at the end of its music video program.

The radio station KKBT in Los Angeles featured a three-hour segment with a few West Coast rappers discussing the rap-on-rap situation. The station aired a similar program on the Sunday morning show "Street Science," hosted by the black radio personality Dominique DiPrima, on March 22, 1997. On March 10, 1997, KPWR of Los Angeles opened their lines to grief-stricken callers who expressed their disbelief of the gang-style execution of The Notorious B.I.G. In a television interview, the West Coast rapper B-Real of Cypress Hill expressed the irony of these deaths: "It's a tragedy because we lost two most important people in this rap industry, which is 2Pac and Biggie. It's ironic because both of them were rivals. And now people are trying to link the two deaths with one another. And they don't really know if that was the case or not" (KTLA News, Mar. 10, 1997).[11]

Other commentators voiced discontent at the authorities' seemingly lax efforts to find Shakur's and Wallace's killers. The host of "Reality Check" on Houston's KBXX, Willie D, a former member of the Geto Boys, compared the manner in which authorities were handling the investigations of these two rap music artists to the way they have nonchalantly investigated drive-by shootings of many black inner-city youth. In a television interview on "BET Talk," hosted by Tavis Smiley on March 11, 1997, Willie D stated that investigators "never came up with a suspect for their deaths. Now if they pursued Tupac Shakur's killer with the same zeal they pursued the Oklahoma City Bomber killer . . . we wouldn't be here [on television discussing this] today."[12] He also admonished those who said that The Notorious B.I.G. and 2Pac "deserved to die" because of the content of their lyrics and the life they perpetrated. He urged people to respectfully mourn their deaths.

Peace efforts resumed on other fronts. On April 3, 1997, hip-hop artists from various parts of the United States joined the Nation of Islam leader, Minister Louis Farrakhan, for a one-day summit meeting in Chicago to discuss and crush the rap-on-rap coastal beefs. The seven-hour meeting, called "Peace in the Streets," was designed to promote unity, atonement, reconciliation, and responsibility in the black community, as reported in the Nation of Islam's newspaper, *The Final Call*. Its hip-hop peace plan included discussion about peace in the Hip-Hop Nation; the production of responsible and positive rap lyrics for uplifting one's people; a hip-hop peace tour; a collaborative album dedicated to 2Pac and The Notorious B.I.G.; and a second-anniversary Million Man March/Day of Atonement on October 16, 1997. The summit meeting comprised not only rappers and members of the black music industry but also Christian clergy, Zulu Nation representatives, and a 1960s Black Nationalist luminary, Kwame Ture (formerly Stokely Carmichael).

Ture, in particular, reminded rappers of their civic duties to the African American struggle by stating that "they are not the inventors of rap, but rather they represent the culture of an oppressed people, [which] must be used to advance the people" (James and William Muhammad 1997:10). The summit ended with hip-hop artists publicly thanking Minister Farrakhan and pledging peace among rappers.

Bambaataa remains hip-hop's central force in resolving conflicts and promoting positive hip-hop images. His endeavors to do so were further promoted by commercial advertising. Coca-Cola featured rap music artists in the 1998 commercial series, "Obey Your Thirst," for the soft drink Sprite. The artists included Common of Chicago, Mack 10 of Los Angeles, Fat Joe of New York, the Goodie MOb of Atlanta, the veteran DJ Jazzy Jay of New York and his mentor, Afrika Bambaataa, and the menacing robotic-transformer, Voltron. One commercial places Bambaataa as the head commander beckoning East and West Coast artists to "obey their thirst" for the sake of unity and hip-hop culture.

Continuing along similar lines, artists from both coasts began recording together as a way to reduce bicoastal tensions. Events such as "Hiphop Appreciation Week," which was established in the late 1990s, promote unity and an effort to form a common bond and purpose. Activities include panel discussions, lectures, film presentations, the International Hiphop Peace Conference event, an award ceremony, and a memorial service for deceased members of the Nation. Some artists left "reality rap" to pursue party-oriented lyrics. Hip-hop's longtime fascination with and affiliation with real-life violence shrunk to a trickle with the premature deaths of two promising artists.[13] The event made members of the hip-hop community aware of their critical stance and the necessity of unifying their nation.

### *"Money, Power, and Respect": The Price of Livin Large*

The impact, complexity, advantages, and disadvantages of materialism also had a profound effect on the shaping of hip-hop culture. Many hip-hop artists view a record deal as a way out of the ghetto. With proper management, many of them achieve a certain level of success and wealth. As they move up the socioeconomic ladder, rap artists generally do not forget their humble beginnings. For instance, in performance rappers will proudly salute their neighborhoods with questions to the audience such as "Is Compton in the house?" or "Is Brooklyn in the house?" During special holiday celebrations, some artists return to their communities to conduct food drives for the needy. Such has been the case with Marion "Suge" Knight, Master P, and The Fugees, to name a few. Other community efforts by hip-hop artists include Jay-Z's generous donation to the Million Family March, Sean Combs's Daddy's House for disadvantaged children, Lauryn Hill's Refugee Project for economically challenged youth in the New Jersey area, and Wyclef Jean's Clef's Kids organization for funding economically challenged youth with music lessons. Because they choose to maintain connections with and deep commitment to their communities, rap artists are exulted as heroes by many inner-city youth. To these admirers, they represent those who are prosperous—livin large—and making an honest living. In this manner, rap music becomes a symbol of success for the average ghetto youth, and most importantly, an example of socioeconomic mobility.

Hip-hop artists express livin large by donning designer fashions and expensive jewelry and driving expensive cars, which they parade in their music videos as well as on- and offstage. Owning these accessories undoubtedly signifies the status and prosperity of the rap artists, but for their fans the desire to acquire these possessions may result in fetishistic obsessions, leading to jewelry snatching, a precursor to concert violence, and assaults on rap stars by crazed fans or stalkers. In an interview, Chuck D discusses the psychology underlying why some hip-hop music fans are obsessed with certain material objects as status symbols and why his group, Public Enemy, refuses to acquiesce to this type of obsession:

> "'Man, I work at McDonald's, but in order for me to feel good about myself I got to get a gold chain or I got to get a fly car in order to impress a sister or whatever, in order to impress myself, in order to make people feel good about me.' We [Public Enemy] show them through the access of the media that this is what we have, no gold chain. You can acquire this, an African medallion, or a clock to know 'what time it is.' But at the same time, you want to be where I'm at, but I have a whole staircase full of knowledge which might put you where I'm at." (quoted in Eure and Spady 1991:362)

In an attempt to downplay gold jewelry, some rap or nation-conscious artists prefer not to don it. Instead, they replace gold jewelry with African leather medallions or other non-gold adornments.

Other rap artists have spoken out against material obsession in their music, as best illustrated in Ice Cube's rap song "Us" (1991), in which he chides youth who prioritize nonsubstantive things like tennis shoes over human life. During the musical interlude of "Us," a voice from a rap music concertgoer asks Ice Cube a question about concert violence: "Yeah, why is it that one motherfucka could ruin it for twenty-two thousand motherfuckas when they wanna come see a good jam?" Ice Cube poignantly responds with a situational rhyme for the interrogator: "'Us' [African Americans] will always sing the blues / 'cause all we care about is hairstyles and tennis shoes. / And if you step on mine you'll push a button, / 'cause I'll beat you down like it ain't nothing."

In further corroboration of fetishistic obsession, I recall an avid rap fan's disappointment with rap music's leading magazine, *The Source,* because of its increased advertisements of name-brand clothing in which models (some of whom are rappers) sport expensive clothes, sending the message that material possessions are the ultimate status symbols and may be, for some fans, desirable at any cost. One reader, in a letter to the editor, states that while the advertised gear is considered "phat," he concurs that they are also too costly (Oscar 1997:14). He suggests that the magazine "try showing some less expensive gear so heads will know they don't have to hustle, steal, or rob and blast shots for the flyness." The reader also states that he was once robbed by some "kids over his fly clothing." By the late 1990s, several incidents involving assaults on rap artists ensued. These incidents received unprecedented attention in the media. Among these included Guru of Gang Starr, who was robbed of his Rolex watch at gunpoint outside a music studio in Queens, Queen Latifah, who was a victim of a carjacking in New York City, Mobb Deep's Prodigy, who was robbed of three hundred thousand dollars' worth of jewelry at gunpoint near a recording studio located near the Queensbridge Project, and Sean Combs, whose protégé Shyne fired a gun inside Club New York in attempt to abate an assault on Combs by a former convict. After a barrage of similar incidents, critics and various rap artists noted on "MTV News [Now] Hard Rhymes: High Stakes" (2001) that rap artists can no longer hang out at certain venues, particularly in their former hoods or clubs that attract hip-hop player haters because there is often someone who will challenge, taunt, or even jack artists. In many instances, such acts occur in the presence of fans; the artists feel humiliated, thus prompting them to physically retaliate by resorting to the street ethic of "keepin it real." Artists who assume a gangsta posture on stage, or the so-called studio gangstas, are often confronted by rivals who fail to distinguish artists' real selves from their fictional ones.

## *"10 Percent Music, 90 Percent Business"*

Regardless of all the negative drama that accompanies the rich and the famous, rap music has undoubtedly opened doors in the music industry to unprecedented numbers of black and Latino youths who often graduate from recording or performing rap to producing, owning their own record labels, or venturing into acting. Examples include Andre Harrell, a former member of the rap duo Dr. Jeckyll and Mr. Hyde, the rapper-turned-actress and talk-show host Dana "Queen Latifah" Owens, the rapper-turned-actor Todd "LL Cool J" Smith, the rapper-turned-actor-and-director O'Shea "Ice Cube" Jackson, and the actor-comedian Will Smith of the rap duo DJ Jazzy Jeff and the Fresh Prince.

The rap mogul Russell Simmons blazed the trail for many hip-hop success stories. Simmons launched his career as a manager of DJ/MC acts on the New York City local circuit during the early 1980s. He teamed up with Rick Rubin to form Def Jam Records and eventually became the sole proprietor of Rush Artist Management.[14] Simmons's success arises from his mastery of an underground promotion tactic known as "street-level production" (see chapter 3). Lauded as "hip-hop's first millionaire entrepreneur" (Stancell 1996:251), Simmons's business acumen was emulated by many of his rap music contemporaries such as the late Eric "Eazy-E" Wright of Ruthless Records, Sean "P. Diddy" Combs of Bad Boy Entertainment, Bill Stephney and Hank Shocklee of SOUL Records, Marion "Suge" Knight of Death Row Records, Queen Latifah of Flavor Unit Records, Andre "Dr. Dre" Young of Aftermath, James Prince of Rap-A-Lot Records, Luther Campbell of Luke Records, and Percy "Master P" Miller of No Limit Records, to name but a few.[15]

The hip-hop community has served as a shelter and training ground for up-and-coming entrepreneurs, attempting to provide its aspiring executives with facts about the music industry and how to avoid its pitfalls in order to become successful in the business of rap. As Yo-Yo cogently stated to *Billboard* following her keynote address on the rap music business at *Rap Sheet* magazine's third annual hip-hop conference in Los Angeles, "'I let people know that this business is not all fun and games. It's 10 percent music and 90 percent business'" (quoted in Reynolds 1996:19). It is for this reason that Wendy Day started the Rap Coalition in March 1992. The Rap Coalition is a nonprofit organization that serves as a watchdog support group on behalf of rap artists. Day outlines the main objectives of Rap Coalition under three broad headings: Information Source, Unity, and Support Network. Through her organization, Day has assisted the professional careers of hip-hop artists such as Common, Master P, Brian and Ron Williams, Eminem, and Tragedy, among many others. Additionally, the advertising sections of many magazines that cater to hip-hop audiences are inundated with various music conventions targeted to the aspiring rap music executive.

But as the old adage goes, "all that glitters ain't gold." The street ingenuity of the rap music industry often conflicts with conventional music practices dominated, controlled, and regulated by performing rights organizations such as the American Society of Composers, Authors, and Publishers (ASCAP) and Broadcast Music Incorporated (BMI) and with music copyright statutes in general.

Digital sampling, one of the primary methods underlying the creation of rap music, has complicated conventional music copyright laws. Prior to rap music, music copyright infringement was limited to the appropriation or use of a copyrighted musical idea that exceeded fair use. By the 1990s, the practice of rap music artists using prerecorded music via digital sampling had begun to fuel much debate among entertainment legal analysts. The most publicized case on digital sampling as "art or theft" centered on the Cold Chillin'/Warner Brothers artist Biz Markie, whose single "Alone Again (Naturally)," from the album *I Need a Haircut,* used eight bars of Gilbert O'Sullivan's 1972 hit "Alone Again (Naturally)" without legal permission. On December 17, 1991, federal judge Kevin Thomas Duffy of the State of New York ruled against Markie et al. for copyright infringement, granted an injunction, and ordered that *I Need a Haircut* be pulled from retail stores. This ruling marked the first time a sampling case had risen to this level in the courts (Russell 1992:1). Pursuant to Markie's case, the music industry established legal guidelines for this type of musical appropriation. Clearing sampled material involved negotiations with the underlying composition's owner, recording artist, or songwriter, music publishers, and the artist who is sampling (Sugarman and Salvo 1991; "New Spin" 1992).

While clearing samples can be tedious, it ensures a profit for all parties involved with the newly created work. The rap music entrepreneur Francesca Spero observes, however, how segments of the industry attempt to benefit from either overcharging hip-hop artists for the use of prerecorded master copies, buying the rights of popular sampled tracks only to file lawsuits against those who use them without clearance, or encouraging the sampled big-name artists to file suit against rap artists—all in the name of "greed" (1992:7). But with court victories such as 2 Live Crew's parodying of Roy Orbison's 1964 hit "Pretty Woman,"[16] deemed by the U.S. Supreme Court as "fair use," subsequent sampling cases were frequently settled out of court.

Bootlegging is the pirating of music tapes and masters. Although piracy is not new to the music industry, some rap artists believe that this practice often results from unauthorized record dealers' discovery of overly produced or defective tapes of rap music, improperly and irresponsibly discarded by a record company. During my fieldwork in New York between 1992 and 1994, the "word on the street"—hip hop's way of saying "the oral tradition"—was that the bulk of bootlegged tapes are those by rap artists. Bootleggers were reproducing tapes and selling them for less than the price in record stores, bypassing the process that delivers royalties to the artists. One could often discern that a tape was pirated by the slightly blurred appearance of the outer edge of the cover (indicating poor printing or photocopying). As a result of bootlegging, rap artists, in contrast to pop artists, are more likely affected by undocumented record sales, those not accounted for by SoundScan.

During the 1990s, there was growing concern over the ability for anyone with access to a computer, the Internet, and the right software to download prereleased music files in MP3 digital format through the online music file-sharing software company Napster. Some hip-hop artists and executives assert that the Internet has only advanced a form of "hi-tech bootlegging" that shortchanges the artists as well as the record companies. Dr. Dre says that Napster is "'enabling people to download my entire album for nothin. I'll go into the studio and spend a year out of my life working on a record, and they are just going to take it and give it away for free?'" (quoted in Edwards 2000:59). Tom Silverman of Tommy Boy Records, however, foresees the Internet as lessening the burdens of distribution for small record labels. Chuck D of Public Enemy, who once recorded on the online music label Atomic Pop, has founded Rapstation.com, described as "a music site that gives exposure to unsigned and lesser-known artists [and] also regards the Internet as a new tool to put control of music in the hands of artists, bypassing record companies" (Holland 2000:10, 118). Since the Internet has been an alternative avenue for advertising and distributing rap in lieu of radio airplay, some artists have argued to include a clause in their contracts that would require digital distribution.[17]

Rap artists sometimes fall prey to other forms of exploitation by the corporate world. Without a doubt, the commercial industry has boosted the careers of rap artists and brought them into the mainstream with popularly consumed products (e.g. Hammer endorsed Pepsi, Heavy D promoted Sprite, and Salt-N-Pepa endorsed Cover Girl products). But there are also commercials that use rap artists as spokepersons for products deemed physically harmful. Of growing concern to the hip-hop community is the use of rappers of color to endorse malt liquors in advertisements targeted at black and Latino working-class communities. The nation-conscious rapper Chuck D once filed a lawsuit against G. Heileman Brewing Company, McKenzie River Corporation, and the marketers of St. Ides Malt Liquor for the misappropriation and unauthorized use of his voice in one of their commercials (Léger 1993:21). While researching malt liquor, Chuck D pondered why these drinks are specifically advertised by and to people of color, and in the process, he discovered,

> "Malt liquor is the fourth most consumed product by the black community. The sad thing is that brothers don't even know what it is. If you look at a bottle of malt liquor, they don't even put the ingredients on the label. Malt liquor is the waste product after they make the real beer. They make beer with hops, barley, fresh oats, and natural spring water. Then they take what's left over, people be washing their hands in it, oil from the machine goes in there, all kinds of dirt fall into a big fat vat. Instead of dumping it in a river . . . they'd just give it to the niggers, like we saw in the *Godfather.* . . . Look at what white boys drink. Heineken and Budweiser." (quoted in Eure and Spady 1991:373–74)

Furthermore, malt liquor has a higher alcohol content than beer. The lawsuit against St. Ides and affiliates was eventually settled out of court. Chuck D interprets his victory as a political statement. He insists that black people as a united force should know that there are button pushers out there, and if they attack the button pushers, they will get more things done (Chuck D interview).

While segments of the hip-hop community rallied vehemently against malt liquor advertisements for black audiences, Ice Cube endorsed St. Ides in exchange for the company's agreement to donate six-digit figures to black inner-city causes. Ice Cube admitted at times that he felt somewhat apprehensive about advertising for St. Ides because of his conversion to Islam, which forbids the use and sale of alcohol. However, after conversing with Dr. Khalid Muhammad, a former cleric of the Nation of Islam, about his uncertainty, Ice Cube was convinced by a paradoxical explanation to view St. Ides as "'a stepping stone . . . to build our Nation. We could use them to donate at least $100,000 a year into all kinds of organizations to help build the Black community'" (quoted in Bernard 1991:33). When continually asked by members of the rap music community if he believed that representing St. Ides advances the stereotype of African American males gulping down forty-ounce bottles of malt liquor, as commonly seen in contemporary urban films,

Ice Cube replied: "'Yeah, that's true. [But] it [St. Ides] puts food on the table for my son. I'm also making them give money to where they wouldn't give it any other way. How else could the Black community come up with $100,000 to help an organization?'" (quoted in Bernard 1991:33).

Although acquiring wealth for one's community in this manner is perceived ambivalently among some members of the hip-hop community, others find that, considering the high incidence of drugs and alcohol in the inner-city communities, the practice is irresponsible and promotes and corroborates the "you gotta get yours, I gotta get mine" attitude.[18] Unfortunately, this ideology has slowly eroded community spirit within the Hip-Hop Nation, breeding anonymity, individualism, and fear.

Prior to the completion of my research in New York City during the summer of 1994, I attended the fifteenth annual New Music Seminar's "Hip Hop Rhythm Cultural Institute" panels. On one panel in particular, "Hip Hop Summit" (July 20, 1994), a discussion ensued around the eroding spirits in hip-hop artists' inner-city neighborhoods. Roxanne Shanté and Afrika Bambaataa recalled a time "when everyone in their projects knew one another, and looked out for each other; but now, when people go outside, they are afraid of getting shot or mugged by someone." Rapper Mia X recounts that during the 1980s living conditions gradually worsened and crime escalated in the Seventh Ward, an area in New Orleans's inner city where she once lived: "'A lot of the people that had been there had either died or moved, so we were getting new people in the area from different parts of town. The present-day Seventh Ward is pure chaos. It's infested with drug dealers, drug users, fugitives on the run. It's just totally different'" (quoted in Braxton 1997:95).

Mia X and the rap panelists' narratives are indicative of those urban African American communities most impacted by the intracommunity epidemics of substance abuse and AIDS. The final section of this chapter delves further into the esoteric beliefs surrounding these epidemics and the manner in which the Hip-Hop Nation addresses the epidemics.

### Intracommunity Epidemics: AIDS Conspiracy Belief Narratives in Hip-Hop

The hip-hop community witnessed the proliferation of AIDS and crack cocaine in the inner city at alarming rates from the mid-1980s through the 1990s. Factors that contributed to the rapid spread of these two epidemics are interrelated and complex. Because the hip-hop community prides itself on

being heterosexual and often believes that AIDS only affects the gay community, such ignorance has led hip-hop heads to engage in unprotected sex.

While AIDS is not exclusive to the homosexual community, "an increasing proportion of diagnosed AIDS cases are from crack-related sex-for-sex
exchanges" (Word and Bowser 1997:68). Sadly, the black inner-city community, where drug dealers are members of local street gangs, has been devas-
tated by the crack epidemic. Crack cocaine is a growing part of the gangs'
subsistence and leads to brutal turf wars. Despite this circumstance, the Hip-
Hop Nation is adamant in its crusade to educate the public about the facts
and fictions of intracommunity epidemics.

In 1991 a few hip-hop artists joined forces with other artists to promote
AIDS awareness on the *Red, Hot, and Blue* (1991) compilation. In *The Source's*
fiftieth anniversary issue (November 1993), a quiz on hip-hop history included a reference to the first mention of AIDS in a rap song, Captain Rapp's "Bad
Times" (1983) with references ranging from gonorrhea and syphilis to doctors afraid to treat a victim of AIDS. Other songs about AIDS were cited in
this issue: Boogie Down Productions' "Jimmy" (1988) and Salt-N-Pepa's
"Let's Talk about Sex" (1990) stand out among those songs that promoted
safe sex practices by encouraging the use of a condom or "jimmy hat."

Despite these songs, segments of the Hip-Hop Nation assumed that AIDS
only affected the gay community. It was not, however, until the AIDS-relat-
ed death of Eazy-E that the hip-hop community realized the disease could
affect them as well. Eric "Eazy-E" Wright, the founder of the group N.W.A.
and Ruthless Records, had boasted about his sexual exploits with women; he
claimed to have fathered seven children with six women (Frank Williams
1995:62). His announcement to fans that he had full-blown AIDS sent shock
waves of disbelief throughout the Hip-Hop Nation. Wright died ten days later
on March 26, 1995. Following his death, I noted to the journalist Frank Williams, "'sometimes a major thing has to happen in rap music before we think
twice. Eazy's situation makes him [now] more human. People will say to
themselves, "if it can happen to a rap star, it can happen to me"'" (quoted
in Frank Williams 1995:62). Since Eazy-E's death, the hip-hop community has
continued to crusade for safe-sex practices. Sponsored by the Red Hot Organization, the CD *America Is Dying Slowly* (1996)—which features rap artists like Wu-Tang Clan, Chubb Rock, and Prince Paul, among others—is recognized as the first hip-hop compilation devoted to combating AIDS.

African Americans have been most affected by these epidemics, according to the Center for Disease Control and Prevention (CDC). African Americans represent 33 percent of patients with AIDS in the United States while

comprising only 12 percent of the population (Word and Bowser 1997:67). Additional statistics from the CDC indicate that black women comprise 58 percent of those classified with AIDS in the United States (Cohen 1999:22). By 1999, the CDC reported that "81 percent of new AIDS cases among women were reported among Hispanic and African-American women. . . . [The rate among] African-American women (49.0 per 100,000) was more than 20 times the rate among Caucasian women (2.3 per 100,000), while the rate among Hispanic women (14.9 per 100,000) was more than six times the rate among Caucasian women" (Ruiz et al. 2001:143). Increasingly, black women living in low-income areas are becoming infected with HIV and AIDS by former prison inmates. Because 33 percent of all state prisoners are African Americans, the number of infected men engaging in unprotected sex with other men is high and may increase the spread of AIDS among heterosexuals when these men are released.

The Hip-Hop Nation argues that AIDS is the result of a governmental conspiracy to eliminate African Americans and Hispanics. As one community spokesperson states, "'I think this is what threatens us the most in terms of a real issue that can devastate black Americans the way Native Americans were decimated'" (Genethia Hayes cited in Fears 1998:28).[19] The folklorist Patricia Turner, in her study *I Heard It through the Grapevine: Rumors in African American Culture* (1993), contends that such conspiracy theories comprise the corpus of contemporary African American legend and rumor narratives. Legends are defined by Turner as "traditionally grounded narratives of belief" consisting of common motifs that circulate in multiple versions and are told as if they are true or at least plausible, whereas rumors are "short, nonnarrative expression of beliefs" (1993:5). Additionally, these narrative types attest to African Americans' beliefs about the powers that be and their penchant for what Turner refers to as "corporal control" of black bodies. Some of these corporal control conspiracy narratives listed by Turner are "the collection of black bodies from Africa via slavery," "the infamous Tuskegee Study" as revisited by the HBO film *Miss Evers' Boys* (1997), the "Atlanta Child Murders,"[20] the Ku Klux Klan and Night Riders stories (Fry 1975), the "AIDS and crack cocaine alleged governmental creations rumors," and the "plotted sterility of black males via certain food products" (Turner 1993).[21] In contrast to what Turner found, I discovered that the AIDS narratives are treated by the hip-hop community as much more than rumors and legends.

In the song "America" (1996), from the compilation album *America Is Dying Slowly,* the Wu-Tang Clan presents rhymes that capture the belief of segments of the hip-hop community that AIDS was manufactured as a genocidal weapon: "AIDS was government made to get Niggaz afraid / So they won't get laid, no babies be made / and the Black population would decrease in a decade." This belief has its precedence in a written source that is widely read by hip-hoppers, as I coincidentally discovered while shopping at a major record store chain in West Los Angeles the fall of 1997. While browsing, I was assisted by a clerk who became intrigued by my assorted collection. The clerk not only informed me of the latest underground recordings but mentioned the most widely read cryptic source among contemporary hip-hoppers, *Behold a Pale Horse* (1991) by Milton William Cooper, a former U.S. Naval Intelligence Briefing Team member. In addition to Cooper's book, the historian A. Ralph Eppersons's *The New World Order* (1990) is deemed as "a must read" work by the Zulu Nation (<http://www.zulunation.com>). Both authors basically discuss what is termed "the illuminati," the basis of a one-world government called the New World Order. The illuminati, or the Illuminated Ones, are etiologicalized by Cooper as evolving from Lucifer, also known in Kemetic (Egyptian) myth as Osiris, a bright (illumined) star that the ancients believed was cast down onto the earth, denoting Lucifer's fall from heaven. The illuminati also manifest themselves in contemporary culture as the Freemasons and other derivatives that are a part of a continuum of ancient secret brotherhoods of the occult, of which many major political leaders are believed to be members. Other evidence of the illuminati, writes Cooper, can be found on the backside of the American dollar bill. These symbols, according to Epperson, are believed to have cryptic meanings that are identified with secret or Masonic societies. The Great Seal, in which the eye within the triangle symbolizes Osiris, is a longtime symbol of the occult and is a Masonic symbol; the unfinished pyramid under the eye intimates work still to be done in creating a New World Order; the eagle is linked to Osiris, and its nine tailfeathers represent the nine beings in the innermost circle of enlightenment in the "Great White Brotherhood," or the Illuminati; and the Latin words on the seal, Novus Ordo Seclorum, translate as "New World Order" (Epperson 1990:133–47). In the Goodie MOb's "Cell Therapy," from their album *Soul Food* (1995), Cee-Lo signifies on the New World Order: "the traces of the new world order / time is getting shorter if we don't get prepared / People it's gon' be a slaughter." In a similar manner, BoogieMonster's "Behold a Pale Horse," from their LP *God Soul* (1997), follow suit: "Our Symbols on the back of their dollars . . . / and spiritually they're unprepared / so we 'gon break them and slaughter in the New World Order."

What becomes most relevant about Cooper's book is his insistence that AIDS is an "infective microorganism" virus created in a laboratory "as a political/ethnic weapon" (1991:446). "It was decided BY THE ELITE that since the population must be reduced and controlled, it would be in the best interest of the human race to rid [itself] of the undesirable element of our society. Specific targeted populations included BLACKS, HISPANICS, and HOMOSEXUALS" (Cooper 1991: 213–14).

### Crack Cocaine and CIA Conspiracy Belief Narratives in Hip-Hop

In tandem with the AIDS epidemic is the growing crack cocaine problem in the hood. Medical science has correlated the rise of AIDS with the growing rate of crack cocaine addiction. According to Carl O. Word and Benjamin Bowser's research, "one can anticipate in coming years that an increasing proportion of diagnosed AIDS cases will be from crack-related sex-for-sex exchanges" (1997:68). The National Household Survey on Drug Abuse infers that crack cocaine use does not necessarily differ by race and ethnicity, rather, environmental influences increase the risk of cocaine use (Cornish and O'Brien 1996). These environmental factors include impoverished conditions where crack is easily available in epidemic proportions among low-income, mostly inner-city African Americans (Lundy et al. 1995:260).

Because the epicenters of crack cocaine remain in the ghetto zones (Davis 1992:315), the reporter Angela Bronner finds that people of color are most likely to be apprehended for its use. There is also a correlation between race and jail sentences: African Americans and Hispanics and dealers are given longer sentences for crack cocaine possession than whites who are apprehended with an equivalent amount of powdered cocaine (Bronner 1996).

In contrast to mainstream society's assumption that hip-hop artists glorify drugs such as blunts and chronic, the Hip-Hop Nation presents prevention-intervention programs such as the "Say No to Drugs" concerts. While conducting fieldwork in New York City during the summer of 1986, I attended a concert at Prospect Park in Brooklyn, where I interviewed several rap artists for the now-defunct magazine *Hip Hop Hit List* (Keyes 1986:9). During one interview, an interviewee informed me that the concert's host, a radio personality DJ, had lost his son to a drug overdose. Later, I heard the grief-stricken DJ mention this tragedy to the audience as a reminder to others about the danger of crack addiction. A primary organizer for this concert was Lumumba Carson, a rap music promoter-turned-rapper known to his fans as Professor X. Several years later Carson, the founder of the rap group X-Clan, premiered the video "Close the Crack House" on the Sony Jumbo-Tron video screen in New York's Times Square on August 16, 1993. This video was part of a rally against drugs sponsored by X-Clan's Blackwatch Movement, WBLS radio of New York City, and the Black Men's Movement against Crack.

From July through September 1994, *The Source* presented a three-part special report documenting crack's tenth anniversary. This report listed more than thirty rap songs about the destructiveness of cocaine and its derivative, crack (Bernard and Dennis 1994:56). Among these songs were Kool Moe Dee's "Crack Monster" (1987),[22] Grandmaster Melle Mel's "White Lines" (1994), MC Lyte's "I Cram 2 Understand U (Sam)" (1988), BDP's "9mm Goes Bang" (1987), Public Enemy's "Night of the Living Baseheads" (1988), Ice Cube's "A Bird in the Hand" (1991), Spice 1's "Runnin' Out Da Crackhouse" (1993), and Too $hort's "Girl (Cocaine) That's Your Life" (1993).

*The Source* also delved into the myths surrounding crack in the hood and the alleged sources of distribution. Belief narratives that circulate in the hip-hop community about the origins of crack cocaine are corroborated similarly to the AIDS conspiracy stories, by written sources, but circulated in the form of an investigative series called "Dark Alliance" by the reporter Gary Webb in the San Jose's newspaper, the *Mercury News*. In 1996, the country was flabbergasted by Webb's story that linked the Central Intelligence Agency to the Nicaraguan Contras' cocaine empires and crises in which crack is distributed by inner-city gang members to earn their subsistence. Although Webb's story was discredited because of allegations that he falsified facts to bolster his career, other sources, such as *XXL,* a nascent hip-hop magazine, and Peter Dale Scott and Jonathan Marshall's *Cocaine Politics: Drugs, Armies and the CIA in Central America* (1998), support the thesis that "the CIA and Washington policy-makers opened the door to the cocaine trade" (Scott and Marshall 1998).[23]

Crack cocaine and gang violence are perceived by some observers to be interconnected. In the foreword to *Uprising: Crips and Bloods Tell the Story of America's Youth in the Crossfire* (Jah and Shah'Keyah 1995), a book written after the Los Angeles gang truce, Ice-T charges that black-on-black crime and gang violence rank foremost among issues facing the African American community. The urban theorist Mike Davis quotes the *Los Angeles Times* (May 15, June 12, 1988; August 4, 1989) on the growth of the crack cocaine enterprise in Los Angeles: "Los Angeles street gangs now dominate the rock [crack] cocaine trade in Los Angeles and elsewhere, due in part to their steady recourse to murderous violence to enforce territorial dealing supremacy, to deter cheating and to punish rival gang members. . . . the LAPD has identified 47 cities, from Seattle to Kansas City to Baltimore, where Los Angeles street gang traffickers have appeared" (Davis 1992:312).

During an informal interview, one rap artist matter-of-factly stated that he used to operate a drug ring. What is most alarming, of course, are the means by which some youth in the hood opt to support livin large by illegal income-producing activities such as drug dealing.[24] Despite this fact, numerous rap songs that seemingly glorify drug use and gangbanging do in turn caution their audiences of the high risk of getting caught or killed. Examples of these songs are "9mm Goes Bang" by BDP (1987), "Deep Cover" (1992) by Dr. Dre and Snoop Doggy Dogg, and "Niggas Bleed" (1997) by The Notorious B.I.G. Films about gangsta life in the hood, referred to by the critic Jacquie Jones as "new jack cinema" (1991), feature rappers who—once privy to the visible manifestations of drug infestations in their communities—bring a sense of realism to their acting. Among these movies are *Colors* (1988), *Boyz 'N the Hood* (1991), *New Jack City* (1991), *Menace II Society* (1993), *Above the Rim* (1994), and *I'm Bout It* (1997). Many of the rap artists who star in these films also wrote the rap soundtracks to these movies. Although these films and sound recordings capitalize on the American entertainment industry's penchant for graphic, violent imagery, they also expose the underlying complexities of a corporate underground economy, where greed has no boundaries.

As the hip-hop community moves into the new millennium the crack cocaine problem has slowly plummeted. The Hip-Hop Nation has undoubtedly served as a conduit by which to educate their communities about intracommunity epidemics, on- and offstage. It exists as a youth arts mass movement whose ideology is conveyed through musical and political avenues. It is embedded in a community-based system called the Zulu Nation, which endeavors to provide inner-city gang members with an alternative to violence. During the formative years of hip-hop, street gangs were replaced by crews of youth who combatted each other artistically rather than violently. Artists dubbed as nation-conscious rappers reinforced the principles espoused by the Zulu Nation, which drew on Black Nationalist principles and the Nation of Islam's beliefs.

By the mid-1980s, rap music attracted the attention of music moguls who brought this inner-city sound to a wider audience. As rap's popularity climaxed during the 1990s, materialism, bicoastal turf wars, and strife in the Hip-Hop Nation peaked and perhaps contributed to the deaths of two prominent rap artists, Tupac Shakur and Christopher "The Notorious B.I.G."

Wallace. Despite violent behavior by some of its members, the Hip-Hop Nation continues to see rap music as a tool for educating its audience and addressing its community's concerns.

In an attempt to mitigate turf wars and corporate exploitation, some artists began using positive or nonviolent lyrics centering around party themes, sponsoring collaborative events for artists from different regions, and proposing to establish hip-hop schools, archives, and a union. These steps and others will lead to the realization of Bambaataa's vision of the Hip-Hop Nation as a symbol of social cohesion and group solidarity.

# Daughters of the Blues: Women, Race, and Class Representation in Rap Music Performance

7

Rap music has been often presented in the media as an urban male phenomenon. This assumption is more apparent when observing the disproportionate representation of female MCs featured in music video programs or on radio compared to that of male artists. Though the presence of female rap artists may seem rather small, particularly during rap's formative years, observers of this form began to notice the proliferation of successful rap female acts during the 1990s. As the rap music journalist Havelock Nelson notes, "While women have always been involved artistically with rap throughout the '80s; artists like [MC] Lyte, [Queen] Latifah, Roxanne Shanté, and [Monie] Love have had to struggle to reach a level of success close to that of male rappers" (1993:77). Like their male counterparts, women rap about aspects of inner-city life and their desire to be "number one"; unlike male MCs, they shed light on everyday realities from a woman's perspective. In challenging the predominance of male rappers, female rap artists have not only proven that they have lyrical skillz, but in their struggle to survive and thrive within this tradition they have created spaces from which to deliver powerful messages from black female and black feminist viewpoints.

Women of rap address issues pertinent to black working-class and ghetto culture in a manner unlike other black women artists in jazz, rhythm and blues, and contemporary pop song styles. While other black women singers deal with topics that conform to the traditional or mainstream idealization of romantic love, women in rap approach love themes and other topics from a viewpoint that is meaningful to black working-class women. Women in rap are more closely allied to the women blues singers, known as classic blues singers, of the 1920s. Similar to women blues singers, female MCs perceive rap as a site from which to contest, protest, and affirm working-class ideologies of black womanhood, notes Angela Y. Davis. "Through the blues, black women were able to autonomously work out—as audiences and performers—a working-class model of womanhood" (1998:46).

Davis concurs with the blues scholar Daphne D. Harrison, who writes that classic blues singers of the 1920s, such as Ma Rainey, Bessie Smith, and Ida Cox, were

> pivotal figures in the assertion of black women's ideas and ideals from the standpoint of the working class and the poor. It reveals their dynamic role as spokespersons and interpreters of the dreams, harsh realities, and tragicomedies of the black experience in the first three decades of this century; their role in the continuation and development of black music in America; their contributions to blues poetry and performance. Further, it expands the base of knowledge about the role of black women in the creation and development of American popular culture; illustrates their modes and means for coping successfully with gender-related discrimination and exploitation; and demonstrates an emerging model for the working woman—one who is sexually independent, self-sufficient, creative, assertive, and trend-setting. (1988:10)

The title of this chapter, "Daughters of the Blues," heralds my assertion that women rappers are part of a continuum established by early female blues singers, who, like female MCs, created a distinctive voice that reflected and celebrated the ethos of working-class black womanhood. Both women's traditions establish "a discourse that articulate[s] a cultural and political struggle over sexual relations: a struggle that is directed against the objectification of female sexuality within a patriarchal order, but also tries to reclaim women's bodies" (Carby 1986:12).

While one will find topics common to several black women's song traditions, including social commentary, political protest, and violence against women, there is a preponderance of prison and ghetto love songs among women blues and rap performers. Most of these songs illustrate the plight of being black and poor under a U.S. justice system that works in favor of the white and well-to-do. Using words uncommon in mainstream romantic pop or jazz songs, women of the blues affectionately refer to their male lovers as "Papa" or "Daddy," while women of rap refer to their male competitors or lovers as "sophisticated thugs" or "niggas." Songs about lesbian relationships are "mainstream" in the blues and rap traditions. Songs celebrating women loving women circulated in the classic blues repertory, for example, Ma Rainey's "Prove It On Me Blues." Similarly, rap music broke ground with a lesbian song by the female artist Queen Pen, who will be discussed in more detail below. Finally, the classic blues singers defied mainstream attitudes about the full-figured black woman, who was often portrayed in patriarchal-controlled media as a mammy, an asexual being. Classic blues singers not only privileged the large-framed black woman, they embraced her as a sexually desirable and sexually active being. Such attitudes about being full-figured, fly, and seductive remain a fixture in hip-hop. Thus I firmly contend that the rise of female MCs in the late twentieth century represents an ongoing musical saga of black women's issues concerning male-female relationships, female sexuality, and black women's representations from a working-class point of view.

Data used in this chapter derive from interviews with "cultural readers"— African American women performers and audience members—and from the comments of black female critics and scholars, who constitute what I refer to as an "interpretive community." In *Black Women as Cultural Readers,* the film critic and scholar Jacqueline Bobo explores the concept of "interpretive community" as a movement comprised of black female cultural producers, critics, scholars, and cultural consumers (1995:22). She writes, "as a group, the women make up what I have termed an interpretive community, which is strategically placed in relation to cultural works that either are created by black women or feature them in significant ways. Working together the women utilize representations of black women that they deem valuable, in productive and politically useful ways" (22). Because much of the criticism of work by black female independent filmmakers stems from male or white perspectives, Bobo finds it necessary to incorporate the views of black women involved in making or consuming these films to accurately assess the intent and effect of the films. Bobo's concept of the "interpretive community" is appropriate to this examination of women in rap because, like film, rap music is a form transmitted by recorded and video performances.

When MC Lyte was asked, for example, if she felt that there was a distinct female rap history, she separated women rappers into crews that reigned in three periods: the early 1980s, the mid-1980s through the early 1990s, and the late 1990s: "Sha-Rock, Sequence, to me, that's the first crew. Then you've got a second crew, which is Salt-N-Pepa, Roxanne Shanté, The Real Roxanne, me, Latifah, Monie [Love], and Yo-Yo. Then after that you got Da Brat, Foxy Brown, Lil' Kim, Heather B" (MC Lyte interview).[1]

In the female rap tradition, four distinct categories of women rappers emerge: "Queen Mother," "Fly Girl," "Sista with Attitude," and "The Lesbian." Black female rappers can shift between these categories, however, or belong to more than one simultaneously. Each category mirrors certain images, voices, and lifestyles of African American women in contemporary urban society.

Queried about specific categories, rap music performers and female audience members frequently used the buzz words "fly" and "attitude" (as in "girlfriend got attitude"), leading me to more clearly discern the parameters of these categories. I revised category of "Black Diva" in early interviews to "Queen Mother" after one female observer convincingly said "diva" denoted a posture of arrogance and pretentiousness as opposed to that of a regal and self-assured woman, qualities that she identified with the Queen Latifah types (Ronda R. Penrice, personal communication, 1995). Let us now examine these four categories or images of black women that female MCs and the interpretive community in general consider representative of and specific to African American female identity in contemporary urban culture.

## Queen Mother

The Queen Mother category comprises female rappers who view themselves as African-centered icons, which is often evoked by their dress. The terms they use to describe themselves—"Asiatic Black Women," "Nubian Queens," "intelligent black women," or "sistas droppin' knowledge to the people"—suggest their self-constructed identity and intellectual prowess. The Queen Mother is associated with traditional African court culture. For instance, in the sixteenth-century Benin kingdom of southeastern Nigeria, she was the mother of a reigning king. Because of her maternal connection to the king, she received certain rights and privileges, including control over districts and a voice in the national affairs of the state. During her son's reign, a commemorative head made of brass, with a facial expression capturing her reposed manner, was sculpted in her honor and adorned with a beaded choker, headdress, and crown.[2]

It is certainly possible that female rap artists know of the historical significance of African queens. Women in this category adorn their bodies with royal or Kente cloth strips, African headdresses, goddess braid styles, and ankh-stylized jewelry. Their rhymes embrace black female empowerment and spirituality, making clear their self-identification as African, woman, warrior, priestess, and queen. Queen Mothers demand respect not only for their people but for black women by men. Among those women distinguished by the interpretive community as Queen Mothers are Queen Kenya, Queen Latifah, Sister Souljah, Nefertiti, Queen Mother Rage, Isis, and Yo-Yo.

Queen Kenya, a member of hip-hop's Zulu Nation, was the first female MC to use "Queen" as a stage name, but the woman of rap who became the first solo female MC to commercially record under the name "Queen" is Dana "Queen Latifah" Owens. Queen Latifah's initial singles, "Princess of the Posse" and "Wrath of My Madness" (1988), followed by her debut album *All Hail the Queen* (1989), established her regal identity. Her songs include lyrics such as, "you try to be down, / you can't take my crown from me" and "I'm on the scene, / I'm the Queen of Royal Badness." Latifah, whose Arabic name means "feminine, delicate, and kind," explains that her cousin, who is a Muslim, gave her the name Latifah when she was eight. "Well in rap, I didn't want to be MC Latifah. It didn't sound right. I didn't want to come out like old models. So Queen just popped into my head one day, and I was like 'me, Queen Latifah.' It felt good saying it, and I felt like a queen. And you know, I am a queen. And every black woman is a queen" (Queen Latifah interview).

Latifah's maternal demeanor, posture, and full figure contribute to the perception of her as a Queen Mother. Although she acknowledges that others perceive her as motherly, she tries to distance herself from this ideal: "'I wish I wasn't seen as a mother, though. I don't really care for that. Just because I take a mature stance on certain things, it gives me a motherly feel . . . maybe because I am full-figured. I am mature, but I'm twenty-one'" (quoted in Green 1991:33).

The ambiguity of Latifah's motherly image follows what the feminist scholars Joan Radner and Susan Lanser identify as a form of coding in women's folk culture called *distraction:* a device used to "drown out or draw attention away from the subversive power of a feminist message" (1993:15). Using distraction allows the artists to deliver strong pro-woman, pro-black messages and have a better chance of being heard. Queen Latifah finds that her stature and grounded perspective cause fans to view her as a person to revere or, at times, fear. However, Latifah attempts to mute her motherly image offstage, indicating to fans that she remains modest, down-to-earth, and an ordinary person in spite of her onstage "Queen of Royal Badness" persona.

In *Black Feminist Thought,* the sociologist Patricia Hill Collins states that in the African American community, some women are viewed as "othermothers": "Black women's involvement in fostering African-American community development forms the basis for community-based power. This is the

Queen Latifah, early 1990s. (Photo by Al Pereira/Michael Ochs Archives)

type of 'strong Black woman' they see around them in traditional African-American communities. Community othermothers work on behalf of the Black community by expressing ethics of caring and personal accountability which embrace conceptions of transformation and mutuality. . . . community othermothers become identified as power figures through furthering the community's well-being" (1990:132).

Queen Latifah's othermother posture is reflected most vividly through her lyrics, which, at times, address political and economic issues facing black women and the black community as a whole. In Latifah's song "The Evil That Men Do" (1989) from *All Hail the Queen,* she "isolates several of the difficulties commonly experienced by young black women [on welfare]" (Forman 1994:44) and depicts how the powers that be are apathetic to black women who are trying to beat the odds:

Here is a message for my sisters and brothers
here are some things I wanna cover.

A woman strives for a better life
but who the hell cares because she's living on welfare?
The government can't come up with a decent housing plan
so she's in no-man's-land.
It's a sucker who tells you you're equal. . . .
Someone's livin' the good life tax-free
'cause some poor girl can't be livin' crack free
and that's just part of the message
I thought I had to send you about the evil that men do.

In "How Do I Love Thee," on Latifah's sophomore LP, *Nature of a Sista* (1991), she uses a seductive vocal style to suggest a young woman in love. The video shows Latifah and a man, as well as other heterosexual couples, embracing one another. The presentation of Latifah in a sexual role was problematic for some of her audience, according to the hip-hop feminist critic Joan Morgan. Morgan opined that some of Latifah's fans were restricted by Latifah's maternal persona, an image associated with nurturing but devoid of sexuality.[3] She contends that "How Do I Love Thee" not only established Latifah's sexuality but also expressed a controlled, nonpromiscuous black female sexuality that defied the white patriarchal myth of the "black Jezebel" or whore (Collins 1990:77). Thus, Latifah's "How Do I Love Thee" asserts that not only can "maternal figures" be sensuous, they can comfortably enjoy eroticism on their own terms.

Latifah's role as Queen Mother of rap was etched in stone with her platinum single "Ladies First" (1989), the first political commentary rap song by a female artist. The lyrics of "Ladies First" defy stereotypes about female MCs' inability to create rhymes:

I break into a lyrical freestyle
Grab the mike, look at the crowd and see smiles
'Cause they see a woman standing up on her own two [feet]
Sloppy slouching is something I won't do.
Some think that we [women] can't flow
Stereotypes they got to go.
I'm gonna mess around and flip the scene into reverse,
with a little touch of ladies first.

The video version is more explicitly political, containing live footage of South Africa's anti-apartheid riots overlaid with photographic stills of the black heroines Harriet Tubman, Frances Ellen Watkins Harper, Sojourner Truth,

Angela Davis, Winnie Mandela, and Rosa Parks.[4] As Queen Mother, Latifah scolds the misinformed and misogynistic and educates her listeners about the diverse and powerful matriarchs who demand respect.

Since Queen Latifah's success, she has sought out other avenues within the entertainment industry. She was an original member of the New Jersey–based MC crew known as Flavor Unit, produced by DJ Mark the 45 King. After the release of her first LP, she transformed Flavor Unit into an artist management enterprise and a record company in the early 1990s. Queen Latifah later appeared as a magazine mogul named Khadijah in the sitcom "Living Single." She has also appeared in several films alongside leading Hollywood actors. In the film *Set It Off* she plays one of the lead women gangstas with Kimberly Elise, Vivica A. Fox, and Jada Pinkett Smith. She also plays a private nurse in the thriller *The Bone Collector,* which stars Denzel Washington. Additionally, Queen Latifah began hosting her own TV talk show in September 1999. Her autobiography, *Ladies First: Revelations of a Strong Woman* (1999), became a bestseller.

Queen Latifah opened the door for other Afrocentric female MCs such as Sister Souljah. A former associate of the Black Nationalist rap group Public Enemy, Souljah launched her first LP in 1992. *360 Degrees of Power* featured the rap single "The Final Solution: Slavery's Back in Effect," in which "Souljah imagines a police state where blacks fight the reinstitution of slavery" (Leland 1992:48). With her candid yet quasi-preachy style of delivery, she earned the title "raptivist" from her followers. Souljah's fame grew after her speech at Reverend Jesse Jackson's Rainbow Coalition Leadership Summit in 1992, where she chided African Americans who murder one another for no apparent reason by figuratively suggesting, "'why not take a week and kill white people?'" (quoted in Leland 1992:48). As a consequence, Souljah was ridiculed as a propagator of hate by presidential candidate Bill Clinton. In the wake of the controversy, her record sales plummeted dramatically while her "raptivist" messages skyrocketed through her appearances on talk shows like "Donahue" and speeches on the university lecture circuit. While Sister Souljah advocates racial, social, and economic parity, she also looks within the community to relationships between black men and women in her lyrics and semiautobiographical book *No Disrespect* (1994:xiv). Sister Souljah also published *The Coldest Winter Ever: A Novel* (1999), which addresses romantic themes from a black working-class woman's perspective.

Nefertiti, Isis,[5] and Queen Mother Rage depict the Queen Mother image via their names and attire. Lauryn Hill earns the title through her lyrics and her community outreach programs like the Refugee Project. Yo-Yo, who is also regarded by the interpretive community as a Queen Mother, uses her lyrics to promote her political ideology of black feminism and female respectability, as advanced by her organization, the Intelligent Black Women's Coalition (IBWC), which she discusses on her debut CD, *Make Way for the Motherlode* (1991). But Yo-Yo's image—long blonde braids, tight-fitting shorts worn by Jamaican dancehall women performers called "batty riders," and her gyrating hips also position her in the next category, "Fly Girl."

### Fly Girl

*Fly* describes someone in chic clothing and fashionable hairstyles, jewelry, and cosmetics, a style that grew out of the black action films (pejoratively called blaxploitation films) of the late 1960s through the mid-1970s. These films include *Shaft* (1971), *Superfly* (1972), *The Mack* (1973), and *Foxy Brown* (1974), a film that inspired one rapper to adopt the movie's title as her moniker. The fly personae in these films influenced a wave of black contemporary youth who resurrected flyness and its continuum in hip-hip culture.

During the early 1980s, women rappers, including Sha Rock of Funky Four Plus One, the group Sequence, and the soloist Lady B, dressed in a way that was considered by their audiences to be fly. They wore miniskirts, sequined fabric, high-heeled shoes, and prominent make-up. By 1985 the commercial recording of "A Fly Girl" by the male rap group Boogie Boys and an answer rap during the same year, "A Fly Guy," by the female rapper Pebblee-Poo, launched a public dialogue of "flyness" in the hip-hop community. In "A Fly Girl," the Boogie Boys describe a fly girl as a woman who wants you to see her name and "her game" and who wears tight jeans or leather miniskirts and abundant gold jewelry and make-up. She has voluptuous curves, but contrary to other "mainstream" images of sexy, acquiescent women, the fly girl speaks what is on her mind.

By the mid-1980s, many female MCs began contesting the fly girl image because they wanted their audiences to focus more on their rapping than on their dress. Despite this changing trend, the female rap trio Salt-N-Pepa canonized the ultimate fly girl posture of rap by donning short, tight-fitting outfits, leather clothing, ripped jeans or punk clothing, glittering gold jewelry (i.e. earrings and necklaces), long sculpted nails, prominent make-up, and hairstyles ranging from braids to wraps to waves in ever-changing hair colors.

Rap's fly girl image is political because it calls attention to aspects of black women's bodies that are considered undesirable by mainstream American standards of beauty (Roberts 1998). Through their performances, Salt-N-Pepa are flippin da script (or deconstructing dominant ideology) by wearing clothes that accent their full breasts, rounded buttocks, and ample thighs, considered beauty markers of black women by black culture but ridiculed or caricatured by the mainstream (Roberts 1998).[6] Moreover, they portray the fly girl as a party-goer, an independent woman, and as an erotic subject rather than an objectified object.

Female rappers' reclamation of the fly resonates with the late Audre Lorde's theory of the erotic as power (Davis 1998:172). In Lorde's seminal essay "Uses of the Erotic" (1984), she reveals the transformative power of the erotic in black women's culture: "Our erotic knowledge empowers us, becomes a lens through which we scrutinize all aspects of our existence, forcing us to evaluate those aspects honestly in terms of their meaning within our lives" (1984:57). The cultural critic and scholar bell hooks claims that black women's erotic consciousness is textualized around issues of body es-

Salt-N-Pepa, left to right: Spinderella, Salt, and Pepa, mid-1980s. (Courtesy of Michael Ochs Archives)

teem. "Erotic pleasure requires of us engagement with the realm of the senses
. . . the capacity to be in touch with sensual reality; to accept and love [our]
bodies; to work toward working self-recovery issues around body esteem;
[and] to be empowered by a healing eroticism" (1993:116, 121–22, 124).

Black fly girls express a growing awareness of their erotic selves by sculpting their own personas and, as the folklorist Elaine J. Lawless (1998) puts it,
"writing their own bodies." For example, Salt-N-Pepa describe themselves
as "'women [who have] worked hard to keep our bodies in shape; we're
proud to show them off. . . . We're not ashamed of our sexuality; for we're
Salt-N-Pepa—sexier and more in control'" (quoted in Rogers 1994:31).

Another aspect of the fly girl persona is independence. Salt notes that
"'the image we project reflects the real independent woman of the '90s'"
(quoted in Chyll 1994:20). But for many women of rap, achieving a sense of
independence in an entrepreneurial sense has not been easy. For instance, it
is common knowledge in the rap community that during Salt-N-Pepa's early
years, their lyrics and hit songs ("I'll Take Your Man," "Push It," "Tramp,"
and "Shake Your Thang") were written mainly by their manager/producer
Hurby "Luv Bug" Azor. For the *Black's Magic* (1990) CD, Salt (Cheryl James)
ventured into writing and producing with the single "Expression," which
went platinum. *Black's Magic* also contained Salt-N-Pepa's "Let's Talk about
Sex" (written by Azor), which Salt rewrote for a public service announcement
song and video, "Let's Talk about AIDS," in 1992.

On Salt-N-Pepa's fourth LP, *Very Necessary* (1993), the group wrote and
produced most of the selections. The celebratory songs "Shoop" and "Whatta Man" from that album deserve note.[7] In the video versions of both songs,
the three women eyeball desirable men. The "Shoop" video presents the trio
as female subjects carefully scrutinizing men they desire, from business types
to ruffnecks (a fly guy associated with urban street culture), thus turning
tables on the male rappers; in it ladies "'see a bunch of bare-chested, tight-
bunned brothers acting like sex *objects,* servicing it up to us in our videos,'"
says Salt (quoted in Rogers 1994:31). In the "Whatta Man" video, Salt-N-Pepa
praise their significant others in the areas of friendship, romance, and
parenting as the female rhythm and blues group En Vogue joins them in
singing the chorus, "Whatta man, whatta man, whatta man, whatta mighty
good man."

Other women whom the interpretive community categorizes as fly are
Left Eye and Yo-Yo. Left Eye is the rapper of the hip-hop/rhythm and blues
hybrid group TLC (*T-*Boz, Left Eye, and Chili). TLC's baggy style of dress runs
counter to the revealing apparel of hip-hop's typical fly girl image, provid-

ing role models they hope will inspire their full-figured audience to do the same. TLC's T-Boz said, "'We like to wear a lot of baggy stuff because for one, it's comfortable, and two, many of our fans don't have the so-called perfect figure; we don't want them to feel like they can't wear what we're wearing'" (quoted in Horner 1993:16). Throughout the 1990s, TLC remained steadfast with the message to women of all sizes regarding mental and physical wellness and body esteem, as underscored in both music and video performances of the single "Unpretty" (1999).

Like Salt-N-Pepa, TLC has made delivering the "safe sex" message a priority. While both groups do so through lyrics, TLC underscores it visually through wearing certain accoutrements. Left Eye wears a condom in place of an eyeglass lens, while other members of the group attach colored condom packages to their clothes. TLC's warning about unprotected sex, emphasized by the condoms they wear, is conveyed powerfully in their award-winning "Waterfalls" from their second LP, *CrazySexyCool* (1994). The message is amplified in the video: a man's decision to follow his partner's wish not to use a condom leads to deadly consequences. Days after this encounter, he notices a lesion on his face, which suggests that he has contacted the virus that causes AIDS. TLC's

TLC, left to right: Chili, Left Eye, and T-Boz, 1994. (Photo by Al Pereira/Michael Ochs Archives)

espousal of fly, sexually independent living in their lyrics and image is firmly entwined with a message of sexual responsibility.

In "His Story," from their debut album, TLC looks beyond the supposedly superficial woman depicted by the fly image to address the real threat of violence that black women face. The unsolved case of Tawana Brawley—who was allegedly raped by white officers of the New York Police Department—becomes emblematic of the murkier intersections of race and gender politics. Race complicates the "virtue question" put to many women who have dared to speak up after being raped. In an interview, Left Eye said, "'It's already hard to be black, but we [black women] got two strikes against us.'" T-Boz added, "'We got the worse end of the stick, being black and female'" (quoted in Mayo 1992:49). While TLC's image is fly, their lyrics are serious, delving into complex social issues facing African American women in contemporary society.

Like TLC, Yo-Yo also delivers a serious message about black womanhood that earns her a place among the Queen Mothers, but her gyrating hips, stylish golden-blonde braids, tight-fitting short outfits, and pronounced makeup also categorize her as fly.[8] Yo-Yo writes about independent, empowered black women, championing African American sisterhood in "The I.B.W.C. National Anthem" and "Sisterland" from *Make Way for the Motherlode* (1991). She takes on sexuality in "You Can't Play with My Yo-Yo" and "Put a Lid on It," which, as suggested by their titles, explore sexual control and responsibility.

In 1996 Yo-Yo moved beyond the shadow of her mentor Ice Cube with her fourth CD *Total Control,* for which she served as executive producer. Following this success, Yo-Yo began a column called "Yo, Yo-Yo" in the hip-hop magazine *Vibe,* in which she addresses questions about heterosexual relationships and interpersonal growth as the representative of the IBWC.

In the late 1990s, the female MC, songwriter, and producer, Missy "Misdemeanor" Elliott joined the fly girl ranks. Mesmerizing viewers with her debut album *Supa Dupa Fly* (1997) and her single "The Rain," which was nominated for three MTV video awards, Elliott has found success with her musical partner Tim "Timbaland" Mosley. Some critics, like Hilton Als, have even called the duo a "'latter-day Ashford and Simpson'" (quoted in Weingarten 1998a:68). In addition to the reverence her creative skills engender, her fans also admire her finger-wave hairstyle, known to some as "Missy waves," and her ability to carry off the latest hip-hop fashions on her full-figured frame. Demonstrating the more typical image of a fly girl as being focused on clothes and looks, in a *Los Angeles Times* cover story Elliott revealed the source of her fashion savvy to fans: "'When I was a kid, I wanted to be like my mother. She's a very classy lady who always wore great clothes and loved

Missy "Misdemeanor" Elliott (right) and her musical partner, Timbaland, perform-ing at 92.3 The Beat Summer Jam at Irvine Meadows Amphitheatre, 1998. (Photo by Alisa Childs)

to wear nice shoes'" (quoted in Weingarten 1998a:68). Elliott has occasion-ally appeared in television advertisements for the youth fashion store The Gap and as a spokesperson for Iman's lipstick line. She succeeds as a full-figured woman, breaking new ground in the "fly arena" that had been off-limits to all but the most slender or "correctly" proportioned women. In staking her claim to rap music's fly girl category, Elliott further reclaims sexuality and eros as healing power for all black women, regardless of size. With her single "She's a Bitch" from her sophomore LP *Da Real World* (1999), Elliott appends another image to her fly girl posture. With her face and hairstyle resembling that of the singer-actress-model Grace Jones—the femme fatale of disco— Elliott's usage of "bitch" makes a declaration about being a mover and shaker, on- and offstage, in rap's male-dominated arena, and thus she shares much in common with the artists of the next category, "Sista with Attitude."

### Sista with Attitude

According to Geneva Smitherman, a scholar of Black English, "'tude, a di-minutive form of attitude, can be defined as an aggressive, arrogant, defiant,

I-know-I'm-BAD pose or air about oneself; or an oppositional or negative outlook or disposition" (1994:228). I group the prototypes of this category according to 'tude: Roxanne Shanté, Bytches with Problems (BWP), and Da Brat are known for their frankness; MC Lyte exudes a hardcore/no-nonsense approach; Boss is recognized for her gangsta bitch posture; and Eve and Mia X are first ladies with 'tude who work in the all-male crews such as Ruff Ryders and No Limit Soldiers, respectively.

In general, Sistas with Attitude comprise female MCs who value attitude as a means of empowerment and present themselves accordingly. Many of these sistas have reclaimed the word "bitch," viewing it as positive rather than negative and using the title to entertain or provide cathartic release. Other women in the interpretive community are troubled by that view. These women refused to be labeled a "bitch" because such appellations merely mar the images of young African American females (Hill 1994; "Female Rappers" 1991). Those who reclaim the term counter with the opinion that "it's not what you're called but what you answer to" (MC Lyte 1993). Some women of rap take a middle road, concurring that "bitch" can be problematic, depending on who uses the term, how it is employed, and to whom one refers. Queen Latifah told me, "I don't really mind the term. I play around with it. I use it with my homegirls like, 'Bitch are you crazy? Bitch is a fierce girl.' Or 'That bitch is so crazy, girl.' Now, that is not harmful. But 'This stupid bitch just came down here talking . . .,' now that is meant in a harmful way. So it's the meaning behind the word that to me decides whether I should turn it off or listen to it" (Queen Latifah interview).

As an "aggressive woman who challenges male authority" (Ronda R. Penrice, personal communication, 1995), the Sista with Attitude revises the standard definition of "bitch" to mean an aggressive or assertive female who subverts patriarchal rule. Lyndah of BWP explains, "We use 'Bytches' [to mean] a strong, positive, aggressive woman who goes after what she wants. We take that on today and use it in a positive sense" ("Female Rappers" 1991). In a similar manner, Trina of the otherwise male crew Slip-N-Slide All-Stars, signifies on the term in her debut LP's title, *Da Baddest B\*\*\*H* (2000).

Another characteristic of this category is the manner in which these sistas refer to their male competitors or suitors as "motherfuckas," "niggas," or "thug niggas." Because the element of signifying is aesthetically appealing in this style of rap, these terms may have both negative and positive meanings, depending on the context.

Roxanne Shanté is a prototype of the Sista with Attitude category. Shanté launched her rappin career at age fourteen with a female answer to UTFO/

Full Force's "Roxanne, Roxanne" in 1984. The single, "Roxanne's Revenge," produced by DJ Marley Marl of Cold Chillin'/Warner Brothers, unleashed Shanté's attitude and foretold her future as a powerful sista. She grabbed her audience's attention by dissin UTFO members. Describing the UTFO member Kangol Kid as not really cute and not knowing how to operate sexually, Shanté garnered the title "The Millie Jackson of Rap" and maintained her bitch image with the follow-up LPs *Bad Sister* (1989) and *Bitch Is Back* (1992).[9] Shanté's "Big Mama," from *Bitch Is Back,* generated controversy because instead of dissin unfaithful male lovers—the standard fare of female rappers—Shanté dared to dis female rappers. She claims that she gave birth to most female MCs and that they, "all bitches," copied her style, "the capital S-H-A-N-T-E." The song "Big Mama" explicitly ridicules prominent female rappers' rhyming skills, hurling insults at Queen Latifah, Monie Love, MC Lyte, Isis, Yo-Yo, and Salt-N-Pepa. MC Lyte responded to Shanté with "Steady F—king" (from *Ain't No Other* [1993]). In this song, Lyte signifies on the male rapper KRS-One's "The Bridge is Over" (1987), which used the words "Steady Fucking" to label Shanté as sexually promiscuous. Shanté's estrangement from female rappers as a result of "Big Mama" has not stopped her from continuing to praise herself as a "bitch." Other sistas with a bitch attitude include BWP, Conscious Daughters, and the solo rapper Boss, popularly known as the "gangsta bitch."

The male rapper Apache introduced this persona in a recording called "Gangsta Bitch" (1993). In this song, the strapped gangsta bitch packs a 9mm gun, drinks forty-ounce beers, and participates in stick-ups with her man. Although rap's first recognized female gangsta was Antoinette, Boss advanced the notion via her dress and use of expletives. Although many women of rap choose the image they feel is most aligned to their real feelings and values offstage, Boss is described by critics to be rather amiable in real life. Brought up primarily in the Midwest, she attended a Catholic college preparatory school in Detroit. On stage, Boss exchanges her middle-class origins and "the straight-up nice girl" image (Pulley 1994:A1) for that of a street gangsta. To perfect this image, she spent months being part of the street scene in Los Angeles and wearing gangsta-like attire. Boss maintains that her choice "to be real" (acquiescing to a street image) is a savvy business decision: "'I know what I'm doing, and I know how to make it in this [rap] business'" (quoted in Pulley 1994:A16).

The female rapper MC Lyte makes only moderate use of expletives and does not directly refer to herself as a "bitch" in her rap songs. Lyte's hardcore stage attitude—tough and aggressive—is intensified through the use of

Roxanne Shanté, late 1980s.
(Courtesy of Michael Ochs
Archives)

expletives but mostly through boisterous speech.[10] Her criticisms of men who
play women for fools in the game of love are more subtle, with the predict-
able defeat of the male. This style is apparent in "Paper Thin," from *Lyte as
a Rock* (1988), and "Lil' Paul" from *Ain't No Other* (1993). In "Paper Thin,"
Lyte addresses a fictitious boyfriend named Sam, who flirts with other women
behind Lyte's back. Catching him in the act on the subway train (seen in the
video version), Lyte precedes to tell Sam that she is aware of his cheating,
delivering her message with punch but without the malice characteristics of
other Sistas with Attitude:

when you say you love me, it doesn't matter.
It goes into my head as just chit chatter . . .
to look into my eyes to see what I am thinking,
the dream is over, your yacht is sinking.
I treat all of you like I treat all of them.
What you say to me is still paper thin. Word!

Regardless of the topic, MC Lyte flaunts her rhyming skill in a quasi-raspy vocal timbre, which she characterizes as "quick, wicked, and buckwild" (from "Ain't No Other" [1993]). The audacity, contempt, and courage with which these Sistas with Attitude claim the microphone undoubtedly paved the way for their contemporaries, who have taken the attitude to newer, more lucrative heights. Three artists worth mentioning here are Da Brat of Chicago, Mia X of New Orleans, and Eve of Philadelphia. Da Brat is acknowledged as the first female solo rap artist to achieve platinum sales with her debut album *Funkdafied* (1994). Introduced to the Atlanta-based producer Jermaine Dupri by the rap duo Kris Kross, Da Brat has the essential traits of a Sista with Attitude. The hip-hop writer Tracii McGregor describes her as a rapper with a "foul mouth, an admitted tom-boy, [who] cusses like there's no tomorrow [but] has made that 'tude work for her" (1996:100).

The Sista with Attitude category includes Mia-X and Eve, first ladies of their respective male crews. Echoing Da Brat's style is Mia X of No Limit Records, whose album *Unlady Like* (1997) garnered more than half a million dollars in sales. In an interview with Thembisa S. Mshaka, Mia X describes herself as "'hard-core, sensitive, and witty'" (quoted in Mshaka 1999:107). Unlike the other Sistas with Attitude, Mia X profiles her full-figure in fly style like Missy Elliott, but her gangsta lyrics—peppered with social commentary about southern ghetto life—temper the superficial femininity.

Eve emerged on the rap scene with the crew Ruff Ryders, led by DMX. Appearing fly with animal paw prints tattooed on her chest, "bleached-blond hair, model good looks, and rugged sound," her self-titled LP *Eve* (1999) sold more than a million copies ("Hottest Females" 2000:58). Top-selling singles from Eve's debut LP include "Love Is Blind," a domestic-violence rap featuring the vocals of Faith, and the single "Gotta Man," which sold over a million copies. Strikingly, "Gotta Man" resonates with Da Brat's "Ghetto Love" (featuring the singer T-Boz of TLC), from her second LP *Anuthatantrum* (1996). Both songs narrate the love and devotion of a woman in love with a very rowdy man. Da Brat and Eve do not present themselves as gangsta bitches; instead they view themselves as loyal, faithful, and devoted women who remain steadfast while their men do jail time. In "Ghetto Love," Da Brat boasts about her drug-dealer lover who showers her with a lavish lifestyle, whereas in "Gotta Man," Eve recalls the times when her incarcerated man draws hearts with her name on the jail cell wall. In the video version of "Gotta Man," Eve's devotion to and support of her man is seen when she pawns her jewelry to post bail for him. Eventually, she picks him up upon his day of release, and he shows his appreciation with a rose and dinner. Eve and Da Brat affectionately refer to their male lovers as "sophisticated thug" and "motherfuckin nigga." While these songs appear to romanticize love with a "sophisticated thug," they contain a deeper message. Both songs capture the ongoing plight of some black males in the hood who, disillusioned with constant unemployment, resort to "underground" means of making a living. Furthermore, these songs reflect the devotion and adoration of some black working-class women for their men as well as the rappers' repudiation of the white patriarchal system's constant lockdown of black men and the poor.

In the late 1990s, the Sista with Attitude category was augmented with the rappers Lil' Kim and Foxy Brown, who conflate fly and hardcore attitudes in erotic lyrics and video performances, thus falling into both the Fly Girl and Sista with Attitude categories. In doing so, they are designated by some as the "'Thelma and Louise of rap'" (Brown quoted in Gonzales 1997:62) and the "bad girls of hip-hop." Foxy Brown, whose name is derived from Pam Grier's 1974 screen character, emulates the powerful and desirable yet dangerous woman: "'I think it's every girl's dream to be fly'" (Brown quoted in Gonzales 1997: 63). While Kim's debut album, *Hard Core* (1996), and Brown's *Ill Na Na* (1997) have reached platinum status, some members of the interpretive community criticize them for being "highly materialistic, violent, lewd" (Morgan 1997:77), an image exacerbated by their affiliation with male gangsta-rap style crews: Lil' Kim is associated with Junior M.A.F.I.A.; Foxy Brown is connected with The Firm. Since their debut works, Foxy Brown and Lil' Kim have released the follow-up LPs *Chyna Doll* (1998) and *Notorious K.I.M.* (2000), Kim's play on her mentor's name, Notorious B.I.G. Lil' Kim has recast herself as a daring fashion setter. At the 1999 MTV Music Awards, she generated controversy by wearing a jumpsuit that exposed her left breast, whose nipple was covered with an appliqué. She posed nude, except for boots and a hat, for a promo poster for her second album, and she characteristically dons blond wigs and blue contact lenses. Lil' Kim has also modeled clothing for top fashion designers like Versace and graced the cover of noted trade magazines including *Essence,* a magazine celebrating black women's issues and culture. Akissi Britton, a critic and research editor for *Essence,* charges that Kim is not making a fashion statement but is instead caught up in a world of make-believe, movie stardom, superficiality—sex, money, and power—the antithesis of female hip-hop figures like Queen Latifah and Sister Souljah. Britton further scolds Lil' Kim for "professing in her lyrics that the ultimate way to 'get yours' is to be a supreme bitch and make men pay for a taste" (2000:115). To some, Lil' Kim has undoubtedly become the epitome of rap's "bad girl."

The bad girl image parallels the "badman" character (e.g. John Hardy, Dolemite, and Stackolee) that is peculiar to the African American oral narrative in the toast, a long poetic narrative form that predates rap.[11] In these narratives, black badmen boast about their sexual exploits with women, wild drinking binges, and narrow brushes with "the law," symbolic of "white power" (Roberts 1989:196). The "empowered female" rendering of "the badman" includes those sistas who brag about partying and smoking blunts (marijuana) with their men; seducing, repressing, and sexually emasculat-

Lil' Kim receives a Lady of Soul Award at the 1997 Soul Train Awards, Los Angeles. (Photo by Alisa Childs)

ing male characters; or dissin their would-be competitors (male and female)—all through figurative speech.[12]

Some female observers I queried felt that these Sistas with Attitude merely
exist on the periphery of rap and are seen as just "shootin' off at the mouth."
Some black female viewers viewed these sistas as misusing sex and feminism
and devaluing black men. In an *Essence* magazine article, the hip-hop feminist Joan Morgan (1997) states that the new "bad girls of rap" may not have
career longevity because "feminism is not simply about being able to do what
the boys do—get high, talk endlessly about their wee-wees and what have you.
At the end of the day, it's the power women attain by making choices that
increases their range of possibilities" (1997:132).[13] Morgan argues that black
women's power—on- and offstage—is sustained by "those sisters who se-
lectively ration their erotic power" (1997:133).

Despite the controversies, Sistas with Attitude have acquired respect from
their peers for their mastery of figurative language and rhyme. They simply
refuse to be second best.

### The Lesbian

While representatives of the Queen Mother, Fly Girl, and Sista with Attitude
categories came into prominence during the mid- to late 1980s, The Lesbian
category emerged from the closet during the late 1990s. Not only does the
female heterosexual audience identify this category as "The Lesbian," but the
artist who has given recognition to this division is among the first to rap about
and address the lesbian lifestyle from a black woman's perspective. Though
other black rap artists rumored to be gay or lesbian have chosen to remain
closeted in a scene described as "'notoriously homophobic'" (Dyson quoted in Jamison 1998:AR34), Queen Pen's "Girlfriend" (1997) from her debut
album *My Melody* represents a "breakthrough for queer culture" (Walters
1998:60).[14]

Although Queen Pen is recognized by her audience as the first female MC
to openly discuss lesbian culture, Laura Jamison writes that ironically Queen
Pen is "somewhat coy about her sexuality in personal interviews" (Jamison
1998:AR34).[15] "Girlfriend" signifies or indirectly plays on black lesbian culture
with Me'Shell NdegéOcello's "If That's Your Boyfriend (He Wasn't Last
Night)." NdegéOcello, who is openly lesbian, appears on "Girlfriend," performing on vocals and bass guitar.[16] In "Girlfriend," Queen Pen positions
herself as the suitor in a lesbian relationship. While this song is a "breakthrough

Queen Pen, 2001. (Used by Permission of Motown Records, a division of UMG Recordings Inc.)

for queer culture," there remain other issues that plague black artists' willingness to openly address gay and lesbian culture in their performances.

Black lesbian culture and identity have been often problematized by issues of race and role-play, according to Lisa M. Walker (1993) and Ekua Omosupe (1991). Drawing upon the critical works of Audre Lorde (1982, 1984), Omosupe notes that lesbian identity, similar to feminism, represents white lesbian culture or white women to the exclusion of women of color. Black lesbians are at times forced to live and struggle against white male patriarchal culture on the one side and white lesbian culture, racism, and general homophobia on the other (Omosupe 1991:105). Corroborating the issue of race privilege raised by the black lesbian community, Queen Pen contends that certain licenses are afforded to openly lesbian white performers, such as Ellen DeGeneres and k. d. lang, who do not have to pay as high a price for their candidness as lesbians of color: "'But you know, Ellen [DeGeneres] can talk about any ol' thing and it's all right. With everybody, it's all right. With "Girlfriend," I'm getting all kinds of questions'" (quoted in Duvernay 1998:88).[17] She continues: "'This song is buggin' everyone out right now. [If] you got Ellen, you got k. d. [lang], why shouldn't urban lesbians go to a girl club and hear their own thing?'" (quoted in Jamison 1998:AR34).

Another aspect of Queen Pen's performance is her play on image, which suggests "role play," an issue crucial to black lesbian culture. Walker asserts that "role-play among black lesbians involves a resistance to the homophobic stereotype . . . lesbian as 'bulldagger,' a pejorative term within (and outside) the black community used to signal the lesbian as a woman who wants to be a man" (1993:886). On her first album cover, Queen Pen exudes a "femme" image through prominent make-up, fly clothing, lipstick, chic hairstyles, and stylish dress. However, in performance, as observed in Blackstreet's video for "No Diggity" (1996), Queen Pen "drowns out" her femme album cover image by appropriating a b-boy hand gesture and a bobbing walk commonly associated with male hip-hop culture. Regardless of issues concerning race privilege and role-play, Queen Pen concludes that "'two or three years from now, people will say I was the first female to bring the lesbian life to light [in an open way] on wax. It's reality. What's the problem?'" (quoted in Jamison 1998:AR34).

▥▨

Women are achieving major strides in rap music by continuing to chisel away at stereotypes about females as artists in a male-dominated tradition and by (re)defining women's culture and identity from a black feminist perspective. Although rap continues to be predominantly male, female MCs move beyond the shadows of male rappers in diverse ways. Some have become exclusively known for their lyrical skillz, while others have used a unique blend of musical styles or a combination of singer-rapper acts, as is apparent with Grammy winners such as Left Eye of TLC and Lauryn Hill.

Women of rap still face overt sexism regarding their creative capabilities. One female MC recalls, "'Only when I led them [male producers] to believe that a man had written or produced my stuff did they show interest'" (quoted in Cooper 1989:80). The mass-media scholar Lisa Lewis notes that in the popular music arena, "the ideological division between composition and performance serves to devalue women's role in music making and cast doubt on female creativity in general" (1990:57). However, female MCs in the 1990s defied sexist repression by writing their own songs, authoring books, producing records, and even starting their own record companies.

While the majority of scholarly studies on female rappers locate black women voices in rap, they present only a partial rendering of female representation.[18] These works tend to focus on females' attitudes and responses to sexual objectification, ignoring the many roles of women and female rappers. Tricia Rose says that female MCs should not be evaluated only in relation to male rappers and misogynist lyrics "but also in response to a variety of related issues, including dominant notions of femininity, feminism, and black female sexuality. At the very least, black women rappers are in dialogue with one another, black men, black women, and dominant American culture as they struggle to define themselves" (1994:147–48). In rap music performance, a "black female-self emerges as a variation of several unique themes" (Etter-Lewis 1991:43).

More importantly, female rappers—most of whom are black—convey their views on a variety of issues concerning identity, sociohistory, and esoteric beliefs shared by young African American women. Female rappers have attained a sense of distinction through revising and reclaiming black women's history and perceived destiny. They use their performances as platforms to refute, deconstruct, and reconstruct alternative visions of their identity. With this platform, rap music becomes a vehicle by which black female rappers seek empowerment, make choices, and create spaces for themselves and other sistas.

# Visualizing Beats and Rhymes

8

If rap music narrates the experiences of contemporary youth culture through aural avenues, rap music videos provide further meaning through their visual texts. Rap music videos draw on physical and intellectual references—encoded culture—that augment the message the rap artist delivers. In contrast to sound recordings, videos are deployed as marketing and advertisement tools by the music industry. Hence, they "depend upon a sensuous approach of marketing, combining inputs from fashion, advertising and the avant garde to lure the viewer into a perpetual state of unfulfilled expectations" (Whiteley 1997:xxxii). More importantly, however, these film vignettes serve an artistic purpose through which rap artists provide a visual interpretation of their songs and create and reenvision their experiences and fantasies. With this medium, viewers can experience hip-hop culture through the lens of its performers. The focus of this chapter is twofold: it provides an interpretive model for analyzing and ascertaining ways by which black youth culture in particular is encoded via the rap video narrative, and it offers insight into the video-making process as explained by the director and producer J. Kevin Swain.

Popular music scholars who analyze music videos are confronted with theories of visual culture that, for the most part, derive from film theory. Andrew Goodwin (1992) and Sean Cubitt (1997) argue that such approaches to music videos are basically dominated by patriarchal structures of looking—centrally voyeuristic and fetishistic—and are shaped entirely for the pleasures of male and heterosexual viewers (Cubitt 1997:295). Drawing on the seminal work of Goodwin, Paul McDonald finds that "commentators have used the concept of the 'classic realist text' in film theory as the yardstick for taking music video as an innovation in audio-visual form, [and] the problem with such a conclusion is that radical breaks are seen in what are actually the conventional forms of popular music performances" (McDonald 1997:281; see also Goodwin 1992:76). I might add that while music videos are "dominated by patriarchal structures of looking," there is little discussion by McDonald, Goodwin, and others of how to interpret those videos that deal specifically with black youth culture and the decision-making processes that occur between directors, black or nonblack, in presenting artists on camera to their perceived audiences.

Film theory does not allow for a musicological interpretation of music videos, where musical and visual texts coalesce. Goodwin finds that interpreting meaning in any music video generally lies in overall visualization—lyrics, music, and performance iconography—whether or not the video's visual narrative belies or amplifies the meaning of a song's narrative. He distinguishes three relationships between song/music and visual texts of music videos: illustration, amplification, and disjuncture. Illustration refers to those video clips in which the visual narrative tells the story of the song lyrics; amplification occurs when the clip introduces new meanings that do not conflict with the lyrics but rather add layers of meaning; and disjuncture describes videos in which imagery has no apparent bearing on the lyrics or may actually contradict the lyrics (Goodwin 1992:87–88). As I concur with Goodwin here, I have adopted his three categories—actually strategies—for my study of the lyrical and visual components of rap music videos.

### Iconic Memory and Rap Music Videos

The imagery of rap music videos documents the history and dreams of urban black youth culture that are specific to its audience. Thus, unique to rap music videos is what I call *iconic memory:* the referencing of place, historical events, and music familiar to hip-hop viewers. These visual cues contain encoded culture, capsules of meaning that add power and depth to the artist's message. The employment of iconic memory is an essential, unifying, and nearly omnipresent trademark of hip-hop videos. Knowledge of the hood and its players is as crucial to understanding the literature of hip-hop as knowledge of Western music theory is to analyzing symphonic scores. As

Tricia Rose notes, "Video themes have repeatedly converged around the depiction of the local neighborhood and the local posse, crew, or support system. Nothing is more central to rap's music video narratives than situating the rapper in his or her milieu and among one's crew or posse" (1994:10). During the preproduction phase, rap video directors scout for location spots, file footage, and photographic stills familiar to the artist and idiosyncratic to the hood. These culture-specific visuals will give texture and depth to the video narrative. Rap music videos often bring viewers from suburban, rural, or mainstream America into the street and hip-hop culture.

Iconic memory is stimulated by the subtle use of visualization via illustration, amplification, and disjuncture in rap video clips. In "The Message" (1982), lauded as the first rap music video, the director Sylvia Robinson uses inner-city images to underscore the lyrical content about harsh ghetto realities. Behind the song's main MC, Melle Mel, and the other members of Grandmaster Flash and the Furious Five, dilapidated buildings appear, reminiscent of impoverished conditions of the South Bronx where the group members grew up. Documentary-style footage of a homeless woman, tow truck, and street arrests reinforce the gravity of ghetto life. Toward the end of this video, as the members of Grandmaster Flash and the Furious Five congregate on a street corner to discuss their party plans, they are apprehended by two white police officers for no reason, illustrating police harassment of African American youth. This particular theme appears frequently in sociopolitical and reality rap music videos.[1]

When the hip-hop veteran Fab Five Freddy directed his first video, "My Philosophy" by KRS-One and Boogie Down Productions, he sought to amplify the artist's Black Nationalist ideas and educate black youth about salient historical and cultural icons. "My Philosophy," from the album *By All Means Necessary* (1988), presents KRS-One as an uncontested MC, a teacher, and a philosopher who possess a wealth of knowledge. KRS-One's album cover signifies on the famous Malcolm X photo in which the Nation of Islam leader is peeping out from a curtain, holding an AK-47 rifle. According to Fab Five Freddy, "'When I did "My Philosophy" I really wanted to take the idea Kris [KRS-One] had started on the album cover and make the video a kind of visual history lesson. Everybody was talking about Marcus Garvey and Bob Marley but most kids didn't even know what they looked like'" (quoted in hampton 1992:36). As KRS-One stands on stage reciting rhymes, photographic stills of Bob Marley and Malcolm X and footage of Malcolm X appear in the background. The raw, grainy film texture, shot in black and white, is typical of early rap music videos, which had minimal operating budgets. But with the major record companies' growing interest in rap, video quality improved. Rawness in texture was, however, relocated and embodied in graphic content, as will be discussed with gangsta rap videos.

In Queen Latifah's video, "Ladies First," which was also directed by Fab Five Freddy, the visual narrative has little or no relation to the lyrics, but certain images amplify the video's meanings. As mentioned in chapter 7, the political content of "Ladies First" is more vivid in its video version. Similar to Freddy's use of photographic stills of famous black male political leaders in "My Philosophy," in "Ladies First" he includes footage of South Africa's apartheid riots and photographic stills of black women political activists: Harriet Tubman, Frances Ellen Watkins Harper, Sojourner Truth, Angela Davis, Winnie Mandela, and Rosa Parks. Pan-Africanism is tacitly evoked with these images of South Africa's political struggle against segregation. A salute to Winnie Mandela, the mother of this struggle, is presented along with African American women, who serve as reminders of black liberation. The bond between women of color is alluded to through the appearance of Monie Love of England, whom Queen Latifah refers to as "my European partner." These images locate Latifah as a "queen mother," and equal partner among those black queens who struggled for the freedom of black people. Latifah's job as the black woman commander-in-charge is further amplified in the video with her appearance in a boardroom, dressed in a white uniform with a black turban-like head wrap. Here Latifah begins to replace the small statues of white persons, symbols of black oppression, on the boardroom table with statues of black fists, symbols of black empowerment.

Other rap music videos employ potent visual text. "Tennessee" by Arrested Development makes visual references to the survival of African roots in the South, racial injustices of Jim Crow, and lynched black men. "By the Time I Get to Arizona" by Public Enemy uses documentary footage of the 1960s civil rights demonstrations, lunch counter sit-ins, and brutal attacks on marchers by armed forces with police dogs and water hoses to illustrate their protest of Arizona's refusal to endorse the federal holiday honoring Martin Luther King Jr. The video also shows Public Enemy's Security of the First World (S1W), an echo of the Black Panthers' security force.[2]

With the emergence of MTV's rap music video program "Yo! MTV Raps" and BET's "Rap City" in the late 1980s, the 1990s ushered in a legion of music video directors in this genre. Among the most celebrated are Philip Atwell, Kevin Bray, Antoine Fuqua, F. Gary Gray, Ron Hightower, Paul Hunter, Diane Martel, Michael Martin, Dave Meyers, Kia B. Puriefoy, Brett Ratner, Chris Robinson, Millicent Shelton, Nzingha Stewart, J. Kevin Swain, and Hype

Williams. Because of his unique vision, personal style, and ability to shape, market, and promote each artist's image, Hype Williams is in high demand by rap and non-rap acts from major and independent labels. As such, he is credited for raising the standard production budget for rap music videos from fifty thousand to two hundred thousand dollars (Swain interview). Millicent Shelton pioneered colorful and heavily stylized videos with her use of fast pacing, or rhythmic editing, as seen in the early Salt-N-Pepa videos (hampton 1992:36). F. Gary Gray and Hype Williams brought attention to the art of rap music video production through the use of fish-eye lenses, unconventional camera angles, scenic backdrops, and kinetic dance movements. Gray garnered several distinguished awards at the 1995 MTV Music Video Awards show, including Video of the Year for his direction of TLC's "Waterfalls." Hype Williams earned several video awards, including six MTV Video Music awards in 1999 for TLC's "No Scrubs." By casting the actress Michelle Pfeiffer in Coolio's 1995 award-winning video for "Gangsta's Paradise," "Antoine Fuqua launched a new way for people to market their movies as a [movie] trailer" (Mukherjee 1998–99:134). Other directors have received international recognition, such as J. Kevin Swain for his video, "Live at the Apollo," for Public Enemy.

The majority of these directors are African Americans who come from similar neighborhoods as those artists they direct. Artistic decisions are often made in collaboration with the featured artist. In an interview with Swain, he told me about the making of 2Pac's video "To Live and Die in LA." He explained how he attempted to capture how 2Pac wished to be represented. Swain explained that it was rather easy to find locations for this project because he was reared in Los Angeles and is therefore familiar with its terrain. The verbal and visual subtext of "To Live and Die in LA" focuses on the African American communities of Los Angeles, including Compton, Watts, Inglewood, and South Central, Swain's neighborhood, and also signifies on the centrality of Los Angeles's Mexican American presence (Swain interview). Similar to directors of mainstream pop videos, hip-hop video directors use their videos to advertise the latest, most fly and expensive street gear, jewelry, hairstyles, and automobiles (lowriders, Mercedes Benzes, Rolls Royces, Bentleys, Jeeps). These commercial endorsements generate income for the artists. As with mainstream videos, companies pay rap artists to wear or show their products in a video. But these videos also support and advertise products of particular interest to hip-hop culture.

Rap artists have also directed their own videos. 2Pac and Dr. Dre, who both have ventured into directing their own music videos, identified with "gangsta rap" or reality rap, a style that exploits pimping, gangbanging, hustling/ drug dealing, police repression, and violence. Though gangsta rap seemingly glorifies black masculinity and bravado, projecting a sense of badness (the unconquerable), it also attempts to convey the reality of life in the hood. Artists usually depict themselves at odds with other gangsta characters, accosted by police officers, or positioned within their own empire in Big Willie style— tailored dress, flashy jewelry, expensive cars—surrounded by beautiful women.

Gangsta rap video narratives are derived from real-life events while also obfuscating the real. Drawing upon Jean Baudrillard's description of the hyperreal, "a situation where the 'contradiction between the real and the imaginary is effaced,' we can see in gangsta rap the continued blurring of the line between fiction and nonfiction" (Boyd 1997:70). Accordingly, rap artists like Snoop Dogg and 2Pac, who had real life run-ins with the law, interpolated these events in their video "2 of Amerikaz Most Wanted" (1996). The video opens with the police apprehending 2Pac and Snoop at a party. Then the camera moves to a courtroom scene in which both artists are on trial. Throughout this video's soundtrack, the chorus repeats "ain't nothin' but a gangsta party." Because both artists' trials were highly publicized, this video narrative flirts with reality and fiction. The hyperreal creates a media image that directs attention away from the actual occurrences (Boyd 1997:71). Following along similar lines as Snoop and 2Pac, Jay-Z, who has had run-ins with the law as well, uses video as a medium to proclaim his innocence in "Guilty Until (Proven Innocent)" (2000). The video reenvisions the events as the artist chooses to depict them.

Whereas some in the mainstream media have charged that "Straight Outta Compton" by N.W.A. and videos like it glorify violence, the rappers themselves claim that the video narratives depict unwarranted police harassment of young, urban black men. The video for "Straight Outta Compton," directed by Michael Martin, opens with a map that places Compton in relation to Hollywood and Beverly Hills, giving context and validity to its existence and to the lives of its inhabitants. The camera pans past a sign stating "Compton Unified Schools" to a storefront with a "bail bonds" sign, a visual subtext of repression. As N.W.A.—dressed in street gang attire—rhyme about life in Compton, the video flashes vignettes of black and white cops, the Los Angeles Police Department's motto "to protect and to serve," and reenactments of young black men frantically running from the cops, only to be apprehended, handcuffed, and detained in paddy wagons. The fusion of black and white officers is a stark reminder that police repression is not distinguished by racial differences.[3]

At the time this video emerged, the LAPD's chief Darryl Gates had implemented "Operation HAMMER," an antigang task force under which almost fifteen hundred black youths in South Central were picked up for "looking suspicious" (Kelley 1996:131). The mainstream media charged that "Straight Outta Compton" glorified violence; for this reason, MTV refused to air the video (Hochman 1989). Unshaken by the resistance, N.W.A.'s Ice Cube said, "'We deal with reality; violence is reality. When you say something like that, it scares people'" (quoted in Hochman 1989:24). Although a video was not made for their single "Fuck tha Police," this song also gives an unblinking account of the menacing behavior of police officers toward young black men. Some members from the black community with whom I informally spoke believed that N.W.A.'s "Straight Outta Compton" and "Fuck tha Police" were clarion calls about police harassment that if heeded could have prevented the 1992 Los Angeles uprising. Following "Straight Outta Compton," N.W.A. made another video that testified to police repression, "100 Miles Runnin."

Other visual themes of the gangsta rap video narrative address the lavish world of the mack, the tragedies of gangbanging, and speculation about the afterlife. The mack subgroup of gangsta rap covers aspects of street hustling—prostitution and illegal drug operations—and the ways they are used to build and maintain empires. For example, Snoop Dogg, who sports a mack image in the video "2 of Amerikaz Most Wanted," expresses his desire "to own a fly casino like [the notorious gangster] Bugsby Siegel." Image is essential to the mack style; macks dress elegantly with a subdued or cool posture. Among rap's celebrated macks are Big Daddy Kane, Too $hort, Snoop Dogg, The Notorious B.I.G., and Puff Daddy (also known as P. Diddy).

Rap's mack/player image resurrects characters from 1970s black action films, such as *Shaft, Superfly,* and *The Mack,* depicting one of the most powerful role models of the underground, a player who lives large and beats the system at its own game and according to mack's terms. Many of these movie characters from the 1970s black action films were "adapted from the work of Black pulp fiction writers of yesteryear like Chester Himes, Iceberg Slim, and Donald Goines" (Ro 1995:46). But the mack's history goes back even farther. Stories about street hustlers are informed by oral poetic narratives like the toasts. Toasts generally celebrate the adventures of the "bad nigga," traditionally embodied in the fictional characters Dolemite and Stackolee (see chapter 7). Most toasts tell how characters like Dolemite and Stackolee outsmart the "law" (or white villain) through clever maneuvering that subverts white patriarchal rule. Hence, these characters' "bad" attitudes make them the urban heroes of African American folklore. The toast-style novels of

Himes, Iceberg Slim, and Goines are based on street hustlers' real-life stories. Iceberg Slim, a former pimp, based such classics as *Pimp, the Story of My Life,* and *The Naked Soul of Iceberg Slim* on his actual experiences as a pimp.[4]

Through the music video medium, artists superimpose or mimic movie scenes depicting their favorite "players" in black action films. In Snoop's video "Doggy Dogg World," directed by Philip Atwell and filmed at Hollywood's Diamond Club (called Carolina West in the video), background music creates a 1970s ambience for viewers through Curtis Mayfield's hit "Freddie's Dead" from *Superfly.* The setting recalls the Player's Ball scene (honoring the Most Valuable Pimp) in *The Mack.* Black actors from the 1970s reappear in Carolina West, playing their familiar "blaxploitation" roles, identified by subtitles. The former professional football player Fred Williamson enters the club as The Hammer. Sitting at their respective tables are the actress Pam Grier as Foxy Brown and the comedian-actor Rudy Ray Moore as Dolemite. Among the crowd of dancers is Fred Berry (familiar to some as Rerun from the sitcom "What's Happening!"), who executes dance moves from his former Los Angeles-based group the Lockers, who received their big break on "Soul Train" during the early 1970s. The actor Antonio Fargas, who played Huggy Bear in the series "Starsky and Hutch," exits a convertible sports car with two women as his trophies. Snoop, accompanied by a harem, attempts to speak to the club's host, TaaDow; resembling Goldie in *The Mack,* Snoop wears a long dark coat with a fur collar, sunglasses, and a wide-brim hat that flattens out his large afro hairstyle. As Parliament's 1970s song "Give Up the Funk (Tear the Roof off the Sucker)" plays, Snoop demonstrates his power over his stable by snapping his fingers, causing the women to disperse. Upon noticing this gesture, TaaDow respectfully responds, "You big old pimp."

Snoop then takes the stage, bringing together the players of the 1970s with those of the 1990s. As he raps over the music "Doggy Dogg World," the lead singer of the 1970s doo-wop ballad group, The Dramatics, bellows "It's a Doggy Dogg World." Dressed as players, Kurupt and Daz, members of Death Row Records' Tha Dogg Pound, join Snoop in the cross-generational conjoining of underground heroes.

In the video "Wanted Dead or Alive," which features scenes of 2Pac and Tim Roth from the 1997 film, *Gridlock'd,* Snoop—appearing in a white suit and beret—is pursued by a squad of police officers and the FBI. Objects of containment such as the estate and the main character's outfit are white. Blackness, as seen in the black gates and the black vehicle Snoop uses to flee his white oppressors, represents a way out of whiteness. The officers throw tear-gas canisters over the gates of Snoop's white Mediterranean-style estate.

The squad climbs over the gates, jumps from the estate's roof, emerges from the swimming pool like a Navy SEAL team on a foreign beach and moves into Snoop's home. Snoop sits and watches their every move via his television monitor, reminiscent of a similar scene in the 1983 movie *Scarface,* starring Al Pacino. The old pro looks over his balcony, grinning at the foolish squad members as they lunge upstairs. He escapes nonchalantly via his secret doorway within seconds, moving through tall, black iron gates and down a hallway. He removes a roll of money and a ring from his wall safe and puts them in a briefcase. While the officers strain toward him from behind the locked gates, Snoop walks calmly toward his black Rolls Royce and drives away.

Although some critics contend that gangsta videos glorify violence, artists like Ice-T and the Houston-based group Geto Boys argue otherwise. Video clips such as Ice-T's "High Rollers" are especially didactic. The narrative illustrates a credible story about street hustling or gangbanging that ends in

Snoop Dogg, 1997. (Photo by Alisa Childs)

tragedy. In "High Rollers," Ice-T plays a drug dealer who appears to be living a young American male's dream. He has a large estate, a swimming pool, and an entourage of friends and beautiful women. Inserted between scenes of partying, documentary footage of drug raids and drug-related homicides reinforces Ice-T's message that a "fast life leads to a quick death." The high roller meets his demise twice in what Ice-T teaches are the only possible endings: a drug bust and a gangland, execution-style murder.

The Geto Boys' video "Six Feet Deep" underscores the tragedy of young gangbangers who do not learn lessons from the wasted lives of their murdered homies, choosing instead to perpetuate the lethal lifestyle. As a group of young black men walks past a store, a man wearing a black hooded sweatshirt fatally shoots one of the men from behind. The song notes the victim is only twenty-eight years old, emphasizing the typically short life expectancy of young black men who grow up in the hood, a common motif of the new jack cinema style (i.e. *Boyz 'N the Hood* and *Menace II Society*). At a New Year's Eve party, a close friend reminiscences about his homie's childhood years through his death, glancing at the deceased's grief-stricken mother, who remains oblivious to her son's gang lifestyle. As the victim's casket is interred and members walk away from the grave, the camera zooms in on the guns that are tucked in the waistbands of the deceased's friends signifying the tragic cliché, "We don't die, we multiply."

Speculations about the afterlife are another common theme in gangsta rap videos, particularly in those lavishly commemorating the abrupt deaths of the rap artists Eazy-E, 2Pac, and The Notorious B.I.G. The videos pose epistemological questions about death, especially about a "ghetto heaven" for one's dead homies. The crossroad motif, recalling the imaginary location where life ends and death begins, also appears in these videos. Videos in which these concepts appear include Bone Thugs-N-Harmony's "Tha Crossroads" in honor of Eazy-E, Richie Rich's "Do G's Get to Go to Heaven," Naughty by Nature's "Mourn You 'Til I Join You," a eulogy to Tupac Shakur, and Puff Daddy's "I'll Be Missing You," in memory of The Notorious B.I.G.

The use of popular folk spirituals in "Tha Crossroads" and "I'll Be Missing You" bring both comfort and historical context to these commemorations of the violent deaths of black men. In the former, a woman's chorus sings "Mary Don't You Weep (Martha Don't You Mourn)." In "I'll Be Missing You," Faith Evans, The Notorious B.I.G.'s ex-wife, sings the spiritual "I'll Fly Away," gesturing toward his final resting place in heaven. In "Tha Crossroads" video, the death angel leads what seemingly are souls up a mountain top. The video concludes as the face of Eazy-E appears against a blue sky, symbolizing his ascension to heaven. The use of the spirituals dignifies the memory of these hip-hop artists, bringing the sacred to where many only see secularism. The sacredness is further amplified with the wearing of white; its symbolism was crucial at a time when hip-hop was brought to a standstill.

But gangsta rap videos have inspired a bevy of imitators whose makers have no direct link to or experience of the context from which this music sprang. Non-black youth adorn themselves in hip-hop fashions, imitate speech patterns, and use gestures in a street style similar to artists in these videos. Elaborating on this notion, the cultural critic Nina Cornyetz (1994) observes that contemporary Japanese youth reconfigure themselves as black based on their reading of hip-hop images. Referring to this occurrence as "Japanese black face," Cornyetz finds a strong link to "the 'white Negro' phenomenon in the United States; but *also* [they] fetishize skin color in an attempt to mask the Japanese self with a realistic black visage" (1994:114). This possibly flattering imitation becomes problematic when hip-hop aficionados associate young black urban culture with violence and romanticize it. A police officer in Davenport, Iowa, noticed "a rise in white gangs whose members dress, walk, and talk in the style of West Coast African-American sets" (Romero 1997:A27).[5]

Some critics find that the so-called archetypes of gangsta rap videos are merely stereotypes, stereotypes that play into the racist, misogynist agenda of white supremacy. So-called realness employed in this manner reinforces black masculinist stereotypes of violence and ultimately offers "neatly packaged and accessible versions of an updated white racial fantasy of the black male as Dolomite in baggies" (Kun 1994:41). Women in gangsta rap videos are objectified and muted, a theme that the feminist critic bell hooks finds is rewarded by a "white supremacist capitalist patriarchy" who "approves [of] and materially rewards" sexism (hooks 1994:122).

Despite such criticism, rap music videos continued to forge ahead and experiment with both content and technology. Gangsta rap videos usually feature L.A. neighborhoods undocumented by Hollywood: Compton (N.W.A., DJ Quik, Compton's Most Wanted), Long Beach (Snoop Dogg), South Central (Ice Cube), and Inglewood (Mack 10). During the late 1990s, videos were no longer limited to scenes from the neighborhood but expanded to more diverse spots—deserts, tropical settings, golf courses, and large bodies of water, as popularized by Bad Boy Entertainment artists. Also significant are videos that summon cultural icons such as the New Orleans Mardi Gras Indians, as seen in TRU's video "Hoody Hoo," or Florida A&M University's Marching 100 band in Trick Daddy's "Shut Up." With the aid of

state-of-the-art equipment, contemporary rap music videos use phantasma-
goria to momentarily suspend viewer's reality, thus propelling the image of
an artist to supernormal status. The director F. Gary Gray won the 1995 MTV
Video Award for TLC's "Waterfalls," in which the group's members are standing on top of water in crystallized form amid the waterfalls.

Hype Williams's video production involves artists portraying multiple
roles. Through the use of elaborate and ever-changing backdrops in "Put Your
Hands Where My Eyes Could See," Busta Rhymes portrays a prince surrounded by a female court, recalling a scene from *Coming to America* (1988),
an African safari hunter chased by a live elephant, and a primordial man amid
male and female dancers who wear grass skirts and whose bodies are adorned
with purple and bright green paint. While the lyrics boast about Busta's lyrical skillz, the video portrays the artist in various comedic skits and shows
his flair for the burlesque. This video, which has no relation to the lyrics, is
an example of disjuncture. Williams also directed Missy "Misdemeanor" Elliott's "The Rain (Supa Dupa Fly)." Elliott, a celebrated full-figure hip-hop
fly girl, is introduced wearing an overblown blimp-like pantsuit made out
of black garbage bags and a silver, galactic-styled headpiece with sunglasses.
Each frame is synchronized to the beat of the music and alternately shows
Elliott performing a bouncy dance step, moving her eyes from side to side,
driving a black Hummer, wearing a long black wig, dressed in a lime-colored
pantsuit, and appearing as a "giant" sitting on the grass. Because the lyrics
are rather sparse in comparison to, for instance, Busta Rhymes's song, Williams's choice of these backdrops in "The Rain" promotes Elliott's image, illustrates the qualities of being "supa dupa fly" (through the costumes of
Elliott and other hip-hop guest stars), and uses the video lens to fill in gaps
during verbal silence.

Videos like "California Love" by 2Pac and Dr. Dre project artists into the
future. The video's imagery derives from the Mad Max movies. Directed by
Hype Williams, "California Love" situates 2Pac and Dre at a party scene in
the year 2095 in barren Oakland, a location known today for its large African American population. This video also features funksters George Clinton
and Roger and the actor-comedian Chris Tucker. Shout outs to other California regions—Long Beach, Inglewood, and South Central—that are mostly
occupied by blacks as well as Latinos occur before the party-goers ride away
in dune buggies across desert sands. Method Man's "Judgement Day," directed by Seb Janiak, is set in the future as well; however, the visual text is apoc-
alyptic in style. Nuclear explosions and mass destruction of cities form the
backdrop as Method Man, dressed in armor, refers in rhyme to the battle of

his own version of Armageddon, where only the verbally fittest survive. At the end of the video, Method Man and his armored crew pass by the fallen head of the Statue of Liberty.

Traditionally, directing jobs are obtained via friendships or intermediate connections with those who are familiar with the artists. Despite all their technical film training, rap music video directors must come foremost with a street sensibility. The music video can also be a billboard for talents seeking to direct feature-length films. Thus, this medium continues to provide avenues for greater economic opportunities, opening Hollywood's inner sanctum to those who usually were sent around to the back door and even then rarely let in. Brett Ratner, the director of *Rush Hour* (1998), attributes Hollywood's interest in rap music video directors to the fact that "'Hollywood execs are much younger. They're affected by MTV'" (quoted in Mukherjee 1998–99:134). Several reputed black hip-hop video directors—including Hype Williams, who debuted as the screenplay writer and director of *Belly* (1998), and F. Gary Gray, who directed *Set It Off* (1996) and *The Negotiator* (1998)—have made strides in the film industry. Other directors who have occasionally directed rap music videos moved on to mainstream television. One such example is Paris Barclay, who directed LL Cool J's "Mama Said Knock You Out" and later became a co-executive producer of the television series *NYPD Blue* and won two Emmys for his directorial work in 1998 and 1999. Rap music videos have functioned as screen tests for numerous artists who would later appear in feature films. These artists include Ice-T in *New Jack City*, Ice Cube in *Boyz 'N the Hood*, Queen Latifah in *Set It Off*, and the late Tupac Shakur in *Juice*. When Ice Cube was asked why rap artists are so appealing as actors in new jack cinema, he responded, "'Movies are fantasy based on reality. And rappers represent reality in the community'" (quoted in "Why Are Rap Stars" 1995:60).

### The Art of Making a Rap Video: A Director's Account

The final section of this chapter includes excerpts from an interview with the music video director J. Kevin Swain. Born in 1963 and raised in South Central Los Angeles, Swain, like many rap music video directors, honed his directing skills in the streets. His directing debut, "We Want Eazy" for the late Eazy-E, was a musical parody of Bootsie Collins's "We Want Bootsie." Following this success, he directed several videos featuring Public Enemy, OutKast, 2Pac, Erykah Badu, and Wu-Tang Clan. In our interview, Swain discussed the vision for two of his videos, "To Live and Die in LA" and "I Ain't Mad at Cha," which were edited shortly after Tupac Shakur's death.

The videos "I Ain't Mad at Cha" and "To Live and Die in LA" captured Shakur's philosophy about death and his adoration of his adopted home. Swain told me that the preparations for "To Live and Die in LA" took days. While flying from Paris to Los Angeles, Swain talked by phone with Suge Knight and 2Pac to determine their ideas for the video: "They wanted to video 'Pac in L.A., but he didn't know L.A., because he was from Baltimore, but raised in the San Francisco Bay Area. Because I was from there, I knew certain aspects of L.A. that had to be in the video. Number one, Compton had to be in the video because Suge was from there. I wanted to represent L.A. as much as I possibly could. I wanted to represent Compton, South Central, Inglewood."

To gather material, Swain sorted through his photo stills to find those that were essential to black Angelenos. He explained, "At the time of the shoot, The Watts Towers were under construction, so I couldn't shoot them. That would have been ideal. But the other shot in the video was what was formerly called Will Rogers Park, and for a person who lives in Watts, that's a major monument. I wanted to shoot monuments. There are certain parts of L.A. that are major to people from L.A.: Roscoe's, one of my favorite hang-outs, a swap-meet sign, and Baldwin Hills [Plaza]." Certain landmarks in "To Live and Die in LA" evoked personal reminiscences for Swain, particularly Angelus Funeral Home, the Black Panthers mural, and the Nation of Islam Temple. He told me,

Angelus Funeral Home is the funeral home in the hood, and it is located in the Crenshaw area. It has been there as long as I can remember. A lot of gang members happened to be funeralized at Angelus. And anyone who knows Crenshaw knows Angelus Funeral Home. The video was specifically done for certain people in my mind because if they were ever away from L.A. and saw "To Live and Die in LA," they were feeling home. The Black Panthers mural I used in the video is the one on Jefferson [Boulevard] and 11th Avenue. The story that happened for me is that I used to live on 9th Avenue and Jefferson. I remember when the artists started painting it. But even further than that, when I was a kid, I lived around the corner from the Southern California Headquarters for Free Angela Davis. I like the symbols of it. For instance, I like the picture of Huey Newton sitting down with the rifle, and Bobby Seale and Angela Davis looking strong. Even today, there is a slight picture of Angela Davis up there. As far as the Black Panthers, I lived around the corner from them. As a child, I liked them a lot. The Nation of Islam temple was on

Jefferson and 7th Avenue. To me that was my neighborhood. Those were
things I saw as my L.A.

Swain brought these political associations up to date with a photographic still
of the 1992 Los Angeles uprising, which he snapped during the riots. Asked
about one of the references—"It wouldn't be Los Angeles without the Mexicans"—2Pac used to remind listeners of rap's respect for and debt to Mexicans, Swain stated,

> I know L.A. And I knew that I wanted a shot, for instance, of a Mexican guy
> selling oranges or brothers [blacks] selling watermelons. I have been in Los
> Angeles all of my life. I feel that Mexicans have been grossly abused here in
> L.A. They are treated like third-class citizens, when this is really their land.
> This is their home. Even though in the original settlement of L.A. there were
> some black people there, of course. But this is still Mexico. If it weren't for a
> few guns and some missionaries, it would still be Mexico. What can I say, this
> is their homeland, including New Mexico and Arizona. 2Pac felt this way. This
> is why I shot the mural "We are the Silent Majority" for the video.

In the video, Swain had Shakur stand between Latinas and African American women while the artist praised the importance of Mexicans in the establishment of Los Angeles.

When the video was filmed, 2Pac wore a blue L.A. hat and blue tank top
with jeans during the scene in which he rides in the back of a car. After
Shakur's death and at the request of Suge Knight, Swain used a Paint Box to
make it appear that 2Pac was wearing a red outfit.[6] Swain estimated the cost
for this change at around twenty thousand dollars.

The "I Ain't Mad at Cha" video was conceived in collaboration with Shakur,
and Swain is still amazed at 2Pac's prophetic contribution. He told me,

> I think there are few people in this world who see their deaths. There are few
> artists who go out with their boots on, so to speak. I think in that respect that
> made him [2Pac] great. Coincidence, if you will, but awfully close. He said
> that this is the concept: "I want to get shot and I want to go to a heaven, where
> I'm talking to my homies." It was real easy to do. In this video, there appeared
> look-and-sound-alikes of deceased luminaries: Redd Foxx, Donny Hathaway,
> Billie Holiday, Miles Davis, Marvin Gaye, Nat King Cole, and Sammy Davis
> Jr. That was the fun part to me, the look-alikes.

Often subjected to judgment by others, 2Pac told Swain that one cannot be
judgmental about who is in heaven. Swain said, "'Pac and I talked about

who's in heaven. One of 'Pac's things is that only God can judge him. So to further that point, we put people in heaven who some would say, 'Oh no, Pac, no way.' You can make cases for all people not deserving to be there. Some of them died from drug overdose, charged violent or suicidal, or a woman beater. So we didn't want to be judgmental about who's in heaven as far as the video was concerned. It was about great artists." Swain further noted, "'Pac knew religion and was a great, insightful guy. And I think often that people who listen to his music are not enlightened because they don't see this. They hear his anger, his rage. They hear his truth and honesty. But I don't think they know from whence it comes. The guy did a lot of reading. Those kind of things never come out, and that's the unfortunate side."

Finally, Swain told me he believes that there is little difference between filmmaking and videomaking techniques: "At the end of the day, it's filmmaking. Back in the day, like with the 'We Want Eazy' video, I used a 16mm camera. But the best quality, be it film- or videomaking, is the 35mm, the best quality, the standard."

The rap music video medium becomes a lens by which rap artists can add layers of meaning through the employment of illustration, amplification, and disjuncture. In doing so, video becomes a means by which rap artists illustrate their deepest sentiments and desires. While the viewers in whom iconic memory is evoked resonate with the deeper or "real" meanings of rap music videos, other viewers are transported outside of their immediate world and introduced to the lore of street and hip-hop culture. Rap music videos undoubtedly shed light on the artists' deepest sentiments and desires. Additionally, rap music videos merge the past with the present by parodying classic scenes from famed films. The rap music video emerges then as "a site for the exploration of postmodernism in the intersection of African-American and mass culture" (Roberts 1996:143).

The advent of music video television in the late 1980s has contributed to a burgeoning of black talents behind as well as in front of the camera. Without a doubt the rap music video narrative has become a lens by which audiences, artists, and directors visualize beats and rhymes.

# Epilogue

I vividly recall when I began researching rap music in 1981 and was told by many that this music was merely a passing fad. Disproving this notion, rap music has stood the test of time. By surpassing other popular music markets—rock, rhythm and blues, and alternative—in record sales, as documented by SoundScan, rap music had succeeded as the most vital and dynamic genre of music by the end of the twentieth century. Because of the overwhelming revenue generated from recordings as well as videos, fashion, advertisements, and concerts, the rap music industry has flourished as a billion-dollar enterprise.

Although the stylistic foundation of rap music is a synthesis of African American and African Caribbean expressive culture, its performance practices have been adopted by non-black artists, thus contributing to rap's hybridity. As evidence of its chameleon appeal, rap and other hip-hop forms are disseminated to a variety of youth communities on the national and international scene by the formation of Zulu Nation chapters within and outside of the United States, the telecasting of music video programs abroad, the exportation of hip-hop cult classic films, and the establishment of rap music record companies globally. Within a form that is predicated upon self-expression and originality through rhymin, non-U.S. artists are finding their unique voices and expressing them in their own language. As the U.S.-based MC Talib Kweli observes, "'hip-hop is a folk music that speaks directly to the people in the language that they are on the street corner speaking'" (quoted in Wong 2001:204).

Hybridity has not only been created by the merging of U.S. rap with international styles but also with other preexisting musical genres from bebop and hard bop to rock and gospel. Hip-hop musicians are reviving the careers of veteran artists of the earlier genres through digital sampling, for example, creating unique musical collages of an Isley Brothers or Aerosmith song with a David Axelrod piece or Earl Palmer's signature drum beat.

Because of rap's overwhelming success in the musical mainstream, hip-hop musicians struggle to remain street-oriented and to maintain an underground essence that keeps rap music separated and distinct from other pop musics. On another front, hip-hoppers have expressed concern about the splintering of hip-hop arts from each other, particularly with respect to privileging one form of hip-hop over the other. I have witnessed those who question the fact that the MC tends to eclipse the DJ in the promotion of rap music. True hip-hop heads claim that focusing too much attention on MCs at the exclusion of DJs, graffiti writers, and b-boy/b-girl dancers may eventually lead to a historical void in one art's history over another. With the ongoing Zulu Nation anniversary celebrations, the rise of hip-hop cultural centers like The Point in the Bronx, KRS-One's hip-hop culture preservation project the Temple of Hip-Hop, and the adaptation of rap and other hip-hop arts in opera, musicals, and symphonic medium, it is hoped that such platforms will continue to serve as important renewal sites for remapping these interconnections.

Hip-hop music and arts have invariably suffered from their commodification and exploitation by the music industry, including efforts to sanitize their presentation by replacing black and brown participants with white ones. For example, critics noted that a black rap act has never received the widespread coverage granted to the white MC Eminem in 2000 and during the pre–Grammy Awards review of March 2001. Without Dr. Dre's Midas touch in music production and Eminem's association with his newly formed record label Aftermath, would Eminem have been the first all-rap act ever to receive nominations for the Best Album of the Year? Ethnicity should not matter when evaluating an individual's mastery of MCing or turntablism. Without a doubt, African Americans and their Latino counterparts "show much love" to those who can flow and appear to be down with them and their causes. However, the appropriation of black cultural productions, primarily nonconformist musical statements like bebop, rhythm and blues, rock, and rap, by whites fosters a sense of suspicion and apprehension among its original creators regarding control and, more importantly, ownership. While American popular music history is saturated with several "black roots, white fruits" accounts, as documented by Steve Chapple and Reebee Garofalo (1977), rap music remains a discursive form in which African American artists continue to be the major creative forces who define its direction.

This study posits that even though rap music began as an outgrowth of black youths' socioeconomic and cultural marginalization within the United States, the music nevertheless functions in a number of positive ways for youth in the street context:

1. Rap music is a display of cultural values and aesthetics. Rap music comprises a complex system in which rules for performance are derived from African performance practices. Artists conceptualize musical and verbal delivery within a systematic framework in which rhyme, poetic logic, vocal quality, flow or rhythm and timing, turntablism, and originality rank as primary areas of significance.

2. Rap music serves as a vehicle for self-expression. Many artists have given testimonies of their stormy past, from brushes with the law and incarceration to near fatal incidents. They have often expressed that during periods of reflection, MCing and DJing have been forums for them to articulate their personal experiences. Rap music serves as an agent for fostering self-esteem, self-knowledge, confidence, and assertiveness among youth.

3. Rap music serves as a vehicle for social control and cohesiveness. Community-based organizations created by rap or hip-hop artists provide alternative solutions to certain crises affecting the members of the Hip-Hop Nation and their respective communities. Thus, it offers youth creative and effective ways to collectively rechannel, redirect, and refocus their energies in lieu of riotous incidents.

4. Rap music serves as a political forum. It emerges as a powerful tool of dissuasion from social ills. Artists utilize rap as a discursive tool through which to discuss social and political issues such as black-on-black violence, police repression, censorship, and the silencing of political prisoners and apathetic treatment of the black and poor by the powers that be.

5. Rap music fosters ethnic pride among its artists. Hip-hop artists often rhyme about their identity and from whence they come. Through the adoption of names that indicate ethnic affiliation and the formation of crews or posses with similar or supportive ethnic groups and nationalities, artists articulate pride in and representation of their respective communities.

6. Rap music represents and reflects personal and economic success. Because of their deep concern and love for their communities, rap artists are exulted as heroes by their followers. To their inner-city admirers, hip-hop artists represent those who are prosperous and making an honest living. Thus it is not surprising that a legion of rap music artists have not only achieved economic success by creating beats and rhymes, but in addition they have taken full control of their careers by creating record companies, management firms, and production teams. Others have used the advertising and music video industry as a portal to Hollywood's film industry. The rap music tradition has therefore come to represent a symbol of success and, more importantly, an example of socioeconomic mobility.

Through the analysis of research for this book, the sociocultural and historical development of rap, the aesthetics of performance of this tradition, and those gender, political, and social issues relevant to the Hip-Hop Nation have been determined. There is, however, much need for further investigation of rap music, particularly its development on the international scene and its influence on dance/club music and whether these arenas continue or break with black musical performance practices. In this regard, the sonic dimensions of hip-hop music and its interconnectedness with electronica, for example, drum 'n' bass, house, and trip-hop, holds much promise for future studies. In addition, yet to be explored in depth is rap's impact on religion, politics, fashion, and other arts, such as the spoken word. Scholars and critics can no longer disregard the cultural merit of this genre. If rap music is to receive equal credibility with the likes of classical or written music traditions and complex improvisatory music in the academy and beyond, scholars and critics must seriously examine the cultural milieu—the streets—from which hip-hop music evolves.

The study presented here is but a single response to defining rap music within contemporary culture from the 1970s to 2000. The implementation of other studies holds much promise for future exploration of rap music as a street phenomenon.

# Glossary of Common Rap Music Terms

*B-boy, B-girl* (n): a breakdancer or a dancer on the hip-hop scene.

*Ballin* (vb): displaying one's wealth while having fun; exhibiting a highrolling or flamboyant lifestyle.

*Beam me up, Scotty* (v imp): addicted to crack or deadly drugs.

*Beef* (n): an argument or feud.

*Benjamins* (n): dollars.

*B.G.* (n): a youngblood or "baby gangster."

*Big Willie* (n/adj): Someone who has an opulent lifestyle; flashy in dress style; or simply pimpin, as in the expression "big pimpin."

*Bite* (vb): to steal someone else's style, rhyme, or beats.

*Bling bling* (n): a term popularized by rapper the B.G. of The Hot Boys to capture the ringing sound produced by a cash register. Also, the term signifies on the sound of jingling jewelry or how much wealth one possesses.

*Blunt* (n): a cigar mixed with marijuana.

*Bone* (vb): to have sex.

*Boom-bap* (n): a sound produced by the "kick" (bass) drum characteristic of the Roland TR-808 drum machine.

*Bum rush* (vt): to take over.

*Bus this* (v imp): pay attention.

*Cat* (n): a term first exploited by bebop artists to refer to a male who is proficient on his instrument. Hip-hop speakers use "cat" very similarly, such as, "This *cat* is slammin on the turntables."

*Cheddar* (n): having lots of money or "cheese."

*Chickenhead* (n): a female groupie who has oral sex with any male. The term refers to the movement of the female's head while performing oral sex.

*Chill-out/chill* (vt): to relax or to calm down (emotionally).

*Chronic* (n): marijuana cigarette laced with cocaine.

*Cipher* (n): a term coined by the Five Percent Nation and adopted by hip-hop speakers to mean knowledge; also refers to a circle of three or more MCs who pass around or trade off rhymes.

*Clockin'* (adj): upset.

*Coochie* (n): vagina; also referred to as *na na.*

*Crash* (vt): to fall asleep.

*Cream* (n): money.

*Crew* (n): rap group members.

*Crib* (n): home.

*Crush* (vb): to put an end to; stop.

*Dead presidents* (n): dollar bills.

*Def* (adj): excellent.

*Def jam* (adj/n): a good record.

*Dis* (vt): to discredit or disrespect someone through insults.

*Dog* (n): a male friend or associate.

*Dope* (adj): great or outstanding.

*Down* (vt): to be connected or associated with.

*Down by law* (adj): considered an expert.

*Down low* (n/adj): the "scoop," "411"; confidential, hush-hush. "You've got to keep
    it on the *down low.*"

*Drama* (n): commotion or disturbance. "We don't need all of this *drama* to solve this
    simple problem."

*Drop* (vb): The date or time something will be released to the masses. "His album
    will *drop* on October 13."

*Drop a dime* (vb): to snitch or tattle on someone.

*Dukey rope* (n): big or thick gold chain necklace.

*Dustin* (adj): intoxicated, drunk; too high.

*Five on it* (n): a five-dollar bag of marijuana, as popularized in a rap song by the Luniz.

*Flippin' da script* (vb): changing the idea; moving to another subject.

*Fly* (adj): a stylish person.

*Flow* (n/vb): one's ability to rhyme without hesitation; or one's personal unique style
    at rhyming.

*Freestyle* (vb): Creating rhymes extemporaneously or in the moment.

*Frontin* (vb): pretending.

*Fresh* (adj): something new or original.

*G* (n): gangsta.

*Gat* (n): a gun.

*ghetto fabulous* (adj): the best or finest of street culture. "Her whole performance,
    dress, and style was *ghetto fabulous.*"

*Glock* (n): a type of 9mm gun.

*Hardcore* (adj): aggressive.

*Heads* (n): people who are highly respected or adherents of hip-hop.

*Hip-hop* (n/adj): an urban youth arts movement comprised of graffiti, emceeing, disc jockeying, and breakdancing; a street attitude displayed through gestures, stylized dress, and language.

*Holla* or *holler back* (inj): an answer back, response, or affirmation to a command.

*Homeboy/girl* (n): friend; someone from the same neighborhood.

*Homie/ey* (n): short for homeboy/girl.

*Hood* (n): the ghetto; an inner-city neighborhood or a diminutive of neighborhood.

*House* (n): a presence in the audience for example, "Is Larry *in the house* tonight?"

*Hyped* (vt): excited.

*Iced* (vb/n): to kill someone; a dead person.

*Ill/Illin* (adj): improper behavior.

*Jack* (vb): to accost or assault. "I heard that he was jacked at the club the other evening."

*Jimbrowski* or *Jimmy* (n): penis.

*Jimmy hat* (n): a prophylactic or condom.

*Jockin* (vt): wanting to associate or be seen with a popular person.

*Juice* (n): someone with clout among peers; or electrical power.

*Knocka* (n): a pest.

*Knock the boot* (n): sexual intercourse.

*Lampin* (adj): relaxing.

*Livin large* (adj): to possess an abundance of material wealth.

*Loc'd out* (adj): erratic behavior or bizarre disposition induced by drugs.

*Loot* (n): Money.

*Megablasts* (n): large consumption of crack.

*Mop* (vt): to steal.

*New Jack* (n): a newcomer on the rap scene.

*Nine* (n): 9mm pistol.

*Off the hook* (adj): spectacular.

*O.G.* (n): original gangsta; a veteran at gangbanging.

*On a mission* (n): something done with serious intent.

*Peep(s)* (vb/n): to observe something; short for people.

*Player hater* (n): one who intentionally seeks out a person whom he or she can dis.

*Posse* (n): a band of rappers or gang members; a crew.

*Project gold* (n): large gold hoop earrings.

*Props* (n): respect or recognition. "She gave *props* to the MC."
*Pumpin* (adj): lively.

*Rank* (vt): to insult.
*Raw* (adj): pure.
*Representin* (adj): the act of representing an ideal or a person.
*Rollin with* (vb): associated with someone or a group.
*Ruffneck* (n): a guy who lives a street lifestyle as apparent by his dress, gestures, and
   language.
*Rock star* (n): drug addict.

*Scopin'* (vt): To examine carefully.
*Shout out* (n): Recognition or "hellos" to a friend, posse, or neighborhood. "He gave
   a *shout out* to his posse."
*Skeeze* (vt): to have sex.
*Skeezer* (n): a sexually promiscuous female groupie or fan.
*Slammin* (adj): outstanding.
*Slippin* (adj): losing effect or popularity.
*Smoke* (vb): to kill someone.
*Static* (n): a disagreement or dispute between two parties.
*Studio gangsta* (vb): a term for an MC who pretends to have lived a gangster lifestyle
   and promotes this falsehood through his or her lyrics.
*Straight up* (adj): honest.
*Strapped* (adj): armed with a gun.
*Step off* (vt): to leave.
*Stupid* (adv): very, as in "*stupid* def."
*Sucker* (n): a square; unfresh or unoriginal person.
*Sweat* (vt): to overpatronize or bother someone. "The guy keeps *sweatin* me."

*Tax* (vt): to physically exhaust; to make excessive demands on a person.
*Trooper* (n): a posse associate.
*Trunk jewelry* (n): big gold jewelry.

*Up North* (n): in jail.

*Wack* (adj): not original; corny.
*Wax* (vt/n): to defeat by outwitting a person; a vinyl record.
*Wildin* (adj): acting recklessly.
*Wild thing* (n): sexual intercourse.
*Word* (inj): affirms the listener has understood or agrees with the speaker.

*Yo* (inj): means "I" or "Me" in Spanish and translated by hip-hoppers as a salutation;
   also used to get someone's attention, such as "*Yo,* I'm talkin to you."

# Notes

## Introduction

1. These films include *Wild Style* (1983), *Beat Street* (1984), *Breakin'* (1984), and *Breakin' 2: Electric Boogaloo* (1984).

2. See note on terminology for an explanation of the spelling of certain words throughout the text.

3. Boots spoke on the panel, "Fight the Power," at Power Moves: A Conference on Hip-Hop, the University of California at Los Angeles, May 10–15, 1999.

4. In 1996 the House of Blues started the Smokin' Grooves exclusively rap music tour. After realizing that rap concerts in the past were "notoriously disorganized affairs, marred by poor production" (Hilburn 1998:F1) and crippled by unprofessional behavior by some acts, Smokin' Grooves improved on these conditions. Smokin' Grooves made use of state-of-the-art production and stipulated standards for professional stage and offstage protocol. As a result, these tours have been quite successful. Additionally, major rap artists and record moguls organized their own concert tours. Among them are Roc-A-Fella's Jay-Z and his Hard Knock Life Tour of 1999, Dr. Dre's Up in Smoke Tour of 2000, and the William Brothers, founders of Cash Money Records, who teamed up with the Ruff Ryder artist DMX to produce the Ruff Ryders/Cash Money Tour of 2000.

5. Death Row Records and its near demise is discussed in chapter 6. For more information see Ro (1998).

6. Ethnomusicology has been heavily influenced by anthropology since its formative years in the United States. Many of the newer perspectives in fieldwork have been impacted by the anthropologist Clifford Geertz, who argued for a shift in anthropology from being "an experimental science in search of law [to] an interpretive one in search of meaning" (1973:5). James Clifford (1986) expanded Geertz's literary model and called for "self-reflexivity," a method of interpretation by which ethnographers document themselves while simultaneously documenting others as a way to eradicate a "partial" rendering of the fieldwork account.

7. While *Shadows in the Field* offers an excellent account of newer dimensions and perspectives on fieldwork in ethnomusicology, ironically it does not include an essay that specifically addresses the constraints of being an "indigenous" or native scholar, nor is Burnim's seminal article mentioned in the text's bibliography.

8. As my fieldwork progressed in the later years, I noticed that established artists rarely sign consent forms because of the industry's skepticism and the prevalence of bootlegging of artists' property, including interviews with nonestablished trade publications.

9. This consultant remains anonymous due to the sensitivity of the matter.

### Chapter 1: The Roots and Stylistic Foundation of the Rap Music Tradition

1. Such a conversation happened after my initial field research in 1986. While attending the Society for Ethnomusicology's annual meeting at the Rochester School of Music in 1986, a prominent sociolinguist poked fun at a similar discussion he had with a rap artist. He said condescendingly that he felt the artist was told or had read about rap's African connection and could not have drawn this connection without having done so. This conversation recalled the "African retention" and "Origins of the Negro Spirituals" debates of the mid-twentieth century.

2. Eric Charry makes a distinction between *jeli* and *jali,* the Mande words equivalent to English "bard". Both words come from the Mande people's language of the "Upper Niger River roughly between Bamako in southwestern Mali and Kouroussa in northeastern Guinea" (2000:1). *Jeli* (pl. *jelilu*) is the Mande word for "bard" as used by those from the Maninka society situated in Mali and Guinea, whereas *jali* or *jalo* (pl. *jalolu*) is the Mande word for bard as used by those from the Mandinka society of Senegal, the Gambia, and Guinea-Bissau. Charry also notes other common uses of the word *Mandinka* as "Mandingo in British writing," and he traces the first use of *griot,* a seventeenth-century word for "bard," to the writings of French travelers (1).

Charry also notes that the *jeli* art (*jeliya*) is not confined to Mande culture but has other counterparts or terms. "Jelis have their analogue in the Wolof *gewel,* Fulbe *gaulo* (*gawlo*), Moorish *iggio* (*iggiw*), and Soninke *jaare,* all of whom come from societies that have had close contact with the Ghana and Mali Empires" (91).

3. Paul Gilroy's employment of "The Black Atlantic" raises excellent points, for the African experience outside of Africa or the "African World" (Clarke 1991) or "diaspora" is not limited to African Americans or African Caribbeans, as is commonly believed, but includes those who live in Europe as well. Throughout this book, I will use the term "black" to refer to those of Africa and the diaspora (Europe, Latin America, the Caribbean, and the United States) and "African American" to refer to blacks in the United States.

4. *Nommo* is a term used among the Dogon of Mali, West Africa, as suggested by the French ethnographer Marcel Griaule. In *Dieu d'eau: entretiens avec Ogotemmêli* (1948) and *Conversations with Ogotemmeli* (1970), Griaule reveals the origins of nommo. According to an interview he conducted with the blind elderly informant Ogotemmêli, the elder translated *nommo* (spelled *Nummo* in the text) as a set of twins created by God and of His divine nature. They were "conceived without untoward

incidents and developed normally in the womb of the earth. The Pair were born perfect and complete; they had eight members, and their number was eight, which is the symbol of speech. The *Nummo* is water and heat, the life-force, which is the bearer of the Word, which is the Word" (1970:18, 138). The Africanists and philosophers Janheinz Jahn (1961) and Paul Carter Harrison (1972) find that the essence of nommo permeates both literature and spoken word produced by Africans and those within the African world (diaspora).

5. For further information about early African American celebrations and holidays see Raboteau (1978), Wiggins (1987), and Southern (1997:52–55).

6. Although slavery was abolished in the North much earlier than in the South, northern blacks still experienced racial segregation from whites. Blacks established their own secular and sacred organizations that, in turn, assisted in the maintenance and continuum of African-derived practices (see Raboteau 1978). Among these organizations were the Free African Society, spearheaded by Richard Allen and Absalom Jones, the Grand Lodge (black Masons), founded by Prince Hall, and religious sects such as the African Methodist Episcopal Church, established by Richard Allen, and the First African Baptist Church, organized by Thomas Paul.

7. The latter type is "peculiar to African Americans and collected most frequently in jails" (Dance 1978:225) and in urban areas. See also Bruce Jackson (1974).

8. "The Signifying Monkey" version I often heard while growing up in Louisiana also appears in Daryl Dance's collection of folk narratives, *Shuckin' and Jivin': Folklore from Contemporary Black Americans* (1978), and a similar rendition of this toast is performed by the comedian Rudy Ray Moore on his album *This Pussy Belongs to Me* (1972).

9. For further readings on Langston Hughes and Sterling Brown, see Rampersad (1986) and Brown (1996).

10. Al Benson's genius in time-brokering is examined in more detail by Mark Newman (1988:82–85).

11. See George (1988b) and Barlow (1999).

12. I posit that the Black Arts Movement ended with Ntozake Shange's play *for colored girls who have considered suicide/when the rainbow is enuf,* which debuted on Broadway in September 1976.

13. According to David Lionel Smith, in the 1970s, "Baraka renounced cultural nationalism, dropped 'Imamu' from his name, and embraced what he called 'Marxism/Leninism/Mao Tse Tung Thought.'" Today he goes by Amiri Baraka (see Smith 1996:262).

14. Veteran African American artists like the visual artist Romare Bearden and the writer Gwendolyn Brooks also embraced the ideas of the Black Arts Movement. In doing so, they shifted their artistic visions from a European canon to an African American one.

15. For further information on the poetic style of Black Nationalist poets, see Stephen Henderson (1973).

### Chapter 2: The Development of the Rap Music Tradition

1. Several of Brown's songs bore the word "funk" in their titles, including "Ain't It Funky Now" (1969), "Funky Drummer" (1970), "Funky President" (1974), and "It's Too Funky in Here" (1979).

2. Robert Farris Thompson traces the etymology of "funk" to the Ki-Kongo word *lu-fuki,* translated as "bad body odor." He also finds that "funk" is interpreted among the Cajun in Louisiana as *fumet,* meaning the aroma of food and wine in French. He contends that the Ki-Kongo word is closer in form and meaning to praising someone for the integrity of their art, for having "worked out" to achieve their aims. Although Thompson states that the Kongo finds positive energy in funkiness, particularly the smell of a hardworking elder as good luck, in jazz/black English earthiness, the word denotes a return to fundamentals. See Thompson (1983).

3. According to the popular music critic Radcliffe A. Joe, "disco" originated from the French word *discothèque.* In the pre–World War II era, the operator of a Parisian bar catering to jazz enthusiasts is said to have used the name "La discotheque" for his establishment. Hence, during and after the war the discotheque concept remained affiliated with Parisian bars that incorporated live and recorded jazz performances. Although the French coined the word, it appears they did not apply it until much later to the concept of dancing in a commercial club to recorded music. Early "discotheque" club owners include Jean Castel, Paul Pacine, and Regina Zylberberg. After Chubby Checker introduced the Twist in the United States in the 1960s, the dance was appropriated in Paris, where discotheques replaced jazz with rhythm and blues. Joe argues that the United States simply borrowed the term rather than the concept of the French. Particularly during the 1970s, disco in the United States centered around the record-spinning DJ and the musical production processes associated with the disco sound (Joe 1980:1). Since making people dance was central to disco, the seven-inch disc was replaced with the twelve-inch, doubling the playing time of a song. Another objective of the twelve-inch disc was to create added space to "enhance and prolong the pulsating tempo of the rhythm and percussions breaks [sections]" for a dance/disco audience (63). The twelve-inch disc concept is credited to Tom Moulton.

4. Some of these fires were actually started by tenants. Disgusted with deteriorating conditions, they hoped that burning their apartments would create government-subsidized opportunities to relocate to new public housing projects and receive up to three thousand dollars for the losses (Rooney 1995:56).

5. With the use of live footage, the documentary *Flyin' Cut Sleeves* (1993) best presents the galvanization of black and Puerto Rican residents. The film indicates that when gang activity eventually subsided in the South Bronx, it was succeeded by positive changes, including the fight for Puerto Rico's independence by both black and Puerto Rican residents.

6. For further information about Afro-Caribbean migration to the United Kingdom, see Thompson (1990).

7. Edward Seaga is worth mentioning because of his political triumph as prime minister of the Jamaica Labour Party in 1980 and his importance as a catalyst in the redefinition of reggae dancehall during this time. Seaga, a Lebanese Jamaican who attained a bachelor's degree in anthropology from Harvard, conducted research on Jamaican folk music, such as Pocomania and Kumina church music.

8. For further information on the PNP and JLP see Gray (1991) and Knight (1990).

9. While Joe finds that disco's twelve-inch disc sensation "enhanced and prolonged the pulsating tempo of the rhythm and percussions breaks," street jockeys used "breaks" in a similar fashion to refer to a percussion vamp section comprised of the timbales, congas, and bongos (1980:63). One of Herc's favorite breaks was "Apache" by the Incredible Bongo Band. By the mid-1980s, breaks or break beats were simply musical motifs from past prerecorded hits used in a rap music mix.

10. Scratching has exploded into a complex craft. See Rice (1998) on various terminologies used in the contemporary scene.

11. In the 1980s, hip-hop DJing, considered primarily a male-dominated craft, expanded to include female artists such as DJ Jazzy Joyce (who studied with Whiz Kid), DJ La Spank, Cocoa Chanel, and Latoya "Spinderella" Hanson (the original DJ for Salt-N-Pepa).

12. Several rap music artists were discovered at Disco Fever, including The Fat Boys, Run-D.M.C., Whodini, The Treacherous Three, Dr. Jeckyll and Mr. Hyde, Grandmaster Flash and the Furious Five, and Kurtis Blow. On April 4, 1986, Disco Fever was forced to close because of a cabaret license violation. Sal Abbatiello started another dance club, The Devil's Nest, in the Bronx. It caters mainly to a teenage Latino clientele and plays Latin popular music, including rap and salsa.

13. I was a panelist for the Rap Music: The Blame or the Burden conference, which was held January 29, 1993, at Medgar Evers College in Brooklyn. Among the panelists was Kool "DJ" Herc, who interjected that a female MC, Pebblee-Poo, also performed with the Herculords.

## Chapter 3: The Explosion of Rap Music in the Musical Mainstream

1. By 1979, with the addition of Raheim and Mr. Ness to Grandmaster Flash and the Three Emcees, the crew renamed themselves Grandmaster Flash and the Furious Five. Funky Four Plus One included KK Rockwell, Lil Rodney Cee, Keith Keith, MC Sha Rock (a woman), and Jazzy Jeff with DJ Breakout.

2. Grandmaster Flash and the Furious Five also recorded "We Rap More Mellow" on Brass Records under the name The Younger Generation.

3. By 1981 the music industry had begun to recognize rap music as a genre distinct from disco.

4. Although "Rapper's Delight" was nearly fifteen minutes long, "Rapping and Rocking" by Funky Four Plus One and "Walk This Way" by Run-D.M.C., both sixteen minutes long, hold the record in rap music history as the longest rap songs.

5. At the time, Blow was managed by Russell Simmons, the cofounder of Def Jam Records and founder of Rush Artist Management, the largest and most successful rap management firm.

6. In November 1988 the Juice Crew formed a rap record label, Cold Chillin' Records, distributed by Warner Bros. Records.

7. Other answer-back raps came from the Juice Crew, including Roxanne Shanté's "Have a Nice Day" (1987), answered by BDP's "I'm Still #1" (1988).

8. The techno-pop sound later provided the musical basis for the following rap songs: "Message II (Survival)" by Melle Mel and Duke Bootee, "Electric Kingdom" by Twilight 22, "Rockin It" by The Fearless Four, "Supersonic" by JJ Fad, "Magic's Wand" by Whodini, "Gonna Make You Sweat" by C+C Music Factory, "Baby Got Back" by Sir Mix-A-Lot, and the music of Mantronix.

9. "I Need Love" set off a wave of mellow style or subdued-in-tone love raps. Among these are A Tribe Called Quest's "Bonita Applebum" on *People's Instinctive Travels and the Paths of Rhythm* (1990) and Common's "The Light" from *Like Water for Chocolate* (2000).

10. De La Soul was embroiled in a $1.7 million lawsuit by the Turtles for the unauthorized use of "You Showed Me" in the trio's song "Transmitting Live from Mars."

11. Jeffrey Louis Decker delves further into the symbolism of "time" as used by Public Enemy. In so doing, Decker shows parallels between Public Enemy's use of time and its use by the Black Arts Movement poet Amiri Baraka in his poem "It's Nation Time" (1993:64–65).

12. This interview appeared in the *Washington Times* (May 22, 1989) by David Mills. For more detail, see Chuck D (1997:205–39).

13. Guzman-Sanchez's two-volume compilation *O.G. Funk Locking* includes a number of funk tunes that were performed by West Coast dancers.

14. See Cross (1993:26–27) for the complete lyrics.

15. Shabba Ranks became the first dancehall star to earn consecutive Grammy awards in 1992 and 1993. His achievements propelled dancehall to international heights.

16. Schoolly D recorded the following albums on Jive records during the 1980s: *Schoolly D* (1986), *Saturday Night* (1987), *Smoke Some Kill* (1988), *Am I Black Enough for You* (1989), *How a Black Man Feels* (1991).

17. Arabian Prince was an original member of N.W.A., but he decided to embark upon a solo career.

18. Tone-Lōc's "Wild Thing" was censured by New York officials as pivotal to the gang rape of a white female in New York City's Central Park by a group of Latino and African American males in April 1989. The *Village Voice* presented a special section featuring various pop culture journalists' take on the racial stereotyping of the rapists and the influence rap music had on the offenders' action. The writers included Linda Goode Bryant, Cathy Campbell, Barry Michael Cooper, Nelson George, Andrea Kannapell, Lisa Kennedy, Joan Morgan, and Greg Tate. For further information see the *Village Voice*, May 9, 1989, 25–39, 53.

19. "Mack" is the anglicized version of *macquereau,* French for a pimp.

20. For additional information about the rise and fall of KDAY, see James (1991).

21. Les Garland, the vice president of programming, brought his experience at MTV to his new position at The Box. He changed the preprogrammed format to one in which viewers could control the programming. The "Music Television You Control" concept was described by *Billboard* as being in the vanguard of the "new interactivity."

22. On November 3, 2000, Johnson sold BET to Viacom for $3 billion. He remains CEO and chair of BET.

23. England-based rap artists include Tarrie B, Monie Love, MC Rebel, Cookie Crew, and the Wee Papa Girls.

## Chapter 4: Expanding Frontiers

1. Also on 2Pac's album *2Pacalypse Now* is "Soulja's Story," an anti–police repression song. In *Davidson v. Time Warner, Inc.,* the plaintiff charged that the lyrics of "Soulja's Story" incited a young black male, Ronald Ray Howard, to fatally shoot a Texas state trooper, William Davidson, on April 11, 1992. The case never went to court.

2. One rap music engineer for an independent record label told me that MTV refused to air videos showing cleavage. The engineer requested anonymity.

3. Biggie Smallz was the first to use this name, which led Christopher Wallace to change his professional moniker from Biggie Small*s* to The Notorious B.I.G.

4. Vanilla Ice responded to critics that he was not familiar with this fraternity, but John Morthland (1991:63) quotes him as saying that the phrase "Ice Ice Baby" is a chant from the Alpha Phi Alpha fraternity.

5. This comment was brought to my attention by a professor at Michigan State University. The day before my participation on a hip-hop panel (February 28, 2001), she told me that she had asked one of her white students what is so appealing about the song "Stan." The student replied that the song is realistic because it captures the average white youth's feelings of loneliness, aloofness, and being misunderstood by his or her parents. Such feelings, she says, result in nihilism, self-mutilation, and, in some cases, suicide. The *Los Angeles Times* featured a front-page story on the life of Eminem prior to his controversial performance of "Stan" with Elton John at the 43rd Annual Grammy Awards on February 21, 2001. The electronic pop singer Dido originally did the vocals sung by John, who performed despite protests from the gay community. The *Los Angeles Times* presents the troubled childhood of Marshall Mathers from his impoverished upbringing in the streets of Detroit and his being "frequently beaten up" by his peers to the dissension between his mother and his former wife, Kim, and to "two incidents in Michigan in which he allegedly brandished an unloaded gun" (Frammolino and Boucher 2001:A18). Despite much debate, Eminem received three Grammy awards for all rap categories: Best Rap Solo Performance for

"The Real Slim Shady," Best Rap Performance by a Duo or Group for "Forgot About Dre" (with Dr. Dre), and Best Rap Album for *The Marshall Mathers LP.*

6. Clubs that hosted open-mic sessions were vital to the post-1960s spoken word movement. The poet Sha-Key refers to the new poetics as "boom poetry." This style of poetry fuses hip-hop and a quasi-scat delivery style executed in freestyle. Among artists of this style are Michael Franti, Reg E. Gaines, Saul Williams, and Ursula Rucker.

7. Scott defines herself as a poet rather than a rappin MC. She delivers rhymes much in the manner of the slam-style poets of the 1990s. Scott's rhyming/poetic skills were honed in intimate sites like coffee houses rather than the more flamboyant freestyle-MC battle venues.

8. In January 1992, Uptown Entertainment sponsored a celebrity charity basketball game in Harlem at the City College of New York at which nine people were crushed to death. This tragedy along with business conflicts led to the estranged relationship between Combs and Harrell.

9. Harrell also produced the film *Strictly Business* (1991) and the television series "New York Undercover." By the mid-1990s he had become president and CEO of Motown Records. He appointed Heavy D to succeed him as president of Uptown Entertainment. Unsatisfied with his work, Motown eventually released Harrell from his contract. Harrell and Combs have since resolved their differences, and in 1998 Harrell became the president of Bad Boy Entertainment. Eventually he left Bad Boy Entertainment to become president of Nu America Records.

10. Former Death Row members attested to these tactics in the MTV documentary "The Rise of Death Row" (1999). See also Farr (1994).

11. Since Shakur's fatal drive-by shooting on September 7 and subsequent death on September 13, 1996, Death Row released an album featuring Shakur's recordings under the name Makaveli, *the don killuminati: the 7 day theory* (1996). Shakur's pseudonym derives from the Italian politician and strategist Niccolò Machiavelli, who is said to have faked his death. 2Pac was so fascinated with Machiavelli that he changed his name to honor him. This coincidence led to an avalanche of urban legends that 2Pac was still alive. 2Pac recorded a wealth of material during his short time with Death Row. Afeni Shakur, Tupac's mother, continued to request ownership of these masters from Death Row. According to her lawyer, 2Pac recorded 151 tracks, but Ms. Shakur had only received 62 as of 1998 (Lodge 1998:66). Since 2Pac's death, several bootlegged tapes of his material have circulated. In the wake of his death, Ms. Shakur launched a record label, Amaru Entertainment Records (Amaru is her son's middle name). Prior to 2001, Amaru released *R U Still Down? (Remember Me)* (1997), *Greatest Hits* (1998), and *Still I Rise* (1999). All four posthumously released albums made the Top 10 and sold over ten million units.

12. On Marion "Suge" Knight and his restructuring of Death Row records, see Anson and Cogan (2001).

13. *The Source* lists Master P in its profile of the thirty top "Hip-Hop Powers." For further information see Mr. Murphy, Lèger, and Fontaine (1999:196).

14. Jay-Z's street-edged album, *Jay-Z Vol. 2 . . . Hard Knock Life,* won a Grammy for the Best Rap Performance in 1999.

15. Turntablism has graduated into a national and international venture, as exemplified by the DJ Battle for World Supremacy, hosted by the New Music Seminar in New York City, the Technics DMC World DJ Championship, and the International Turntablist Federation Championship competitions, among others.

16. In *Representing: Hip Hop Culture and the Production of Black Cinema* (1998), S. Craig Watkins explores "new jack" films and black filmmaking during the post–Civil Rights movement era.

17. *The Source* presented a special section on the global hip-hop scene in its one hundredth issue (January 1991). The rap music/hip-hop magazines *Hip-Hop Connection* and *XXL* include monthly sections on regional and global hip-hip scenes. I might add that the establishment of Zulu Nation chapters abroad—commonly known as the Universal Zulu Nation—have also contributed to the dissemination of hip-hop arts (see chapter 6).

### Chapter 5: Street Production

1. Postwar black popular music styles include rhythm and blues, soul, funk, and ballad style; the performance practices of all of these are based in the gospel-blues tradition. The context from which most of these styles emerged was the black church; singers in these traditions initially performed music associated with the traditional black church before exclusively affiliating with the popular music scene. Among these are Sam Cooke of the Soul Stirrers, Jackie Wilson of the Dominoes, Dinah Washington, Ruth Brown, Aretha Franklin, Patti LaBelle, Gladys Knight, Larry Graham, Wilson Picket, and Whitney Houston, to name but a few. Rap music artists, however, claim that their music started in the streets and do not see their musical beginnings or style as deriving from the black sacred tradition.

2. For further information on these updates see Fab Five Freddy (1992), Major (1994), and Smitherman (1994).

3. For more detailed discussion about the Five Percenters, refer to chapter 6.

4. The ethnomusicologist Alpha Balde compares a cipher to a ring-shout. Commenting on the seminal discussions of Sterling Stuckey (1987) and Samuel J. Floyd Jr. (1995), Balde concurs that the ring-shout is a signifier on the unbroken circling of African-derived ideas. Thus it is "a narrative trope or the (re)construction and continuation of African-American cultural values and symbols" in the Western world (1999:82).

5. According to Carl "Butch" Small, Snoop's mother used to refer to him as Snoopy, the little dog featured in the *Peanuts* cartoon series. Once Snoop became older, he added Doggy Dogg to his name to indicate his adult status. Small summarizes that

"as he evolved, Snoopy was cute, but Snoopy wanted to become a man. So the name changed into Snoop Doggy Dogg" (Small interview). After leaving Death Row Records for No Limit in the late 1990s, Snoop changed his name to Snoop Dogg.

6. 2Pac had the acronym "THUG LIFE" tattooed on his abdomen, which he translates as "The Hate U Gave Lil' Infants Fuck Everybody" (Light 1997:29).

7. Regarding flow as an overarching aesthetic common to all hip-hop arts, see Rose (1994:38–39).

8. Raggamuffin is used interchangeably in England and other international markets for reggae dancehall music.

9. Singles that make use of Jamaican dancehall style rap include "9mm Goes Bang," from *Criminal Minded* (1987) by Boogie Down Productions, "Princess of the Posse," from *All Hail the Queen* (1989) by Queen Latifah, and "Chain Gang-Rap" and "Gimme No Crack," from *Unity* (1988) by Shinehead.

10. During the early commercial years of rap music, go-go music produced by Trouble Funk and the E.U. Band created a rap hybrid.

11. "The Message" ranks as the first politically toned rap in the annals of popular music history. According to Sugar Hill Records cofounder Joe Robinson, it was written and performed by Melle Mel and Duke Bootee, a percussionist in the house band of Sugar Hill Records.

12. On his debut album *2Pacalypse Now* (1991), 2Pac decodes each letter of N.I.G.G.A. (Never Ignorant Getting Goals Accomplished) in the sociopolitical song "Words of Wisdom."

13. "Two minute motherfucka" is a phrase used in the song "Two Minute Brother" by Bytches with Problems to describe a man who cannot sustain lovemaking past two minutes.

14. A "house nigga" is a black person who reports to whites or outsiders about the black community's intimate affairs and a black person who responds passively to white patriarchal rule. This term is also the name of a song by Boogie Down Productions ("House Niggas" [1991]).

15. "Sucka Nigga" is a song from A Tribe Called Quest's LP *Midnight Marauders* (1993) that explores the various meanings of this word.

16. LL Cool J continues to participate in many disses/signifyin duels. On his 1997 LP *Phenomenon,* he disses Canibus, a younger rap artist, who indicated his desire to figuratively "rip" the microphone tattoo off of LL Cool J's right biceps. In "4,3,2,1" LL disses Canibus by calling him "Lil Shorty" and telling him that the mic never leaves his (LL's) side. He taunts Canibus by clarifying that Canibus doesn't really want to borrow LL's mic but just idolizes it. Canibus comes back with much hyperbole in "Second Round K.O." on his 1998 self-titled LP. He responds to LL Cool J by telling him to watch him rip the tattoo from his arm (on the back of LL Cool J's LP, there is a photograph highlighting his tattoo). Canibus mockingly parades a similar tattoo on the back of his LP.

17. Numerous rap songs have exposed police brutality. Among these are N.W.A.'s "Fuck tha Police," from *Straight Outta Compton* (1988); Ice Cube's "Endangered Species (Tales from the Darkside)," from *AmeriKKKa's Most Wanted* (1990), and "Who Got the Camera," from *The Predator* (1992); 2Pac's "Soulja's Story," from *2Pacalypse Now* (1991), and "Strictly 4 My N.I.G.G.A.Z.," from *Strictly 4 My N.I.G.G.A.Z* (1993); "Behind Closed Doors," from *Ain't a Damn Thang Changed* (1991), featuring Coolio of W.C. and the Maad Circle; Cypress Hill's "Pigs," from *Cypress Hill* (1991); Ice-T and Body Count's "Cop Killer," from *Body Count* (1992); and Kid Frost's "I Got Pulled Over," from *East Side Story* (1992). Some of the most popular rap music LPs with sexual content include *Eazy-Duz-It* (1988) by Eazy-E and the controversial album *As Nasty As They Wanna Be* (1989) by 2 Live Crew (see chapter 6). Themes of sociopolitical commentary, Black Nationalism, and drug addiction are discussed in chapters 6; rap songs dealing with feminist issues are examined in more detail in chapter 7.

18. For further discussion of turntable techniques (e.g. beat-juggling, chirps, rubs, etc.) via the cross-fader, see Rice (1998), Brewster and Broughton (2000), and "The History of Turntablism" (2000).

19. Glazer (1999) profiles DJs Dummy and Doo Wop and their opinions of both models.

20. The term "wall of noise" derives from a 1960s music production concept, "wall of sound," coined by the songwriter-producer and girl-group mogul Phil Spector. The term was adopted by the rap music journalist S. H. Fernando Jr. in his discussion of the musical production of the hip-hop DJs Rza of Wu-Tang Clan and Timbaland and the British trip-hop producer Tricky (Fernando 1998: 146).

21. Jazz/rap fusion was first labeled among English DJs as "acid jazz" in the 1980s. Since the 1990s, U.S.-based artists who fuse jazz with rap do not refer to their music as "acid jazz," but the term is employed by the music industry as a label for this type of rap.

22. For further information about the popularity of platinum jewelry and a profile of jewelry worn by members of The Hot Boys see Ogunnaike (2000).

23. The high flat-top has occasionally been referred to as a "cameo," a fade-like hairstyle worn by the singer-drummer Larry Blackmon of the group Cameo during the mid-1980s.

### Chapter 6: Issues, Conflicts, and Conspiracies

1. Vivid examples of this type of exploitation within the hip-hop community include Luke Campbell's Peep Show, a pay-per-view X-rated adult program that started in 1996, and the use of porno actors in videos such as 2Pac's "How Do You Want It" (1996). In 2001 Snoop Dogg released *Snoop Dogg's Doggystyle,* an X-rated rap music video, produced by Larry Flynt's *Hustler* magazine corporation.

2. After the gang culture subsided in New York City during the early 1970s, blacks and Latinos worked together for Puerto Rico's statehood. For further information refer to the video *Flyin' Cut Sleeves* (1993), which shows footage of this political effort.

3. Refer to "The Beliefs of the Universal Zulu Nation" (1993:49) or the Zulu Nation's Web site <http://www.zulunation.com>.

4. Queen Latifah, who is not a Five Percenter, comments on this masculinist concept by referring to herself as an "Asiatic black woman" in the rap song "Come into My House" (1989).

5. For further information on the proliferation of the Five Percenters ideology in rap music, see Allen (1996).

6. *Rap Sheet* (December 1992) presented a special issue on rap music radio programming and the ways in which contemporary urban radio (a.k.a. "churban") stations were forced to decrease playing rap. The stations included WPGA and WFXA, of Macon and Augusta, Georgia, respectively; WILD of Boston; WGCI of Chicago; KDAY of Los Angeles; and KYOK of Houston, Texas.

7. 2 Live Crew won all of their court cases through testimonies of expert witnesses hired by their lawyer. Among the expert witnesses was Henry Louis Gates Jr., a scholar of black culture and literature. Gates testified that 2 Live Crew were simply utilizing the art of signifyin, which he describes as parody, "one of the most venerated forms of art" in African American vernacular speech. For further information about the details of Gates's testimony, see Rimer (1990); Kitwana (1994).

8. At the time of the meetings, Interscope, a record label housed under Time-Warner, was a distributing arm for Death Row Records. The meetings focused attention on Death Row Records as a producer of gangsta rap recordings. Eventually, Interscope Records was bought by Universal Music Group of Seagram. Because of the controversy and pressure exerted by anti–gangsta rap activists, Seagram pressured Interscope to sever all distribution ties with Death Row Records in August 1997.

9. Many celebrities donated money to the making of the "Self-Destruction" video. See George (1990:10–19).

10. *Vibe* magazine featured cover stories on the feud between Tupac of Death Row Records and Sean "Puffy" Combs and The Notorious B.I.G. The rapper Chubb Rock also discusses the bicoastal rap turf war in Eure and Spady's *Nation Conscious Rap* (1991:189). Other references to the instigation of the media and rap turf wars can be found in the editorial section of *The Source* (January 1997).

11. A few months after the death of The Notorious B.I.G., KPWR started a talk show, hosted by Ice-T, called "One Nation," in an effort to shed more light on community issues, including black-on-black crime and rap turf wars.

12. At the present time FBI investigations are pending. Media reports have stated that witnesses to the fatal shootings of Shakur and Wallace were afraid to come forward because they feared retaliation.

13. By June 2001, new developments in the murders of Tupac Shakur and The Notorioius B.I.G. were presented by Randall Sullivan in *Rolling Stone*. Extracted from

the investigation of Russell Poole, a former LAPD detective, Sullivan reports that LAPD's Rampart Division corruption scandal erupted as a result of the shooting of an officer by another officer in 1997 and the intentional entrapment of known drug offenders by some officers of the LAPD, who, in turn, were drug dealing. Sullivan also discloses Poole's theory that when these officers were off duty, they occasionally worked as security for Death Row Records' events. Based on further evidence, Poole suggests that these officers have first-hand knowledge of the murders of Tupac and The Notorious B.I.G. A few years before Sullivan's article, Death Row Records' CEO Marion "Suge" Knight was sentenced to nine years in a California federal prison for a probation violation, and the FBI launched an investigation into whether the convicted drug dealer Michael Harris invested his money in Death Row Records, as Knight alleged. Knight was released from prison on good behavior in August 2001. As a result of Sullivan's article, Knight planned to sue *Rolling Stone* for defamation of character. For further information, see Ro (1998), Sullivan (2001), and Philips (2001).

14. In 1994, Simmons's Def Jam Recording Group had a major disagreement with Sony Music and was soon acquired by Polygram's Mercury Records Division for distribution. The Seagram Company purchased Polygram—including Def Jam Recordings—for $10.4 billion in May 1998.

15. In 1998 the rap entrepreneurs Master P and Sean "Puffy" Combs and the rapper-actor Will Smith were among the forty highest-paid entertainers listed in *Forbes* magazine (September 21, 1998). Master P, who refers to himself as the "Ghetto Bill Gates," ranked tenth, grossing $56.5 million; Puffy Combs ranked fifteenth, earning $53.5 million; Smith ranked thirty-sixth, with an estimated $34 million.

16. The U.S. Supreme Court ruled on March 7, 1994, that 2 Live's Crew's use of Orbison's "Pretty Woman" in "Clean as They Wanna Be" was simply a parody of Orbison's song and therefore considered fair use.

17. See Babcock (1999).

18. This line is adapted from MC Breed's song "Gotta Get Mine" (1993).

19. When Surgeon General Dr. David Satcher appeared on the July 15, 1998, edition of "BET Tonight," hosted by Tavis Smiley, he referred to the AIDS epidemic as an "epidemic of color" because of its high incidence in the African American community. According to his statistics, blacks make up 13 percent of the U.S. population (rather than 12 percent as quoted by Word and Bowser), yet they make up 57 percent of AIDS cases. It was also reported that AIDS is the leading cause of death among African Americans between the ages of twenty-five and forty-four. The rate of infection among women is rising at an alarming rate.

20. Also see Noel (1997).

21. For further discussion of the conspiracy theories surrounding AIDS in the African American communities, see Cohen (1999:186–219).

22. On Kool Moe Dee's self-titled album, this song is listed as "Monster Crack."

23. Gary Webb was fired from the *Mercury News* several months later. However,

he published his work about the CIA, the Nicaraguan Contras, and the crack cocaine triangle in his book, *Dark Alliance: The CIA, the Contras, and the Crack Cocaine Explosion* (1998). California Congresswoman Maxine Waters wrote the book's foreword.

24. For further reading on black youths and street hustling or "income-producing activities" and the U.S. legal system, see Ruth Wilson Gilmore (1998).

### Chapter 7: Daughters of the Blues

An earlier version of this chapter appeared as "Empowering Self, Making Choices, Creating Spaces: Black Female Identity via Rap Music Performance," in *Journal of American Folklore* 113:449 (Summer 2000):255–69.

1. Other female MCs include Antoinette (Next Plateau), Bahamadia (EMI), Doggy's Angels (Dogghouse), Charli Baltimore (Sony), Conscious Daughters (Priority), Finesse and Synquis (MCA), Gangsta Boo (Relativity), Heather B (MCA), Lady of Rage (Death Row), Ladybug (Pendulum), MC Smooth (Crush Music), MC Trouble (Motown), Nikki D (Def Jam), Nonchalant (MCA), Oaktown's 3–5–7 (Capital); Solé (Dreamworks), T-Love (Down Low), and Trina (Slip-N-Slide).

2. The custom of sculpting the queen mother's head was established in Benin by King Oba Esigies during the sixteenth century. Sieber and Walker note that during Esigies's reign, he commissioned a sculpted bronze head of his mother, Idia, and placed it in his palace to commemorate her role in the Benin-Idah, thereby including queen mothers in the cult of royal ancestors for the first time (1987:93). In addition to Sieber and Walker's work, refer to Ben-Amos (1995) and Ben-Amos and Rubin (1983) for photographs and a brief discussion of queen mother heads in Benin.

3. Joan Morgan was among the women panelists at the "Sexuality in Rap Music" forum held at Tisch School of the Arts Auditorium at New York University on December 5, 1992.

4. For further discussion of this video see chapter 8.

5. Isis, formerly affiliated with X-Clan, records under the name of Lin Que.

6. In 1986 Salt-N-Pepa recorded "Shake Your Thang" for their second LP, *Salt with a Deadly Pepa*. In the video version, Salt-N-Pepa are seen gyrating their hips and shaking their buttocks during musical interludes. Since the 1990s, several rap songs and video performances by male artists celebrate and/or exploit black women's buttocks in bumping-and-grinding or rump-shaking dance movements. These songs include Sir Mix-A-Lot's "Baby Got Back" (1991), Wreckx-N-Effect's "Rump Shaker" (1992), Juvenile's "Back That Azz Up" (1998), and Mystikal's "Shake It Fast" (2000), to name a few. The focus on black women's buttocks in hip-hop culture is predated by Jamaican dancehall musical culture. For further discussion of this phenomenon, see Carolyn Cooper (1989).

7. "Whatta Man" is adapted from Linda Lyndell's 1968 hit "What a Man."

8. On Yo-Yo's first LP she spells her name with a hyphen; on her subsequent re-

cordings she deletes the hyphen from her name. I will use the initial spelling of her name throughout.

9. Millie Jackson is a rhythm and blues singer who garnered the attention of listeners during the 1970s with her flair for sexually explicit songs about male/female relationships. During the musical introductions or interludes of her songs, Jackson employs sexual metaphors in a conversational manner over musical accompaniment. She is considered a role model not only by Shanté but also by other female rappers, including Lil' Kim, Foxy Brown, and Da Brat, whose third LP, *Unrestricted,* recalls Millie Jackson's 1997 album *Totally Unrestricted: The Millie Jackson Anthology.* Also see Pearlman (1988) and Saxon (1997).

10. During MC Lyte's early career, she wore no makeup, dressed in sweatsuits with sneakers, and used hardcore facial expressions (i.e. grimacing), mirroring the male hardcore image. Since her first album, *Lyte as a Rock* (1988), she has maintained her hardcore image, but, as she says, "'I've grown and I'm becoming a woman, slowly but surely. I'm finding my feminine qualities; it's okay to wear makeup and lipstick; it's something I like to do now'" (quoted in Lady G 1992:42).

11. For further information about the toast, see Abrahams (1970) and Dance (1978).

12. Sistas with Attitude accomplish this emasculation by referring to their male competitors or suitors as "motherfuckers," "niggas," and "suckers." Since the element of signifyin is aesthetically appealing in this style of rap, the former two terms may have both negative and positive meanings, depending on the context; the latter is used as an insult for men lacking in verbal or sexual skills. Examples of rap songs that portray those distinct characteristics of Sistas with Attitude include the following: "I Don't Give a Fuck" and "Mai Sista Izza Bitch" (1993), by Boss on *Born Gangstaz;* "Two Minute Brother" and "Shit Popper" (1991), by Bytches with Problems on *The Bytches;* "Da Shit Ya Can't Fuc Wit" and "Fire it Up" (1994), by Da Brat on *Funkdafied;* "Ill Na Na" and "Letter to the Firm" (1997), by Foxy Brown on *Ill Na Na;* "Big Momma Thang" and "Spend a Little Doe" (1996), by Lil' Kim on *Hard Core;* "Paper Thin" (1988) by MC Lyte on *Lyte as a Rock;* "Steady F—king" (1993), by MC Lyte on *Ain't No Other;* and "Big Mama" (1992), by Roxanne Shanté on *Bitch Is Back.*

13. Morgan speaks further about the use and abuse of sexuality by women of hip-hop in the chapter "from fly girls to bitches and hos" from her book *when chickenheads come home to roost: my life as a hip-hop feminist* (1999).

14. See Chideya (2000) for further discussion of hip-hop and homophobia.

15. While Queen Pen is a play on "kingpin," she also uses this moniker to indicate that she "pens" (or writes) her own lyrics, a skill that some have believed that female MCs lack. Although "Girlfriend" and other selections on her LP were co-written and produced by Teddy Riley, her real name (Lynise Walters) is credited on all songs. In the music industry, it is not unusual for producers to take co-writing credit on their mentees' debut works.

16. "Girlfriend" was co-written and produced by Teddy Riley, the inventor of new jack swing style (rap/rhythm and blues hybrid) and the leader of the group Black-

street, in which Queen Pen performs a rap. Riley's input on "Girlfriend" is discussed by Jamison (1998).

17. When asked about "Girlfriend," Queen Pen asserts that her debut album, *My Melody*, contains nonlesbian songs, including "Get Away," which discusses domestic violence (Duvernay 1988:AR34).

18. For more on this topic see Guevara (1987), Berry (1994), Forman (1994), Goodall (1994), and Rose (1994).

### Chapter 8: Visualizing Beats and Rhymes

1. For other analyses of rap music videos dealing with the issue of police harassment, see Tricia Rose's analyses of BDP/KRS-One's "Who Protects Us from You?" and LL Cool J's "Illegal Search" (1994:107–14). The theme of police repression of African American youth dominates in West Coast reality or gangsta raps. For further details see Kelley (1996).

2. "By the Time I Get to Arizona" provoked protest by civil rights followers because of certain scenes, such as Public Enemy's Security of the First World marching with rifles, which some viewers felt was contrary to King's belief in nonviolence.

3. A similar motif from John Singleton's movie *Boyz 'N the Hood* (1991) is seen in the video "Growing Up in the Hood," by Compton's Most Wanted (1991). Viewers witness via visual text the belligerent treatment of a young black male by a black police office, who holds a gun to the youth's throat.

4. Iceberg Slim, Donald Goines, Robert H. deCoy (author of *The Nigger Bible*) were among the most celebrated black writers to pen a legion of raw street stories published by Holloway House of Los Angeles. Holloway House was founded by the white publishers Bently Morris and Ralph Weinstock in 1959. Some of their writers and staff were solicited from the Watts Writers Workshop. Because of the popular demand for Holloway House's books, Iceberg Slim's *Pimp, the Story of My Life*, for example, has been translated into Spanish, French, Italian, Dutch, Swedish, and Greek. For further information, see Gilstrap (1998).

5. Japanese youth who imitate black popular cultural forms like hip-hop are called "niggernese" in Japan. White youth of the United States who do the same are ridiculed by some observers as "wiggers," similar to Norman Mailer's usage of "white Negro," who are essentially "Negro wannabes."

6. In many interviews, Suge Knight has identified himself with the Bloods gang in Los Angeles, whose color is red. Their rivals, the Crips, wear blue.

# Selected Discography

Afrika Bambaataa and the Soul Sonic Force. 1982 (reissued 1992). "Planet Rock." *Don't Stop . . . Planet Rock* (Tommy Boy 1052).

Anthrax. 1991. "Bring the Noise." *Attack of the Killer B's* (Island 314-510-318-2).

Antoinette. 1989. *Who's the Boss?* (Next Plateau 1015).

Arrested Development. 1992. *3 Years, 5 Months & 2 Days in the Life of . . .* (Chrysalis 21929).

Beastie Boys. 1986. *Licensed to Ill* (Def Jam/Polygram 27351).

———. 1989. *Paul's Boutique* (Capitol 91743).

———. 1992. *Check Your Head* (Grand Royal/Captiol 98938).

———. 1994. *Ill Communication* (Grand Royal/Capitol 28599).

———. 1994. *Some Old Bullshit* (Grand Royal/Capitol 89843).

Beck. 1994. "Loser." *Mellow Gold* (David Geffen Company 24634).

———. 1996. *Odelay.* (David Geffen Company 24823).

Big Daddy Kane. 1988. *Long Live the Kane* (Cold Chillin'/Warner Bros. 25131).

———. 1989. *It's a Big Daddy Thing* (Cold Chillin'/Warner Bros. 26303).

Biz Markie. 1988. *Goin' Off* (Cold Chillin'/Warner Bros. 25675).

———. 1989. *The Biz Never Sleeps* (Cold Chilln'/Warner Bros. 26003).

———. 1991. *I Need a Haircut* (Cold Chillin'/Warner Bros. 26648).

Blowfly. 1980. *Rap Dirty.* 12-inch single (T.K. Records 438).

Bone Thugs-N-Harmony. 1995. "Tha Crossroads." *E. 1999 Eternal* (Epic 5539).

Boogie Boys. 1985 (reissued 1987). "A Fly Girl." *Rap vs. Rap: The Answer Album* (Priority 9506).

Boogie Down Productions. 1987. "The Bridge Is Over." *Criminal Minded* (B Boy 4787).

———. 1988. "My Philosophy." *By All Means Necessary* (Jive/Novus 10974-7).

———. 1989. *Ghetto Music: The Blueprint of Hip-Hop* (Jive/Novus 1187).

———. 1992. *Sex and Violence* (Jive/Novus 41470).

BoogieMonsters. 1997. *God Sound* (EMI 56045).

Boo-Yaa T.R.I.B.E. 1990. *New Funky Nation* (4th & B'Way 4017).

Boss. 1993. *Born Gangstaz* (Def Jam/Columbia 52903).

Brand Nubian. 1990. *One for All* (Elektra 60946).

———. 1993. *In God We Trust* (Elektra 61381).

Brown, James. 1996. *JB40: 40th Anniversay Collection* (Polydor 533409).

Brown, Sterling. 1995. *The Poetry of Sterling Brown* (Smithsonian/Folkways SF 47002).

*Bulworth* (soundtrack). 1998. (Interscope 90160).

Busta Rhymes. 1997. *When Disaster Strikes . . .* (Elektra 62064-2).

Bytches with Problems (BWP). 1991. *The Bytches* (No Face/RAL 47068).

Canibus. 1998. *Can-I-Bus* (Universal UD-53136).

Captain Rapp. 1983. "Bad Times (I Can't Stand It)." 12-inch single (Becket 517).

Clinton, George. 1977. "P-Funk." *Parliament Live: P-Funk Earth Tour* (Casablanca 7053).

Compton's Most Wanted. 1991. *Straight Checkn'em* (Epic 47926).

Coolio. 1995. "Gangsta's Paradise." *It Takes a Thief* (Tommy Boy 1141).

The Coup. 1993. *Kill My Landlord* (Wild Pitch 89047).

Cypress Hill. 1991. *Cypress Hill* (Ruffhouse/Columbia 47119).

———. 1993. *Black Sunday* (Ruffhouse/Columbia 53931).

Da Brat. 1994. *Funkdafied* (Chaos/Columbia 66164).

———. 1996. *Anuthantrum* (So So Def/Columbia 67813).

———. 2000. *Unrestricted* (So So Def/Sony 69772).

Da Lench Mob. 1992. *Guerillas in the Mist* (Street Knowledge/Atco 7 92206-2).

Das EFX. 1992. *Dead Serious.* (EastWest 91827-47).

Davis, Miles. 1992. *Doo-Bop* (Warner Bros. 4-26938).

De La Soul. 1989. *3 Feet High and Rising* (Tommy Boy 1019).

———. 1991. *De La Soul Is Dead* (Tommy Boy 1029).

Def Jef. 1989. *Just a Poet with Soul* (Delicious Vinyl 92199).

Digable Planets. 1993. *Reachin' (A New Refutation of Time and Space)* (Pendulum 961414-2).

Digital Underground. 1990. *Sex Packets* (Tommy Boy 1026).

DJ Quik. 1991. *Quik Is the Name* (Profile 1402).

———. 1995. *Safe + Sound* (Profile 1462).

Tha Dogg Pound. 1995. *Dogg Food* (Death Row 50546).

Doug E. Fresh. 1996. "All the Way to Heaven." *The Greatest Hits, Vol. 1* (Bust It Records 76002).

Dr. Dre. 1992. *The Chronic* (Death Row/Interscope 57128).

Eazy-E. 1988. *Eazy-Duz-It* (Ruthless 57100).

EPMD. 1988. *Strictly Business* (Sleeping Bag/Priority 57135).

———. 1989. *Unfinished Business* (Sleeping Bag/Priority 57136).

———. 1991. *Business as Usual* (Def Jam/Columbia 47067).

Eminem. 1999. *The Slim Shady LP* (Aftermath/Interscope 90287).

———. 2000. "Stan." *The Marshall Mathers LP* (Aftermath/Interscope 490629).

Eric B. and Rakim. 1987. *Paid in Full* (4th & B'Way 4005).

———. 1988. *Follow the Leader* (Uni UNID-3).

Eve. 1999. "Gotta Man." *Let There Be . . . Eve—Ruff Ryders' First Lady* (Ruff Ryders/Interscope 490453).

Foxy Brown. 1997. *Ill Na Na* (Def Jam 540728).

———. 1998. *Chyna Doll* (Def Jam 558933).

Freestyle Fellowship. 1993. *Innercity Griots* (4th & B'Way 162-444-0550-2).

Fugees. 1996. *The Score* (Ruffhouse/Columbia 67639).

Funkadelic. 1978. *One Nation under a Groove* (Priority 53872).

Funky Four Plus One. 1980. "Rapping and Rocking the House." *Great Rap Hits* (Sugar Hill 246).

Gang Starr. 1989. *No More Mr. Nice Guy* (Wild Pitch 98709).

Geto Boys. 1990. *Grip It! On That Other Level* (Rap-A-Lot 40371).

———. 1993. "Six Feet Deep." *'Til Death Do Us Part* (Rap-A-Lot 40372).

Giovanni, Nikki. 1970 (reissued 1993). *Truth on Its Way* (Collectables Col 6506).

God's Property. 1997. "Stomp." *Kirk Franklin & Nu Nation* (B-Rite Music/Interscope 90093).

Goodie MOb. 1995. *Soul Food* (LaFace Records AC 6018).

Graham Central Station. 1975. *Release Yourself* (Warner Bros. 56062).

Grandmaster Flash. 1981. *Adventures of Grandmaster Flash on the Wheels of Steel* (Sugar Hill SH-557A).

Grandmaster Flash and the Furious Five. 1979. *Freedom.* 12-inch single (Sugar Hill SH-249).

———. 1982. *The Message.* 12-inch single (Sugar Hill SH-584).

*Gridlock'd* (soundtrack). 1997. (Death Row 90114).

Guru. 1993. *Jazzmatazz: Volume 1* (Chrysalis 21998).

Hammer. 1988. *Let's Get It Started* (Capitol 90924).

———. 1990. *Please Hammer Don't Hurt 'Em* (Capitol 92857).

———. 1994. *The Funky Headhunter* (Giant 24545).

Hancock, Herbie. 1983. *Future Shock* (CBS 38814).

———. 1994. *Dis Is Da Drum* (Mercury P2 22681).

HardKnox Productions. 1994. *By All Means Necessary* (Double "B" OC1212).

Hayes, Isaac. 1969. "By the Time I Get to Phoenix." *Hot Buttered Soul* (Stax S-4114).

Heavy D. 1997. *Waterbed Hev* (Universal 53033).

Heavy D and the Boyz. 1987. *Livin' Large* (Uptown/MCA 5896).

———. 1989. *Big Tyme* (Uptown/MCA 42302).

Hill, Lauryn. 1998. *The Miseducation of Lauryn Hill* (Ruffhouse/Columbia 69035).

House of Pain. 1992. *House of Pain* (Tommy Boy 1064).

Hughes, Langston. 1995. *The Voice of Langston Hughes* (Smithsonian/Folkways SF 46001).

Ice Cube. 1990. *AmeriKKKa's Most Wanted* (Priority 57120).

———. 1991. *Death Certificate* (Priority 51744).

———. 1992. *The Predator* (Priority 57185).

Ice-T. 1987. *Rhyme Pays* (Sire/Warner Bros. 25602).

———. 1988. "High Rollers." *Power* (Sire/Warner Bros. 25765).

———. 1991. *O.G. Original Gangster* (Sire/Warner Bros. 26492).

Ice-T with Body Count. 1992. *Body Count* (Sire/Warner Bros. 26878).

Isis. 1990. "To the Crossroads." *Rebel Soul* (4th & B'Way 444-030-4).

Jackson, Millie. 1997. *Totally Unrestricted: The Millie Jackson Anthology* (Rhino 72863).

Jay-Z. 1998. *Vol. 2 . . . Hard Knock Life* (Roc-A-Fella/Polygram 314 558 902-2).

———. 2000. *The Dynasty: Roc La Familia (2000– )* (Roc-A-Fella/Universal P2 48202).

JJ Fad. 1988. *Supersonic* (Atco 90929).

Jones, Quincy. 1989. *Back on the Block* (Qwest/Time Warner 26020).

Jungle Brothers. 1988. *Straight out of the Jungle* (Warlock 2704).

Juvenile. 1998. *400 Degreez* (Cash Money/Universal 53262).

Kid Frost. 1990. *Hispanic Causing Panic* (Virgin 86169).

Kid 'N' Play. 1988. "Rollin' with Kid 'N' Play." *Rollin' With Kid 'N' Play* (Select 21628).

Kool and the Gang. 1973. "Funky Stuff." *Wild and Peaceful* (Mercury 522082).

Kool Moe Dee. 1988. "Let's Go." *How Ya Like Me Now* (Jive 1079-J).

Kris Kross. 1992. *Totally Krossed Out* (Ruffhouse/Columbia 48710).

Kurtis Blow. 1980. *The Breaks*. 12-inch single (Mercury 4010).

———. 1980. *Kurtis Blow* (Mercury 6337137).

———. 1994. *Best of Kurtis Blow* (Mercury 522456).

Lady B. 1980. "To the Beat Y'all." *Great Rap Hits* (Sugar Hill 246).

Last Poets. 1970. *The Last Poets* (Douglas 3).

Lightin' Rod. 1984. *Hustler's Convention* (Celluloid 6107).

Lil' Kim. 1996. *Hard Core* (Big Beat Records/Atlantic 92733-2).

———. 2000. *Notorious K.I.M.* (Atlantic 92840).

Limp Bizkit. 2000. *Chocolate Starfish and the Hotdog Flavored Water* (Interscope 490770).

LL Cool J 1986. *Radio* (Def Jam/Columbia 40239).

———. 1987. "I'm Bad." *Bigger and Deffer* (Def Jam/Columbia 40793).

———. 1988. *Jack the Ripper*. 12-inch single (Def Jam/Columbia 44 07563).

———. 1990. *Mama Said Knock You Out* (Def Jam/Columbia 46888).

———. 1997. *Phenomenon* (Def Jam/Polygram P2 39186).

Lords of the Underground. 1993. *Here Come the Lords* (Pendulum 61415).

Love Unlimited/Barry White. 1974. *Rhapsody in White* (Mercury 558201).

Makaveli. 1996. *the don killumanati: the 7 day theory* (Death Row 90039).

Marley Marl. 1988. *In Control, Volume One* (Cold Chillin'/Warner Bros. 25783).

———. 1991. *In Control, Volume II: For Your Steering Pleasure* (Cold Chillin'/Warner Bros. 26257).

Marsalis, Branford. 1994. *Buckshot LeFonque* (Columbia 57323).

Master P. 1996. *Ice Cream Man* (No Limit 53978).

———. 1998. *MP Da Last Don* (No Limit 53538).

MC Lyte. 1988. "I Am Woman," "Paper Thin." *Lyte as a Rock* (First Priority Music 7 90905-1).

———. 1993. *Ain't No Other* (First Priority Music 7 92230-4).

————. 1996. *Bad as I Wanna B* (Elektra 61781-2).

Melle Mel. 1985. *World War III.* 12-inch single (Sugar Hill SH-32039).

Mellow Man Ace. 1989. *Escape from Havana* (Capitol/EMI 91295).

Method Man. 1998. "Judgment Day." *Tical 2000: Judgement Day* (Def Jam 558920).

MFSB. 1974 (reissued 2000). "T.S.O.P." *Soul Train 1974* (Rhino 79930).

Mia X. 1997. *Unlady Like* (Priority 50705).

————. 1998. *Mama Drama* (No Limit 53502).

Missy "Misdemeanor" Elliott. 1997. *Supa Dupa Fly* (Elektra 62062-2).

Moore, Rudy Ray. 1972. *This Pussy Belongs to Me* (Kent Records/Comedy Series, KST-002).

Mos Def. 1999. "Fear Not of Man." *Black on Both Sides* (Rawkus 1159).

Parliament. 1975. *Mothership Connection* (Casablanca/Mercury 824502).

Nas. 1994. *Illmatic* (Columbia 57684).

————. 1996. *It Was Written* (Columbia 68633).

————. 1999. "Nas Is Like." *I Am: The Autobiography* (Columbia 67015).

Naughty by Nature. 1991. "Ghetto Bastard." *Naughty by Nature* (Tommy Boy 1044).

————. 1999. "Mourn You 'Til I Join You." *Nature's Finest: Naughty by Nature's Greatest Hits* (Tommy Boy 1310).

Nelly. 2000. *Country Grammar* (Universal UD 57857).

The Notorious B.I.G. 1994. *Ready to Die* (Bad Boy/Arista AC 3000).

————. 1997. *Life after Death.* (Bad Boy/Arista 78612-73011-4).

N.W.A. 1988. *Straight Outta Compton* (Ruthless 57102).

————. 1991. *Efil4zaggin* (Ruthless 57126).

Onyx. 1993. *Bacdafucup* (JMJ/Columbia 472980).

Osby, Greg. 1993. *3-D Lifestyles* (Blue Note 98635).

OutKast. 1994. *Southernplayalisticadillacmuzik* (LaFace/Arista 26010).

————. 1996. *ATLiens* (LaFace/Arista 6032).

————. 1998. *Aquemini* (LaFace/Arista 6053).

————. 2000. *Stankonia* (LaFace/Arista 6073).

Paris. 1991. *The Devil Made Me Do It* (Tommy Boy 1030).

————. 1993. *Sleeping with the Enemy* (Scarface SCR007-100-2).

The Pharcyde. 1992. *Bizarre Ride II: The Pharcyde* (Delicious Vinyl 92222).

Poor Righteous Teachers. 1990. *Holy Intellect* (Profile 1289).

Public Enemy. 1987. *Yo! Bum Rush the Show* (Def Jam/Columbia 40658).

————. 1988. "Don't Believe the Hype." *It Takes a Nation of Millions to Hold Us Back* (Def Jam/Columbia BFW 44303).

————. 1989. "Fight the Power." *Do the Right Thing* (soundtrack) (Motown 6272).

————. 1990. *Fear of a Black Planet* (Def Jam/Columbia 45413).

Puff Daddy and the Family. 1997. "I'll Be Missing You." *No Way Out* (Bad Boy 73012-2).

Queen Latifah. 1989. *All Hail the Queen* (Tommy Boy 1022).

————. 1991. *Nature of a Sista* (Tommy Boy 1035).

————. 1993. *Black Reign* (Motown 6370).

Queen Pen. 1997. "Girlfriend." *My Melody* (Lil' Man/Interscope 90151).

Rage. 1997. *Necessary Roughness* (Death Row 90109).

Rakim. 1997. *Rakim: The 18th Letter* (Universal 53113).

The Real Roxanne with Howie Tee. 1986. *Band Zoom (Let's Go Go)*. 12-inch single (Select 62269).

R.E.M. 1991. "Radio Song." *Out of Time* (Warner Bros. 9-26496-2).

Richie Rich. 1996. "Do G's Get to Go to Heaven?" *Seasoned Veteran* (Def Jam 533471).

The Roots. 1994. *Do You Want More?!!!??!* (David Geffen Company 24708).

———. 1999. *Things Fall Apart* (MCA 11948).

Roxanne Shanté. 1992. *Bitch Is Back* (Livin' Large 3001).

———. 1995. "Roxanne's Revenge." *Roxanne Shanté's Greatest Hits* (Cold Chillin'/ Warner Bros. 5007).

Run-D.M.C. 1984. "Sucker M.C.s" and "Rock Box." *Run-D.M.C.* (Profile 1202A).

———. 1986. "Hit It Run" and "Peter Piper." *Raising Hell* (Profile 1217A).

Salt-N-Pepa. 1986. *Hot, Cool & Vicious* (Next Plateau/London 422-828362-2).

———. 1990. *Black's Magic* (Next Plateau/London 422-828352-2).

———. 1993. *Very Necessary* (Next Plateau/London P2-28392).

Schoolly D. 1986. *Schoolly D* (Jive 1338).

———. 1988. *Smoke Some Kill* (Jive 1101).

———. 1989. *Am I Black Enough for You* (Jive 1237).

Scott, Jill. 2000. *Who Is Jill Scott?* (Hidden Beach Recordings/Epic EK 62137).

Scott-Heron, Gil. 1970. "Plastic People." *A New Black Poet: Small Talk at 125th and Lenox* (Flying Dutchman Stereo FD 10131).

*Self-Destruction.* 1989. 12-inch single (Jive 1178-4).

Sequence. 1981. "Funk You Up." *Funky Sounds* (Sugar Hill SH-561).

Shabazz, Lakim. 1988. *Pure Righteousness* (Tuff City Records 5557).

Shinehead. 1988. "Chain Gang-Rap." *Unity* (African Love 60802-4).

Silver, Horace. 1953. "Opus de Funk." *Horace Silver Trio* (Blue Note 81520).

Sir Mix-A-Lot. 1992. *Mack Daddy* (Rhyme Cartel 26765).

Sister Souljah. 1992. "The Final Solution: Slavery's Back in Effect." *360 Degrees of Power* (Epic 48713).

Slick Rick. 1988. *The Adventures of Slick Rick* (Def Jam/Columbia 40513).

Sly and the Family Stone. 1970. *Greatest Hits* (Epic 30325).

Smith, Will. 1997. *Big Willie Style* (Columbia 68683).

———. 1997. *Men in Black* (soundtrack single) (Columbia 86824).

Snoop Doggy Dogg. 1993. *Doggystyle* (Death Row 06544).

Sparky Dee. 1986. *Don't Make Me Laugh.* 12-inch single (Next Plateau 50039).

Spearhead. 1994. *Home* (Capitol 8 29113-2).

Stetsasonic. 1988. *In Full Gear* (Tommy Boy 1017).

Sugarhill Gang. 1996. *The Best of Sugarhill Gang* (Rhino 71986).

3rd Bass. 1989. *The Cactus Album* (Def Jam 45415).

Tim Dog. 1991. *Penicillin on Wax* (Columbia 48707).

TLC. 1992. *Oooooooohhh . . . On the TLC Tip* (Laface/Arista 26003-2).

———. 1994. *CrazySexyCool* (Laface/Arista 6009).

———. 1999. "Unpretty." *Fanmail* (LaFace/Arista AC 26055-4).

Tone-Lōc. 1989. *Lōc-ed After Dark* (Delicious Vinyl 92197).

Too $hort. 1988. *Born to Mack* (Jive 1100).

———. 1989 *Life is . . . Too $hort* (Jive 1149; clean version, Jive 1218).

———. 1990. *$hort Dog's in the House* (Jive/RCA 1348).

———. 1992. *$horty the Pimp* (Jive 41467).

———. 1993. *Get in Where You Fit In* (Jive 41526).

A Tribe Called Quest. 1991. *The Low End Theory* (Jive 1418).

———. 1993. *Midnight Marauders* Jive 1490.

Trick Daddy. 2000. "Shut Up." *Book of Thugs* (Slip-N-Slide Records/Atlantic 83287).

Trinia. 2000. *Da Baddest B***H* (Slip-N-Slide Records/Atlantic 83212-2).

2 Live Crew. 1989. *As Nasty as They Wanna Be* (Luke 91651).

2Pac. 1991. "Soulja's Story." *2Pacalypse Now* (Interscope 91767-4).

———. 1993. *Strictly 4 My N.I.G.G.A.Z.* (Interscope 92209-2).

———. 1995. *Me against the World* (Interscope 92339-4).

———. 1996. "2 of Amerikaz Most Wanted" and "I Ain't Mad at 'Cha." *All Eyez on Me.* (Death Row 314-524-204-2).

———. 1997. *R U Still Down? (Remember Me)* (Amaru/Jive 1630).

The Unknown Rapper. 1980. "Election '80 Rap." 12-inch single (ALA 114-A).

US3. 1993. *Hand on the Torch* (Blue Note/Capitol 580883).

Vanilla Ice. 1990. *To the Extreme* (SBK 95325).

Warren G. 1994. *Regulate . . . G-Funk Era* (RAL 314 523 335-4).

W.C. and the Maad Circle. 1991. *Ain't a Damned Thang Changed* (Priority 57156).

Whodini. 1984. *Escape* (Jive 8-8267-SB).

———. 1986. *Back in Black* (Jive 8-8407).

Wu-Tang Clan. 1993. *Enter the Wu-Tang (36 Chambers)* (Loud/BMG BG4-66363).

———. 1996. "America." *America Is Dying Slowly* (compilation) (EastWest 61925-2).

Wyclef Jean/Refugee All-Stars. 1997. *Wyclef Jean Presents the Carnival, featuring the Refugee All-Stars* (Refugee Camp Records/Columbia 67974).

X-Clan. 1990. *To the East Blackwards* (4th & B'way, 444-019-4).

Young MC. 1989. *Stone Cold Rhymin'* (Delicious Vinyl 422-842375-2).

Yo-Yo. 1991. *Make Way for the Motherlode* (EastWest 91605).

———. 1996. *Total Control* (EastWest/Atlantic 61898).

## Selected Rap Music Compilations

*'80's Underground Rap: Don't Believe the Hype.* 1998. (Rhino Records 75280).

*Kurtis Blow Presents the History of Rap.* 1997. 3 vols. (Rhino Records 72851, 72853, 71986).

*Lyricist Lounge 2.* 2000. (Rawkus 26131).

*Old School Rap* (Vols. 1–3). 1994, 1995, 1996. (Thump 4510, 4520, 4530).
*O.G. Funk: Underground Dance Masters Music Series—Locking.* 1997/1998. 2 vols. VRL
   Muzic (451-410-001-2, 451-410-002-2).
*Rap vs. Rap: The Answer Album.* 1987. (Priority 9506).

## Selected Videography

*Freestyle: The Art of Rhyme.* 2000. Dir. Keven Fitzgerald (Organic Films).
*Flyin' Cut Sleeves.* 1993. Dir. Rita Fecher and Henry Chalfant (New York Cinema
   Guild).
*I'll Make Me a World: Not a Rhyme Time.* 1999. Prod. Sam Pollard. (Blackside, Inc.
   and Film and Television Productions).
*Keepin' Time.* 2001. Dir. Brian "B-Plus" Cross (B-Plus Productions).
*Nobody Knows My Name.* 1999. Dir. Rachel Raimist (Unleashed Entertainment).
*MTV News [Now] Hard Rhymes: High Stakes.* 2001. (MTV Productions).
*History of Rock'n'Roll.* Vol. 5: "Looking for the Perfect Beat." 1995 (WGBH/BBC).
*Rap City Rhapsody.* 1990. Prod. Akili Buchana (KQED Inc.).
*Rhyme and Reason.* 1997. Dir. Peter Spirer (Asian Pictures/City Block/Miramax Films).
*Scratch.* 2001. Dir. Doug Pray (Firewalks Film).
*The Show.* 1995. Dir. Brian Robbins (Savoy Pictures).
*Style Wars.* 1984. Dir. Tom Silven (New Day Films).
*Underground Dance Masters: History of a Forgotten Era* (VRL Muzic 1998).
*Wild Style.* 1983. Dir. Charlie Ahearn (Pow Wow Productions/First Run Features).

# Works Cited

## Interviews

Copies of the interview tapes have been deposited at the Ethnomusicology Archive, University of California at Los Angeles. All interviews were conducted in person by the author.

Abbatiello, Sal (owner of Disco Fever in the Bronx and founder of Fever Enterprise), June 3, 1986

Adler, Bill (rap publicist), Manhattan, May 23, 1986

Bambaataa, Afrika (DJ and founder of the Zulu Nation), Manhattan, June 10, 1986

Blake, Mark (DJ), Long Island, August 24, 1986

Brothers of a Young Nation (underground rap trio), Brooklyn, March 3, 1993

Carson, Lumumba (producer, MC), Brooklyn, June 16, 1986

Chuck D. (MC and author), Manhattan, April 25, 1994

Courtland, Ocie (a.k.a. Cool DJ OC; owner of OC Records and DJ) and Anthony Knox (a.k.a Ant Knox–MC), East Lansing, Mich., August 13, 1995

Davis, Jermaine (MC), Los Angeles, August 25, 1995

DJ Hollywood (MC and DJ), Harlem, August 18, 1986

DJ Red Alert (rap radio personality/DJ), Manhattan, July 14, 1986

Doug E. Fresh (MC), Manhattan, August 19, 1986

Dynasty (MC and Entrepreneur), Manhattan, May 23, 1986

Grandmaster Flash (DJ), Harlem, March 4, 1993

KRS-One (MC/hip-hop artist, author, and entrepreneur), Bowling Green, Ky., October 14, 1991

MC Lyte (MC), Irvine, Calif., August 11, 1996

Melle Mel (MC), Manhattan, June 7, 1986

Mr. Magic (rap radio DJ), Manhattan, July 11, 1986

Positive K (MC), Manhattan, July 15, 1986

Queen Latifah (MC, actress), Jersey City, July 8, 1993

The Real Roxanne (MC and model), Brooklyn (telephone interview), July 30, 1986

Robinson, Darren (a.k.a. The Human Beat Box of The Fat Boys), Brooklyn (telephone interview), May 22, 1986

Robinson, Joe (cofounder of Sugar Hill Records), Englewood, N.J., August 19, 1986

"Say No to Drugs" interviewees (rap artists and radio DJs: Cut Master D.C., Divine Sounds, Eric B. and Rakim, The Freshman, Paradise, Stetsasonic, Supreme Force, Ultimate Three, Vandy C), Prospect Park, Brooklyn, June 21, 1986

Singleton, Cedric (founder of Black Market Records), Manhattan, October 12, 1992

Shaw, Dennis (former promoter) and Lumumba Carson, Brooklyn (telephone interview), July 12, 1986.

Simmons, Russell (rap music mogul), Brooklyn, August 5, 1986

Small, Carl "Butch" (musician and producer), Los Angeles, September 11, 1995

Smith, Larry (musician and producer), Brooklyn (telephone interview), July 12, 1986

Spicer, Jimmy (MC), Manhattan, May 23, 1986

Stephney, Bill (music entrepreneur/founder of StepSun Music) Manhattan, May 23, 1986

Swain, J. Kevin (music video director), Los Angeles, January 13, 1999

Turkkan, Leyla (music entrepreneur/artist management), Manhattan, November 23, 1992

Vicki and Valerie (audience members at The Underground), Manhattan, July 15, 1986

### Published and Other Sources

Abrahams, Roger. 1970. *Deep Down in the Jungle: Negro Narrative Folklore from the Streets of Philadelphia.* Chicago: Aldine Publishing.

Abu-Lughod, Lila. 1990. "Can There Be a Feminist Ethnography?" *Women and Performance: A Journal of Feminist Theory* 5(9): 7–27.

Adler, Jerry, Jennifer Foote, and David Gates. 1990. "Rap Rage." *Newsweek,* March 19, pp. 56–64.

Ahrens, Richard. 1995. "Rap: Music? Not!" *Los Angeles Times,* June 24, p. F6.

Alert. 2000. "Best Kept Secret." *The Source,* January, pp. 106–13.

Alim, H. Samy. 2000. "360 Degreez of Black Art Comin at You: Sista Sonia Sanchez and the Dimensions of a Black Art Continuum." In *BMa: The Sonia Sanchez Literary Review* 6(1): 15–33.

Allen, Earnest Jr. 1996. "Making the Strong Survive: The Contours and Contradictions of Message Rap." In *Droppin' Science: Critical Essays on Rap Music and Hip Hop Culture.* Ed. William Eric Perkins. 159–91. Philadelphia: Temple University Press.

Allen, Harry. 1988. "Hip-Hop Hi-Tech." *Village Voice* (Consumer Electronics Special Section), October, pp. 10–11.

———. 1994. "Time Bomb: Clocking the History of Hip Hop 15 Years after 'Rapper's Delight.'" *Vibe,* December, pp. 71–75.

———. 1996. "The Mic, the Star and the Crescent: Hip-Hop and the Message of Islam." *Radio 1* (BBC Radio), September 1.

Anderson, Benedict. 1983. *Imagined Communities: Reflections on the Origin and Spread of Nationalism.* London: Verso.

Anderson, Elijah. 1992. *Streetwise: Race, Class, and Change in the Urban Community*. Chicago: University of Chicago Press.

Anson, Sam Gideon, and David Cogan. 2001. "Knight Moves." *Vibe*, October, pp. 100–108.

Anyanwu, Chukwulozie K. 1976. *The Nature of Black Cultural Reality*. Washington, D.C.: University Press of America.

Atwood, Brett. 1995. "MTV Expands Its Online Programming." *Billboard*, July 29, pp. 8, 16.

Austerlitz, Paul. 1997. *Merengue: Dominican Music and Dominican Identity*. Philadelphia: Temple University Press.

Averill, Gage. 1997. *A Day for the Hunter, a Day for the Prey: Popular Music and Power in Haiti*. Chicago: University of Chicago Press.

Babcock, Jay. 1999. "My MP3 Weighs a Ton." *Vibe*, May, p. 49.

Baber, Ceola. 1987. "The Artistry and Artifice of Black Communication." In *Expressively Black: The Cultural Basis of Ethnic Identity*. Ed. Geneva Gay and Willie L. Baber. 75–108. New York: Praeger.

Baker, Houston A. Jr. 1993. *Black Studies: Rap and the Academy*. Chicago: University of Chicago Press.

Balde, Alpha Alimou. 1999. "The Art of Words: Freestyling in African-American Musical Culture." Master's thesis, University of California at Los Angeles.

Bambaataa, Afrika. 1986. "The Destruction of the Hip-Hop Culture." *Jack the Rapper*, October 22, pp. 1–2.

Barlow, William. 1999. *Voice Over: The Making of Black Radio*. Philadelphia: Temple University Press.

Barz, Gregory F., and Timothy J. Cooley, eds. 1997. *Shadows in the Field: New Perspectives for Fieldwork in Ethnomusicology*. Chicago: University of Chicago Press.

Baugh, John. 1983. *Black Street Speech: Its History, Structure, and Survival*. Austin: University of Texas Press.

"The Beliefs of the Universal Zulu Nation." 1993. *The Source*, May, pp. 32–36.

Ben-Amos, Paula Girschick. 1995. *The Art of Benin*. Rev. ed. Washington, D.C.: Smithsonian Institution Press.

Ben-Amos, Paula, and Arnold Rubin, eds. 1983. *The Art of Power, the Power of Art: Studies in Benin Iconography*. Los Angeles: Museum of Cultural History.

Benesch, Connie. 1994. "The Good, the Bad, and the Censored." *Billboard* (Rap Spotlight Issue), November 26, pp. 42, 44.

Berger, Harris M. 1999. *Metal, Rock, and Jazz: Perception and the Phenomenology of Musical Experience*. Hanover, N.H.: Wesleyan University Press.

Berger, Stephen D. 1970. *The Social Consequences of Residential Segregation of the Urban American Negro*. MARC Paper no. 2. New York: Metropolitan Applied Research Center.

Bernard, James. 1991. "Ice Cube Building a Nation." *The Source*, December, pp. 32–34.

Bernard, James, et al. 1992. "A Newcomer Abroad, Rap Speaks Up" and "The Many Accents of Rap around the World." *New York Times,* August 23, sec. 2, pp. 1, 22–23.

Bernard, James, and Reginald C. Dennis. 1994. "A Megablast from the Past: Cocaine's Greatest Hits." *The Source,* July, p. 56.

Berry, Venise T. 1994. "Feminine or Masculine: The Conflicting Nature of Female Images in Rap Music." In *Cecilia Reclaimed: Feminist Perspectives on Gender and Music.* Ed. Susan C. Cook and Judy S. Tsou. 183–201. Urbana: University of Illinois Press.

Bird, Charles. 1976. "Poetry in the Mande: Its Form and Meaning." *Poetics* 5(2): 89–100.

The Blackspot. 1996. "Stakes Is High." *Vibe,* September, pp. 100–104.

Blassingame, John W. 1979. *The Slave Community: Plantation Life in the Antebellum South.* New York: Oxford University Press.

Bobo, Jacqueline. 1995. *Black Women as Cultural Readers.* New York: Columbia University Press.

Boehlert, Eric. 1999. "'98 Goes Boom: Hip-Hop Leads the Way in Album-Sales Growth." *Rolling Stone,* February 18, pp. 15, 24.

Boucher, Geoff. 1999. "Pop Takes a Little R&R." *Los Angeles Times* (Calendar Section), July 10, pp. F1, F10.

Boyd, Todd. 1995. "To the Player's Ball and Beyond: Right On." *Los Angeles Times* (Calendar Section), October 1, pp. 26–28.

———. 1997. *Am I Black Enough for You: Popular Culture from the 'Hood and Beyond.* Bloomington: Indiana University Press.

Braxton, Charlie R. 1997. "Mia X: All Tru Woman." *XXL* 1(1): 95–98.

Braxton, Greg, and Jerry Crowe. 1995. "Black Leaders Weighing In on Rap Debate." *Los Angeles Times,* June 14, pp. F1, F8.

Brewster, Bill, and Frank Boughton. 2000. *Last Night a DJ Saved My Life: The History of the Disc Jockey.* New York: Grove Press.

Britton, Akissi. 2000. "To Kim with Love: Deconstructing Lil' Kim." *Essence,* October, pp. 112–15, 186.

Brodeur, John M. 1995. "Dole Indicts Hollywood for Debasing Culture." *Los Angeles Times,* June 1, pp. A1, A15.

Brodeur, Scott. 1995. "The Life of Eazy-E: A Chronological Retrospective." *The Source,* June, pp. 54–57, 60–62.

Bronner, Angela. 1996. "Scarface vs. Big Willie." *The Source,* February, p. 23.

Brown, Ann. 1999. "Hip-Hop Indie Films." *The Source,* February, pp. 160–64.

Brown, H. Rap. 1981. "Street Smarts." In *Mother Wit from the Laughing Barrel: Readings in the Interpretation of Afro-American Folklore.* Ed. Alan Dundes. 353–56. New York: Garland.

Brown, Sterling A. 1996. *A Son's Return: Selected Essays of Sterling Brown.* Ed. Mark A. Sanders. Boston: Northeastern University Press.

Bryant, Linda Goode, Cathy Campbell, Barry Michael Cooper, et al. 1989. "The Central Park Rape." *Village Voice,* May 9, pp. 25–39, 52.

Burley, Dan. 1981. "The Technique of Jive." In *Mother Wit from the Laughing Barrel:*

*Readings in the Interpretation of Afro-American Folklore.* Ed. Alan Dundes. 206–21. New York: Garland.

Burnim, Mellonee V. 1985a. "The Black Gospel Tradition: A Complex of Ideology, Aesthetic, and Behavior." In *More Than Dancing: Essays on Afro-American Music and Musicians.* Ed. Irene V. Jackson. 147–67. Westport: Greenwood Press.

———. 1985b. "Culture Bearer and Tradition Bearer: An Ethnomusicologist's Research on Gospel Music." *Journal of the Society for Ethnomusicology* 29(3): 432–47.

"Busta Rhymes, Missy Elliott among Rappers under New Management Partnership." 2000. *Jet,* February 14, p. 48.

Carby, Hazel. 1986. "It Just Be's Dat Way Sometime: The Sexual Politics of Women's Blues." *Radical America* 20(4): 9–22.

Chang, Kevin O'Brien, and Wayne Chen. 1998. *Reggae Routes: The Story of Jamaican Music.* Philadelphia: Temple University Press.

Chapple, Steve, and Reebee Garofalo. 1977. *Rock 'n' Roll Is Here to Pay: The History and Politics of the Music Industry.* Chicago: Nelson-Hall.

Charry, Eric. 2000. *Mande Music: Traditional and Modern Music of the Maninka and Mandinka of Western Africa.* Chicago: University of Chicago Press.

Chernoff, John Miller. 1979. *African Rhythm and African Sensibility: Aesthetics and Social Action in African Musical Idioms.* Chicago: University of Chicago Press.

Chideya, Farai. 2000. "Homophobia: Hip-Hop's Black Eye." *Step into a World: A Global Anthology of the New Black Literature.* Ed. Kevin Powell. 95–100. New York: John Wiley and Sons.

Chuck D., with Yusuf Jah. 1997. *Fight the Power: Rap, Race, and Reality.* New York: Delacorte Press.

Chyll, Chuck. 1994. "Musical Reactions: Sexy Rap or Credibility Gap?" *Rap Masters* 7(7): 19–20.

Clarke, John Henrik. 1991. *Africans at the Crossroads: Notes for an African World Revolution.* Trenton, N.J.: African World Press.

Clifford, James. 1986. "Introduction: Partial Truths." In *Writing Culture: The Poetics and Politics of Ethnography.* Ed. James Clifford and George E. Marcus. 1–26. Berkeley: University of California Press.

Cohen, Cathy J. 1999. *The Boundaries of Blackness: AIDS and the Breakdown of Black Politics.* Chicago: University of Chicago Press.

Coleman, Bill. 1988. "Female Rappers Give Males Run for the Money." *Billboard,* May 21, pp. 1, 29.

Collins, Glen. 1988. "Now Rap Is 'Bum-Rushing' the Mainstream." *New York Times,* August 29, pp. C15, C17.

Collins, Patricia Hill. 1990. *Black Feminist Thought: Knowledge, Consciousness, and the Politics of Empowerment.* Boston: Unwin Hyman.

Coker, Cheo H. 1995–96. "What a Rush." *Vibe,* December–January, pp. 86–90.

Connor, Walker. 1978. "A Nation Is a Nation, Is a State, Is an Ethnic Group, Is. . . ." *Ethnic and Racial Studies* 1(4): 379–88.

"Conversation with Ed Gordon." 1994. *Black Entertainment Television Network,* September 21.

Cooley, Timothy J. 1997. "Casting Shadows in the Field: An Introduction." In *Shadows in the Field: New Perspectives for Fieldwork in Ethnomusicology.* Ed. Gregory F. Barz and Timothy J. Cooley. 3–19. Chicago: University of Chicago Press.

Cooper, Carol. 1989. "Girls Ain't Nothin' but Trouble." *Essence,* April, pp. 80, 119.

Cooper, Carolyn. 1989. "Slackness Hiding from Culture: Erotic Play in the Dancehall." *Jamaican Journal* 22(4): 12–31.

———. 1995. *Noise in the Blood: Orality, Gender, and the "Vulgar" Body of Jamaican Culture.* Durham, N.C.: Duke University Press.

Cooper, Milton William. 1991. *Behold a Pale Horse.* Sedona, Ariz.: Light Technology Publishing.

Copeland, Lee. 1997. "Fear of a Rap Concert." *The Source,* May, pp. 98–106.

Cornish, James W., and Charles P. O'Brien. 1996. "Crack Cocaine Abuse: An Epidemic with Many Health Consequences." *Annual Review of Public Health* 17:259–73.

Cornyetz, Nina. 1994. "Fetishized Blackness: Hip Hop and Racial Desire in Contemporary Japan." *Social Text* 41:113–39.

Crenshaw, Kimberle. 1991. "Beyond Racism and Misogyny: Black Feminism and 2 Live Crew." *Boston Review,* December, pp. 6, 30–33.

Cross, Brian. 1993. *It's Not about a Salary . . . : Rap, Race, and Resistance in Los Angeles.* New York: Verso.

Cubitt, Sean. 1997. "Rolling and Tumbling: Digital Erotics and the Culture of Narcissism." In *Sexing the Groove: Popular Music and Gender.* Ed. Sheila Whiteley. 295–316. London: Routledge Press.

Cummings, Sue. 1986. "Burning the Kingdom." *Spin,* July, pp. 57–61, 73.

Dallek, Robert. 1984. *Ronald Reagan: The Politics of Symbolism.* Cambridge, Mass.: Harvard University Press.

Dance, Daryl C. 1978. *Shuckin' and Jivin': Folklore from Contemporary Black Americans.* Bloomington: Indiana University Press.

Davis, Angela Y. 1998. *Blues Legacies and Black Feminism: Gertrude "Ma" Rainey, Bessie Smith, and Billie Holiday.* New York: Pantheon Books.

Davis, Gerald L. 1985. *I Got the Word in Me and I Can Sing It, You Know: A Study of the Performed African-American Sermon.* Philadelphia: University of Pennsylvania Press.

Davis, Mike. 1992 [1990]. *City of Quartz: Excavating the Future in Los Angeles.* New York: Vintage Books.

Davis, Thulani. 1994. "The Artist in Society." Keynote address. National Endowment for the Arts Conference, Chicago, April 14.

Decker, Jeffrey Louis. 1993. "The State of Rap: Time and Place in Hip Hop Nationalism." *Social Text* 34:53–84.

del Barco, Mandalit. 1996. "Rap's Latino Sabor." In *Droppin' Science: Critical Essays on Rap Music and Hip Hop Culture.* Ed. William Eric Perkins. 63–84. Philadelphia: Temple University Press.

Diallo, Yaya, and Mitchell Hall. 1989. *The Healing Drum: African Wisdom Teachings.* Rochester, Vt.: Destiny Books.

Diawara, Manthia. 1992. "Black Studies, Cultural Studies: Performative Acts." *After-Image,* October, p. 47.

Doctor Dre. 1988. "How to Talk B-Boy." *Spin,* October, p. 47.

Drewal, Margaret Thompson. 1992. *Yoruba Ritual: Performers, Play, Agency.* Bloomington: Indiana University Press.

Duvernay, Ava. 1998. "Queen Pen: Keep 'em Guessin'." *Rap Pages,* May, pp. 86–88.

Dyson, Michael. 1993. *Reflecting Black: African-American Cultural Criticism.* Minneapolis: University of Minnesota Press.

———. 1994. "Shaping Our Responses to Violent and Demeaning Imagery in Popular Music." Testimony at the Hearing before the Subcommittee on Juvenile Justice of the Committee on the Judiciary, U.S. Senate, 103d Cong., 2d Sess., February 23, serial no. J-104-43.

———. 1996. *Between God and Gangsta Rap: Bearing Witness to Black Culture.* New York: Oxford University Press.

Edgerton, Robert B., and L. L. Langness. 1974. *Methods and Styles in the Study of Culture.* San Francisco: Chandler and Sharp.

Edsall, Thomas Byrne, with Mary Edsall. 1992. *Chain Reaction: The Impact of Race, Rights, and Taxes on American Politics.* New York: W. W. Norton.

Edwards, Shawn. 2000. "The Digital Dilemma." *The Source,* September, pp. 59–60.

Elliot, Mike. 1988. "Public Enemy: Prophets of Rage." *Krush,* August–September, p. 15.

Emery, Andrew. 1998. "Cutting Edge: Who Is the Greatest Deejay Ever?" *Hip-Hop Connection,* May, pp. 26–28.

Epperson, A. Ralph. 1990. *The New World Order.* Tucson: Publius Press.

Erlmann, Veit. 1991. *African Stars: Studies in Black South African Performance.* Chicago: University of Chicago Press.

———. 1996. *Nightsong: Performance, Power, and Practice in South Africa.* Chicago: University of Chicago Press.

Etter-Lewis, Gwendolyn. 1991. "Black Women's Life Stories: Reclaiming Self in Narrative Texts." In *Women's Words: The Feminist Practice of Oral History.* Ed. Sherna Berger Gluck and Daphne Patai. 43–59. New York: Routledge.

Eure, Joseph D., and James G. Spady. 1991. *Nation Conscious Rap.* Philadelphia: PC International Press.

Fab Five Freddy. 1992. *Words and Phrases of the Hip-Hop Generation.* Stamford, Conn.: Longmeadow Press.

———. 1995. "Tupac Shakur: The Final Chapter." *Vibe* (Mail Section), August, pp. 25–29.

Farr, Jory. 1994. *Moguls and Madmen: The Pursuit of Power in Popular Music.* New York: Simon and Schuster.

Fears, Darryl. 1998. "AIDS among Black Women Seen as a Growing Problem." *Los Angeles Times,* July 24, pp. A1, A28.

Fee, Debi. 1988. "Rap Producers: Taking on the Challenge of Creating a Sense of Longevity Amid Change." *Billboard,* December 24, pp. R8, R21.

"Female Rappers Invade the Male Rap Industry." 1991. *The Phil Donahue Show.* Transcript no. 3216, May 29.

Fernando, S. H. 1994. "Spinning Isn't Everything." *The Source,* September, pp. 54–56.

———. 1998. "Beat You Down." *Vibe,* September, pp. 146–49.

Fikentscher, Kai. 2000. *"You Better Work!" Underground Dance Music in New York City.* Hanover, N.H.: Wesleyan University Press.

Fischer, Paul D. 1996. "The PMRC: The 1994 Congressional Hearing on Music Lyrics and Commerce." *Journal of Popular Music Studies* 8:43–55.

Floyd, Samuel A., Jr. 1995. *The Power of Black Music: Interpreting Its History from Africa to the United States.* New York: Oxford University Press.

Flores, Juan. 2000. *From Bomba to Hip-Hop: Puerto Rican Culture and Latino Identity.* New York: Colombia University Press.

Ford, Robert Jr. 1979. "Jive Talking N.Y. DJs Rapping Away in Black Discos." *Billboard,* May 5, pp. 3, 54.

Forman, Murray. 1994. "Movin' Closer to an Independent Funk: Black Feminist Theory, Standpoint, and Women in Rap." *Women's Studies* 23: 35–55.

Fox, Steve. 1981. "Rappin' to the Beat." *20/20* (transcript), July 9, pp. 11–14.

Foxxx, Freddie. 1992. "A Cut-by-Cut Breakdown of *Sex and Violence* by KRS-One." *The Source,* April, p. 36.

Frammolino, Ralph, and Geoff Boucher. 2001. "Rap Was Eminem's Roots and Road out of Poverty." *Los Angeles Times,* February 21, pp. A1, A18.

Franklin, John Hope, and Alfred A. Moss Jr. 1994. *From Slavery to Freedom: A History of African Americans.* 7th ed. New York: Alfred A Knopf.

Frederic, Stephanie. 1997. "Do Like Superfly." *XXL* 1(2): 112–13.

Fry, Galdys-Marie. 1975. *Night Raiders in Black Folk History.* Knoxville: University of Tennessee Press.

Fuentes, Annette. 1985. "The Hollis Rappers: Hometown Boys Make Good." *City Limits,* December, pp. 16–21.

Gates, Henry Louis Jr. 1988. *The Signifying Monkey: A Theory of African-American Literary Criticism.* New York: Oxford University Press.

Gaunt, Kyra D. 1993. "An' It Ain't Mozart: Hip-Hop, Polytextuality, and Reconstruction in the Music of Public Enemy." Paper presented at the 38th Annual Meeting of the Society for Ethnomusicology, Oxford, Mississippi, October 29–31.

Gay, Geneva. 1987. "Expressive Ethos of Afro-American Culture." In *Expressively Black: The Cultural Basis of Ethnic Identity.* Ed. Geneva Gay and Willie L. Baber. 1–16. New York: Praeger.

Geertz, Clifford. 1973. *The Interpretation of Cultures.* New York: Basic Books.

George, Nelson. 1983. "City Sounds Lead to Rap Contest." *Billboard,* October 8, p. 1.

———. 1985. "Rap Hit Spawns Many Answers: Roxanne, Roxanne, Rocks On." *Billboard,* February 9, p. 50.

———. 1988a. "Controversy Arises: Is It Sampling or Stealing?" *Billboard,* January 16, p. 23.

———. 1988b. *The Death of Rhythm and Blues.* New York: Plume.

———. 1989. "Hammer Hits Hard with New Jack Moves." *Billboard,* February 25, p. 24.

———. 1990. "Making Self-Destruction." In *Stop the Violence: Overcoming Self-Destruction.* Ed. Nelson George. 10–19. New York: Pantheon Books.

———. 1992. *Buppies, B-Boys, Baps and Bobos: Notes on the Post-Soul Black Culture.* New York: HarperCollins.

———. 1993. "Hip-Hop's Founding Fathers Speak the Truth." *The Source,* November, pp. 46–50.

Gil, John. 1998. "Rhyme and Reason: OutKast's *Aquemini.*" *The Source,* December, pp. 46, 48.

Gillespie, Dizzy. 1979. *To Be, or Not . . . To Bop.* Ed. Al Fraser. Garden City, N.J.: Doubleday and Company.

Gillespie, Marcia. 1983. "Sylvia Robinson: Rap Music Queen." *Ms.,* October, pp. 32–33.

Gilmore, Ruth Wilson. 1998. "From Military Keynesianism to Post-Keynesian Militarism: Finance Capital, Land, Labor, and Opposition in the Rising California Prison State." Ph.D. dissertation, Rutgers University.

Gilroy, Paul. 1993. *The Black Atlantic: Modernity and Double Consciousness.* Cambridge, Mass.: Harvard University Press.

Gilstrap, Peter. 1998. "The House That Blacks Built." *The New Times,* October 15–21, pp. 11–21.

Glasgow, Douglas. 1980. *The Black Underclass: Poverty, Unemployment, and Entrapment of Ghetto Youth.* San Francisco: Jossey-Bass.

Glazer, Max. 1999. "Test-driving the New Gemini Turntable." *Blaze,* January, pp. 58–59.

Goldstein, Patrick. 1998. "Hanging with Warren B." *Los Angeles Times* (Calendar Section), May 3, pp. 8–9; 91–92.

Gonzales, Michael A. 1997. "Mack Divas." *The Source,* February, pp. 62–67.

Goodall, Nakati. 1994. "Depend on Myself: T.L.C. and the Evolution of Black Female Rap." *Journal of Negro History* 79(1): 85–93.

Goodwin, Andrew. 1988. "Sample and Hold: Pop Music in the Digital Age of Reproduction." *Critical Quarterly* 30(3): 34–39.

———. 1992. *Dancing in the Distraction Factory: Music Television and Popular Culture.* Minneapolis: University of Minnesota Press.

Gray, Herman. 1995. *Watching Race: Television and the Struggle for "Blackness."* Minneapolis: University of Minnesota Press.

Gray, Obika. 1991. *Radicalism and Social Change in Jamaica, 1960–1972.* Knoxville: University of Tennessee Press.

Green, Kim. 1991. "The Naked Truth." *The Source,* November, pp. 32–34, 36.

———. 1996. "Brooklyn Keeps on Takin' It." *The Source,* October, pp. 78–80, 82.

Gregg, Richard, A., Jackson McCormick, and Douglas J. Pedersen. 1969. "The Rhetoric of Black Power: A Street Level Interpretation." *Quarterly Journal of Speech* 55 (April): 151–60.

Grein, Paul. 1990. "Bustin' the Beat: Rap Milestones Rewriting Pop Chart History Weekly." *Billboard* (Rap Music Spotlight Issue), November 24, pp. R12, R20.

Griaule, Marcel. 1970 [1965]. *Conversations with Ogotemmeli: An Introduction to Dogon Religious Ideas.* London: Oxford University Press.

Groh, George. 1972. *The Black Migration: The Journey to Urban America.* New York: Weybright and Talley.

Guevara, Nancy. 1987. "Women Writin' Rappin' Breakin'." In *The Year Left 2.* Ed. Mike Davis et al. 160–75. New York: Verso Press.

Guilbault, Jocelyne. 1993. *Zouk: World Music in the West Indies.* Chicago: University of Chicago Press.

Guralnick, Peter. 1986. *Sweet Soul Music: Rhythm and Blues and the Southern Dream of Freedom.* New York: Harper and Row.

Hager, Steven. 1984. *Hip Hop: The Illustrated History of Break Dancing, Rap Music, and Graffiti.* New York: St. Martin's Press.

Hale, Thomas A. 1998. *Griots and Griottes: Masters of Words and Music.* Bloomington: Indiana University Press.

Haley, Alex. 1976. *Roots: The Saga of an American Family.* New York: Dell.

hampton, dream. 1992. "Four Minutes of Pleasure: Making Fly Videos." *The Source,* March, pp. 33–39, 54–55.

Hanley, Shawn. 1980. "Rap Records Inducing Listener Participation." *Billboard,* July 19, pp. 51, 53.

Harrison, Daphne Duval. 1988. *Black Pearls: Blues Queens of the 1920s.* New Brunswick, N.J.: Rutgers University Press.

Harrison, Paul Carter. 1972. *The Drama of Nommo.* New York: Grove Press.

Hebdige, Dick. 1979. *Subculture: The Meaning of Style.* New York: Methuen and Company.

———. 1987. *Cut 'N' Mix.* London: Comedia.

Henderson, Alex. 1988a. "Active Indies: Rap's Cutting Edge Seeks Next New Creative Frontiers to Stay Sharp and Successful." *Billboard,* December 24, pp. 6, 16, 20.

———. 1988b. "Artists of Image: Rappers Answer Critics, Pinpoint Resistance to Youth Wave." *Billboard,* December 24, pp. 5–6, 13.

Henderson, Stephen. 1973. *Understanding the New Black Poetry.* New York: William Morrow.

Herskovits, Melville. 1958 [1941]. *The Myth of the Negro Past.* Boston, Mass.: Beacon.

"Hey DJ: KKBT Los Angeles O.G." 2000. *Rap Pages,* July, pp. 112–16.

Hilburn, Robert. 1989. "No Longer under Raps: Explosive Sounds Rock Pop Music Mainstream with Tales of Black Pride Frustrations." *Atlanta Constitution,* April 4, pp. 1E, 4E.

———. 1998. "Grooves by the Clock." *Los Angeles Times,* August 15, pp. F1, F8.

Hill, Lauryn. 1994. Panelist for "Hip-Hop Summit." New Music Seminar 15, Manhattan, July 20.

Hinckley, David. 1986. "You Can 'Run,' but You Can't Hide." *Daily News,* July 16, p. 21.

Hirschberg, Lynn. 1996. "Does a Sugar Bear Bite?" *New York Times Magazine,* January 14, pp. 24–31, 39–40, 50–57.

"The History of Turntablism." 2000. <http://www.scratchdj.com/history.shtml>.

Hochman, Steve. 1989. "N.W.A. Cops an Attitude: L.A. Rappers Portray the Violence of Ghetto Life." *Rolling Stone,* June 29, p. 24.

Holland, Bill. 2000. "Chuck D, Others Testify on Web's Pros and Cons." *Billboard,* June, pp. 10, 118.

Honey, Martha. 1997. "Cocaine Business Controls America: How the CIA Started the Crack Epidemic." *XXL* 1(2): 104–10, 116.

hooks, bell. 1993. *Sisters of the Yam: Black Women and Self-Recovery.* Boston: South End Press.

———. 1994. *Outlaw Culture: Resisting Representations.* New York: Routledge.

Horner, Cynthia. 1993. "TLC: The Homegirls with Style!" *Right On!* February, pp. 16–17.

"The Hottest Females in Rap Music." 2000. *Jet,* February 21, pp. 58–62.

Hunt, Dennis. 1989. "The Rap Reality: Truth and Money." *Los Angeles Times* (Calendar Section), April 2, pp. 80–87.

Hurston, Zora Neale. 1981. *The Sanctified Church: The Folklore Writings of Zora Neale Hurston.* Berkeley, Calif.: Turtle Island.

Jackson, Bruce. 1987. *Fieldwork.* Urbana: University of Illinois Press.

———, comp. 1974. *Get your ass in the water and swim like me: Narrative Poetry from Black Oral Tradition.* Cambridge, Mass.: Harvard University Press.

Jackson, Joyce Marie. 1981. "The Black American Folk Preacher and the Chanted Sermon: Parallels with a West African Tradition." In *Discourse in Ethnomusicology II: A Tribute to Alan P. Merriam.* Ed. Caroline Card et. al. 205–22. Bloomington: Indiana University Press.

———. 1988. "The Performing Black Quartet: An Expression of Cultural Values and Aesthetics." Ph.D. dissertation, Indiana University at Bloomington.

Jackson, Kenneth. 1985. *Crabgrass Frontier: The Suburbanization of the United States.* New York: Oxford University Press.

Jah, Yusuf and Sister Shah'Keyah, eds. 1995. *Uprising: Crips and Bloods Tell the Story of America's Youth in the Crossfire.* New York: Scribner.

Jahn, Janheinz. 1961. *Muntu: An Outline of the New African Culture.* Trans. Marjorie Grene. New York: Grove Press.

James, Darryl. 1991. "KDAY: The Quiet Murder of a Radio Station." *The Source,* September, p. 20.

Jamison, Laura. 1998. "A Fiesty Female Rapper Breaks a Hip-Hop Taboo." *New York Times,* January 18, p. AR34.

Jenkins, Sacha. 1996. "Short Stop." *Vibe,* April, pp. 63–64.

Jewell, K. Sue. 1993. *From Mammy to Miss America and Beyond: Cultural Images and the Shaping of U.S. Social Policy.* New York: Routledge.

Joe, Radcliffe A. 1980. *The Business of Disco.* New York: Billboard Books/Watson-Guptil.

Joe, Radcliffe, and Nelson George. 1979. "Rapping DJs Set a Trend." *Billboard,* November 3, pp. 4, 64.

Johnson, John W. 1980. "Yes, Virginia, There Is an Epic in Africa." *Research in African Literatures* 11(3): 308–26.

Jones, Jacquie. 1991. "The New Ghetto Aesthetic." *Wide Angle* 13(3 and 4): 32–43.

Jones, James T. 1990. "M.C. Hammer: More Than a Rap Star." *Louisville Courier-Journal* (The Scene), July 16, p. 13.

Jones, Lisa. 1988. "Pussy Ain't Free." *Village Voice* (Hip-Hop Nation Special Section), January 19, pp. 34–35, 37.

Jones, Quincy. 1990. *Listen Up: The Many Lives of Quincy Jones.* New York: Warner Books.

Keil, Charles, and Steven Feld. 1994. *Music Grooves: Essays and Dialogues.* Chicago: University of Chicago Press.

Kelley, Robin. D. G. 1996. "Kickin' Reality, Kickin' Ballistics: Gangsta Rap and Postindustrial Los Angeles." In *Droppin' Science: Critical Essays on Rap Music and Hip Hop Culture.* Ed. William Eric Perkins. 117–58. Philadelphia: Temple University Press.

Kemp, Mar. 1989. "Name That Tune: Sampling—Whose Music Is It Anyway?" *Option,* May–June, pp. 66–69, 129.

Keyes, Cheryl L. 1982. "Verbal Recollections." Unpublished memoirs.

———. 1984 "Verbal Art Performance in Rap Music: The Conversation of the '80s." *Folklore Forum* (17:2): 143–52.

———. 1986. "Say No to Drugs!" *The Hip-Hop Hit List,* July 14–30, p. 9.

———. 1992. "Rap Music: Its Roots and Traditions in Detroit, Michigan." In *1992 Festival of Michigan Folklife.* 36–38. East Lansing: Michigan State University.

———. 1996. "At the Crossroads: Rap Music and Its African Nexus." *Ethnomusicology* 40(2): 223–48.

———. 2000. "Empowering Self, Making Choices, Creating Spaces: Black Female Identity via Rap Music Performance." *Journal of American Folklore* 113(449): 255–69.

Kgositsile, Ipeleng. 1997. "High Risk: The Reality of AIDS." *The Source,* November, pp. 28–30.

Kisliuk, Michelle. 1997. "(Un)Doing Fieldwork: Sharing Songs, Sharing lives." In *Shadows in the Field: New Perspectives for Fieldwork in Ethnomusicology.* Ed. Gregory F. Barz and Timothy J. Cooley. 23–44. Chicago: University of Chicago Press.

Kitwana, Bakari. 1994. *The Rap on Gangsta Rap: Who Run It? Gangsta Rap and Visions of Black Violence.* Chicago: Third World Press.

Knight. Franklin W. 1990. *The Caribbean: The Genesis of a Fragmented Nationalism.* Chapel Hill: University of North Carolina Press.

Kochman, Thomas. 1981. *Black and White Styles in Conflict.* Chicago: University of Chicago Press.

Kubik, Gerhard. 1972. "Oral Notation of Some West and Central African Time-Line Patterns." *Review of Ethnology* (3:22): 169–76.

Kun, Josh. 1994. "The Sound of Blacknuss: Rapping Master/ Counternarratives of the Hip Hop Imagi-Nation." *RepercussionsRepercussions* 3(2): 5–49

Labov, William. 1972. *Language in the Inner City.* Philadelphia: University of Pennsylvania Press.

Lacey, Terry. 1977. *Violence and Politics in Jamaica, 1960–1970: Internal Security in a Developing Country.* Manchester: Manchester University Press.

Lady G. 1992. "I Want Everybody to Know." *Rap Pages,* April, pp. 40–43.

Lawless, Elaine J. 1998. "Claiming Inversion: Lesbian Constructions of Female Identity as Claims for Authority." *Journal of American Folklore* 111(439): 3–22.

Léger, Dimitry. 1993. "Takes This to Quart: Chuck D is Moving Forward with His Lawsuit against St. Ides." *The Source,* September, p. 21.

Leland, John. 1992. "Souljah on Ice." *Newsweek,* June 29, pp. 46–52.

———. 1994. "Our Bodies, Our Sales." *Newsweek,* January 31, pp. 56–57.

Leland, John, and Steve Stein. 1988. "What It Is." *Village Voice* (Hip Hop Nation Special Section), January 19, pp. 26–30.

Levine, Lawrence W. 1977. *Black Culture and Black Consciousness.* New York: Oxford University Press.

Levtzion, N., and J. F. P. Hopkins, eds. 2000 [1981]. *Corpus of Early Arabic Sources for West African History.* Trans. J. F. P. Hopkins. Princeton, N.J.: Markus Wiener Publishers.

Levy, J. Allen. 1988. "DJ Jazzy Jeff and the Fresh Prince Get Stupid." *Spin,* October, pp. 45–46.

Lewis, Lisa. 1990. *Gender Politics and MTV: Voicing the Difference.* Philadelphia: Temple University Press.

Light, Alan, ed. 1996. *Tupac Shakur.* New York: Crown.

Lipsitz, George. 1994. *Dangerous Crossroads: Popular Music, Postmodernism, and the Poetics of Place.* London: Verso.

List, George. 1963. "The Boundaries of Speech and Song." *Ethnomusicology* 7(1): 1–16.

Lodge, Veronica. 1998. "Jackin' Beats." *Rap Pages,* September, pp. 64–67.

Lomax, Frank III. 1990. "Crime Is Not a Part of Our Heritage." In *Stop the Violence: Overcoming Self-Destruction.* Ed. Nelson George. 20–22. New York: Pantheon Books.

Lorde, Audre. 1982. *Zami: A New Spelling of My Name.* Trumansburg, N.Y.: Crossing Press.

———. 1984. *Sister Outsider: Essays and Speeches.* Trumansburg, N.Y.: Crossing Press.

Lott, Tommy. 1992. "Marooned in America: Black Urban Youth Culture and Social Pathology." In *The Underclass Question*. Ed. Bill E. Lawson. 71–89. Philadelphia: Temple University Press.

Loza, Steven. 1993. *Barrio Rhythm: Mexican American Music in Los Angeles*. Urbana: University of Illinois Press.

Lundy, Allan, Edward Gottheil, Ronald D. Serota, Stephen P. Weinstein, and Robert C. Sterling. 1995. "Gender Differences and Similarities in African-American Crack Cocaine Users." *Journal of Nervous and Mental Disease* 183(4): 260–66.

Major, Clarence. 1994 [1970]. *Juba to Jive: A Dictionary of African-American Slang*. New York: Penguin.

Majors, Richard, and Janet Mancini Billson. 1992. *Cool Pose: The Dilemmas of Black Manhood in America*. New York: Touchstone Books.

Malanowski, Jamie. 1989. "Top Hip-Hop." *Rolling Stone*, July 13–27, pp. 77–78.

Manuel, Peter. 1988. *Popular Musics of the Non-Western World: An Introductory Survey*. New York: Oxford University Press.

———. 1993. *Cassette Culture: Popular Music and Technology in North India*. Chicago: University of Chicago Press.

Marriott, Robert. 1994. "The Resurrection of the Jester King." *The Source*, August, pp. 74–80.

Marriott, Rob, James Bernard, and Allen Gordon. 1994. "Reality Check." *The Source*, June, pp. 64–68, 70, 74–75.

"Marsalis Rips Rap and Heavy Metal Musicians." 1989. *Jet*, November 6, p. 22.

Maultsby, Portia K. 1979. "A Health Diversity Evolves from Creative Freedom." *Billboard* (Black Music Spotlight Issue), June 9, pp. BM10, 22, 28.

———. 1990. "Africanisms in African-American Music." In *Africanisms in American Culture*. Ed. Joseph E. Holloway. 185–210. Bloomington: Indiana University Press.

Mayo, Kierna. 1992. "2 Proud to Quit: Sisterhood in Baggies and Big Hats." *The Source*, June, pp. 46–49, 61.

Mbiti, John S. 1970. *African Religions and Philosophies*. Garden City, N.Y.: Doubleday.

McCall, Nathan. 1994. *Makes You Wanna Holler: A Young Black Man in America*. New York: Vintage Books.

McDonald. Paul. 1997. "Feeling and Fun: Romance, Dance, and the Performing Male Body in the Take That Videos." In *Sexing the Groove: Popular Music and Gender*. Ed. Sheila Whiteley. 277–94. London: Routledge Press.

McGregor, Tracii. 1996. "Sittin' on Top of the World." *The Source*, October, pp. 98–104.

———. et al. 1998. "Worldwide, Worldwide." *The Source*, January, pp. 109–38.

McKinney, Rhoda E. 1989. "What's Behind the Rise of Rap?" *Ebony*, January, pp. 66–70.

MC Lyte. 1993. *The Arsenio Hall Show* (musical guest), October 8.

McNeil, W. K. 1986. "Hambone." In *The New Grove Dictionary of American Music*. Vol. 2. Ed. H. Wiley Hitchcock and Stanley Sadie. New York: MacMillan Press.

Merriam, Alan P. 1964. *The Anthropology of Music*. Evanston, Ill.: Northwestern University Press.

"A Message in Their Music." 1983. *Right On!* Winter, pp. 27–28, 53.

Mills, David. 1989. "The Hard Rap on Public Enemy" and "Professor Griff: 'The Jews Are Wicked.'" *Washington Times*, May 22, pp. E1–E2.

Mitchell-Kernan, Claudia. 1981. "Signifying." In *Mother Wit from the Laughing Barrel: Readings in the Interpretation of Afro-American Folklore*. Ed. Alan Dundas. 310–28. New York: Garland.

Mollenkopf, John. 1983. *The Contested City*. Princeton, N.J.: Princeton University Press.

Mollenkopf, John, and Manuel Castells, eds. 1991. *Dual City: Restructuring New York*. New York: Russell Sage Foundation.

Moon, Tom. 1991. "Public Enemy's Bomb Squad." *Musician*, October, 69–72, 76

Moore, Robin. 1997. *Nationalizing Blackness: Afrocubanismo and Artistic Revolution in Havanna, 1920–1940*. Pittsburgh: University of Pittsburgh Press.

Morgan, Joan. 1992. "Sexuality in Rap Music." Forum at Tisch School of the Arts, New York University, December 5.

———. 1997. "The Bad Girls of Hip-Hop." *Essence*, March, pp. 76–77, 132, 134.

———. 1999. *when chickenheads come home to roost: my life as a hip-hop feminist*. New York: Simon and Schuster.

Morthland, John. 1991. "Yo, Y'all." *Texas Monthly*, February, pp. 60–63.

Mr. Murphy, Dimitry Elias Léger, and Smokey D. Fontaine. 1999. "Masters of the Universe." *The Source*, February, pp. 179–96.

Mshaka, Thembisa S. 1999. "Mama Mia." *Blaze*, December/January, pp. 106–8.

Muhammad, James, and William Muhammad Jr. 1997. "Atonement, Reconciliation, Foundation for Rap Summit." *The Final Call*, April 15, pp. 9–10.

Muhammad, Richard. 1997. "Peace in the Streets: Minister Farrakhan and Rappers Announce Peace Strategy." *The Final Call*, April 15, pp. 3, 8.

Mukherjee, Tiarra. 1998–99. "Straight Shooters." *Vibe*, December–January, pp. 60–63.

Nathan, David. 1988a. "The Majors: Marketing Campaign Yields Spectacular Results as Activated Labels Gear Up for Record Year." *Billboard*, June 18, pp. B3, 14, 22.

———. 1988b. "Major Labels are Suddenly Singing a Different Tune While Indies Grow Stronger as Rap Emerges as the Most Popular and Vital New Music Form of the '80s." *Billboard*, December 24, pp. R4–5, 10, 14, 18–19.

Narayan, Kirin. 1993. "How Native Is a 'Native' Anthropologist?" *American Anthropologist* 95(3): 671–86.

Nelson, Havelock. 1988. "Stetsasonic: A Sampling Supporter." *Billboard*, November 12, p. 28.

———. 1989. "Kid-N-Play Get Serious with Gold Album, Film Project" *Billboard*, July 8, p. 27.

———. 1991. "Marley Marl: Soul Controller, Sole Survivor." *The Source*, October, pp. 36–39.

———. 1993. "New Female Rappers Play for Keeps. *Billboard*, July 10, pp. 1, 77.

Nelson, Havelock, and Michael A. Gonzales. 1991. *Bring the Noise: A Guide to Rap Music and Hip-Hop Culture*. New York: Harmony Books.

Nettl, Bruno. 1964. *Theory and Method in Ethnomusicology*. New York: Schirmer Books.

———. 1983. *The Study of Ethnomusicology: Twenty-Nine Issues and Concepts*. Urbana: University of Illinois Press.

Newman, Mark. 1988. *Entrepreneurs of Profit and Pride: From Black-Appeal to Radio Soul*. Westport, Conn.: Praeger.

Newman, Melinda, and Chris Morris. 1991. "Sampling Safeguards Follow Suit." *Billboard*, May 23, pp. 1, 80.

"A New Spin on Music Sampling: A Case for Fair Play." 1992. *Harvard Law Review* 105(3): 726–44.

Nketia, J. H. Kwabena. 1962. "The Problem of Meaning in African Music." *Journal of the Society for Ethnomusicology* 6 (Fall): 1–7.

———. 1974. *The Music of Africa*. New York: W. W. Norton and Company.

Noel, Peter. 1997. "Atlanta Child Murders: 'Rumors of War.'" *The Source*, November, 126–36.

Norris, Chris. 1993. "Old School, New School, Cool School." *Option*, September–October, pp. 82–87.

Nuruddin, Yusuf. 1994. "The Five Percenters: A Teenage Nation of Gods and Earths." In *Muslims Communities in North America*. Ed. Yvonne Yazbeck Haddad and Jane Idleman Smith. 109–32. Albany: State University of New York Press.

Ogunnaike, Lola. 2000. "The Iceman Cometh." *Vibe*, May, p. 102.

Oliver, Paul. 1968. *Screening the Blues: Aspects of the Blues Tradition:* London: Cassell.

———. 1970. *Savannah Syncopators: African Retentions in the Blues*. New York: Stein and Day.

Olsen, Jack. 1967. *Black Is Best: The Riddle of Cassius Clay*. New York: Dell.

Olson, Yvonne. 1988. "As Rap Goes Pop, Some Say Black Radio Is Missing Out." *Billboard*, June 18, pp. 1, 69.

Omosupe, Ekua. 1991. "Black/Lesbian/Bulldagger." *differences: A Journal of Feminist Cultural Studies* 3(2): 101–11.

Oscar. 1997. "Music vs. Fashion" (letter to the editor). *The Source*, May, p. 14.

Owen, Frank. 1988."Crime as a Metaphor," "Homeboy Fashion: Up for the War," and "Hip Hop Bebop." *Spin*, October, pp. 48, 52, 61.

Pacini Hernandez, Deborah. 1995. *Bachata: A Social History of a Dominican Popular Music*. Philadelphia: Temple University Press.

Palmer, Ransford W. 1995. *Pilgrims from the Sun: West Indian Migration to America*. New York: Twayne Publishers.

Pappas, Ben. 1998. "The Rap Pack." *Forbes*, September 21, p. 224.

Pearce, John Ed. 1990. "Rapping Rap." *Courier-Journal Magazine,* July 29, pp. 14–15.

Pearlman, Jill. 1988. "Girls Rappin' Round Table." *Paper,* Summer, pp. 25–27.

Peña, Manuel. 1985. *The Texas-Mexican Conjunto: History of a Working-Class Music.* Austin: University of Texas Press.

Perkins, Eugene. 1975. *Home Is a Dirty Street: The Social Oppression of Black Children.* Chicago: Third World Press.

Perkins, William Eric, ed. 1996. *Droppin' Science: Critical Essays on Rap Music and Hip Hop Culture.* Philadelphia: Temple University Press.

Philips, Chuck. 1997. "Hip-Hop Has Really Got the House Jumpin'." *Los Angeles Times,* July 24, pp. D1, D4.

———. 2001. "Death Row Records Founder Out of Prison After 5 Years." *Los Angeles Times,* August 7, pp. C1, C6.

Plastino, Goffredo. 1996. *Mappa delle voce: Rap, Raggamuffin e tradizione in Italia.* Rome: Meltemi editore.

Potter, Russell A. 1995. *Spectacular Vernaculars: Hip-Hop and the Politics of Postmodernism.* Albany: State University of New York Press.

Powell, Kevin. 1995. "Tupac Shakur." *Vibe,* April, pp. 50–55.

———. 1996. "Live from Death Row." *Vibe,* February, pp. 44–50.

Prévos, André. J. M. 1996. "The Evolution of French Rap and Hip Hop Culture in the 1980s and 1990s." *French Review* 69(5): 713–25.

Pulley, Brett. 1994. "How a 'Nice Girl' Evolved into Boss, the Gangster Rapper." *Wall Street Journal,* February 3, pp. A1, A16.

Queen Latifah. *Ladies First: Revelations of a Strong Woman.* New York: William Morrow.

Raboteau, Albert J. 1978. *Slave Religion: The "Invisible Institution" in the Antebellum South.* New York: Oxford University Press.

Radner, Joan Newlon, and Susan S. Lanser. 1993. "Strategies of Coding in Women's Culture." In *Feminist Messages: Coding in Women's Folk Culture.* Ed. Joan Newlon Radner. 1–29. Urbana: University of Illinois Press.

Rampersad, Arnold. 1986. *The Life of Langston Hughes.* New York: Oxford University Press.

"Rap Attack." 1986. *Positively Black* (NBC-TV, New York), December 7.

"Rap Records: Are They Fad or Permanent." 1980. *Billboard,* February 16, pp. 57, 59.

Reid, Vernon. 1993. "The Vibe Q: George Clinton." *Vibe,* November, pp. 44–49.

Reynolds, J. R. 1996. "Hip-Hop Meet? Aims for Unity." *Billboard,* November 6, pp. 19, 22.

Rice, David Wall. 2000. "Platinum Jewels: Bling Bling." *Blaze,* March, pp. 72–74.

Rice, Doc. 1998. "The Language of Scratching." *Rap Pages,* September, p. 30.

Rice, Timothy. 1997. "Toward a Mediation of Field Methods and Field Experience in Ethnomusicology." In *Shadows in the Field: New Perspectives for Fieldwork in Ethnomusicology.* Ed. Gregory F. Barz and Timothy J. Cooley. 101–20. Chicago: University of Chicago Press.

Rickelman, Melinda. 1989. "Rap: A Layman's Guide." *The Crisis,* May, pp. 8–9.

Rimer, Sara. 1990. "Rap Band Members Found Not Guilty in Obscenity Trial." *New York Times,* October 21, pp. A1, A30.

Ro, Ronin. 1991. "Prince Paul." *The Source,* August, p. 22.

———. 1995. "Pulp Fiction." *The Source,* March, 46–48, 82.

———. 1996. *Gangsta: Merchandising the Rhymes of Violence.* New York: St. Martin's Press.

———. 1998. *Have Gun Will Travel: The Spectacular Rise and Violent Fall of Death Row Records.* New York: Doubleday.

Roberts, Deborah. 1998. "Beautiful Women." *20/20 Monday.* Transcript no. 1796, March 30.

Roberts, John W. 1989. *From Trickster to Badman: The Black Folk Hero in Slavery and Freedom.* Philadelphia: University of Pennsylvania Press.

Roberts, Robin. 1996. *Ladies First: Women in Music Videos.* Jackson: University Press of Mississippi.

Robinson, Cedric J. 1983. *Black Marxism: The Making of the Black Radical Tradition.* London: Zed Press.

Rogers, Charles E. 1983. "The Magic of Radio Rap." *Right On!* Winter, pp. 8–10.

———. 1994. "The Salt-N-Pepa Interview." *Rap Masters,* July, pp. 30–31.

Romain, Louis. 1992. "X-Clan: Roots and Boots." *The Source,* May, pp. 32–36.

Romero, D. James. 1997. "Influence of Hip-Hop Resonates Worldwide." *Los Angeles Times,* March 14, pp. A1, A27.

Rooney, Jim. 1995. *Organizing the South Bronx.* Albany: State University of New York Press.

Rose, Tricia. 1994. *Black Noise: Rap Music and Black Culture in Contemporary America.* Hanover, N.H.: Wesleyan University Press.

Rosen, Craig. 1990. "Bilingual Rap Is Translating into Sales." *Billboard,* September 8, pp. 1, 70.

Ross, Andrew. 1995. "Back on the Box." *ArtForum,* May, pp. 17, 112.

Ruiz, Monica S., Alicia R. Gable, Edward H. Kaplan, Michael A. Stoto, Harvey V. Fineberg, and James Trussell, eds. 2001. *No Time to Lose: Getting More from HIV Prevention.* Washington, D.C.: Institute of Medicine.

Russell, Deborah. 1992. "Judge Clips Biz Markie on Sampling Issue." *Billboard,* January 4, p. 1

Saxon, Shani. 1997. "Feelin' Bitchy." *Vibe,* February, pp. 78–79.

Schloss, Joe. 1997. "'A Handshake Business': The Ethics of Hip Hop Mix Tapes." Paper presented at the 42nd Annual Meeting of the Society for Ethnomusicology, Pittsburgh, October 22–26.

———. 2000. "Making Beats: The Art of Sample-Based Hip-Hop." Ph.D. dissertation, University of Washington.

Schoolly D. 1988. "The Meaning of Gold." *Spin,* October, p. 52.

Scott, Peter Dale, and Jonathan Marshall. 1998 [1991]. *Cocaine Politics: Drugs, Armies and the CIA in Central America.* Berkeley: University of California Press.

Shaw, Arnold. 1986. *Black Popular Music in America: From the Spirituals, Minstrels, and Ragtime to Soul, Disco, and Hip-Hop.* New York: Schirmer Books.

Sieber, Roy, and Roslyn Adele Walker. 1987. *African Art in the Cycle of Life.* Washington, D.C.: Smithsonian Institution Press.

Simmons, Ken. 1983. "Rap Music is More Than Black and White." *Right On! Focus,* Winter, pp. 48–51.

Sister Souljah. 1994. *No Disrespect.* New York: Random House.

———. 1999. *The Coldest Winter Ever: A Novel.* New York: Pocket Books.

Smith, David Lionel. 1996. "Amiri Baraka." In *Encyclopedia of African-American Culture and History.* Vol. 1. Ed. Jack Salzman, David Lionel Smith, and Cornel West. 261–63. New York: MacMillan.

Smith, R. J. 1998. "Lock, Pop, and Quarrel." *Vibe,* September, pp. 267–68.

Smitherman, Geneva. 1986 [1977]. *Talkin and Testifyin: The Language of Black America.* Detroit: Wayne State University Press.

———. 1994. *Black Talk: Words and Phrases from the Hood to the Amen Corner.* New York: Houghton Mifflin.

Southern, Eileen. 1997 [1983]. *The Music of Black Americans: A History.* 3d. ed. New York: W. W. Norton and Company.

Spaulding, Norman W. 1981. "History of Black Oriented Radio in Chicago 1929–1963." Ph.D. dissertation, University of Illinois at Urbana-Champaign.

Spero, Francesca. 1992. "Sampling Greed Is Hurting Hip-Hop Business." *Billboard,* December 5, p. 7

Stancell, Steven. 1996. *Rap Whoz Who: The World of Rap Music.* New York: Schirmer Books.

Stanley, Lawrence A., ed. 1992. *Rap, the Lyrics: The Words to Rap's Greatest Hits.* New York: Penguin Books.

Stark, Phyllis. 1993. "Gangsta Rap under the Gun." *Billboard,* December 18, pp. 1, 103.

Stolzoff, Norman. 2000. *Wake the Town and Tell the People: Dancehall Culture in Jamaica.* Durham, N.C.: Duke University Press.

Stone, Ruth M. 1982. *Let the Inside Be Sweet.* Bloomington: Indiana University Press.

———. 1985. "In Search of Time in African Music." *Music Theory Spectrum* (7): 139–48.

———. 1988. *Dried Millet Breaking: Time, Words, and Song in the Woi Epic of the Kpelle.* Bloomington: Indiana University Press.

Stuart, Dan. 1986. "Whodini Is Back in Black and Better Than Ever!" *Black Beat,* August, pp. 21–22.

———. 1988. "The Rap against Rap at Black Radio: Professional Suicide or Cultural Smokescreen?" *Billboard,* December, pp. R8, 21.

Stuckey, Sterling. 1987. *Slave Culture: Nationalist Theory and the Foundation of Black America.* New York: Oxford University Press.

Sugarman, Robert G., and Joseph P. Salvo. 1991. "Sampling Gives Law a New Mix." *National Law Journal* 14(10): 21–23.

Sullivan, Randall. 2001. "Who Shot B.I.G.?" *Rolling Stone,* June 7, 86–106, 124–25.

Taha, Kofi. 1999. "Moon Struck." *The Source,* April, pp. 124–30.

Tapley, Mel. 1988. "Does Rap Music Create Violence or Is It Just a Bad Rap?" *Amsterdam News,* October 15, pp. 28, 30.

Tate, Greg. 1988. "It's Like This, Y'all." *Village Voice* (Hip-Hop Nation Special Section), January 19, p. 21.

Taylor, Clyde. 1977. "The Language of Hip: From Africa to What's Happening Now." *First World,* January–February, pp. 25–32.

Thomas, Don. 1986. "Puttin' the Rap on 'Rap Attacks.'" *Big Red,* July 26, pp. 20–21.

Thompson, Mel. E. 1990. "Forty-and-One Years On: An Overview of Afro-Caribbean Migration to the United Kingdom." In *In Search of a Better Life: Perspectives on Migration from the Caribbean.* Ed. Ransford W. Palmer. 39–70. New York: Praeger.

Thompson, Robert Farris. 1983. *Flash of the Spirit: African and Afro-American Art and Philosophy.* New York: Vintage.

———. 1990. "Kongo Influences on African-American Artistic Culture." In *Africanisms in American Culture.* Ed. Joseph E. Holloway. 148–84. Bloomington: Indiana University Press.

Titon, Jeff Todd. 1994 [1977]. *Early Downhome Blues: A Musical and Cultural Analysis.* 2d. Ed. Chapel Hill: University of North Carolina Press.

Toop, David. 2000 [1984]. *Rap Attack #3: African Rap to Global Hip Hop.* 3d. ed. London: Serpent's Tail.

Turino, Thomas. 2000. *Nationalists, Cosmopolitans, and Popular Music in Zimbabwe.* Chicago: University of Chicago Press.

Turner, Patricia A. 1993. *I Heard It through the Grapevine: Rumors in African-American Culture.* Berkeley: University of California Press.

Vigil, James Diego. 1994 [1988]. *Barrio Gangs: Street Life and Identity in Southern California.* Austin: University of Texas Press.

"Violator Bio." 2001. <http://www.sonymusic.com/artists/Violator/bio/html>.

Wade, Carlton. 2001. "More Bounce to the Ounce." *Vibe,* January, p. 52.

Waldron, Clarence. 1990. "Could Students Learn More If Taught with Rap Music?" *Jet,* January 29, pp. 16–18.

Walker, Lisa M. 1993. "How to Recognize a Lesbian: The Cultural Politics of Looking Like What You Are." *Signs: Journal of Women in Culture and Society* 18(4): 866–89.

Walkowitz, Daniel J. 1990. "New York: A Tale of Two Cities." In *Snowbelt Cities: Metropolitan Politics in the Northeast and Midwest since World War II.* Ed. Richard M. Bernard. 189–208. Bloomington: Indiana University Press.

Wallace, Michele. 1992. "When Feminism Faces the Music, and the Music Is Rap." In *Reading Culture: Contexts for Critical Reading and Writing.* Ed. Diana George and John Trimbur. 25–28. New York: HarperCollins.

Wallis, Roger, and Krister Malm. 1984. *Big Sounds from Small People: The Music Industry in Small Countries.* New York: Pendragon.

———. 1992. *Media Policy and Music Activity.* London: Routledge.

Walters, Barry. 1998. Review of Queen Pen, *My Melody. Advocate,* March 17, pp. 59–60.

Waterman, Christopher. 1990. *Jùjú: A Social History and Ethnography of an African Popular Music.* Chicago: University of Chicago Press.

Watkins, S. Craig. 1998. *Representing Hip Hop Culture and the Production of Black Culture.* Chicago: University of Chicago Press.

Watkins, William H. 1984. *All You Need to Know about Rappin'! From Grandmaster Blaster.* Chicago: Contemporary Books.

Webb, Daniel L. 1992. "'They're Trying to Destroy Hip-Hop All Over the World': Afrika Bambaataa's Busy Importing Rap to Europe . . . and Beyond!" *Rap Pages,* April, pp. 54–57.

Webb, Gary. 1998. *Dark Alliance: The CIA, the Contras, and the Crack Cocaine Explosion.* New York: Seven Stories Press.

Webley, Susan A. 1994. "Will the Real Spinderella Please Raise Her Hand?" *Rap Masters,* July, pp. 8–9.

Weingarten, Marc. 1998a. "All Made Up, Ready to Go." *Los Angeles Times* (Calendar Section), February 1, pp. 5, 68–69.

———. 1998b. "Large and In Charge." *Los Angeles Times* (Calendar Section), July 26, pp. 8–9, 81.

Wepman, Dennis, Ronald B. Newman, and Murray B. Binderman. 1976. *The Life: The Lore and Folk Poetry of Black Hustler.* Philadelphia: University of Pennsylvania Press.

West, Cornel. 1994. *Race Matters.* New York: Vintage Press.

White, Miles. 1996. "The Phonograph Turntable and Performance Practice in Hip Hop Music." <http://www.research.umbc.edu/efhm/2/white/index.html>.

Whiteley, Sheila. 1997. Introduction. to *Sexing the Groove: Popular Music and Gender.* Ed. Sheila Whiteley. xiii–xxxvi. New York: Routledge.

"Why Are Rap Stars So Appealing as Actors?" 1995. *Jet,* July 31, pp. 58–61.

Wiggins, William H. Jr. 1987. *O Freedom! Afro-American Emancipation Celebrations.* Knoxville: University of Tennessee Press.

Williams, Frank. 1995. "Eazy-E: The Life, the Legacy." *The Source,* June, pp. 52–62.

———. 1997. "Only in Cali." *The Source,* November, pp. 76–82.

Williams, Gilbert A. 1986. "The Black Disc Jockey as a Cultural Hero." *Popular Music and Society* 10(3): 79–90.

Williams, Hype. 1995. Interview with Fab Five Freddy. *Yo! MTV Raps,* February 11.

Williams, Juan. 1989. "Fighting Words." *Washington Post,* October 15, pp. G1, G8–9.

Wilson, Olly. 1974. "The Significance of the Relationship between Afro-American Music and West African Music." *Black Perspective in Music* 2 (Spring): 3–22.

———. 1983. "Black Music as an Art Form." *Black Music Research Journal* 3:1–22.

Wong, Celine. 2001. "Native Tongues: Hip Hop's Global Domination." *The Source,* March, pp. 202–9.

Word, Carl O., and Benjamin Bowser. 1997. "Background to Crack Cocaine Addiction and HIV High-Risk Behavior: The Next Epidemic." *American Journal of Drug Alcohol Abuse* 23(1): 67–77.

Zook, Krystal. 1992. "Reconstructions on Nationalist Thought in Black Music and Culture." In *Rocking the Boat: Mass Music and Mass Movements.* Ed. Reebee Garofalo. 255–66. Boston: South End Press.

# General Index

Page numbers in boldface refer to illustrations and music examples.

Abbatiello, Sal, 61, **61,** 124
Above the Law, 95
*Above the Rim* (film), 184
Abu-Lughod, Lila, 11
Adler, Bill, 43, 132
Aerosmith, 80, 108, 227
aerosol artists. *See* graffiti artists/writers
aesthetics: bounce, 114–15; Chicano identity, 89, 152; Dirty South, 114–15; disco, 43–44; funk, 41–42, 238n2; gangsta rap (reality rap), 89–90, 92; G-Funk, 88; human beat box, 77; Jamaican dancehall (sound system culture), 51–54; Miami Bass, 115; naming, 125; new jack films, 118; New School, 75; Old School, 74; rap music production, 74, 81; rap-rock fusion, 80–81; rhyme, 126–28; slackness, 90; sound, 147–50; street culture, 5–6, 122–53; style, 6, 12, 126; underground, 122
African American folklore themes (in hip-hop): badman, 24, 34, 205; bad nigga, 216; conspiracy belief narratives, 178–84; crossroads, 27–28; night riders stories, 180; rumor, 180; spirituals, 219; toasts, 34; trickster figure, 86; (urban) legend, 180; vernacular expressions, 30, 115. *See also the glossary*
African-derived concepts (of rap music): call and response, 20, 26–27; celebrations and holidays, 237n5; coolness, 153; crossroads, 27–28; libation, 151, 162; *nommo* (*nummo*), 22, 236–37n4; queen mother's head, 248n2; spiritualism, 161–62; time, 140–41; tonal speech, 26
Afrika Islam, 59, **60,** 92, 162
Aftermath, 108, 113, 174, 228

Ahmad, 162
AIDS and the hip-hop community, 164, 196–97; conspiracy belief narratives, 178–82; illuminati theory, 181–82 (*see also* Cooper, Milton William; Epperson, A. Ralph; New World Order); rap songs, 4, 196–97; statistics, 180, 247n19
Al-Amin, Jamil Abdullah. *See* Brown, Hubert "Rap"
Ali, Muhammad, 31
Alpha Phi Alpha, 107, 241n4
Als, Hilton, 198
al-'Umarī, 19
Amaru, 242n11
American Society of Composers, Authors, and Publishers (ASCAP), 175
AMG. *See* Artists Management Group
AMG (artist), 105
Anderson, Benedict, 159
Ant Banks, 117
Anthrax, 108
Anti-Defamation League, 163
Ant Knox, 131
Antoinette, 248n1
Apache, 112, 162, 201
Arabian Prince, 89, 240n17
Armaggedon, 117. *See also* Fat Joe and his Terror Squad
Amil, 117
Armstrong, Stretch, 73
Arrested Development, 115, 158, 213
"The Arsenio Hall Show," 153
Art Blakey and the Messengers, 110
Artists Management Group (AMG), 119
ASCAP. *See* American Society of Composers, Authors, and Publishers
ATL. *See* Mellow Man Ace
Atwell, Philip, 213, 217

281

# Index of Recordings and Music Videos

Cheryl L. Keyes is an associate professor of ethnomusicology at the University of California at Los Angeles as well as a composer, songwriter, and performer. She has published articles on rap in *Ethnomusicology,* the *Journal of American Folklore,* and the anthology *Feminist Messages: Coding in Women's Folk Culture* (1993).

Music in American Life

Bibliographical Handbook of American Music   *D. W. Krummel*
Goin' to Kansas City   *Nathan W. Pearson, Jr.*
"Susanna," "Jeanie," and "The Old Folks at Home": The Songs of
   Stephen C. Foster from His Time to Ours (2d ed.)   *William W. Austin*
Songprints: The Musical Experience of Five Shoshone Women   *Judith Vander*
"Happy in the Service of the Lord": Afro-American Gospel Quartets
   in Memphis   *Kip Lornell*
Paul Hindemith in the United States   *Luther Noss*
"My Song Is My Weapon": People's Songs, American Communism, and
   the Politics of Culture, 1930–50   *Robbie Lieberman*
Chosen Voices: The Story of the American Cantorate   *Mark Slobin*
Theodore Thomas: America's Conductor and Builder of Orchestras, 1835–1905
   *Ezra Schabas*
"The Whorehouse Bells Were Ringing" and Other Songs Cowboys Sing
   *Guy Logsdon*
Crazeology: The Autobiography of a Chicago Jazzman   *Bud Freeman,
   as Told to Robert Wolf*
Discoursing Sweet Music: Brass Bands and Community Life in Turn-of-the-
   Century Pennsylvania   *Kenneth Kreitner*
Mormonism and Music: A History   *Michael Hicks*
Voices of the Jazz Age: Profiles of Eight Vintage Jazzmen   *Chip Deffaa*
Pickin' on Peachtree: A History of Country Music in Atlanta, Georgia
   *Wayne W. Daniel*
Bitter Music: Collected Journals, Essays, Introductions, and Librettos
   *Harry Partch; edited by Thomas McGeary*
Ethnic Music on Records: A Discography of Ethnic Recordings Produced in
   the United States, 1893 to 1942   *Richard K. Spottswood*
Downhome Blues Lyrics: An Anthology from the Post-World War II Era
   *Jeff Todd Titon*
Ellington: The Early Years   *Mark Tucker*
Chicago Soul   *Robert Pruter*
That Half-Barbaric Twang: The Banjo in American Popular Culture   *Karen Linn*
Hot Man: The Life of Art Hodes   *Art Hodes and Chadwick Hansen*
The Erotic Muse: American Bawdy Songs (2d ed.)   *Ed Cray*
Barrio Rhythm: Mexican American Music in Los Angeles   *Steven Loza*
The Creation of Jazz: Music, Race, and Culture in Urban America
   *Burton W. Peretti*
Charles Martin Loeffler: A Life Apart in Music   *Ellen Knight*
Club Date Musicians: Playing the New York Party Circuit   *Bruce A. MacLeod*
Opera on the Road: Traveling Opera Troupes in the United States, 1825–60
   *Katherine K. Preston*

The University of Illinois Press
is a founding member of the
Association of American University Presses.

---

Composed in 10.5/13 Minion
with Eurostile display
by Jim Proefrock
at the University of Illinois Press
Designed by Paula Newcomb
Manufactured by Thomson-Shore, Inc.

University of Illinois Press
1325 South Oak Street
Champaign, IL 61820-6903
www.press.uillinois.edu